# THE IMAGE
# OF MAN

A STUDY OF THE IDEA OF HUMAN DIGNITY IN CLAS-
SICAL ANTIQUITY, THE MIDDLE AGES, AND THE
RENAISSANCE

# THE IMAGE OF MAN

A STUDY OF THE IDEA OF HUMAN DIGNITY IN CLASSICAL
ANTIQUITY, THE MIDDLE AGES, AND THE RENAISSANCE

## by Herschel Baker

*Plato having defined man to be a two-legged animal without feathers, Diogenes
plucked a cock and brought it into the Academy, and said, "This is Plato's man."
On which account this addition was made to the definition, "With broad flat nails."*

GLOUCESTER, MASS.

PETER SMITH

1975

*For*

*Hyder Edward Rollins*

HARPER TORCHBOOKS / The Academy Library
*Advisory Editor in The Humanities and Social Sciences: Benjamin Nelson*

THE IMAGE OF MAN

# PREFACE

THIS BOOK UNDERTAKES TO DISCUSS, if only fragmentarily, one of the perennial topics in the history of thought—the dignity of man. To trace the rationalizations that constitute the history of this idea is extremely difficult. Such a subject is obviously too big for one book, or for a series of books, and the only comfort one can take in presuming to treat it at all is to remember Voltaire's remark that the secret of being a bore is to tell everything. But the temptation to tell everything is in this instance not very strong, simply because no one, and least of all I, is capable of treating adequately even the major topics suggested by such a subject.

Therefore I have written this book with considerable diffidence and discontent, knowing that every paragraph could be a chapter, every chapter a book—and that there are many things that, either through ignorance or because life is short, I have left unsaid altogether. I have tried to mitigate my presumption with the implication of modesty in the subtitle; for although I have tried to write a more or less continuous exposition, I knew that I could treat merely a sampling of the relevant topics. Hoping to suggest some of the main lines of development in the history of the idea of human dignity, I have sacrificed thoroughness for scope. And inevitably, in organizing what I have to say under the chronological headings of classical antiquity, the Middle Ages, and the Renaissance, with the corresponding thematic headings of philosophy, theology, and literature, I have imposed an arbitrary order on material that everywhere cuts across such artificial lines. None the less, as the virtual exclusion of Greek literature (and especially the beguiling figure of Homer) shows, I have tried to limit myself to my self-imposed categories. The most conspicuous of my voluntary omissions has been the development of late Renaissance skepticism and naturalism: although they were to have a corrosive effect on man's traditional evaluation of himself, these topics belong more properly to the crucial seventeenth than to the sixteenth century. I hope presently to devote a whole book to their bearing on this subject in the seventeenth century, but to treat them here would be to disrupt (although not, I hope, to demolish) my thesis that in its estimate of human nature the Renaissance marked no radical departure from the late Middle Ages.

A good many of us, perhaps, are not warmed by Augustine's theology, but we should all admit that he was a born writer. At the close of the *De*

*Civitate Dei*—a book whose only similarity to this one is that it too was on too big a subject—he spoke for everyone who has ever been beguiled into literary composition: "Let those who think I have said too little, or those who think that I have said too much, forgive me; and let those who think that I have said just enough join me in giving thanks to God."

# ACKNOWLEDGMENTS

Surely the most pleasant of an author's duties is to thank those who through their knowledge and generosity have lightened his labors. The dedication of this book signalizes, if inadequately, my sense of obligation to a man who as both friend and teacher has put me lastingly in his debt. Henry Nash Smith permitted himself to become involved in the very conception of this work, and I have probably profited more than I myself realize from his fine sense of history and his generous interest. Theodore Spencer and Douglas Bush took the trouble not only to read a bulky manuscript but through their detailed suggestions to give it virtues it would otherwise have lacked. D. T. Starnes was good enough to give the third section the benefit of his close knowledge of Renaissance literature. The Syndics of the Harvard University Press and Mr. Roger Scaife, the Director, have undertaken to publish without subsidy a book from which, in the nature of things, they can expect no great return; and their agents, particularly Mrs. Cedric Whitman, have been unfailingly coöperative. A grant from the Research Council of the University of Texas afforded me a couple of months of blissful leisure for composition. Finally, I shall defy convention by thanking my wife for something other than her typing, excellent as it is. Although her services in behalf of this book will be nameless, it must be said that without them it would probably never have been written.

H. B.

Harvard University
21 November, 1946

# CONTENTS

## PART I

## *The Classical View of Man*

I. THE PRE-SOCRATIC QUEST     3
*Ionian Naturalism; Pythagorean Mysticism; The Challenge of the Eleatic Absolute; The Culmination of Naturalism: the Atomists*

II. THE PROBLEM OF ETHICAL ABSOLUTES: SOCRATES AND THE SOPHISTS     16
*Permanence as Law; Sophistic Relativism; The Socratic Refutation*

III. PLATONIC HUMANISM     37
*Metaphysics: Permanence as Idea; Ethics*

IV. ARISTOTELIAN HUMANISM     53
*Metaphysics: Permanence as Actuality; Psychology; Ethics*

V. THE ETHICS OF STOICISM     69
*The Cosmos; The Individual; Roman Stoicism: The Notion of Law*

VI. THE DECAY OF HUMANISM     84
*Epicurus; Skepticism; Neoplatonism*

VII. RETROSPECT     100

## PART II

## *The Christian View of Man*

VIII. THE RELIGIOUS ATTITUDE     109
*Religion and Philosophy; Orphism*

IX. THE CHRISTIAN FRAME OF REFERENCE     120
*Certum est, quia impossibile est; The Metamorphosis of Jesus; The Seed of Salvation; The Rejection of Paganism*

X. THE WINDS OF DOCTRINE     142
*The Ontology of God; Gnosticism; The Incarnate God; The Council of Nicaea*

XI. AUGUSTINE AND THE MEDIEVAL VIEW OF MAN     159
*The Glory of God; The Infamy of Man; God and Man*

XII. AUGURIES OF CHANGE     187
*Realism and Nominalism; The Natural Theology of Aquinas*

## PART III

# The Renaissance View of Man

XIII. VIS INERTIAE IN THE RENAISSANCE 203
The Point of View; The Conservative Revolutionists; Toward a Definition of the Renaissance

XIV. THE BEST OF ALL POSSIBLE WORLDS 223
The Principle of Order; The Sanctity of Due Degree; A Little Lower than the Angels

XV. THE USES OF NEOPLATONISM 241
Florentine Neoplatonism; Bellezza del Spirito; The Eclectic Optimism of the Faerie Queene

XVI. CHRISTIAN HUMANISM 258
Christ and Cicero; Erasmus and Luther; "Pryuate Studys"

XVII. THE NATURALISTIC VIEW OF MAN 275
The Body-Soul Relationship; The Vegetable Soul; The Sensitive Soul; The Rational Soul

XVIII. SIXTEENTH-CENTURY ETHICS AND THE DEVELOPMENT OF NEO-STOICISM 293
"Right Reason" as an Instrument of Christian Virtue; Neo-Stoicism

XIX. THE PROTESTANT VIEW OF MAN 313
The Revival of Augustinian Individualism; The Economic Sanction

EPILOGUE 335

BIBLIOGRAPHY 339

INDEX 361

# PART I

*The Classical View of Man*

# I

## THE PRE-SOCRATIC QUEST

### IONIAN NATURALISM

WHEN ARISTOTLE, in that admirable history of philosophy that forms the opening of his *Metaphysics,* said that philosophy began with wonder, he must have been thinking of the Ionians of the sixth century. For they wondered much, and from Aristotle's day to this, most accounts of organized European thought have started with them. Because posterity has always been charmed with Athens, it has sometimes forgotten that Athens imported philosophical speculation along with the alphabet and literature from the eastern periphery of the Hellenic world. That remarkable group of Ionians of the sixth century from Thales on should be remembered not because they answered questions, but because they first asked questions that perhaps cannot be answered. Whatever their limitations—Thales' cosmology construes the earth as a flat disc floating on circumambient waters—their minds, as Mr. Whitehead has said, were infected with an eager generality; their curiosity is characteristic of Greek thought at its best.

True, their influence has always been oblique. For one thing, they were neophytes in conceptual thought, and hinted where Aristotle was to expound; for another, their work has come down to us in the sorriest shreds and patches. Nonetheless, their importance is great. They introduced into European thought that habit of mind that was later to be called naturalism, and thus presaged both the success of the atomists and the magnificent refutation of Socrates. More basic than this, however, were the principles of simplicity and order with which they tried to explain the blooming welter of the universe. It is not too much to say that the Greek reverence for law can be traced as clearly to the assumptions of the Ionians as to the contemporary constitution of Solon. They explained the universe variously, but their explanations all proceeded on the assumption of an inherent and permanent order, regularity, and pattern subsisting beneath the changes and chances of appearance. Permanence and change were to become the two great themes of Greek philosophy, and the Ionians were the first to realize the significance of the themes. From Thales to Plotinus the assumption of permanence (of various sorts) runs steadily: it informs not only Greek metaphysics and cosmology, but also ethics; and it is the most powerful single factor in determining the Greek view of man.

The Ionians, interested mainly in matter and its transformations, show a candid indifference to those ethical and moral problems that were to dominate post-Socratic thought. They were plain men—some, as we know from Aristotle's gossip about Thales' successful speculation in oil-presses, men of shamelessly practical affairs; and, like many plain men since, they refused to entertain any vexing questions that could not be given a plain answer. Dr. Johnson kicked a stone, and thus refuted Berkeley. Likewise the Ionians looked about and assumed that the universe was made up of things extended in space. They bowed to no priest, read no sacred book, and were commercially prosperous enough to indulge their bent for speculation.[1] By definition, the supernatural did not entice them, for what was above or outside the natural they made no attempt to accommodate. To them, everything—the universe and all it contained, including (ostensibly) themselves—was natural. Living on the fringe of Asia, they must have encountered those nebulous mystery religions that the East has showered on Europe; but notions of guilt and sin, of deific interventions in the affairs of men, of cajoling an arbitrary supernatural creature or prostrating oneself before it, of the Mithraic taurobolium, of Mazda and Ahriman, of Attis and Osiris, of the Orphic mysteries, did not divert their quizzical attempts to understand the world. On the great premise that all things are material and as such subject to a natural sequence of cause and effect, they excluded the spiritual and the transcendental. Their universe was to be philosophically understood, not religiously venerated and worshipped for its mystery.[2]

Specifically, the Ionians were intent on defining the primary stuff that they took to be the material basis of all things—the *arché*, the irreducible element which underlies all appearances and manifestations of sense.[3]

---

[1] See F. M. Cornford, "Mystery Religions and Pre-Socratic Philosophy," *The Cambridge Ancient History*, IV (1926), 538. In the interests of economy—and perhaps to facilitate the reading of a heavily documented book—I have throughout used as short a reference as possible for the notes. Complete bibliographical data will be found in the Bibliography (pp. 339 ff.).

[2] See F. M. Cornford, *Before and After Socrates* (1932), pp. 14 ff. The standard collection of the pre-Socratic fragments is Hermann Diels (ed.), *Die Fragmente der Vorsokratiker*, 3 vols., 1934-1938. Many of the fragments are translated in John Burnet's indispensable *Early Greek Philosophy* (1930). Other useful compilations are Charles M. Bakewell, *Source Book in Ancient Philosophy* (1909), T. V. Smith (ed.), *Philosophers Speak for Themselves* (1934), and Milton C. Nahm (ed.), *Selections from Early Greek Philosophy* (1934).

[3] On the use of the term *arché* (which is really Aristotelian) see F. M. Cornford, *From Religion to Philosophy* (1912), p. 4, n. 1.

Their pursuit, it must be emphasized, was wholly materialistic; their goal was to discover the mechanism by which natural objects derived from the *arché*, and they, unlike their posterity, were mainly untroubled by the distinction between *natura naturata* and *natura naturans*. They thought, as Aristotle records, that

the principles which were of the nature of matter were the only principles of all things. That of which all things that are consist, the first from which they come to be, the last into which they are resolved (the substance remaining, but changing in its modifications), this they say is the element and this the principle of things, and therefore they think nothing is either generated or destroyed, since this sort of entity is always conserved.[4]

The search for this "element and principle of things" to which the Ionians variously reduced all phenomena led Thales to posit water as the *arché*, and Anaximenes to posit vapor; but it led Anaximander, a very powerful thinker, to the concept of the Boundless (*apeiron*) from which, by the action of heat and cold, were distilled the elements of matter. In this pregnant concept of primordial permanence which subsumes the *dynamis* of all coming into being and passing away lie the germs of much Greek philosophy.[5] The *diké* or order which governs the transformations of matter implies sequence, pattern, direction, and coherence as the necessary modes of all mechanism. Anaximander explains even "living creatures" (not exempt from the natural material order) as rising from the elemental "moist air as it was evaporated by the sun." And man—proud man—"was like another animal, namely, a fish, in the beginning."[6] If we take naturalism to imply both the exclusion of the transcendental as a principle of explanation and the assumption that all phenomena are explainable in terms of "matter, conceived as extended, impenetrable, eternally existent, and susceptible of movement or change of relative position,"[7] then the doctrine of Anaximander must be held to crown the Ionian attempt to render a naturalistic account of the universe.

The importance of this attempt becomes clearer when we remember its historical context. The Ionians refused to enter the tantalizing area of the supernatural. It remained for their great contemporary Pythagoras, on the other, Italic, side of the Greek world, to develop philosophically the converse spiritual attitude toward the universe. But back of both the Ionian

---

[4] *Metaphysica*, 983.

[5] Burnet, *Early Greek Philosophy*, pp. 53 ff.; cf. Werner Jaeger, *Paideia: the Ideals of Greek Culture* (1939), I, 156 ff.

[6] Burnet, *Early Greek Philosophy*, p. 70.

[7] James Mark Baldwin (ed.), *Dictionary of Philosophy and Psychology* (1901-1905), II, 45.

and the Italian schools (to use a distinction of Aristotle's) lay the abyss of prehistorical animism, magic, and spiritualism. Back of them both lay also the chthonic and mystery cults which we shall presently survey. Mr. Bradley has said that metaphysics is merely finding bad reasons for what we believe upon instinct: we should, then, perhaps lamely conclude that while Ionia was somehow producing a race of tough-minded materialists, southern Italy and Sicily were somehow nourishing a wide variety of Orphics, cultists, and mystical Pythagoreans who feared and derogated matter as instinctively as the Ionians celebrated it.

## PYTHAGOREAN MYSTICISM

The concept of *psyché* (soul) is so germane to primitive thought, Greek and other, that its origins are concealed in prehistory, and lie in the province of folklore and anthropology rather than philosophy.[8] Certainly, men had very early established a crude dichotomy between the body that extends in space and reacts to external stimuli and the mysterious phenomena attendant on dreams and breath and death. The spirit-world, beyond the limitations of sense, was early associated by the Greeks with the *alter ego*, itself perhaps corporeal, that subsisted with the body but nonetheless had an identity and existence of its own. Ancient legends attest to this dualism, which is reaffirmed by Homer and Hesiod—to say nothing of the Rig-Veda and the Pyramid texts.[9] Its emergence into urbane, organized belief was theologically signalized in Hellas by the Eleusinian and Orphic cults and philosophically by the teachings of Pythagoras. The dread and secret rites of the mysteries, based on the myths of Demeter and the orgiastic Dionysos, had as their theme the superiority of soul to body; and Orphism centered about the principle of *ekstasis* (stepping out) —the severance of soul from body in order to escape the terrible reincarnations of the wheel of birth and to achieve the divinity of a bodiless existence.

Although the Pythagoreans were intensely sympathetic to such doctrines, the Ionians could only have thought them odd. In seeking a material element for "all things" they ignored the spirit-world and man's traffickings with it—precisely because it lay in the realm of the supernatural and (by implication) the arbitrary, and thus transcended order and sequence. By implication at least (for their fragments are innocent of

---

[8] See the brilliant discussion in Cornford, *From Religion to Philosophy*, chaps. III-IV. The standard account is Erwin Rohde, *Psyche: The Cult of Souls and Belief in Immortality among the Greeks* (1925); cf. John Burnet, "The Socratic Doctrine of the Soul," *Proceedings of the British Academy (1915-1916)*, pp. 235-259.

[9] Henry Osborn Taylor, *Ancient Ideals* (1913), I, 16 ff.

ethical or humanistic bias) they reduced man to the uniform level of all things, enlisting no divinities or theologies to account for him. The soul, they seemed to agree, was of a subtle and rarefied materiality with the attributes of perception and location, but these attributes were merely high organizations and distillations of matter. Thales, like Empedocles much later, was inclined to ascribe motion to the soul, which he believed dispersed throughout the whole universe;[10] Anaximenes, of course, identified it with air.[11] Not until the seventeenth century of our era was a first-rate thinker to wound man's dignity comparably, by suggesting, like the Ionian physicists, that he was after all nothing more than a certain configuration of material elements. And everyone knows the vilification Hobbes got for his pains.

Pythagoras of Samos (582-510?) could not be satisfied with the materialism of the older Ionians. Their thought was essentially secular, his essentially religious, and so his system was profoundly dissimilar to theirs. Thus this very great man (whose influence is in inverse ratio to our knowledge of him) symbolizes the first attempt to make philosophy something more than the natural science of the physicists. Inherently religious, a powerful mathematician, the quasi-holy founder of a cult, he could not accept the monotheism that might be derived from Anaximander's *apeiron*. He, who invented the word "philosophy," could not use wisdom merely to satisfy his curiosity; instead, like Socrates who echoes him so often, he could use it only in the achievement of virtue.

Pythagoras, a man of many talents, was both a scientist and a mystic,[12] but he was careful to use his mathematics to buttress his profound religious impulses. (Later, and inevitably, his followers split into two factions, one modernist and scientific, the other mystic.) For Pythagoras himself, so far as we can reconstruct his own thought, mathematics was never an end in itself: the Pythagoreans, as Aristoxenus reminds us, were a religious brotherhood: "In all their definitions of conduct, their aim is communion [or converse, *homilia*] with the divine. This is their starting-point; their whole life is ordered with a view to following God; and it is the governing principle of their philosophy."[13] Pythagoras construed philosophy as a religious regimen, thus anticipating Plato in the *Phaedo* and even Aristotle in his paean of pure speculation. Because we actually

---

[10] Aristotle, *De Anima*, 405, 411.

[11] Burnet, *Early Greek Philosophy*, p. 75.

[12] See F. M. Cornford, "Mysticism and Science in the Pythagorean System," *Classical Quarterly*, XVI (1922), 137-50.

[13] Quoted by Cornford, "Mystery Religions and Pre-Socratic Philosophy," *Cambridge Ancient History*, IV, 546.

know almost nothing of Pythagoras' religious teachings—except that they included such doctrines as transmigration and the kinship of all living creatures—Grote's unpretentious summary is doubly welcome:

Of his spiritual training much is said, though not upon very good authority: we hear of his memorial discipline, his monastic self-scrutiny, his employment of music to soothe disorderly passions, his long novitiate of silence, his knowledge of physiognomy which enabled him to detect even without trial unworthy subjects, his peculiar diet, and his rigid care for sobriety as well as for bodily vigour.[14]

There were, inevitably, certain taboos imposed upon the cult, such as abstinence from beans and from flesh, but dogma perhaps played no important part in the brotherhood. As Aristotle explained, "the initiated are not supposed to learn anything, but to be affected in a certain way and put into a certain frame of mind." [15] Whatever the religious practices of the cult, which was established at Crotona about 532, it presently became so potent politically that the secular authorities discouraged it by the blunt expedient of setting fire to many of the prominent brethren.

Although Pythagoras' original impulse, in spite of his Ionian birth, must have been sincerely religious, he takes his place among the world's great thinkers as a scientist. His achievement was to substitute a philosophy of form and relationship for the Ionians' philosophy of matter. For him, reality was something other than a material *arché*: it was mathematical harmony and proportion in which numbers represented qualitative essences or absolutes rather than quantitative relationship.[16] Pythagoras construed mathematics rather as the Orphics construed ritual initiation, as a means by which man could achieve purification and escape the wheel of birth.[17] In his complicated system, concord or harmony (e.g. as in a musical scale, or as between the microcosm and the macrocosm) is the foundation of both science and ethics. The intricate mathematics of the Pythagoreans, symbolized by the numerology of the tetractys, assumes metaphysical significance. Because, as Aristotle reports, everything in nature seemed to be "modelled on numbers, and numbers seemed to be the first things in the whole of nature, they [the Pythagoreans] supposed the elements of numbers to be the elements of all things, and the whole heaven to be a musical scale and a number." [18] The soul, thus, is merely

[14] George Grote, *A History of Greece* (Everyman's Library), V, 102.
[15] Quoted by Burnet, *Early Greek Philosophy*, p. 84.
[16] See Jaeger, *Paideia*, I, 161.
[17] On the vexed question of the relationship between the Orphics and the Pythagoreans, see Theodore Gomperz, *Greek Thinkers*, I, 123.
[18] *Meta.*, 985; cf. Rohde, *Psyche*, pp. 374 ff.

the harmonious relationship of the elements of warm and cold, dry and moist.[19] Like all other things, it represents the effect of limit or form operating on the Boundless or the Infinite, a concept inherited from Anaximander. This basic dualism suggests all the dualisms of nature: right and left, masculine and feminine, light and dark, square and oblong.[20] This system, based upon a sophisticated mathematics, presages much— the massive dualisms of Plato's ideas and particulars, Aristotle's form and matter, the Christian cleavage of body and soul, as well as the mumbo-jumbo of Neo-Pythagorean and Alexandrian numerology and assorted modern quackeries.[21] One has only to read the *Phaedo,* and note its repercussions in Christian theology, to realize the power of Pythagorean thought through the whole Hellenic world.

### THE CHALLENGE OF THE ELEATIC ABSOLUTE

Ionian naturalism and Pythagorean mysticism, both products of the sixth century, represented the two major kinds of answer to the question of permanence and change: naturalism and mysticism. Also they posed the kinds of problems that philosophers of the fifth century addressed themselves to, and suggested the main lines that philosophical speculation was either to follow or attack. Heraclitus and Parmenides, each in his own way, undermined both the older metaphysics, but the atomists worked out the implications of Ionian materialism with extraordinary success. At any rate, by the time the Sophists appeared, about the middle of the fifth century, the distrust of abstruse ontological pronouncements was widespread; it remained for Socrates to introduce into philosophy an entirely new line of ethical inquiry.

Heraclitus of Ephesus (fl. 500) marks the deliquescence of Ionian naturalism. The "dark philosopher" who has defied definitive analysis to this day was haunted by the fact of change. Most men who aspire to the title of philosopher are *au fond* teased with the riddle of permanence and change. Certainly the Ionians were, but most of them assumed since (empirical investigation had to wait on technology) a material permanence behind the transformations of matter. Heraclitus' notorious dictum, known to everybody through Walter Pater's citation, declared cryptically that all flows and nothing remains. Paradoxically, he found a certain constant in the universality of mutation. The principle of eternal flux— "you could not step twice in the same rivers; for other and yet other

---

[19] Plato, *Phaedo,* 86-87; cf. Burnet, *Early Greek Philosophy,* pp. 295-96.

[20] Aristotle, *Meta.,* 986. Aristotle, always the systemizer, explains that there are "ten principles, which they [the Pythagoreans] arrange in two columns of cognates."

[21] See George Boas, *The Major Traditions of European Philosophy* (1929), pp. 100 ff.

waters are ever flowing on" [22]—has been a perennially popular answer to the question of ontology; currently the notion that reality is a process and not a thing has the support of some of our most eminent philosophical scientists. But the dialectic of Heraclitus, in which everything is as real as everything else, and in which the key to the dynamics of reality lies in the tension of opposites,[23] was as destructive to the Pythagoreans' concept of mathematical absolutes as to the Ionians' of material absolutes. "Opposition unites. From what draws apart results the most beautiful harmony. All things take place by strife." [24]

If Heraclitus was haunted by the fact of change, his contemporary, Parmenides, was haunted by the fact of permanence. Though bred an orthodox Pythagorean, he was unable to derive any sort of pluralistic universe from the latent monism of Pythagoras: for him, the real had to be one. The Eleatic absolutism of which he is the most brilliant spokesman rejects, therefore, both naturalism and Pythagorean mysticism. Parmenides himself was so obsessed with the notion of rest, unity, and wholeness that he could only conceive of reality as possessing such attributes. He and his fellow Eleatics, though metaphysicians, have profoundly influenced many subsequent theologies (including Plato's) in reserving for reality the attributes of permanence and unity that clearly do not belong to the objects of sensation.[25] Xenophanes (fl. 536), for instance, was perplexed by the absurdities of the Olympic pantheon. In Euripides' day when skepticism had become fashionable, only the very pious or the very blind could still cringe at the blasphemies of dying Hippolytus,[26] or at Creusa's denunciation of her seducer Apollo.[27] But a century earlier Xenophanes had dared to ridicule anthropomorphic deities. Like the prophets of Israel, he was trying to formulate a monotheism: "God is one, supreme among gods and men, and not like mortals in body or mind." [28]

Parmenides' absolutism is the philosophic coördinate of Xenophanes'

[22] Nahm, Selections, p. 91.

[23] See Burnet, Early Greek Philosophy, pp. 165-67.

[24] Nahm, Selections, p. 91.

[25] It is not odd, for instance, to find so religious a man as Boethius (The Consolation of Philosophy, III.12) quoting Parmenides with approval. Parmenides' simple Being is, says Boethius, the "very form of the Divine Substance."

[26] See Clifford Herschel Moore, The Religious Thought of the Greeks (1916), pp. 133 ff.

[27] Ion, 885.

[28] Nahm, Selections, p. 109. About six centuries later, Clement of Alexandria ("Exhortation to the Greeks" II.27) sounded the same note (a common one in early Christian writers): "Now listen to the loves of these gods of yours; to the extraordinary tales of their incontinence; to their wounds, imprisonments, fits of laughter, conflicts, and periods of servitude. Listen, too, to their revels, their embraces, their tears, passions and dissolute pleasures."

monotheism. Reality for Parmenides could include nothing less than the divine attributes of unity, eternity, and immutability. Since change was repellent to him, he inferred that what is timeless and unchanging must be real. Against Heraclitus, who held reality to be essentially dynamic, Parmenides maintained a rigid, static monism. The one made stability inconceivable; the other made change impossible. Parmenides insisted on the existence of one immutable Being as the unique object of knowledge. What *is* consists of a corporeal plenum, aboriginal and spherical and motionless; therefore the phantasmagoria of sensation is illusion and absurdity. Everything that is, is part of Being; what is not is unthinkable. *Ex nihilo nihil fit.* "So it is necessary that being either is absolutely or is not. Nor will the force of the argument permit that anything spring from being except being itself. Therefore justice does not slacken her fetters to permit generation or destruction, but holds being firm." [29]

When Parmenides substitutes simple Being for the various specialized forms of being, he suggests an almost Platonic distinction between the intelligible and the sensible world. But also he reaffirms the common pre-Socratic belief in a permanent material reality. The ambiguities of his position are ambiguities still: the concept of finite, spatial, globe-shaped Being, found in the world of thought and not of sense, can be and has been interpreted variously as materialistic or idealistic.

One path only is left for us to speak of, namely, that *It is.* In this path are very many tokens that what is is uncreated and indestructible; for it is complete, immovable, and without end. Nor was it ever, nor will it be; for now *it is,* all at once, a continuous one.[30]

But it seems likely that Parmenides, going even further than the mystical Pythagoreans who had found the highest reality in super-sensibles and in mathematical abstractions, suggested an idealism so absolute as to make the objects of sense impossible. Otherwise, would Plato have thought him so great a man?

Parmenides' destruction of the physical universe made necessary a reconstruction of philosophic pluralism. Anaxagoras, the intimate of Pericles, restated the Ionian tradition which was so brilliantly worked out by the atomists, while Empedocles (fl. 450) attempted to accommodate philosophically Parmenides' absolutism and the pluralistic universe forced upon us by our senses. Chronologically, both Empedocles and Anaxa-

[29] Nahm, *Selections,* p. 116. The celebrated paradoxes of such derivative Eleatics as Zeno show the lengths to which Parmenides' absolutism could be pushed.
[30] Burnet, *Early Greek Philosophy,* pp. 174-75.

goras inherited the contradiction between the Heraclitean flux and the Eleatic absolute. Empedocles' thought had many facets. The religious doctrine of his *Purifications,* revolving about the principle of transmigration, is almost Orphic; but philosophically he shows the influence of both the absolutists and the pluralists, and bows in deference to both schools. To account for a basic stability he proposed the four "roots"—earth, air, fire, water—which combine to form all things; to explain the dynamics of the world of sense he predicated continual change in the way the four elements alter their relationships. By the twin principles of Love and Strife, attraction and repulsion (which themselves assume the status of elements) Empedocles was able to accommodate both the absolutes of real being and the ceaseless flux of sensation.[31]

Anaxagoras, who also modified Ionian naturalism under the influence of Parmenides, enjoys two biographical distinctions. He first brought philosophy to Athens, and he shared with Socrates the obliquy of being tried and found guilty of a bogus charge of immorality by the citizens of that enlightened city. But philosophically he is significant because he, like Empedocles, attempted a compromise between pluralism and monism. His solution is not radically new in principle; instead of four elements he demanded an infinite number of irreducible and inert particles of reality: "all things were together, infinite both in number and in smallness." [32] But his concept of *nous* (mind), the complement of matter, led him to a dualism adumbrated in Empedocles' Love and Strife. Like Empedocles, and unlike the early Ionians, he felt the need to explain the motion of matter, and this philosophic maturity, says Aristotle, made him "seem like a sober man in contrast with the random talk of his predecessors." [33] *Nous* originates motion and imposes order upon motion: it is to the universe as the mind is to the body. "All things were together; then mind came and set them in order." [34] It is Anaxagoras' achievement to have conceived mind as a metaphysical concept with the status of an Eleatic absolute. Of the two ultimate realities, mind is superior to matter; it is the unmixed purity, the "Prime Mover" regulating the infinite alterations of material things. "It exists alone by itself," [35] and because it is unmixed

[31] On some of the interesting scientific implications to be deduced from Empedocles' dicta (e.g. the circulation of the blood and the theory of evolution), see John Martyn Warbecke, *The Searching Mind of Greece* (1934), pp. 67 ff.

[32] Burnet, *Early Greek Philosophy*, p. 258.

[33] *Meta.*, 984.

[34] Quoted by William L. Davidson, *The Stoic Creed* (1907), p. 4.

[35] Nahm, *Selections*, p. 150. As to the actual corporeality of the mind, Anaxagoras is not clear. See W. Windelband, *A History of Philosophy* (1931), p. 98; Rohde, *Psyche*, pp. 386 ff.

while matter is complex, it is not mechanistically determined. Indivisible into parts or faculties, mind (or soul) is everywhere the same—the principle of life in both plants and animals that varies only quantitatively.

All other things partake in a portion of everything, while Nous is infinite and self-ruled, and is mixed with nothing, but is alone, itself by itself . . . For it is the thinnest of all things and the purest, and it has all knowledge about everything and the greatest strength; and Nous has power over all things, both greater and smaller, that have life.[36]

Thus Anaxagoras' concept of *nous* marks, in Aristotelian terms, the concept of an efficient cause transcending matter; the concept is the first philosophic formulation of a dualism in which mind controls matter. The respect with which both Plato and Aristotle treated it merely corresponds to its importance in most subsequent theologies. By escaping from the persistent question of *how* the universe is as it is, and substituting for it the question of *why,* Anaxagoras raised the curtain on the great period of Greek philosophy. His injection of teleology into cosmology is a prognostic of the direction which Hellenic thought was to follow.

### THE CULMINATION OF NATURALISM: THE ATOMISTS

While one line of thinkers under the influence of Parmenides was gradually modifying the Milesian's materialism, another was strengthening it. Leucippus and Democritus, the latter a young man in Socrates' prime, achieved in their atomism a thoroughly mechanistic rationale of the contradiction of permanence and change; Epicurus later revived and popularized their physics with enormous success, and finally Lucretius immortalized atomism in poetry. Its exclusion of God, mind, or direction must have attracted a disillusioned Roman like Lucretius as strongly as it repelled Socrates. The atomists' pluralism assumed a universe composed of infinite discrete and homogeneous particles between which no qualitative distinction could be made. Because the atoms were corporeal and eternal, they represented permanence; because they hurtled from one aggregation to another, their activity represented change. By the concept of the void—the empty space in which atoms operate—the atomists escaped some of Parmenides' untenable doctrines of motion; to his plenum they adduced an equally necessary vacuum to make activity possible. What appears to us as the objects of sense are configurations of atoms, themselves too small to be seen; however the combinations may flow together and apart again in the void, the atoms persist unchanged. Motion

---

[36] Burnet. *Early Greek Philosophy,* pp. 259-60.

depends not on a prime mover (such as Anaxagoras' *nous*), but is itself primary and eternal. Like the Heraclitean flow, it is an ultimate attribute of reality.

This atomism did not demand a universe of chance and chaos. The configurations of the atoms, as Leucippus said, are not fortuitous: "Nothing occurs at random, but everything for a reason and by necessity." [37] The agitation of the particles in the void, far from being capricious, is "definite, necessary, reasonable, grounded in the total situation." [38] The cosmic planning is not conscious, or superimposed by some superior force on the hurrying of atomic groupings. It is inherent in the process of change itself; it is wholly natural, wholly mechanistic, and merely expresses the attraction of like for like that impels the configurations of structure.[39]

The soul, obviously, cannot be qualitatively distinguished from the universal corporeal reality. It too is composed of atoms (distinctively round and smooth, however) distributed throughout the body. Even though these atoms, like all others, are eternal, they do not permanently retain their special configuration. The soul is not immortal: its components flow back into the vast matrix of nature, whence they presently form new allocations. The atoms of the mind are congregated in the brain, and are unmixed. The soul, like the brain, is the source of knowledge, since knowledge arises from the contact of atom with atom. Sensation occurs when a film or effluence (*eidolon*) from external atoms encounters those within the body by entering the interstices of the void. When these *eidola* persist, we have memory; when they fade and dissolve, forgetfulness. Those effluences too finely rarefied to affect the soul atoms pass on to the brain; there they impinge on the mind atoms and the result is thought. Thus thought itself is a matter of touch, the mutual materialistic action of body on body.[40] This means that the knowledge gained through the soul is grosser and less reliable than that resulting from thought. Real knowledge, said Democritus, is of the atoms and the void, and comes only, if at all, from intellection. The data of sensation, concerning the variables

[37] Cyril Bailey, *The Greek Atomists and Epicurus* (1928), p. 85. This is the only extant fragment of Leucippus.

[38] Warbecke, *The Searching Mind of Greece*, p. 85.

[39] See Diogenes Laertius' account of Leucippus, *The Lives and Opinions of Eminent Philosophers* (Bohn's Classical Library, 1901), pp. 388-90.

[40] Aristotle discusses this psychology in *De Anima*, 403. The ethics of Democritus, preserved in the "Golden Sayings," are largely aphoristic. Happiness, the highest good, comes of an awareness of one's place in the cosmic structure. Material possessions are derogated, for genuine well-being consists in "uprightness and fulness of understanding." See Smith, *Philosophers Speak for Themselves*, pp. 40-43; Diels, *Die Fragmente der Vorsokratiker*, II, 154 ff.

of temporary atomic groupings, are fleeting and misleading, and in no way concerned with permanent reality.

The succession of thinkers which had begun with Thales, a contemporary of Solon, and had ended with Democritus, who long survived Socrates, had sketched in the lines that Greek thought was to follow. Most subsequent philosophy was to oscillate between the extremes of Ionian naturalism and Italic mysticism. The relevance of these Pre-Socratics to the problem of this work—which is the nature of man—is oblique, but important. Although they were mainly interested in cosmology and ontology, they provided a frame of reference for the great period of Greek ethics. After all, ethics is a subordinate branch of philosophy, and when later and greater thinkers began to concern themselves with it, they adjusted their ethical systems to the metaphysics they had borrowed or adopted from the Pre-Socratics. As we shall see, in the history of ethics it has mattered greatly whether one is generically an Ionian materialist or an Italic idealist. Therefore a synoptic account of these two basic attitudes will perhaps be useful in tracing the development of Greek ethical theory. At any rate, Plato and Aristotle were not ashamed to acknowledge their indebtedness to the men who had first posed the necessary questions of philosophy.

# II

## THE PROBLEM OF ETHICAL ABSOLUTES

### PERMANENCE AS LAW

MOST MEN ARE NOT PHILOSOPHERS, and philosophic concepts generally lie beyond the comprehension and interests of most men. Certainly, the cosmogonies of the sixth and fifth centuries cannot be said to have influenced the daily life of contemporary Greeks: after Parmenides, philosophy became so abstruse and conceptual as to be the business of only a few dozen specialists. Nevertheless, it is useful to trace the course of philosophic speculation because any philosophy—and to an extraordinary degree Greek philosophy—derives from the attitudes and habits of thought common to a group of people at a given time. Ordinarily the correlation between "professional" philosophy and secular activity seems tenuous, and almost always it is difficult to formulate, but it always exists. Stoicism in the Roman Empire was peculiarly congenial to a people who reverenced law and whose genius was for juridical administration; the roots of Locke's thought lie deeply embedded in English constitutional history; the various vitalistic systems of modern times, from Schopenhauer to Bergson, signalize a widespread distrust (apparent in many departments of thought, and most notably in science) of traditional *a priori* rationalism. Thus, to understand the significance of the pre-Socratic quest for permanence should help us understand how the Greeks viewed themselves and their universe.

The various metaphysical and cosmological systems of the sixth century sought to define the element of permanence in a universe ostensibly characterized by change. The importance of the attempt is that the Greeks after Thales seem to have had a supremely high regard for order, and a compulsion to express that regard in all their institutions. The concept of order implies, of course, the mutual relation of the parts and the whole, and it is the concept that explains what is most typical in all Greek activity —in metaphysics, ethics, politics, and art. The fact that men so widely dissimilar as Thales and Pythagoras felt the need to state philosophically the nature of permanence and the relationship of the permanent to the impermanent suggests a characteristic Greek attitude: a deep reverence for the pattern, design, and recurrence that are the surest indices of permanence in a world of change. Plato's concept of the Ideal and Aristotle's of form are the most significant metaphysical formulations of this concept in Greek thought; but they answer, in a more sophisticated and complex way, the same question that had teased the Ionian physicists, the Pythagoreans, the Eleatics, and that was to tease the Stoics and the Epicureans.

As Herodotus shows, the Greeks had an incorrigible interest in themselves as humans, but it was subordinated to their interest in the universe as a whole. Their wish was always to understand themselves, but only as parts of the universe: thus the extraordinary significance of their concept of the *polis*—the city-state which embraces all individual citizens, and in reference to which the status of each individual was determined. Later, Alexander and the Stoics made possible a universalized concept of citizenship which, as developed by the Romans, has been the most powerful legacy of pagan antiquity. When Aristotle said that the state is a creation of nature and that man is by nature a political animal,[1] he was stating in political terms those recurrent factors of all experience: the general and permanent, and the idiosyncratic and individual. The harmonious relationship between the two, based upon a proper comprehension of the *physis* or nature of the two, was to the Greek the highest desideratum, in politics as in ethics. It is better, Pericles told the Athenians, "for individuals themselves that the citizens should suffer and the state flourish than that the citizens should flourish and the state suffer."[2]

In Greek political institutions the concept of order appears in the idealization of law or 'fixed measure' (*diké*). What the Ionians had sought to formulate cosmologically, Solon and Clisthenes sought to formulate politically. Plato, the metaphysician who resented so desperately the disorderly world he lived in, met the same problem and so construed virtue itself in terms of harmony, proportion, and order. "The virtue of each thing," Socrates tells Callicles, "whether of body or soul, instrument or creature, when given to them in the best way, comes to them not by chance, but as the result of the order and truth and art which are imparted to them. Am I not right? I maintain that I am. And does not the virtue of each thing depend on order or arrangement? Yes, I say."[3] Centuries later, Boethius, overwhelmed by affliction and aghast at the intellectual darkness settling over the world, posed the old question and reaffirmed the old answer. "Thinkest thou that this world is governed by haphazard and chance? Or rather dost thou believe that it is ruled by reason?" Boethius, nurtured in the Greek tradition, made the inevitable answer: he

---

[1] *Politica,* 1253.
[2] Thucydides, II.60.
[3] *Gorgias,* 506.

could "in no manner imagine that such certain motions are caused by rash chance. And I know that God the Creator doth govern His work, neither will I ever think otherwise." [4]

This belief in an essentially systematic—and, to the Greek, therefore rational—universe is the touchstone of Greek thought. Homer's Alcinous remarks that it is good to observe a certain seemliness in all things[5]—a gnomic tag that, developed into the majestic ethical principle of moderation, itself is a corollary of the concept of order. As early as the *Odyssey* the notion of *areté* (nobility) was made to include something other than the valor and military honor of the *Iliad;* in the later epic, which reflects a later and more mature culture, virtue assumes social implications involved in the ownership of land, respect for tradition, and communal obligations. The subsequent virtues of Solon's *polis*-culture are, naturally, those virtues of civil righteousness which were to be codified in Plato's tetralogy of courage, godliness, righteousness, and prudence.[6] And significantly, above them all looms the splendid, cumulative virtue of justice, which governs the relation of the parts to the whole.

Even Heraclitus, the philosopher of flux, celebrates that order that "always was, and is, and ever shall be, an ever-living fire, kindling according to fixed measure, and extinguished according to fixed measure." [7] Fixed measure is clearly the dominating concept behind Solon's constitution. Thus his magnificent eulogy of law as the creator of "order and harmony":

It maketh rough things smooth, it checketh inordinate desires, it dimmeth the glare of wanton pride and withereth the budding bloom of wild delusions; it maketh crooked judgments straight and softeneth arrogant behavior; it stoppeth acts of sedition and stoppeth the anger of bitter strife. Under the reign of law, sanity and wisdom prevail ever among men.[8]

In later and more perilous days, Demosthenes cited Solon's denunciation of those who disregard the innate principle of law, of which the state is

---

[4] *Consolation,* I.6.

[5] The *Odyssey,* VII. 312-13. Likewise Heraclitus (Nahm, *Selections,* p. 94): "To be temperate is the greatest virtue; and it is wisdom to speak the truth and to act according to nature with understanding."

[6] See Jaeger, *Paideia,* I, 15 ff., 103 ff. On the four cardinal virtues see Constantin Ritter, *The Essence of Plato's Philosophy* (trans. Adam Alles, 1933), pp. 306 ff.

[7] Nahm, *Selections,* p. 90.

[8] Ivan M. Linforth, "Solon the Athenian," *Classical Philology,* VI (1919), 143. This volume includes both a biography (pp. 3-127) and the text and translation of the extant fragments (pp. 129-171). On the Solonic code see F. E. Adcock, "The Reform of the Athenian State," *Cambridge Ancient History,* IV, 41 ff.; Grote, *A History of Greece,* III, 305 ff.

the political embodiment: woe to those who "pay no heed to the unshaken rock of holy Justice, who, though she be silent, is aware of all that happeneth now or hath happened in the past, and, in the course of time, surely cometh to demand retribution." [9]

Solon had brought order out of chaos by implicitly accepting the principle of order and articulating it in politico-economic terms. There are, he said, four classes of free men in Athens: the *pentakosiomedimni* (those with an annual return of five hundred bushels), the *hippes,* the *zeugitai,* the *thetes.*[10] Each class had its duties and its functions, and each found its voice in such groups as the Areopagus, the Council of Four Hundred, the *ekklesia.* The scheme, frankly a compromise of democracy, oligarchy, and timocracy, may seem mathematically rigid;[11] but Solon's constitution (594) persisted, *mutatis mutandis,* as the pride of Athens and the very fabric of its *polis*-culture. Through all the upheavals and reversals that followed—the "tyranny" of Pisistratus (who actually spoke for the restive middle class against the landed aristocracy), the democratic "reforms" of the high-born Cleisthenes, the apotheosis of the fifth century, the slow rot of the Peloponnesian War, the ignominy before the power of Macedonia—the Solonic constitution continued to express politically that sense of order and proportion so basic to the Greek mind. Winckelman and Lessing, in the eighteenth century, bowed reverently before Hellenistic sculpture: in it they found, as they thought, genuine classicism—the synthesis of rest and motion, strength and beauty, the part with the whole. In short, order and design. And even when Greece was slipping into moral and political decadence we hear Xenophon, a professional soldier, urging that shoes and clothes, properly arranged on a shelf, may induce something like aesthetic pleasure; for even pots, he says, "have a graceful appearance when they are placed in regular order." [12] He, like Solon, was a true Greek.

From this basic notion of society as the just and reciprocal relation of parts sprang the complex and sometimes perplexing stratification of Greek life. The paradox of slavery existing among a people who achieved the first democracy and whose humanism has been the envy of posterity has been frequently deplored. Yet given the Greek view of the universe (the

---

[9] Linforth, p. 141.

[10] Some of these classes were, of course, relics from the period of the Eupatrid oligarchs. The *hippes* were owners of horses (i.e. knights), the *zeugitai* owners of oxen, the *thetes* hired laborers.

[11] Note Herodotus' interesting discussion (III.80-82) of the three forms of government in the dialogue of Otanes, Mogabyzus, and Darius.

[12] *Oeconomicus,* VIII.18-19. For a discussion of some of the semantic implications of *diké* see Kenneth Burke, *A Grammar of Motives* (1945), p. 15.

macrocosm) and of society (the microcosm) the paradox is resolved. The concept of static, hierarchal degrees which lay at the basis of every Greek's thought and which was codified by Aristotle has had a long life in the intellectual history of Europe. Our own humanitarian and democratic concepts of the equality and the dignity of men derive from both Greek humanism and from Christianity, but they have been powerfully sustained, since the Renaissance, by the idea of progress. Perfectibility demands some sort of change for the better. Any glorification of change was an idea foreign to the Greeks. They, with Parmenides, held the static and the immutable higher than that which fluctuates. Aristotle's pure being and Plato's Ideas were far removed from those impermanent realms of becoming and of sense; and as these metaphysics mirrored the Greek ideal, so did Greek politics. Whatever change society exhibited was, to their thinking, deterioration and not progress. Plato dated the ideal commonwealth some 9000 years before Solon, and Aristotle held it axiomatic that any modification in the social system was undesirable.[13] Hence the sanction of a social *order* that is static, in which each element has its place determined by its relation to other and different elements. Plato, as his seventh epistle makes clear, had been lamentably disheartened by attempts at social leveling: of all things he feared a genuine democracy the most, and even Aristotle had his doubts. The *Republic* insists upon a stratified society of sharp demarcations, governed by the philosopher-king whose distinction it is to perceive the divine order of the universe.

For he, Adeimantus, whose mind is fixed upon true being, has surely no time to look down on the affairs of earth, or to be filled with malice and envy, contending against men; his eye is ever directed towards things fixed and immutable, which he sees neither injuring nor injured by one another, but all in order moving according to reason; these he imitates, and to these he will, as far as he can, conform himself.[14]

The Athenians, then, were not alarmed by the fact that at the close of the fourth century there were four slaves for every citizen. As Aristotle explains, slaves are like animals: both use their bodies to minister to the needs of life.[15] And because manual labor was beneath the free man, Plato—very justly, as he must have thought—refused to grant citizenship to the artisans of his ideal commonwealth, for they are only partial men.[16] "For that some should rule and others be ruled is a thing not only neces-

[13] See J. B. Bury, *The Idea of Progress* (1932), pp. 10-11.
[14] *Republic*, 500.
[15] *Pol.*, 1254.
[16] *Republic*, 495.

sary, but expedient," Aristotle remarks; "from the hour of their birth, some are marked out for subjection, others for rule." [17] Only Euripides, the subversive, mocking Euripides, dared suggest that slavery was an accident of environment, and not a law of nature. But he, as Aristophanes never tires of telling us, was the son of a greengrocer. And Plato and Aristotle were the intimates of monarchs.

It is a commonplace that a leisure class necessitates a slave class. Whatever the lot of the lowly born or the unfortunate, the citizen of Athens could only consider the world as his oyster. He was the ideal object of humanistic cultivation. His privileges were matched only by his obligations to the state that made his privileges possible. He was the complete man, zealous alike of wisdom and pleasure, of physical strength and of intelligence. Asceticism was unknown to the Greek: just as the health of the state depended on the harmony and just relationship of the parts, so man's health depended on the fullest employment of all his capacities in accordance with reason, his highest quality. Plato's symposium had little in common with the *agapé* of the early Christians, for luxury was not abhorrent to the Greek. The "health and beauty and well-being of the soul" which Socrates calls virtue implies the complete man.[18] Simonides, so typically Hellenic in his zest for life and in his weary wisdom of life's tragedy, named man's goods as health, beauty, wealth, and friendship. "For what human life, nay, what throne, is desirable without pleasure? Without her the life of a very God is not to be envied." [19] The tone of ineffable pathos in the Greek Anthology derives mainly from the bittersweet of remembered pleasure, the wholesome acceptance of life's fragile goods that are so soon decayed. Thus Pericles, the paragon of Hellas. A hearty man, he is not ashamed to praise the games and religious festivals, the refinements of life, the general well-being enjoyed by the Athenian citizen. "Because of the greatness of our city the fruits of the whole earth flow in upon us; so that we enjoy the goods of other countries as freely as our own." [20] Certainly, says Aristotle, no one will deny that the happy man must enjoy all possible goods—"external goods, goods of the body, and goods of the soul." [21] Those famous words that Thucydides

---

[17] *Pol.*, 1254. On slavery in Greece see W. G. De Burgh, *The Legacy of the Ancient World* (1924), pp. 151 ff.; Marcus Tod, "The Economic Background of the Fifth Century," *Cambridge Ancient History*, V (1927), 6-11; Ernest Barker, *Greek Political Theory* (1918), pp. 29-33.

[18] *Republic*, 444.

[19] *Lyra Graeca*, II, 363 (frag. 69).

[20] Thucydides, II.38.

[21] *Pol.*, 1323; cf. *Magna Moralia*, 1204 ff., where Aristotle elaborately refutes obscurantists who would divorce pleasure from virtue; note Pericles' boast (Thucydides, I.6) that "we cultivate the mind without loss of manliness."

puts into the mouth of Pericles must stand as the most comely expression
of this Greek humanism:

To sum up: I say that Athens is the school of Hellas, and that the individual
Athenian in his own person seems to have the power of adapting himself to the
most varied forms of action with the utmost versatility and grace.[22]

While the Ionians were groping for a naturalistic cosmology based upon
the concept of permanence, Solon was formulating a cognate naturalism in
politics as exemplifying the notion of immanent law. As Werner Jaeger
has pointed out, the same attitude informs Athenian tragedy a century
later.[23] *Diké* is eternal, and injustice is followed by misery, according to
fixed measure. "For there really is," Aristotle insists, "as every one to some
extent divines, a natural justice and injustice that is binding on all men,
even on those who have no association or covenant with each."[24] This is
the theme that Aeschylus develops like a Bach fugue. "Nay, the law is
sternly set," says Zeus in denying Orestes' plea for tranquillity:

> Blood-drops shed upon the ground
> Plead for other bloodshed yet;
> Loud the call of death doth sound,
> Calling guilt of olden time,
> A Fury, crowning crime with crime.[25]

Greek tragedy is predicated upon the naturalistic assumption that effect
follows cause. Retributive justice is as eternal as Parmenides' absolute.
The protagonist must realize that his disaster occurs because he has done
this or that for which he alone is responsible, and also that he can be
neither victimized by a capricious deity nor protected by supernatural
agencies that will deflect the normal sequence of events for his benefit.[26]
Antigone's catastrophe is thus inevitable, no matter which course she
chooses. When charged by Creon with breaking his law, she answers that
she has obeyed a higher law—"the unwritten and unfailing statutes of
heaven."[27] Aeschylus, as monolithic as a Hebrew prophet, never aban-
dons the theme. His Furies chant:

[22] II.40-41.
[23] *Paideia*, I, 143.
[24] *Rhetorica*, 1373.
[25] *The Choephori*, 298 ff. (*The Complete Greek Drama* ed. Whitney J. Oates and Eugene
O'Neill Jr., 2 vols., 1938, I, 243). This and following citations from *The Complete Greek
Drama* are quoted by permission of Random House, the publishers.
[26] See Boas, *The Major Traditions of European Philosophy*, pp. 4-6; cf. A. H. Butcher,
"The Melancholy of the Greeks," *Some Aspects of the Greek Genius* (1893), pp. 133-76.
[27] *Antigone*, 450 ff. (*Complete Greek Drama*, I, 433).

Stern and fixed the law is: we have hands t'achieve it,
Cunning to devise.
Queens are we and mindful of our solemn vengeance.
Not by tear or prayer
Shall a man avert it.[28]

The enormous interest that still attaches to Greek drama—written for a theatre, and in a language, strange to us—largely lies in the dialectic between the universal and the individual: the intense humanism of the dramatists is a corollary to their innate reverence for moral law. This humanism is in clear contrast to the passivity and asceticism of the Orient; the dominant mood in the shield of Achilles is one of activity, of man functioning in his natural habitat. The *Iliad,* though the epic of a relatively barbarous age of warfare, is profoundly humanistic in the pathos it derives from man's struggle in his context of inevitable cosmic forces. Greek drama insistently develops the same theme, for it juxtaposes the concept of man's dignity and free will to that of a universe governed by a necessary law infinitely beyond man's ability to alter. "Wonders are many," says Sophocles in his beautiful hymn, "and none is more wonderful than man." Clearly preëminent in his physical and mental prowess, and in his conquest over nature, yet his greatest victory is his submission to law—"when he honors the laws of the land, and that justice which he has sworn by the gods to uphold, proudly stands his city: no city hath he who, for his rashness, dwells with sin." [29]

The civic, Olympian religion of the Greeks—so closely associated with their drama—reveals a similar attitude towards law. The aboriginal chthonic cults of Pelasgo-Mycenaean origin, which the Dorians had no doubt found flourishing as they swept down to the Peloponnesus after the twelfth century, continued to hold a strong appeal for the lower classes; but their influence, like their gods, was subterranean. For the most part, the Olympian pantheon of the invaders had been superimposed on the older chthonic religion and, sanctified by Homer and Hesiod, had become the official public religion of the *polis-*culture. As such, it represents a characteristic Greek attitude towards deity, an attitude tersely stated in a fragment of Philemon's:

Kings have their servants, but submit to gods:
God, to necessity. Considered well,
All things in their degree give place, the small
By nature's law made subject to the greater.[30]

---

[28] *The Eumenides,* 285 ff. (*Complete Greek Drama,* I, 284).
[29] *Antigone,* 332 ff. (*Complete Greek Drama,* I, 432).
[30] Trans. T. F. Higham, *The Oxford Book of Greek Verse in Translation* (Oxford: At the Clarendon Press, 1938), p. 525.

The Olympian gods, like the temples erected to them, are elements in the open, sunny landscape—public, accessible, and parts of the whole.

As Mr. Whitehead has said, " 'Canst thou by searching find out God?' is good Hebrew, but it is bad Greek." [31] Far from being inscrutable and beyond the understanding of man, *diké* and the gods who themselves are subject to it lie well within his comprehension. Like him, his gods are elements in a larger whole, and between him and his gods there is a reciprocal relation under eternal law. It is, moreover, man's high privilege and greatest good to know that law rules all. To the Greek his gods were his superiors, just as the powerful *pentakosiomedimni* were the superiors of the ignoble *thetes;* and his relation to his gods was similarly legal. Certainly, in the civic religion (for Orphism was, as we shall see, quite another matter), there was no element of mystery and no need for debased adoration. Everything was perfectly regular and comprehensible. Even in Homer, where there is so much animism and polytheism,[32] Zeus is by and large (as in the deific counsels which open the first and fifth books of the *Odyssey*) conceived of as the agent of law and cosmic order. As such, even in the implied monotheism of Aeschylus and Sophocles, he elicits admiration and respect, but not prostration.

The Periclean Greek was not tortured by conscience or sin in the Christian sense; he did not even have a word for sin, for the *hamartia* of the New Testament meant no more than error (literally, 'missing the mark'). Nor did he exhibit the characteristic *inwardness* of the Christian.[33] His gods were domesticated, like himself in shape and appetites, and his relation to them was not soul-searing and guilt-conscious. His obligations to them were contractual: in return for man's rites, sacrifices, and festivals the gods would, through oracles and by divinations, look after man's interests. The sacrifices were to keep the gods favorably disposed (even to avert their jealousy), but they were not to signalize atonement or remorse. Religious observances were, as even Aeschylus suggests, little more than a civic duty, like taxation. For above the gods loomed *moira* (fate, destiny, justice) and *diké* to which even the gods were subordinate and subject, and of which even Zeus, the mightiest of them, was merely an agent.[34] Nothing—least of all the sportive deities

---

[31] *Adventures of Ideas* (1935), p. 132.

[32] For instance, the nature myths of Scylla and Charybdis (*Ody.*, VII.70 ff.).

[33] See G. Lowes Dickinson, *The Greek View of Life* (1919), pp. 15 ff.

[34] It was this juridical, unemotional aspect of Greek religion that Nietzsche characterized as "precision and clarity" in his *Birth of Tragedy* (The Modern Library, n.d., p. 220). He interpreted the contrast between the Apollonian and the Dionysian as the contrast between the rational and the vitalistic, and he excoriated Socrates, the father of rationalism, as the greatest scoundrel in history.

of Olympus—could stay the inevitable punishment of the House of Atreus: in an essentially just and orderly universe crime was followed by retribution. Homer sounds like Aeschylus when he has Zeus deplore men's folly in charging against the gods "the evils (far beyond our worst dooming) which their own exceeding wantonness has heaped upon themselves." [35]

Thus variously but insistently the Greeks restated their fundamental conception of a permanent order inherent in the cosmos—an order, or justice, to which man, as part of nature, was subject.[36] This notion was not like Israel's: that law was imposed by an inscrutable and suprarational deity, a jealous god who warmed and cooled towards his wayward "children" and who dealt with them tenderly or harshly as he willed. Such an impositional law would have seemed chaos to the Greek; he placed even his gods within the cosmic order, and not above it. Zeus, after all, did not create the world, but as the supreme deity his functions as the preceptor of moral laws (*themistes*), as the purifier, as the guardian of both social and political order were clear. From the crude materialism of Thales to the conceptual grandeurs of Plato and Aristotle the theme ran: that law is immanent and inherent in the cosmos and that therefore things stand in a certain orderly relation to each other.[37] "Wherefore the temperate man is the friend of God," says the aged Plato after a lifetime of speculation on the subject, "for he is like Him; and the intemperate man is unlike Him, and different from Him, and unjust." [38]

### SOPHISTIC RELATIVISM

It has been not uncommon for historians of philosophy to derogate the Sophists—mainly, perhaps, because their mighty opponent Socrates so overshadows them. Those highly cultivated professional teachers, most advantageously represented by Protagoras (481?-411) and Gorgias (485?-380?), found it expedient to make expediency the supreme virtue. But they also (and this fact is sometimes neglected) held that man is the measure of all things; thus they gave philosophic statement to the basic humanism of the Greeks. In deriving their ethics and their epistemology

---

[35] *Ody.*, I.35 ff.

[36] At the close of the *Nicomachean Ethics*, where questions of ethics merge with those of politics, Aristotle defends civil law as the necessary discipline in virtue. See *Ethica Nicomachea*, 1179 ff.

[37] On this concept of immanent law, see Mr. Whitehead's brilliant discussion in *Adventures of Ideas*, pp. 152 ff. He takes as his text Plato's pronouncement (*Sophist*, 247) that the definition of being is power, which implies the interdependence of all things. See also, W. T. Stace, *The Destiny of Western Man* (1942), p. 29.

[38] *Laws*, 716.

from a fundamental attitude towards the human race, they marked a reaction against the cosmological and metaphysical theorizing of their predecessors. At the same time, they made themselves odious to unsympathetic critics like Plato whose thought was increasingly theocentric rather than anthropocentric.[39]

Historically, the Sophists were inevitable. From Protagoras, older by a generation than Democritus, until the glory of Athens collapsed before Spartan fascism, they symbolized both the weakness and the strength of Hellenic thought: the strength of a very urbane skepticism with which the rather shapeless intellectual accumulations of Greece were evaluated and codified; the weakness of a venal and often cynical subjectivism which could, and apparently did, induce something very like moral anarchy. The charges brought against them—they had the misfortune of making powerful enemies—sound suspiciously like the charges brought against all "radicals" by all "conservatives," and in judging them we must not forget either the temper of the times that produced them or their very considerable contributions to Greek culture. It would not do to denounce out of hand those men who represent the very clarity, logic, and precision that we so much admire in Greek thought; who made grammar and literary style legitimate objects of study; who, like Voltaire and Butler, dared to expose traditional stuffiness and sham.

The Sophists were genuine relativists. The course of events in the fifth century had challenged belief in absolutes, and the assaults against the Solonic constitution—from such men as Harmodios and Aristogeiton, for instance—had seemed to make untenable any affirmation of cosmic law mirrored in human institutions. In the sixth century the great political power and intellectual prestige of Ionia had begun to fail before the Persian advance, and the destruction of Miletus (494-93) had disillusioned and terrified all Hellas. True, at the beginning of the fifth century, Marathon and Salamis had saved Europe from Asiatic despotism and ushered in the blazing noon of Greek glory. But the glory was relatively short-lived: the suicide of Greece in the Peloponnesian War (431-404), accompanied by all the internal disasters and the moral anarchy which Thucydides has recorded, made it inevitable that by the end of the fourth century all Greece should lie prostrate before Macedonia.

Those were centuries of miraculous achievement and of miraculous change; and to intelligent men like the Sophists they must have seemed as profoundly disturbing as our own century seems to us. The march of events refused to conform to the old ideologies. How could a sensible man, the Sophists must have wondered, still find solace in absolutes—

[39] See Werner Jaeger, *Humanism and Theology* (1943), *passim*.

either metaphysical or ethical? Justice, like the *arché* of the Ionians, could be nothing more than an empty verbalization. Do not babble about justice, the brazenly opportunist Corinthians tell the Athenians; remember "that in the event of war something else is expedient; for the true path of expediency is the path of right." [40] Thucydides grimly develops all the variations of this sorry theme; and although we must not mistake the Sophists for the formulators of state policy, they were the mentors of men who were. Was not Alcibiades the pupil of Protagoras? The descendants of those Athenians who early in the century had applauded Aeschylus confessed, before the century was over, that their motives were ambition, fear, and interest.

We are not the first who have aspired to rule; the world has ever held that the weaker must be kept down by the stronger. And we think that we are worthy of power; and there was a time when you thought so too; but now when you mean expediency you talk about justice. Did justice ever deter anyone from taking by force whatever he could? [41]

We have only to look at Euripides and Aristophanes, those two mighty opposites, to see some diverse consequences of the Sophistic *Aufklärung*. Euripides, the skeptical and the radical, threw all in doubt. He questioned the moral justice of slavery (the best and oldest families had slaves), he sympathized with the hard lot of women, he even dared to wonder if the Olympians had any claim to a good man's worship. An intensely moral man, he was—to his sorrow—honest enough to explore the implications of the relativism so characteristic of the late fifth century.

> Doth some one say that there be gods above?
> There are not; no, there are not. Let no fool,
> Led by the old false fable, thus deceive you.
> Look at the facts themselves, yielding my words
> No undue credence: for I say that kings
> Kill, rob, break oaths, lay cities waste by fraud,
> And doing thus are happier than those
> Who live calm pious lives day after day. . . .
> All Divinity
> Is built up from our good and evil luck. [42]

In Aristophanes' incessant drubbing of Euripides we see the passionate anger of the conservatives against the radicals. For Aristophanes was

[40] Thucydides, I.42.
[41] *Ibid.*, I.76.
[42] A fragment of *Bellerophon* trans. J. A. Symonds, *The Oxford Book of Greek Verse in Translation* (Oxford: At the Clarendon Press, 1938), p. 457.

essentially the *laudator temporis acti.* With scabrous malice he laughed—
that he might not weep—at the innovations of his age. He detested democratic leveling and he abhorred religious skepticism. In the lost *Baby-
lonians* (426) his attack on Cleon (Pericles' successor) was so sharp that
he was fined; and in the *Knights* (424) the butt Demos (i.e. democracy)
was so grossly caricatured that only Aristophanes himself would dare
play the part. He thought the Sophists the enemies of the state and the
corrupters of morals; hence the attack, in the *Clouds,* on Socrates, who
owed more to Sophistic dialectic than he would perhaps admit. His unreasoned and vitriolic assaults on Euripides, both in the *Frogs* and the
scatological *Thesmorphoriazusae,* show, among other things, how un-
reasonable a man of genius might become.

Euripides, however, was a realist: he mourned the decay of morals, but
he admitted the decay. That, of course, makes for unpopularity. His
*Trojan Women,* produced in 415 shortly after the Athenian rape of
neutral Melos, voices the despair at the loss of political honor and justice.
"Oh heart of a beast where law is none," wails Hecuba,

> Where all things change so that lust be fed,
> The oath and the deed, the right and the wrong,
> Even the hate of the forkèd tongue.[43]

He announces the Hellenistic age, when *Tyché* (chance) displaced the
justice of Aeschylus' Zeus. He would nod in sad agreement with these
lines from a lost play:

> Poor Virtue, she's but words,—a vain romance
> I took for truth; ᴐ slave of Circumstance.[44]

The same note is struck repeatedly in Thucydides' superbly ironical account of Athenian depravity. Justice and honor, say the Athenians to the
Melian delegation, are only words. "The powerful exact what they can,
and the weak grant what they must." [45] To read Thucydides—and was
there ever a greater historian?—is to understand both the old and the new,
the justice of Solon and Aeschylus and the ethical relativism of Thrasymachus and Alcibiades. The litany of Thucydides memorializes the moral
deliquescence that Socrates tried to check. The Athenians who praised
democracy were as shifty and amoral as the Spartans who praised oligarchy. They were all men of labels, not principles.

[43] 281 ff. (*Complete Greek Drama,* I, 971).
[44] *The Oxford Book of Greek Verse in Translation,* p. 464.
[45] V.85.

For the leaders on either side used specious names, the one party professing to uphold the constitutional equality of the many, the other the wisdom of an aristocracy, while they made the public interests, to which in name they were devoted, in reality their prize. Striving in every way to overcome each other, they committed the most monstrous crimes; yet even these were surpassed by the magnitude of their revenges which they pursued to the very utmost, neither party observing any definite limits either of justice or public expediency, but both alike making the caprice of the moment their law.[46]

It is perhaps not too much to say, then, that the Sophists learned their philosophical relativism from the political and ethical decay which they had helped foster. They had learned the hard lesson of practical morality: that to seize the main chance was the highest good in a world where no value was objective, and where no principle—except to have no principle— was permanently valid. Their humanism, which made men rather than absolute truth the main concern of humans, was forced upon them. In a universe characterized by strife, and devoid of moral implications, they as men could only cultivate those interests that seemed momently efficacious for man. Not that this was entirely deplorable, for they marked a new advance in the humanism latent in all Greek thought. As so profound an apologist as Werner Jaeger has said, they were genuine and skilful educators who gladly learned and gladly taught.[47] But compared to that of greater Greeks like Plato and Aristotle, their brand of humanism was thin. However favorably they are viewed—as, for instance, in Gomperz' celebrated defense—they are still liable to Plato's indictment that in cultivating the parts of knowledge they neglected the whole of knowledge. They knew all there was to know, except what Socrates knew—that cultivation of the inward life or of the *psyché* by which man has access to objective and permanent reality.

In their heyday from the middle of the fifth to the middle of the fourth centuries, the Sophists were available for instruction in all the useful arts and sciences. Some, like Protagoras, specialized in literature; others, like Tesias and Corex and most notably Gorgias, specialized in rhetoric.[48] But all concurred in their distrust of metaphysics. They had learned that the sciences of geometry and astronomy were showing practical consequences; that the Orphic and Eleusinian mysteries had challenged the orthodox pantheon of Homer and of Hesiod; that the skills of rhetoric and dialectic were more useful than abstruse philosophizing. As acknowledged professionals in learning, they appealed to the characteristic pragma-

---

[46] Thucydides, III.82.
[47] See *Paideia*, I, 283 ff.
[48] See Leonard Whibley (ed.), *A Companion to Greek Studies* (1916), p. 195.

tism of the Greeks when they announced that they could teach the art of survival—or, euphemistically, the useful accomplishments of a gentleman.[49] Plato, who detested the Sophists and from whom unfortunately most of our information about them comes, insinuated that they manufactured the learned wares they purveyed.[50] But Protagoras' own career was a testimonial: he began as a porter, passed to itinerant teaching, and at last, wealthy and esteemed, was a personage of importance throughout all Hellas.[51] He might even have ended his days in Athens but for his notorious jibe about the gods—he did not choose to speak of them: the subject was obscure, and life was short. For that widely circulated remark, one of his few extant, the seemingly pious Athenians sent him packing. But in general the Sophists were everywhere welcomed. They were expensive but useful. As teachers of grammar, rhetoric, logic, law, literature, geometry, and varied subjects, the Sophists, as Heinrich Meier has it, "fühlten sich als die Bahnbrecher der modernen Kultur, und als die Fackelträger einer neuen Wissenschaft." [52] Certainly, the long *apologia* which Plato puts in Protagoras' mouth remains, in spite of Plato's obvious irony, a brilliant defense of Sophistic humanism.[53]

Although the Sophists, with their urbane insistence on man and his concerns, formulated a humanism that has never lost its charms—it is congenial to modernists of all ages—they went further. If man is the measure of all things, as Protagoras said, then the objective reality sought by the Ionians, Pythagoreans, and Eleatics, becomes nonsensical, or at least unattainable by humans. The incipient idealism in the notion that the real is real only in relation to the cognitive mind notoriously leads to solipsism, as Berkeley was long afterwards to demonstrate. Plato, in fact, specifically charged Protagoras with this.[54] But the ethical implications of Sophism were equally repellent to ocrates and his disciples. If what is real is so only for me, then there can be no objective and enduring standards, not even a *sensus communis* by which to regulate conduct. One

---

[49] Note the speech of Polus (*Gorgias*, 448) commending the "experience" and "proficiency" of the rhetorician. See *Protagoras*, 313.

[50] *Sophist*, 231.

[51] Diogenes Laertius, pp. 397 ff.

[52] *Sokrates, sein Werk und Seine Geschichtliche Stellung* (1913), p. 195. Protagoras, according to the acidulous report of Diogenes Laertius (p. 398), "was the first person who demanded payment of his pupils; fixing his charge at a hundred minae. He was also the first person who gave a precise definition of the parts of time; and who explained the value of opportunity, and who instituted contests of argument, and who armed the disputants with the weapons of sophism. He it was too who first left facts out of consideration, and fastened his arguments on words; and who was the parent of the present superficial and futile kinds of discussion."

[53] *Protagoras*, 320 ff.

[54] *Theaetetus*, 152 ff.

man's meat is another man's poison; each man's virtue is his own, and truth is relative and subjective, valid only for him whose purpose it suits at the moment. Morality, therefore, cannot rightly be distinguished from flute-playing or debating, for each could serve practical ends and each could be taught by the Sophists' latest approved methods.

Epistemological skepticism and ethical relativism are the results. Protagoras in asserting that our senses are the only valid measures of experience, and the only avenues to each man's private knowledge, called forth Socrates' great refutation—the refutation which inaugurated the high period of Greek philosophy. Ethical relativism made necessary the quest for the objective, permanent, and formal reality. As one man, the great post-Sophistic thinkers rose against Protagoras and his fellows. The wisdom of the Sophists, Aristotle decreed, was sham wisdom, and wise only because it is ostensibly expedient: "Sophistic is what appears to be philosophy but is not." [55] Gorgias is a case in point. A teacher of that rhetoric which Socrates condemned because it creates a belief about the just and unjust, but gives no instruction about them, he was especially chary of cosmological generalizations. According to Sextus Empiricus, his treatise maliciously entitled *On Nature, or the Non-Existent,* pushed skepticism to the point of nihilism. Nothing exists; if anything did exist, we could know nothing of it; if we did know something, we could not describe it to our fellows.[56]

However reputable Protagoras and Gorgias may have been as citizens— and they were both public-spirited men of wide esteem—their followers drove home the uncivil implications of Sophistic relativism. As we know from Plato, the opportunist Callicles could seriously maintain that since there is no basic, objective moral norm, what passes for virtue is a creed shackled to the strong by the weak, for the purpose of restraining superior persons. A sensible morality would, as nature demonstrates, make it proper for the strong to exploit the weak; justice would then consist "in the superior ruling over and having more than the inferior." [57] The famed Thrasymachus, whose very name has become a byword, denied his colleague's implication of even a "natural" morality. There is no particular justice in the superiority of the strong, for it is merely by chance that they are fortunate. In a capricious universe, blown about by winds of chance, nothing is right or wrong, just or unjust. Things are merely as they are.[58]

[55] *Meta.*, 1004.
[56] *Against the Logicians,* I.65.
[57] *Gorgias,* 483.
[58] It should be remembered that the Sophists were the first practicing Greek moralists (or immoralists, Plato would say). The cosmologists had shown no concern with ethics; their scattered gnomic dicta add little to the unreasoned if stirring precepts of Homer. The

### THE SOCRATIC REFUTATION

Greek ethical thought was at the sorry stage represented by Thrasymachus when Socrates appeared to do battle, in his own disarming way.

Socrates remains one of the riddles of philosophy. A man, like Jesus, who wrote nothing, he has, by the sheer force of his personality, been one of the creators of occidental thought; yet to determine his own identity is difficult. How are we to disengage his ideas from Plato's, or even to be sure that the Socrates of the dialogues is not a creation of Plato's? Was Socrates merely the first great Greek to concern himself with ethical rather than cosmological problems, or was he (as Plato suggests) the author of those concepts of Ideas, preëxistence, the ideal state—in short, "the father of European metaphysics"? [59] So eminent a Hellenist as Werner Jaeger takes a median position: he sees Socrates as "the central point in the making of the Greek soul" and as "the greatest teacher in European history." But, he adds, if we "attempt to find his greatness in the field of theory and systematic philosophy, we shall either concede him too much and Plato too little, or else end in disbelieving in it altogether." [60]

By assuming, however, that the *Republic* is entirely and characteristically Platonic, we may still ascribe to Socrates the refutation of Sophistic relativism and the brilliantly argued belief (if not demonstration) that human conduct should conform to objective standards based on an objective reality. Socrates asserted, with a force that is still felt, the existence of Eleatic absolutes in a world of Heraclitean changes. [61] Such absolutes were for him the sole objects of rational knowledge, and his real objection to the Sophists, as the *Protagoras* shows, was that they made no provision for the soul, the instrument of rational knowledge by which we may discern the eternal behind the flux of sensation. "Knowledge is the food of the soul," Socrates tells young Hippocrates who is so enchanted by Pro-

---

early Greeks had neither a Job nor a Confucius, even if they did have an Aeschylus. The Pythagoreans, it is true, had tried to apply numerology to the sphere of conduct: they would equate justice, thought of as equal retribution, with a square number, and would construe health and virtue as "harmonies." But the conduct of the exclusive brotherhoods was apparently regulated by dietary taboos and the like. Otherwise, the Pre-Socratics, like Heraclitus, had contented themselves with sporadic exhortations. See Henry Sidgwick, *Outlines of the History of Ethics for English Readers* (1939), pp. 14 ff.; for a favorable, and classical, account see Gomperz, *Greek Thinkers,* I, 412 ff., which might be compared to the learned defense of Werner Jaeger's, already cited. Grote's evaluation (VIII, 312 ff.) is still indispensable.

[59] Jaeger, *Paideia,* II, 26.

[60] *Paideia,* II, 27. See Arthur Kenyon Rogers, *The Socratic Problem* (1933), pp. 29-54 for a detailed discussion, and also the admirable presentation of the evidence by Arthur O. Lovejoy, *The Great Chain of Being: A Study in the History of an Idea* (1936), pp. 31 ff.

[61] See Boas, *The Major Traditions of European Philosophy,* p. 43.

tagoras; "and we must take care, my friend, that the Sophist does not deceive us when he praises what he sells, like the dealers wholesale or retail who sell the food of the body." [62] In Socrates' judgment, the soul was neither Homer's *eidolon* (the pale shade of Hades) nor the soul-daemon of the Orphics.[63] His analysis, moreover, was innocent of those eschatological factors introduced by Plato in the *Phaedo*. Socrates seems to mean by the soul one of man's two aspects of being: like the other, physical aspect, it has its own *physis* and its own nutriment. As wealth and strength are goods of the body, courage, piety, justice, and prudence are goods of the soul—and these goods depend upon knowledge.[64] Such knowledge has as its object something very much like metaphysical absolutes. Thus, for the anthropocentric humanism of Protagoras, Socrates attempted to formulate a theocentric humanism that would link man with what Aquinas was to call *aeterna veritas*.[65]

Socrates brought to philosophical speculation something of the skepticism so characteristic of both Pyrrho and the Sophists. His success in questioning and finally demolishing commonly held notions, no less than the whole movement of the Socratic dialectic, shows this plainly. Like the Sophists, he was uninterested in cosmological theorizing; his inquiry was not into the *physis* of material things, but into the *physis* of human conduct. Thus Aristophanes portraying him, in *The Clouds,* as a Sophist, was not entirely off the mark.[66] *Fas est et ab hoste doceri.* For like the Sophists, Socrates was really a very practical man. As the philosopher of the *agora,* he was concerned with determining the basis of the good life. As Cicero said, he was the first to introduce philosophy into the houses of men, and he inaugurated the passion for ethical speculation that characterized subsequent Greek thought. His defiant rationalism is as uncompromising as what Mr. More has called his spiritual affirmation, or as the naturalism of the Ionians. For the material reality of the atomists, he urged the conceptual reality of form, relationship, and generality which, rational in nature and discernible through reason (the faculty of soul) is both the only valid object of knowledge and the only valid basis of a good life.[67]

[62] *Protagoras,* 313.
[63] See John Burnet, "The Socratic Doctrine of the Soul," *Proceedings of the British Academy 1915-1916,* pp. 235-259.
[64] See Jaeger, *Paideia,* II, 40 ff.
[65] See Jaeger, *Humanism and Theology,* pp. 42 ff.; Plato, *Laws,* 716; *Theaetetus,* 176.
[66] Grote says (VIII, 315) that if, during the Peloponnesian War, a stranger had asked an Athenian who was the principal Sophist, Socrates would have been named first.
[67] See Ernest Barker, *Greek Political Theory* (1918), pp. 58 ff. For an interesting explanation of the shift from cosmology to ethics as a psychological phenomenon see Franz Alexander, *Our Age of Unreason* (1942), pp. 25 ff.

Since the relativism of the Sophists stemmed from their epistemology of sense, which meant a denial of any objective and universal object of knowledge, Socrates by affirming the existence of absolutes over and above the subjective data of sensation struck at the root of their ethics. Through his efforts, reason as an epistemological device supplanted the notoriously erratic perceptual knowledge that the Sophists had regarded as ultimate.[68] In declaring knowledge a matter of concepts, Socrates made the gigantic intellectual stride from the purely sensual and private to the conceptual and objective. Man through this kind of knowledge is enormously ennobled: his importance derives from his capacity to pierce the mask of appearances and to approach the world of absolutes. With access to the immutable, the timeless, the good, he acquires a new dignity and elevation. Socrates' humanism, thus, is rooted not in skepticism and self-interest, but in man's link with the transcendental and the formal.[69]

In all of Plato's charming early dialogues, Socrates is presented as trying to define some aspect of virtue. Temperance is the theme of *Charmides,* bravery of *Laches,* holiness of *Euthyphro,* friendship of *Lysis.* But the only conclusion reached about any of them is that the customary opinion is unsatisfactory. With the skepticism that delights in demolishing dogmatic opinions, Socrates also exhibits a tendency to consolidate all the separate virtues into one inclusive virtue, and to make that, in some way, dependent on knowledge. In the *Protagoras,* this tendency becomes articulate. "Now I want you to tell me truly," Socrates says, "whether virtue is one whole, of which justice and temperance and holiness are parts; or whether all these are only the names of one and the same thing." [70] When Protagoras answers, like a good Sophist, that the virtues are distinct, Socrates has little trouble in showing them to be merely aspects of a master virtue, and that to be knowledge. For instance, courage is not, as Protagoras has urged, the inclination to approach the frightful. There are *kinds* of frightful things: the wise man fears dishonor, but the coward, in his ignorance, fears death. Therefore, knowledge determines our estimate of a situation, and courage is, in effect, the "knowledge of that which is and is not dangerous." [71] But Socrates goes further. Since all men instinctively seek pleasure and shun pain, he suggests that a life designed to nurture the one and to avoid the other is the most virtuous

---

[68] Thus Aristotle's distinguishing Socrates (*Meta.,* 1078) for originating inductive reasoning and universal definitions.

[69] See Meier, *Sokrates,* pp. 183 ff.

[70] *Protagoras,* 329.

[71] *Protagoras,* 360.

life. Knowledge, then, is the necessary condition for a rational hedonism that enables a man to calculate, in terms of good and bad, the effects of experience. It is conceptual evaluation.[72]

Socrates had thus attempted the demonstration of a great ethical tenet: no man does wrong knowingly. But he could not be content to rest with a hedonistic ethics, and in the *Gorgias,* with yet another unregenerate Sophist as his victim, he pursues his dialectic mercilessly. Gorgias, the butt, thumps out his doctrine roundly. "I plainly assert, that he who would truly live ought to allow his desires to wax to the uttermost, and not to chastise them; but when they have grown to their greatest he should have courage and intelligence to minister to them and to satisfy all his longings. And this I affirm to be natural justice and nobility." [73] All of which leads to the desperate conclusion: "Luxury and intemperance and license, if they be provided with means, are virtue and happiness—all the rest is a mere bauble, agreements contrary to nature, foolish talk of men, nothing worth." [74] But with this Gorgias has played into the hands of Socrates, who relentlessly explores the implications of such a hedonistic ethics. When Gorgias is aghast at his antagonist's commendation of the life of a successful catamite, Socrates can only remark that unless one distinguishes good from bad pleasures, his moral scruples are untenable. Scruples imply values, and values are determined with reference to a norm. Since pleasure and pain are not necessarily concomitant with good and evil, as even Gorgias admits,[75] the argument is virtually over. Socrates has only to enunciate his ringing conclusion, one of the peaks of Greek ethical thought: the good always involves the temperate and the orderly, and the temperate man, by definition just and courageous and holy, "cannot be other than a perfectly good man, nor can the good man do otherwise than well and perfectly whatever he does; and he who does well must of necessity be happy and blessed, and the evil man who does evil, miserable. . . . Such is my position, and these things I affirm to be true." [76] Rational knowledge, whose object lies in the realm of the absolute rather than the relative, is thus the cumulative virtue, the reservoir from which flow courage, temperance, and all the others.

The work of Socrates, so curiously fragmentary and elliptical in view of

[72] *Protagoras,* 351 ff.; cf. Rogers, *The Socratic Problem,* pp. 80-81.

[73] *Gorgias,* 491-92.

[74] *Gorgias,* 492; cf. *Republic,* 348.

[75] A man cannot enjoy both good and evil fortune simultaneously, which is not true of pleasure and pain, as the alleviation of thirst indicates.

[76] *Gorgias,* 507. Gorgias' discomfort is matched in the *Republic* (350)—a charming scene in which Thrasymachus, after undergoing vivisection at the hands of Socrates, is actually seen to blush.

its immense influence, now was over. Like most great men, he was really a simple man—a fact we sometimes forget in winding through Plato's sophisticated reconstruction. But in the *Apology,* if anywhere, we see Socrates face to face, and hear the tones of his voice. In his own words, his creed sounds almost as simple—and as millennial—as the Sermon on the Mount:

Men of Athens, I honour and love you; but I shall obey God rather than you, and while I have life and strength I shall never cease from the practice and teaching of philosophy, exhorting any one whom I meet and saying to him after my manner: You, my friend,—a citizen of the great and mighty and wise city of Athens,—are you not ashamed of heaping up the greatest amount of money and honour and reputation, and caring so little about wisdom and truth and the greatest improvement of the soul, which you never regard or heed at all? . . . For I do nothing but go about persuading you all, old and young alike, not to take thought for your persons or your properties, but first and chiefly to care about the greatest improvement of the soul.[77]

The materialism that since Thales had proved so attractive had been countered, and a grand strategy of combat had been sketched. It remained for Plato—and, in his own way, for Aristotle—to complete the case for rational knowledge, the food of the soul, and to posit it in an astral sphere far above the irrational and ceaseless flux of the sensible world.

[77] *Apology,* 29-30.

# III

## PLATONIC HUMANISM

### METAPHYSICS: PERMANENCE AS IDEA

SOCRATES' ACHIEVEMENT had been very great. In asserting, against the Sophists and the moral relativism they symbolized, the objectivity of virtue, he had in effect restated the old belief in permanence. Thus he was in the major tradition of Greek thought. But his thinking was philosophically incomplete. He had failed—perhaps he wished it so—to formulate a system. He had, for instance, given no clear conception of the nature of the absolute, and he had failed, as his great pupil Plato was to fail, to show the correlation between the noumenal and the phenomenal, or between the absolute and the world of sense. Moreover, he had not made clear how man has knowledge of the absolute. But he had affirmed his intense emotional conviction that such knowledge was attainable, and that it was necessary for virtue. He had given Greek humanism a new set of coördinates—or revived an old set—by linking man with the eternal, and thus had ennobled him beyond the comprehension of the Sophists. But for Socrates and his glorification of the knowledge that is virtue, Boethius, nearly a thousand years later, could not have said of man that "he who, leaving virtue, ceaseth to be a man, since he cannot be a partaker of the divine condition, is turned into a beast." [1]

Nevertheless, Socrates had left the question of virtue in suspension. Since he had insisted on generalizing the notion of justice by pushing discussion into the realm of concepts that would have individual application, it was clear that knowledge, which is identical with virtue, lay in some sort of formal relationship rather than in the particulars that characterize a virtuous act. Plato took up the task, at this point, of extending this logical realism to the rarefied metaphysics that sought *the* good for the whole universe. He agreed with his master in seeking the particular end which for individuals constitutes well-being—that is, in adapting means to ends—but he wished to go further, and demonstrate how the complex network of private goods is in some way related to the cosmic good. This led him into the far reaches of cosmology and metaphysics which Socrates, perhaps in revulsion from the Ionians, had never entered.

---

[1] *Consolation,* IV.3.

On his answer to the question, "What is knowledge?" Plato reared the whole of his vast edifice of thought. As the *Theaetetus* shows, he could find knowledge neither in sensation nor opinion. Thus his rejection of Sophistic relativism: if the individual is, as Protagoras had urged, the measure of all things—

. . . if truth is only sensation, and no man can discern another's feelings better than he, or has any superior right to determine whether his opinion is true or false . . .[2]

—then clearly the judgment of the wisest man is no better than that of a tadpole or of a dog-faced baboon. In his obsession with absolutes—and how many men has it ruined?—Plato could only share Socrates' belief that sensory data are relativistic, often contradictory (as when a straight stick seems crooked under water), and admitting no proof.[3] As for opinion, it may be grounded on misleading intuition, and is thus both subjective and fallacious.

Knowledge, then, can be only knowledge of concepts—the generalized images which, transcending and including particulars, are the keys to permanent and objective truth.[4] By his rational comprehension of such concepts man classifies and groups the swarming, unstable particulars; they come into being and pass away, but the ideas or concepts which subsume them are immutable, perfect, eternal. Knowledge must necessarily have a permanently valid object.

But if the very nature of knowledge changes, at the time when the change occurs there will be no knowledge; and if the transition is always going on, there will always be no knowledge, and, according to this view, there will be no one to know and nothing to be known. . . .[5]

Such a condition is patently intolerable to Plato. Man is a rational being, and must therefore have knowledge. The object of his knowledge must be, consequently, concepts or Forms, for they alone are absolute and eternal. The idea *horse* remains, even though this or that horse may perish. Such mathematical concepts as triangles and circles are ideas that are permanently valid whether or not perfect triangles or circles exist as objects of sense. Similarly, all abstraction, as of pity or courage or beauty,

---

[2] *Theaetetus*, 161.
[3] See W. T. Stace, *A Critical History of Greek Philosophy* (1920), pp. 177 ff. There is a sprightly discussion of the problems of sensation in C. E. M. Joad's *Guide to Philosophy* (n.d.), pp. 23-125.
[4] *Republic*, 509.
[5] *Cratylus*, 440.

must exist as transcendent to particulars.[6] Even though they are not apprehended by organs of sense, the mind, "by a power of its own, contemplates the universal in all things." [7]

For Plato these Forms are metaphysically and ontologically valid. They are substantial, and not the products of our thought (for Plato does not fall into Berkeleian idealism). Their identity depends upon nothing other than themselves, but they are the origin of subsequent identities. They are universals that cause—just how, Plato could never explain, as Aristotle obligingly pointed out—the existence of sensibles. They are unchanging and eternal, the archetypes of being. Most important of all, they are rational, and as such not apprehended through our senses. Whereas the external world of trees and stones and things is known through sensation, the realm of the universal conceptual Forms is known through reason. Like Heraclitus, Plato holds that the sphere of becoming—the sensible world that represents merely flux and transition, but not the permanence and perfection of Formal being—can give rise only to sensation, whose objects change even as they are being contemplated. Rational knowledge, however, has as its object the objective reality of Forms, and it is superior to sensation as the Forms are to sensibles. Moreover, it is the very fount of ethics: the rational knowledge of Forms becomes, ultimately, an apprehension of the culminative idea of the Good—the rational, creative force of the universe, the basic eternal verity. Without this knowledge, Plato concludes, "any other knowledge or possession of any kind will profit us nothing." [8] Here the quest for absolutes finds the very seamark of its utmost sail.[9]

Thus Plato, as Aristotle pointed out, shapes into his metaphysics various strains of earlier Greek thought. His realm of Forms is strongly reminiscent of Eleatic Being; his notion of the perceptual world (which he so consistently deprecates as a metaphysician if not as a humanist) suggests the Heraclitean Becoming; and finally, his emphasis on conceptual knowledge is merely an extension of Socrates' answer to the Sophists.[10] When he identifies the Socratic concepts with Eleatic Being, there emerges his own distinctive theory of Forms, and these Forms, as anyone who has detected Plato the mathematician lurking behind Plato the philosopher must realize, serve virtually the same metaphysical function as Pythag-

---

[6] *Phaedo*, 65.
[7] *Theaetetus*, 185.
[8] *Republic*, 505.
[9] Plato's serpentine inconsistency is notorious. His emerging notions of the theory of Forms winds in and out of nearly all the dialogues, and for a meager summary as ours, specific citation is difficult. See the *Republic, Parmenides, Theaetetus,* and *Timaeus, passim.*
[10] *Meta.,* 987 ff.

orean number. Reduced to its simplest terms—something which Plato himself was reluctant to do—the theory of Forms apparently means that relationship, or the abstract pattern and framework within which events are perceived, is the ultimate object of man's knowledge.[11]

Plato was, among other things, a consummate man of letters who thought metaphorically. *Form* itself seems to be a metaphor, and the difficulty in explaining it accounts in great measure for the extreme divergence of opinion among Plato's willing interpreters. The theory of Forms seems, at any rate, to mean this: that the true object of knowledge lies not in the sensibles of perceptual experience, but in the realm of the "real," the timeless, the Eleatic absolute, of which sensory data are merely shadows. A knowledge of this true reality will inevitably involve a knowledge of right conduct: Plato is in the main tradition of Greek thought, from Homer to Socrates, in making the wise man the good man. The highest wisdom is that of Forms, which means that the peak of moral excellence is the contemplation of Ideas, far above the ceaseless flux of sensation. Plato's metaphysics thus involves his epistemology, which in turn embodies an ethical attitude—one, like Parmenides', of rejection of the world of sense. Good living yearns to transcend sense; it is the art of escaping the bondage of gross sensual experience. Therefore the true philosophers, those who most piously seek the knowledge of Forms by freeing themselves from the shackles of desire that sensory knowledge entails, "are always occupied in the practice of dying." [12] On occasion, Plato's metaphysics is almost undistinguishable from theology; not for nothing has he so profoundly affected the evolution of Christian dogma. The knowledge of Forms, however, is not for everyone, for few men are capable of a life of pure contemplation. To achieve a regimen for practical conduct and to live virtuously in this our life are lesser but more immediate problems, and to Plato's solution of them we must now turn in order to place him in the tradition of Greek humanism.

ETHICS

The fact that justice occupies a central position in both Plato's ethics and politics suggests his continuity with the tradition represented by Solon and Aeschylus. For he, like them, construes justice as determining the relationship of the parts and the whole. Politically, the ideal state is the whole of which various degrees of citizens are the parts; ethically and psycho-

---

[11] The mathematical implications of Plato's philosophy could be properly discussed by a mathematician and a philosopher, and I am neither. Mr. Jaeger (*Paideia*, II, 166-70, 288 ff., 301-9), on this topic as on so many others, is very helpful.
[12] *Phaedo*, 67.

logically, man's soul is the whole of which his various faculties and appetites are the parts. Thus it is natural that so much of the inexhaustibly rich *Republic,* Plato's masterpiece, is devoted to finding a satisfactory definition of justice: for the macrocosm of the state and for the microcosm of man, justice should properly be the cardinal concept.

If we grant Plato's contention that the state thrives by the division of labor resulting in a ruling class, a fighting class, and a producing class (to meet the three main requirements of government, defense, and nurture), then it follows that the health of the state consists in each class functioning according to its characteristic capacity. The traditional cardinal virtues of *polis*-culture are best exemplified when the rulers are wise, when the soldiers are brave, when the workers are temperate in having their passions and desires regulated for the good of the whole.[13] In a larger view, temperance resides in the entire state: it "runs through all the notes of the scale, and produces a harmony of the weaker and the stronger and the middle class."[14] But the fourth cardinal virtue, justice, is not far off. It is the result of one man following one thing, "the thing to which his nature was best adapted."[15] Justice comes when, in a grand harmony of the whole, each part achieves its function that contributes to the general good. Thus the state has a horizontal order that makes for the organic whole, a vertical order that makes for the sharp stratification of social classes.[16] So much for the civil virtues. When they are given individual application, Plato promises, the subsequent general well-being "may possibly strike a light in which justice will shine forth, and the vision which is then revealed we will fix in our souls."[17] Even in the chaotic fourth century, and even loathing democracy as he did, Plato was enough of a Greek to interpret the state as both the model and repository of private virtues—the organic whole which mirrored the rational order of the cosmos and exemplified the order which each man should seek to establish within himself.

It is nothing less than a painful duty to examine the political implications which Plato derives from his quest for absolutes. We must be careful, in reading the dialogues, not to let ourselves be seduced either by his vast reputation or by his sheer verbal brilliance. In spite of all the adulatory nonsense that has been written about him, the fact is that he, like many great men, makes severe demands on his admirers' affection. Basically, Plato appears to have been an insufferable snob: although he was too

[13] *Republic,* 429 ff.
[14] *Republic,* 432.
[15] *Republic,* 433.
[16] See Raphael Demos, *The Philosophy of Plato* (1939), pp. 358 ff.
[17] *Republic,* 435.

good a Greek to break from the tradition of humanism, it is quite apparent that as he grew older he entertained less and less regard for the dignity of man. And finally, in the *Laws,* that dour memorial of his intransigent old age, he did not scruple to urge a political system that today could be called nothing less than fascistic. His progress toward that sorry end is apparent even in the great *Republic;* for when Plato, like certain notable contemporary advocates of "order," supports a stratified society as a bulwark against social chaos the drift of his political thought is toward a kind of *Ordnung* that to most of us sounds suspiciously like National Socialism. When Plato tried to articulate his metaphysics of absolutes in political terms, he ended with an outrageously totalitarian state.

Our modern fascists, professed and otherwise, like to talk in terms of an *élite* below which are spread, in hierarchal array, the lesser manifestations of life. Being himself of the *élite,* socially and intellectually, Plato lovingly develops the same idea. His birth was exalted: his mother's family was descended from Solon; she was the sister of Charmides and the niece of Critias. Born with such impeccable connections and educated expensively as a scion of Athenian nobility, Plato at the age of twenty-three witnessed the oligarchic revolution of 404 in which his high-born relatives were leaders.[18] For a year the Thirty Tyrants expressed their contempt for democracy in very forcible terms: they scandalously wasted public funds, they slaughtered fifteen hundred democrats and exiled five thousand, they ruthlessly suppressed all upstart notions of civil liberties, they made Athenian life intolerable by imposing their kind of order upon it. If we may judge by his subsequent strictures on democracy, Plato must have approved of all this. At any rate, when he saw the restoration of democracy under Thrasybulus (403) and the well-deserved death of his reactionary kinsmen, he suffered an emotional shock from which he apparently never recovered. The trial and death of Socrates climaxed his disgust of all things democratic, and he fled from Athens in moral revulsion. While he wandered over the Mediterranean during the next ten years, the democrats and *nouveaux riches* at Athens were confirming his hatred. Even after he returned to open his academy he never relented.

Democracy, thought Plato, "comes into being after the poor have conquered their opponents, slaughtering some and banishing some, while to the remainder they give an equal share of freedom and power." [19] To a man of delicate sensibility, to a man who yearned almost erotically for absolutes, what could be more repugnant than a leveling movement that eradicated all distinctions between men, and that even enthroned the

[18] See Grote, *A History of Greece,* VIII, 213.
[19] *Republic,* 557.

Sophistic fallacy of making one man's judgment equal to another's? Like Aristophanes, Plato thought the system was pernicious, and with masochistic glee he itemizes the tokens of corruption. The teacher is no better than his pupils, the wisdom of age is held to be no better than the folly of youth, the slave is as good as his master, and even women are thought the equals of men.

The son is on a level with his father, he having no respect or reverence for either of his parents; and this is his freedom, and the metic is equal with the citizen and the citizen with the metic, and the stranger is quite as good as either.[20]

Worst of all, men lose respect for their superiors: "they chafe impatiently at the least touch of authority and at length, as you know they cease to care even for the laws, written or unwritten; they will have no one over them." [21] But they live in a fool's paradise, losing their odious liberty as soon as they get it. For all the fine and futile promises of democracy are forgotten by the knaves who lead the mob. The tyrant exalts himself to trample down the very freedom that produced him, and the outcome is despotism, the rule of one fool over many. "The excess of liberty, whether in States or individuals, seems only to pass into excess of slavery." [22] The excess of liberty is, in fact, the key to all disorder: through it, aristocracy deteriorates into timocracy (where honor rather than virtue implies preeminence), timocracy into oligarchy (where wealth confers preëminence), oligarchy into democracy, and democracy into tyranny.[23]

The antidote for this "charming form of government, full of variety and disorder, and dispensing a sort of equality to equals and unequals alike," [24] is a hierarchal state controlled by an *élite* of carefully trained intellectuals. Plato's *Übermensch* is a titan of intellect rather than will, but an *Übermensch* none the less. He is both the product and the guardian of the state, and it is his function to rule as the philosopher-king, the sage who superimposes order and discipline on the chaos of the ordinary man's communal life. At the end of twenty years of public education, the (mentally) unfit youths are culled out to become artisans or tradesmen. The more promising pass to higher studies, and ten years later the inferiors are again eliminated while the *aristoi* pass on to the study of philosophy. Finally, at the age of fifty—after a brief apprenticeship in the world of men and affairs—they assume their proper place at the head of the state.

[20] *Republic*, 562-63.
[21] *Republic*, 563.
[22] *Republic*, 564.
[23] See Barker, *Greek Political Theory*, pp. 251 ff.
[24] *Republic*, 558.

The state itself becomes a mechanical monster, as we learn from the *Laws*. This grim dialogue, written after Plato's depressing experience with Dionysius II of Syracuse (who he had hoped would be a true philosopher-king), shows the old philosopher even more antidemocratic, more totalitarian, more mathematically rigid in his prescriptions for Utopia. The ideal commonwealth will permit no indigents or beggars, for "he is not to be pitied who is hungry." [25] A comic poet who satirizes a citizen ("either in anger or without anger") will be either exiled or fined,[26] and whoever is audacious enough to harbor an exile will surely die.[27] There shall be 5040 free citizens, no more and no less, who will be landowners and not sully themselves with trade.[28] No funeral—even of him of the highest class—shall cost more than five minae, and the scale of expenditures shall be mathematically reduced in accordance with the rank of the *honoré*. The state shall, of course, appoint a commissioner of funerals to supervise all details: he should not forbid mourning, "but he may forbid cries of lamentation, and not allow the voice of the mourner to be heard outside the house." [29] A religious skeptic will mercifully, while in prison, be given the opportunity for orthodoxy, and unless he defers to the wisdom of his betters he will perish.

And when he is dead let him be cast beyond the borders unburied, and if any freeman assist in burying him, let him pay the penalty of impiety to any one who is willing to bring suit against him.[30]

And so on, *ad absurdum*.

Plato's ideal commonwealth is a totalitarian nightmare, and we can forgive it only if we remember that the end for which he proposed it was moral. That is, Plato was a genuine rationalist who believed that man's rational faculty should guide him. The principle is impeccable, but its political implications are ruinous. At least, as Plato worked them out they meant the denial of the noblest strain of Greek thought—its high regard for man as a rational animal. Actually, the analogy between man the microcosm and the state the macrocosm is untenable. When Plato descends from political theory to ethics, although he pushes the analogy very hard, he is a much more appealing person, as we shall see. It is one thing to urge that man is a creature of conflicting principles, of which the high-

---

[25] *Laws*, 936.
[26] 935.
[27] 955.
[28] 919.
[29] 959-60.
[30] 909.

est should govern in achieving a proper balance of personality; but quite another to personify that highest principle, reason, as a political ruling class which despotically repudiates the claims of the individual citizen to any sort of humanistic freedom. As a practical moralist Plato divests himself of both his Pythagorean, mystical asceticism and history—not to say fascist—contempt for the common man. He becomes one of the most winsome spokesmen for the humanistic tradition. But, as he unfortunately never realized, the order and balance and symmetry that are the goals of humanistic cultivation for the individual present an odious aspect when they are transformed into the order and symmetry of a totalitarian state. But let us turn to Plato the humanistic moralist.

Just as justice or rational equilibrium is the necessary condition for the health of the state, so it is for the virtuous conduct of the individual. Although the path of a commentator is devious, it is sometimes leaf-fringed. In the *Phaedrus,* for instance, occurs this celebrated purple passage:

Of the nature of the soul, though her true form be ever a theme of large and more than mortal discourse, let me speak briefly, and in a figure. And let the figure be composite—a pair of winged horses and a charioteer. Now the winged horses and the charioteer of the gods are all of them noble and of noble descent, but those of other races a.e mixed; the human charioteer drives his in a pair; and one of them is noble and of noble breed, and the other is ignoble and of ignoble breed; and the driving of them of necessity gives a great deal of trouble to him. I will endeavour to explain to you in what way the mortal differs from the immortal creature. The soul in her totality has the care of inanimate being everywhere, and traverses the whole heaven in divers forms appearing:—when perfect and fully winged she soars upward, and orders the whole world; whereas the imperfect soul, losing her wings and drooping in her flight at last settles on the solid ground—there, finding a home, she receives an earthly frame which appears to be self-moved, but is really moved by her power; and this composition of soul and body is called a living and mortal creature.[81]

This "figure" means many things, as Plato's long and beautiful exegesis indicates; but its psychology signifies one of the recurring conceptual achievements of Plato. The driver is reason; the right-hand horse, a superb white steed with a haughty neck and an aquiline nose, needs not a whip but only a word for guidance; the dark nag on the left, crooked and lumbering, "shag-eared and deaf," is with difficulty restrained through force. When the charioteer beholds a desirable object and "has his whole soul warmed through sense," the obedient horse, "then as always under the government of shame, refrains from leaping on the beloved." But not so the other. Heedless of discipline, it plunges towards the lure. If the

[81] 246. See J. A. Stewart, *The Myths of Plato* (1905), pp. 336 ff.

pull of desire is too strong, the whole chariot is swept madly earthward; but if the driver remembers the rational ideal of pure beauty, he restrains the black beast and, aided by the white, turns the chariot from its downward flight.[32]

Concealed in this allegory lies much of what Plato thought about human nature and right conduct. The soul of man, far from being a unit, is a whirling mass of mixed principles and mixed allegiances. Just as men in social units are normally (unless restrained by law) each other's enemies, so each man is privately his own.[33] The terrible consciousness of internal strife, which is universal and organic (as Heraclitus had suggested), signifies a basic dualism: the tension between the higher and the lower elements of the soul, between that which checks or restrains action and that which urges action.[34] These two forces are antithetical. The nobler tends towards the Ideal, and induces the supreme function of pure contemplation; but the other impels towards the pleasure derived from sensible objects. The higher is a divine faculty of judgment, discrimination, and (Platonic) recollection; but the lower is mortal, violent, stimulated by the desire of trivial externals and uncertain of consequences.[35]

In the *Republic* Plato gives a rather bleaker statement of the psychology implicit in the *Phaedrus* myth.[36] The tripartite division of the soul which he here advances corresponds in all essentials to the charioteer and the two horses. Reason is the "forbidding principle" that reflects before it inhibits; desire is the unreflecting appetite for presumably pleasurable objects or for gratification of sense; and spirit (*thymos*) is the assertive element that makes for leadership and achievement—the propulsive faculty that, although distinct from the other two, is the agent of reason, "transmitting the verdict of reason to the appetite, and making that verdict effective by the use of force upon appetite."[37]

Actually, it becomes very easy to misconstrue Plato at this point—as, for that matter, at nearly all points. And it is not too much to say that the assimilation and transmogrification he underwent during the early centuries of the Christian era ignore both the facts and the humanistic im-

---

[32] Note a cognate passage in the *Phaedrus* (246-48): "When the better elements of the mind which lead to order and philosophy prevail, then they pass their life here in happiness and harmony—masters of themselves and orderly—enslaving the vicious and emancipating the virtuous elements of the soul."

[33] See the *Laws*, 626.

[34] *Republic*, 439; cf. 426, 440, 488.

[35] *Phaedrus*, 237.

[36] 439 ff. Here the categories of reason, spirit, and appetite are clearly analogous to the corresponding elements of the state.

[37] Demos, *Plato*, p. 310.

plications of his ethics. Historically, Plato's ethical influence in the Occident is reflected by Augustine's dichotomy of the earthly and celestial cities. That is, he was made the great pagan representative of the characteristic Christian dualism between the body and soul, flesh and spirit, earth and heaven. It is easy to see how Plato's persistent metaphysical dualism could beguile one into a sheep-and-goats frame of mind; and indeed there are certain dialogues (such as the Pythagorean *Phaedo*) that suggest ethical correspondences to Plato's metaphysical dualism. The *Phaedo*, for instance, must be accounted a powerful influence on early Christendom: it poses very sharply the contrast between the body and soul that informs so much early Christian asceticism. The soul is of the realm of Forms, the corruptible body of the realm of sensibles, and between them no good man should hesitate.

For the body is a source of endless trouble to us by reason of the mere requirement of food; and is liable also to diseases which overtake and impede us in the search after true being: it fills us full of loves, and lusts, and fears, and fancies of all kinds, and endless foolery, and in fact, as men say, takes away from us the power of thinking at all. Whence come wars, and fightings, and factions? whence but from the body and the lusts of the body? Wars are occasioned by the love of money, and money has to be acquired for the sake and in the service of the body; and by reason of all these impediments we have no time to give to philosophy; and, last and worst of all, even if we are at leisure and betake ourselves to some speculation, the body is always breaking in upon us, causing turmoil and confusion in our inquiries, and so amazing us that we are prevented from seeing the truth. . . . In this present life, I reckon that we make the nearest approach to knowledge when we have the least possible intercourse or communion with the body, and are not surfeited with the bodily nature, but keep ourselves pure until the hour when God himself is pleased to release us.[38]

Nonetheless, this rigid—almost mystical—dualism is not congruent to the ethical ideal of harmony and justice that is so organic in the later dialogues. However diffuse and sporadic Plato may be in arriving at his final conception of the soul, and of a practical morality, he does at length arrive at a genuine humanism. The soul is tripartite, and spirit, man's characteristic faculty mediating between appetite, which man shares with beasts, and reason, which man shares with the eternal, is the fulcrum on which the extremes of conduct must be poised. Certainly there is in the *Republic* nothing to suggest an Augustinian dualism between reason and appetite; rather thay are to be reconciled and adjusted to the ends of good conduct by the agency of spirit. Spirit itself becomes Plato's symbol for the

---

[38] *Phaedo*, 66 ff. See the famous allegory of the cave, *Republic*, 514 ff.; cf. Gorgias, 82-83.

specifically human factor in conduct.[39] As a moralist, if not as a metaphysician, he was unwilling to view the flesh and its desires as wholly bad, the mind and its rational contemplation of the Ideal as wholly good. For either requires the implementation of spirit (motor activity?) to become effective in human conduct. Man acts well when he uses his superior faculty of reason to regulate, through the agency of spirit, the turbulence of desire. Regulation does not mean eradication, however. Certain desires (e.g. for food and for sexual satisfaction) must be gratified to insure health and even survival for the organism; but unless spirit imposes the limits set by reason, and thus maintains moderation and justice, the organism perishes—just as the state would perish if the working class usurped the control rightly exercised by the ruling class.[40]

Although Plato's conception of the soul, with its hierarchal gradations and mutual interactions, is characteristically complex, it is consistently humanistic. The three levels of reason, spirit, and appetite are matched, for instance, by the three attributes of motion, *eros,* and mixture. The soul possesses motion because it is the life-principle of becoming; the self-mover that supplies movement to other things, it animates the entire universe. It possesses *eros* because of its propulsion towards the beauty that, as the beautiful *Symposium* shows, culminates at last in the teleological realization of value that embraces not only sensual beauty but also metaphysical truth and goodness; thus Plato's concept of *eros*—which suggests such modern vitalistic principles as the Freudian id and the *élan vital* of Bergson—makes possible the sublimation of desire into rational knowledge.[41] The soul possesses mixture because it is, through its hierarchal complexity, the very principle of interrelatedness, thus linking sensibles to Form and desire to reason. The chariot of the *Phaedrus* myth, with its two steeds, exemplifies these coördinates of the sensuous and the conceptual, and the reason which guides them therefore embraces both poles of being.[42] In

[39] Spirit is not reason, as Plato points out (*Republic,* 441), because it is found in infants and dumb animals. When Homer says, "He smote his breast, and thus rebuked his soul," he has "clearly supposed the power which reasons about the better and the worse to be different from the unreasoning anger which is rebuked by it."

[40] For a restatement of the tripartite division of the soul, see the *Timaeus,* 69-70, where Plato locates reason in the skull, spirit in the thorax, and desire in the bowels. For modifications of this psychology, see the *Republic,* 475, 511, 533-34; *Sophist,* 263 ff:; *Philebus,* 33-34.

[41] See Jaeger, *Paideia,* II, 179 ff. The concept of *eros,* the vitalistic urge by which man passes from sensual gratification to rational knowledge, complicates (or, perhaps, contradicts) the common Platonic notion that reason is the principle of inhibition and negation which limits action. See Paul Elmer More, *Platonism* (1917), pp. 139 ff.

[42] For an extended and rewarding discussion, see Demos, *Plato,* pp. 78 ff., 309 ff.; cf. Paul Shorey, *What Plato Said* (1933), pp. 194 ff. In the *Timaeus* (35 ff.) Plato correlates the cosmic soul (reason) and the mortal soul as two circles, revolving congruently, "centre to

its highest function, then, the soul gives man insight into the ultimate order and intelligence which governs the universe. The cosmos is essentially rational, and man, through the activity of his soul, can comprehend its rationality. Plato, like Socrates, constructs a theocentric humanism that correlates man's rational faculty with the guiding principle of the universe. Even though man is bound by desire, he can pass from desire to rational contemplation of the eternal Forms: he is, in short, both man and god. At the very beginning of creation, the primary dichotomy between reason and necessity was resolved when reason triumphed by imposing limit and (geometric) form on matter.[43] Man, the microcosm, follows the same pattern: through his capacity for conceptual and rational knowledge, "which contemplates the universals in all things," [44] he can comprehend the eternal Forms of reality and thus impose order and teleological significance on the irrational urges of his fleshly nature.

At the close of the ninth book of the *Republic,* Socrates permits himself to imagine that man has so adjusted the diverse faculties of his soul that he is "like the composite creations of ancient mythology." When this balance and proportion are attained, man will have achieved the humanistic ideal. He will then conduct his life so as

to give the man within him in some way or other the most complete mastery over the entire human creature. He should watch over the many-headed monster like a good husbandman, fostering and cultivating the gentle qualities, and preventing the wild ones from growing; he should be making the lion-heart his ally, and in common care of them all should be uniting the several parts with one another and with himself.[45]

This perfect equilibrium—which should characterize both the ideal man and the ideal state, for they correspond to one another—is perhaps not humanly attainable, as Socrates admits. But no matter: in heaven there is the pattern, "which he who desires may behold, and beholding, may set his own house in order." [46] If Augustine had read and understood that as sympathetically as he did the *Phaedo,* perhaps he would have considered Plato as something other than the least damned among the heathen philosophers.

centre." The perfect synchronization is broken only when sensation mars the harmony. When, through discipline and the exercise of his reason, man again attunes his soul to the cosmic soul, he attains the "fulness and health of the perfect man."

[43] See Léon Robin, *Greek Thought and the Origin of the Scientific Spirit* (trans. M. B. Dobie, 1928), pp. 229 ff.

[44] *Theaetetus,* 185.

[45] 588-89.

[46] *Republic,* 592.

Plato's epistemology derives from a series of negations. Knowledge is not thus or thus. Likewise his ethics are constructed to deny the pernicious suggestion that virtue is pleasure. The same reasons obtain in both instances. He cannot accept the relativity of virtue any more than the relativity of knowledge; he cannot accept the tacit identification of one man's good with another man's evil; he cannot believe that pleasure, which comes from the gratification of sensual desires, is cognate with that virtue appropriate to the conceptual realm of universals or Forms; he cannot believe that morality is not an end in itself, quite unlike the mercenary Sophistic skill for attaining some extrinsic end.[47] Knowledge, universal and unchanging, is *the* good. "The greatest ignorance is when a man hates that which he nevertheless thinks to be good and noble, and loves and embraces that which he knows to be unrighteous and evil." [48]

In Plato's view, virtue, like knowledge, is thoroughly rational. It has a definite goal which is the *summum bonum* of both epistemology and ethics: the rational knowledge by which one attains harmony and equilibrium. Although Plato's theory of Forms would impel him towards a harsh renunciation of the world of sensibles (including the all-too-earthly demands of our earthly nature), and towards an ascetic orgy of pure contemplation, as a moralist he actually advances no such regimen for the good life. The *Philebus,* that rather ponderous and arid dialogue which wrestles with the problem of what constitutes right conduct, concludes that the only good for man is a mixed life ignoring neither knowledge nor pleasure, but maintaining a just relation between the two. Such passions as anger, envy, grief, and jealousy are based on belief in future states of pain or pleasure;[49] and Plato, the humanist to whom nothing human was alien, insists on a cognitive element even in passion. He distinguishes it from reason not in the exclusion of thought, but in the level of thought; the difference between reason and passion is one of degree, not of kind. The pursuit (*eros*) of both is towards the good, but passion, because its object is variable, is vacillating; reason is steady. Since appetite is concerned with pleasure or pain, it can never be consistent, for when pleasure is followed by pain, we at once desire a new pleasure; our shifting satisfactions can be but wavering and spasmodic.[50] But as the object of desire becomes higher, *eros* becomes more rational; presently it is the contemplation of pure Form.[51]

---

[47] See Stace, *Critical History of Greek Philosophy*, pp. 217-19; cf. *Philebus*, 31 ff.; *Republic*, bk. IV, *passim*.

[48] *Laws*, 689.

[49] *Philebus*, 47.

[50] Plato classifies desire variously as hunger, thirst, and lust (*Laws*, 782), or as necessary and unnecessary (*Philebus*, 35).

[51] In his theory of recollection Plato states in another way the process by which we attain

"Are we not cup-bearers?" asks Socrates; "and here are two fountains which are flowing at our side: one, which is pleasure, may be likened to a fountain of honey; the other, wisdom, a sober draught in which no wine mingles, is of water unpleasant but healthful; out of these we must seek to make the fairest of all possible mixtures." [52]

The essential humanism in Plato's thinking is nowhere revealed more clearly than in his ethics. He urges man to ignore none of his natural faculties, but to develop his highest. If we may consider the *Phaedo* (whose Pythagorean and mystical overtones are unmistakable) as a temporary but aesthetically beautiful aberration from the main line of his ethical thought, it seems clear that he refined and brought to philosophic maturity the central Greek concepts of moderation and justice. Plato, as a moralist, refused to preach a violent renunciation of what was germane to man; he could suggest no more sensible basis for good conduct than temperance and a rational harmony of the parts. Like Democritus, whose metaphysics he detested, he declared for "symmetry of life" as every good man's highest obligation. When a successful balance between the pulls of reason, spirit, and desire is achieved, then man, through the education and discipline that strengthens the superior faculty of reason and controls the inferior faculty of desire, will be a healthy organism, and free. When reason controls, man is linked to the inherent rational order of the cosmos and by knowledge arrives at virtue; but when the whips and stings of passion drive him, he is "the slave of self and unprincipled." [53] As the *Republic* makes clear, the individual, like the well-ordered state, puts his spirit, a good soldier, under the command of reason in order to check the desires that would, unleashed, "overturn the whole life of man." To each part, as to each citizen, its own business and function, but always under the benevolent and ennobling aegis of reason.

For the just man does not permit the several elements within him to interfere with one another, or any of them to do the work of others,—he sets in order his own inner life, and is his own master and his own law, and at peace with himself; and when he has bound together the three principles within him, which may be compared to the higher, lower, and middle notes of the scale, and the intermediate intervals—when he has bound all these together, and is no longer many, but has become one entirely temperate and perfectly adjusted nature, then he proceeds to act, if he has to act, whether in a matter of property, or in the treatment of the body, or

rational knowledge. Man remembers, from the realm of Ideas which is the home of the soul, the Forms abstracted from sensory data. If the right questions are asked, the right answers will be forthcoming—as Socrates' subtle questioning of the slave in the *Meno* demonstrates. On the implications of immortality, see *Phaedo*, 73 ff.

[52] *Philebus*, 61.
[53] *Republic*, 431.

in some affair of politics or private business; always thinking and calling that which preserves and co-operates with this harmonious condition, just and good action, and the knowledge which presides over it, wisdom, and that which at any time impairs this condition, he will call unjust action, and the opinion which presides over it, ignorance.[54]

The chariot races forward, the steeds together straining to achieve the goal of the proud and comely driver.

[54] *Republic*, 443-44; cf. *Laws*, 850. On the Pythagorean influences in this soul-harmony, see Burnet, *Early Greek Philosophy*, 295-96.

# IV

## ARISTOTELIAN HUMANISM

### METAPHYSICS: PERMANENCE AS ACTUALITY

ARISTOTLE, WHO LIKE PLATO has been all things to all men, has to an uncommon degree suffered misinterpretation, the price of greatness. Because the anti-Scholastic polemic of Bacon still appeals to many, nothing need be added to the opprobrium so fashionably heaped on the Schoolmen and their master: at the best they were unduly but subtly agitated over questions that since the Renaissance have lost significance; at their worst their pious dullness is undistinguishable from a kind of perverse stupidity. But M. Jourdain's toplofty master of philosophy is not to be confused with the sage whom he quotes so glibly. Aristotle himself, Dante's master *di color' che sanno,* remains one of the shapers of the mind of the Occident. For all the distortion of his misguided exegetes, some of his ideas and ways of thought have worked themselves inextricably into the mind of Christendom. With these we shall be concerned.

However widely the two great figures of Greek philosophy may have differed in their metaphysics, in ethics they are in most essentials agreed. Both call for the humanistic exploitation of man's highest faculty. Aristotle's coldly uttered rationale of the good life represents a codification and systematic development of what Plato in his abundance had scattered so richly through the dialogues. With his incomparable gift for analysis and schematic statement, Aristotle, in large measure, formally organized the broad ethical principles advanced by Plato.[1]

Plato, obsessed with the vision of pure contemplation of Form—which afforded little guidance for the traffickings of daily life—only incidentally attempted a common-sense program for good conduct: his concept of Form is, after all, hardly a key to practical morality; an art of dying is not a plausible enchiridion. It is on the metaphysical implications of this point, indeed, that Aristotle attacked him repeatedly in the *Metaphysics.*

[1] See Sidgwick, *Outlines of the History of Ethics,* pp. 51 ff. This is one of the themes of Werner Jaeger's *Aristotle: Fundamentals of the History of His Development* (1934). For instance (p. 372): "Everything that Plato's spirit touched has a certain plastic roundness, than which nothing more strenuously resists the analytical urge of Aristotle's thought, which is to Plato's as the anatomical diagram is to the plastic human form. Perhaps this shocks the aesthetic and the religious man. Anyhow it is characteristic of Aristotle."

If Plato's Forms are self-subsistent and transcendent, then what can be the relation between them and the world of sensibles? Plato insisted that Ideas are the essences of things, and yet he committed the error of placing those essences outside the things, thus leaving unexplained the ways in which sensibles and Forms interact. His vague metaphor of perceptual data "participating" in Ideas is merely a metaphor that does not withstand close analysis.[2] Aristotle's task, as he saw it, was to solve the problem left unanswered by his teacher: to bridge the gap between permanence and change, and, by explaining the world as we know it, to make philosophy practical in the highest sense of the word. As we have seen, Plato as a moralist had to compromise his metaphysics; but Aristotle, whose thought was extraordinarily homogeneous, resorted to no such bifurcation. His ethics are rooted in his metaphysics.

"*We* must begin with things known to *us*."[3] Aristotle's great legacy to western Europe is his respect for the objects of perceptual knowledge. Although Plato had turned from them with something like aesthetic revulsion, Aristotle embraced the mean, the common, and the low. His passion for cataloguing and itemizing is antipodal to Plato's lofty, earth-fleeing speculation. Plato is the introvert, Aristotle the extrovert whose first concern was the observation and ordering of fact. In his emphasis on the system and methodology of observation he was to exert enormous influence in the Alexandrian age of scholarship—an influence which has not yet run its course.[4] Conceptual knowledge and the juggling of universals could, for Aristotle, rest only on close factual scrutiny. "It is the mark of an educated man to look for precision in each class of things just so far as the nature of the subject permits."[5]

The first problem he attacks as a metaphysician is, therefore, one of generic importance: are the things that we experience bodiless and transitory shadows of a higher reality, as Plato held? Are they merely states of mind, inherent in the observer and of no validity apart from his mind? Are they substances, somehow separate and somehow related, with identity and reality of their own?[6] Aristotle unflaggingly maintained the doctrine of substance. Reality for him consists in the essence unfolded in the phenomena, in the inclusive quality (of horseness or whiteness) that pertains to and is generalized from a given number of individual instances.

[2] See G. R. G. Mure, *Aristotle* (1932), p. 37.

[3] *Eth. Nich.*, 1095.

[4] See Whitehead, *Adventures of Ideas*, p. 136. See Cornford, *Before and After Socrates*, pp. 86 ff.

[5] *Eth. Nich.*, 1094.

[6] See the excellent article by Thomas Case, "Aristotle," *The Encyclopaedia Britannica*, 11th ed. (1910), II, 501-22.

Is there, then, a sphere apart from individual spheres or a house apart from the bricks? Rather we may say that no 'this' would ever have been coming to be, if this had been so, but that the 'form' means the 'such,' and is not a 'this'—a definite thing. . . . Obviously, then, the cause which consists of the Forms (taken in the sense in which some [e.g. Plato?] maintain the existence of the Forms, i.e. that they are something apart from the individuals) is useless, at least with regard to comings-to-be and to substances.[7]

Reality is firmly tied to substance, which is the corporeal *thingness* of the universe.[8] Since the form and function are the determining factors in the identity of substance, Aristotle's elaborate teleology is merely a critique of the ways in which substance manifests itself, potentially and actually.

For the nature of form must first be sought in sensible things. "One must start from that which is barely knowable but knowable to oneself, and try to know what is knowable without qualification, passing . . . by way of those very things which one does know."[9] Plato's Forms, existing not in things, but somehow over and above them, seemed meaningless to Aristotle. "What on earth," he asks sharply, do such Forms contribute to sensibles? "For they cause neither movement nor any change in them."[10] Since substance, to Aristotle, is that which is never a predicate, but to which all predicates are applied, Plato's universals or Forms cannot properly be called substances; the universal, after all, is merely a generic predicate for many objects of a class.[11] Moreover, particulars are not substances because any given particular has certain qualities in common with a larger grouping or a class; stripped of these qualities, the particular ceases to have meaning. Thus a bronze bust without weight or color or density or malleability is no longer bronze. Therefore, Aristotle concludes, substance can be affirmed only of the union of the particular with its qualities (or attributes or predicates), the manifestation of the universal in the concrete specimen. Aristotle was enough of a Greek to believe that the highest kind of knowledge is conceptual knowledge, but it can be attained only by passing from the individual to the universal. "For without the universal it is not possible to get knowledge; but separating the universal from the individual is the cause of the objections that arise with regard to the Platonic theory of Ideas."[12]

Although Aristotle, it might be said, redirected philosophy to the world of things, he was anything but a primitive naturalist. For he developed

[7] *Meta.*, 1033.
[8] See the *Meta.*, 980-83, *passim*.
[9] *Meta.*, 980.
[10] *Meta.*, 991; cf. Jaeger, *Aristotle*, p. 381.
[11] See Stace, *Critical History of Greek Philosophy*, p. 265.
[12] *Meta.*, 1086.

enormously Anaxagoras' suggestion that the transformation of matter is purposeful and meaningful—not the aimless fall of atoms through the void. His thought is basically teleological. Everything that is represents the operation of four causes: the material, the efficient, the formal, and the final. To employ Aristotle's own favorite example, when a sculptor is working a piece of bronze, the bronze itself is the material cause of the finished article (a statue); the sculptor, shaping the metal, is the efficient cause; the concept or preëstablished notion of the finished product is the formal cause; and the statue itself, the end towards which the others coincide, is the final cause.[13] Thus Aristotle develops the *why* rather than the *how* of philosophical speculation with an enthusiasm that would have bewildered the Ionian physicists. But he acknowledged that earlier thinkers had suggested, in various ways, each of these causes. The Ionians, so much agitated over the question of matter, were actually trying to isolate the material cause of the universe. When men began to wonder how aboriginal matter—such as the Boundless—was transformed into the objects of sense, they were seeking an efficient cause, for which both Empedocles and Anaxagoras, to their great honor, advanced explanations. Formal cause was adumbrated not only in the Pythagorean concept of numbers as universals but more significantly in Plato's theory of Forms— which, however, implied a dualism of sensibles and Ideas deprived of efficient cause. In point of fact, it was Anaxagoras, a wise man in the midst of babblers, who dimly perceived the importance of formal cause, and therefore formulated the notion of cosmic intelligence (*nous*). "Those who thought thus stated that there is a principle of things which is at the same time the cause of beauty, and that sort of cause from which things acquire movement." [14]

Aristotle was not content, however, merely to itemize the kinds of causes, for he held all change to be teleological; consequently reality must somehow be implicit in the concept of cause. By reducing the four causes to two, he arrives at form (which includes the formal, efficient, and final causes) and matter (the material cause)—the antithetical ultimates in a teleological universe, and therefore the proper base for metaphysics.

Form and matter are never to be thought of as separate. They are inextricably merged, and to abstract either is to commit Plato's error of isolating a realm of pure Form whose relation to matter cannot be explained. Form is universal, matter is particular; and by their fluid mutual relationship one flows into the other. That which is in a state of becoming is matter; that which it finally becomes is form. "Substance is the indwell-

[13] *Meta.*, 1013 ff.
[14] *Meta.*, 984.

ing form, from which and the matter the so-called concrete substance is derived; e.g. concavity is a form of this sort, for from this and the nose arise 'snub-nose' and 'snubness.' " [15] The concept of form thus not only embraces the shape of a thing (as a statue of Hermes), but all its internal organization, network of relationships, qualities, and even functions (its final cause). What is left is matter, the formless which, since it has no qualities or attributes, is the anonymous, homogeneous, undifferentiated stuff on which form must operate to bring it to identity. Matter is the substratum, the passive receptacle of coming-to-be and of passing-away. But both matter and form are eternal, "for everything that changes is something and is changed by something and into something. That by which it is changed is the immediate mover; that which is changed, the matter; and that into which it is changed, the form. The process, then, will go on to infinity." [16] Or again, matter is potentiality, form actuality; and wherever activity or change or motion occurs, it is merely potentiality becoming actuality, matter becoming form. When the potentiality of matter is successfully developed and shaped by form, then entelechy or completeness is attained.

And thus we arrive at Aristotle's basic reality, the end of all creation. It is form, the first principle which is both the source of all movement and the goal towards which all movement tends. Like Plato's Idea, Aristotle's form is the ultimate object of knowledge—not, as Plato thought, because form is transcendent, but because, being inherent *in* things, it determines their kind or species.

Obviously, then, the actuality or the formula is different when the matter is different; for in some cases it is the composition, in others the mixing, and in others some other of the attributes that we have named. And so, of the people who go in for defining, those who define a house as stones, bricks, and timbers are speaking of the potential house, for these are the matter; but those who propose 'a receptacle to shelter chattels and living beings,' or something of the sort, speak of the actuality. Those who combine both of these speak of the third kind of substance, which is composed of matter and form (for the formula that gives the differentiae seems to be an account of the form or actuality, while that which gives the components is rather an account of the matter); and the same is true of the kind of definitions which Archytas used to accept; they are accounts of the combined form and matter. E.g. what is still weather? Absence of motion in a large expanse of air; air is the matter, and absence of motion is the actuality and substance. What is a calm? Smoothness of sea; the material substratum is the sea, and the actuality or shape is smoothness. It is obvious then, from what has been said, what sensible substance is and how it exists—one kind of it as matter, another as form or actuality, while the third kind is that which is composed of these two.[17]

[15] *Meta.*, 1037; cf. 1064.          [16] *Meta.*, 1069-70.          [17] *Meta.*, 1043.

The cosmos represents all the infinite gradations of matter and form: at the very lowest, brute matter, at the very top, pure form (if such abstractions could be). Form in its more rarefied essence is, in a strangely anomalous expression for Aristotle, God—the actuality, the absolute end, the idea, the first mover who is Himself unmoved and free of all qualitative change whatever.[18] God is pure thought; "its thinking is a thinking on thinking." God is the perfection of form, the thought of thought whose eternal blessedness is the contemplation of its own perfection. Beyond the *ens perfectissimum* there is no further excellence; it is the goal of all the teleological striving and the fulfillment of all potentiality.[19]

PSYCHOLOGY

Aristotle's psychology is anchored to his metaphysics. In the vast chain of being—the teleological panorama that sweeps from matter to form—man finds his natural place. Aristotle's is not a meager anthropocentric universe that exists for the sake of man alone; rather, man is himself one of the configurations of actuality and matter in the ascending scale mounting towards the pure realization of form. This concept of continuity, as Mr. Lovejoy has called it, is intrinsic in Aristotle's thought; it establishes his title of the most systematic thinker of the ancients as well as the tutelary deity of modern biological science.[20]

Matter is inorganic, passive, inert, and irrational. Ranged above it in the mounting cosmic scale are all those higher manifestations of form shaping into ever more complex organisms the brute material or creation. Organic matter signalizes the emergence of soul, and soul, to Aristotle, is merely the function or form of the body. It is form working on matter, actuality molding potentiality; and it distinguishes the animate from the inanimate—that whose end is outside itself from that whose end is within itself.[21] The differences between plants, animals, and men are merely the differences of degree of soul they possess. Since soul is the function, or life-process, of the body, and not some *thing* injected into it as a sword into a scabbard, it is obvious that one is unthinkable without the other. There is no place in Aristotle's system for the Pythagorean and Platonic notion of reincarnation. How, indeed, could the function of Socrates become the function of a toad, or a tiger?[22] In defining soul as the first

---

[18] See *Meta.*, bk. XII, *passim*.

[19] On potentiality (or potency) see *Meta.*, bk. IX, *passim*. For a characteristically derogatory analysis of Aristotle's concept of God see Paul Elmer More, *Hellenistic Philosophies* (1923), pp. 208 ff.

[20] See A. O. Lovejoy, *The Great Chain of Being*, pp. 55 ff.

[21] See Stace, *Critical History of Greek Philosophy*, p. 296.

[22] Soul is that "which makes a body what it is; supposing that instruments had a natural

actuality of a natural body potentially possessing life, Aristotle extends significantly the scope of soul, and makes it operative through the whole scale of animate creation.[23]

Aristotle makes the hierarchal gradation of soul characteristically precise. The lowest kind, possessed by plants, is the nutritive soul whose activity is self-preservation achieved through nutrition and reproduction. But with the level of animals, the sensitive soul appears. Sensation, the property of "being moved or acted upon," [24] is a qualitative change by which the sensory organs assimilate form without matter. Because sensation, though incorporeal itself, involves both body and soul (a stimulus and a recipient) [25] Aristotle insists that it is the basis of knowledge. *Nihil est in intellectu quod non prius in sensu.* Without the potentiality of sensation, the actuality of knowledge, achieved through thought and reason, could never emerge.[26]

Plants have a nutritive soul, animals both a nutritive and a sensitive soul, but only man has, in addition to the other two, a rational soul. It is his highest distinction. Because of his unique attribute of reason, he links the lower to the higher planes of formal organization, just as his substantial nature lies between the substance of inanimate things and that of God. Man is part matter, part form;[27] and although he has the human capacity of rational thought, he cannot share the deific one of pure speculation. Such knowledge as he has, however, is significant: by sense he knows particulars, and by intellect or reason he knows universals. Thus, while he receives through sensation the impression of whiteness from individual things in the external world, he can apprehend and conceptualize whiteness as an essence.[28] It is the function of reason to generalize the form of whiteness, but only in discrete things known through sense. Man, therefore, exemplifies the emergence of reason or form, which in the lower brackets of the soul cannot pierce the confines of matter. Thus among all animals he is unique.

---

body, for instance an axe: the substratum of the axe would be that which makes it an axe, and this would be its soul; suppose this were removed, and it would no longer be an axe in the ordinary sense of the term" (*De Anima*, 412). See E. E. Spicer, *Aristotle's Conception of the Soul* (1934), pp. 31 ff.

[23] See Spicer, pp. 29-42.

[24] *De Anima*, 416.

[25] On the physiology of sensation see *De Anima*, II.4-III.3; cf. W. D. Ross, *Aristotle* (1930), pp. 136-42; Mure, *Aristotle*, pp. 102 ff.

[26] Sensation involves awareness of pleasure and pain, and, through movement, makes it possible to seek one and avoid the other. For Aristotle, pleasure is unimpeded activity, pain the obstruction of activity. See *De Anima*, 433.

[27] *Meta.*, 1045.

[28] *De Anima*, 431.

The rational soul has various faculties, but not, as Plato thought, "parts." How can the soul, an organic and indivisible life-force, be arbitrarily chopped into segments? Rather should one think of activities that emerge and develop even as the soul rises from the nutritive to the rational level. For instance, common sense is the lowest faculty of the rational soul, and by it man compares, distinguishes, and ranks the inrushing data of sense.[29] A secondary characteristic of common sense is imagination (*phantasia*), whose function is to retain and recall images derived from sense-impressions. It is neither thought nor sensation, but a bridge between; lacking the truthfulness of the one and the omnipresence of the other, it occupies in Aristotle's psychology a place rather like that of "decaying sense" in Hobbes'. The passive imagination may merely perceive images, but the active imagination may reconstruct and distort them, and thus produces not only art (which is essentially mimetic) but also fantasies and monstrous untruths.[30] Memory, a faculty superior to imagination, both recalls sense-images and recognizes them as veracious copies of past sensory experience; but recollection, yet higher in the faculties of the rational soul, may consciously and purposefully recall past images which memory seizes only at random.[31]

The most elevated and benign attribute of all, of course, is reason itself, the glory of man. On its passive level it is merely the latent but unexercised capacity for conceptual thought; but active reason is thought itself, that supreme faculty by which we enter the universal realm of relationship, essence, quality, and form. Like all other functions of soul, reason derives ultimately from the data of sense: it is the highest development of the psychological process by which potentiality is progressively developed into actuality. But for the active intellect Aristotle seems to indulge in special pleading. Since all other faculties of soul are inextricably associated with body, being its form, they must be supposed to perish with the body; the two are like convex and concave. But the active intellect comes from God, its reservoir and source, and to God it must return. It comes to man from without, and departs when he is no more. It is an eternal part of that eternal cosmic reason of the supreme entelechy, pure form.

Actual knowledge is identical with its object: in the individual, potential knowledge is in time prior to actual knowledge, but in the universe as a whole it is not prior

---

[29] Common sense—the *sensus communis*—employs such tools as the concepts of shape, size, unity, number, motion, rest, and time; Locke was one day to call these the primary qualities. See John Isaac Beare, *Greek Theories of Elementary Cognition from Alcmaeon to Aristotle* (1906), pp. 250 ff.

[30] *De Anima*, III.3, *passim;* cf. Ross, *Aristotle*, pp. 142 ff.

[31] See Spicer, p. 93.

even in time. Mind is not at one time knowing and at another not. When mind is set free from its present conditions it appears as just what it is and nothing more: this alone is immortal and eternal (we do not, however, remember its former activity because, while mind in this sense is impassible, mind as passive is destructible), and without it nothing thinks.[32]

### ETHICS

From this psychology Aristotle derives his ethics, the most warmly and genuinely humanistic of antiquity. In comparison, Socrates' are toplofty and even mystical, Plato's are abstract and unsystematic, the Stoics' dourly repellent. For Aristotle brought to ethical thought sanity, clarity, and practicality. Just as his metaphysics is developed from a basic interest in things of experience, his psychology from the realistic view that man's soul is his function, so his ethics is developed from the primary common-sense assumption that man must be considered as man, and not as angel or devil. "Clearly the virtue we must study is human virtue." [33]

The object of ethics, then, as well as the object of good living, must be *eudaimonia*—an untranslatable word that means some sort of happiness or (if that term is too much incrusted with Augustinian and Calvinistic opprobrium) well-being. It is the satisfaction resulting from moral conduct, "an activity of the soul in accordance with perfect virtue." [34] In explaining the nature (or *physis*) of moral conduct, Aristotle never departs, as Plato often tends to, from the secular, common-sense attitude that morality is a matter of daily living. Virtue is, therefore, not a transcendental Ideal, not a set of deific and superimposed restrictions, not Kantian duty, not arbitrary Blue Laws; it is nothing more than the proper functioning of reason, man's unique and highest faculty of soul; it is a final good that is an end, and not a means to an end. If man possessed only the sensitive soul, then sensation would be the entelechy of his nature; but because he enjoys the active intellect, reason is his entelechy, and rational conduct is virtuous conduct.[35]

Aristotle is not seduced by an ethics of impracticable elevation.[36] Man is not purely rational: he is a mixed animal with a nutritive and a sensitive soul beneath his rational soul, and their functions cannot legitimately be ignored or denied. If a hand is amputated, its function of

---

[32] *De Anima*, 430. Did Aristotle, in this difficult passage, declare his belief in a personal immortality? As we shall see, the question was to become theologically momentous in the late Middle Ages. See Stace, pp. 302 ff., Ross, pp. 15 ff.

[33] *Eth. Nich.*, 1102.

[34] *Eth. Nich.*, 1102.

[35] The conduct of an animal is nonmoral, no matter with what human terms we burden it; because an animal lacks reason, morality is impossible for it.

[36] For Aristotle's objections to Plato's ethics, see *Eth. Nich.*, 1096-97.

grasping is vitiated, and it is actually no longer a hand. Likewise, if a man drastically suppresses any natural function, he is no longer a complete man. Our natural—human, all too human—characteristics have been studiously abused by many eminent men, but not by Aristotle. His view is naturalistic. Man's functions, from nutrition and reproduction to conceptual thought, are all organic; and as a complex organism he should attempt to synthesize virtuously (i.e. rationally) all the complex functions of his nature. He possesses passions, "feelings that are accompanied by pleasure or pain"; faculties by which he satisfies his desires; and states of character, "the things in virtue of which we stand well or badly with reference to the passions"; and these multiple parts have to be adjusted into a well-functioning whole.[37]

As a Greek and a rationalist, Aristotle distinguishes degrees of moral excellence. Like Plato, he has a special regard for a life of pure thought, and this he calls dianoetic or intellectual virtue. Such virtue transcends the sphere of practical morality to soar into an almost Platonic realm of pure intellection; the speculative reason deals only with conceptual formal knowledge, and its truth is absolute because the object of its speculation never changes. On the other hand, practical or calculative reason, expressed by the twelve moral virtues, concerns the "variable" objects of sense and is therefore deliberative and, in a sense, expedient for good conduct.

And let it be assumed that there are two parts which grasp a rational principle—one by which we contemplate the kind of things whose originative causes are invariable, and one by which we contemplate variable things; for where objects differ in kind the part of the soul answering to each of the two is different in kind, since it is in virtue of a certain likeness and kinship with their objects that they have the knowledge they have.[38]

The functions of the highest or speculative intellect are scientific knowledge, intuitive reason (*nous*), and philosophic wisdom (*sophia*). Science, whose objects are constant, starts with the known, and either inductively or syllogistically proceeds ever upwards to those conceptual abstractions that both embrace and transcend the data of sense. It leads to that knowledge which Socrates, more emotionally and less schematically, had worshipped with a kind of religious fervor. But because some things are incapable of demonstration, we often use as a spring-board to higher intellection the truths revealed to us by intuitive reason. It puts us in "the

[37] *Eth. Nich.*, 1105. For an extended discussion of the passions, see the *Rhetoric*, II.1-11, *passim*.
[38] *Eth. Nich.*, 1139.

states of mind by which we have truth and are never deceived about things invariable or even variable." [39] But the apex of man's intellection, and "plainly the most finished of the forms of knowledge," [40] is philosophic wisdom, which synthesizes intuition and scientific knowledge. This, for Aristotle as for Plato, is the attribute of the true philosopher who transcends practicality.

This is why we say Anaxagoras, Thales, and men like them have philosophic but not practical wisdom, when we see them ignorant of what is to their own advantage, and why we say that they know things that are remarkable, admirable, difficult, and divine, but useless; viz. because it is not human goods that they seek. [41]

This kind of wisdom, Aristotle is quick to add, is not for the common man.

Practical wisdom on the other hand is concerned with things human and things about which it is possible to deliberate; for we say this is above all the work of the man of practical wisdom, to deliberate well, but no one deliberates about things invariable, nor about things which have not an end, and that a good that can be brought about by action. [42]

Here Aristotle appears at his most characteristic best, in framing an ethics for practical morality that may achieve goods brought about by action. His is the most urbane kind of humanism, one that candidly names as its object an attainable good. "The man who is without qualification good at deliberating is the man who is capable of aiming in accordance with calculation at the best for man of things attainable by action." [43] Such a man attains the good by relying on those ethical or moral virtues which serve a constabulary purpose of harmonizing, not eradicating, the functions of the lower levels of soul under the control of reason. By exercising our moral virtues we achieve the highly practical goal of good behavior, or, in Aristotle's characteristically civic view, social conduct.

The best life for the average man, therefore, lies in blending dianoetic and moral virtue, in being a rational creature as well as a responsible member of a good society. He who lives (if such be possible) only on the nutritive level cannot be happy, for he ignores his higher functions of sensation and

[39] *Eth. Nich.,* 1141; cf. 1139; *Meta.,* 993; Spicer, pp. 190 ff. Some of the obvious functions of practical reason are art and practical wisdom (*phronesis*), because they are subject to that kind of intellection that accepts, rejects, and balances.
[40] *Eth. Nich.,* 1141.
[41] *Eth. Nich.,* 1141.
[42] *Eth. Nich.,* 1141.
[43] *Eth. Nich.,* 1141.

intellection. Happiness can mean nothing other than the most nearly complete functioning of the soul in its highest capacity: it is the just and orderly composition of those activities—and how often Aristotle uses this word—that "give life its character." [44] Moral virtue involves, then, the rational discipline of passion. The functions of our lower souls are to be regulated, but not (Stoically) suppressed. Even though the mass of mankind, Aristotle candidly admits, prefers a "life suitable to beasts" [45] to one of rational equilibrium, any one, through training and habit, can achieve rational, and therefore virtuous conduct without resorting to a vicious asceticism. Calvin's belief in the total depravity of man would appear to Aristotle repellent and unintelligent, for reason is as innate in man as sensual desire. So long as each fulfills its proper function, virtue and well-being result.

The verbalization of this characteristic Greek attitude is Aristotle's doctrine of the mean. By it, conflicting parts are reconciled into a harmonious whole; moderation is a virtue, excess is a vice. The wise man will determine his own mean, for no *a priori* norms, Pythagorean numerology, or superimposed Platonic Forms can achieve a balanced life for all men. To find the ethical mean between sensual bestiality and ascetic theorizing is difficult: "*that* is not for everyone, nor is it easy: wherefore goodness is both rare and laudable and noble." [46] The most that Aristotle will commend, by way of moral precept, is what he calls "insight." Arising from the exercise of virtue and tending towards future virtue, it is the acquired judgment, tact, and good sense that makes morality essentially human. It is the last attainment of the wise man who is also, and inevitably, the good man. To feel the passions "at the right times, with reference to the right objects, towards the right people, with the right motive, and in the right way, is what is both intermediate and best, and this is characteristic of virtue." [47] And thus Aristotle prepares for his celebrated pronouncement: virtue "is a state of character concerned with choice, lying in a mean, i.e. the mean relative to us, this being determined by a rational principle, and that principle by which the man of practical

[44] *Eth. Nich.*, 1100. Aristotle charges Socrates with positing *a priori* a transcendental "knowledge" as the referent of all particular virtues—this in spite of his ostensibly inductive dialectic. Aristotle is more pragmatic in maintaining that practice or habit, inculcated by unremitting self-discipline, is the only weapon against dangerously passionate action. Ethics, Aristotle the philologist points out (*Eth. Nich.*, 1103), is cognate with *ethos* (habit). Education and training are the surest guides to good conduct, for they buttress and enforce the dictates of reason.

[45] *Eth. Nich.*, 1095; cf. Stace, p. 317.

[46] *Eth. Nich.*, 1109.

[47] *Eth. Nich.*, 1106.

wisdom would determine it." [48] Man's reason permits rational choice, and his distinction lies in his ability to choose rationally with respect to the well-being of his whole complex nature. Humanism has never been argued more soundly, or stated more appealingly.

The famous list of moral virtues exemplifying the mean—and how many dreary imitations it has spawned—has been vastly influential with later moralists, perhaps because it is so precise about matters usually treated with imprecision. If Aristotle's analysis appears clinical, at least it avoids Plato's error of melting all virtues into one nebulous, transcendental, undefinable, and virtually unattainable master-virtue. Relating to conduct and motive and dependent on deliberation and choice, the twelve moral virtues comprise the modes of a good man's activity. Courage and temperance, the custodians of the irrational parts of the soul,[49] characterize the citizen-soldier and the man who with self-respect can indulge his appetites for food and drink and sexual intercourse. In liberality and magnificence Aristotle urges especial moderation, partly, no doubt, as a social corrective for the Athenian *nouveaux riches*. The remaining eight moral virtues are similarly concerned with man in a given social or cultural pattern. Honor and ambition are proper to the affable, solvent, and patriotic citizen who takes a proper pleasure in making his way in the world. Good temper enables one to succumb to anger "at the right things and with right people, and, further, as he ought, when he ought, and as long as he ought." [50] Friendliness, truthfulness, and wit are all clearly social virtues. Shame, hardly a virtue at all, is encountered properly only in young people "because they live by feeling and therefore commit many errors." [51] And justice, the last of all and the sum total of all the others, is the "complete" virtue because he who "possesses it can exercise his virtue not only in himself but towards his neighbor also." [52]

The difference between Aristotle the realist and Plato the visionary absolutist is nowhere more obvious than in their approach to politics. Plato, as we have seen, allowed his quest of the absolute to lead him into political despotism; Aristotle, with much more experience in the world of men and certainly with a more basic humanistic comprehension of man,

---

[48] *Eth. Nich.*, 1106; cf. 1140. Some passions (e.g. spite, shamelessness, envy) and some actions (e.g. adultery, theft, murder) patently do not admit of a mean. "For all these things and such like things imply by their names that they are themselves bad, and not the excess or deficiencies of them" (*Eth. Nich.*, 1107).

[49] *Eth. Nich.*, 1117.

[50] *Eth. Nich.*, 1125.

[51] *Eth. Nich.*, 1128.

[52] *Eth. Nich.*, 1129.

made his political theory consonant with his ethics. Because his approach to both politics and ethics was practical rather than theoretical, he was willing to forego absolutes. Instead of seeking them, he said, we must be content with conclusions that are only approximately true, and workable.[53] Plato, however, never forgot his moral shock of the democracy that had dispossessed his powerful relatives, and in his old age he found a sort of vicarious revenge in theoretically legislating democracy out of existence. But Aristotle, in shaping his views about man as a political animal, proceeded to scrutinize, with characteristic and painful thoroughness, man's political activity. He studied and wrote analyses of one hundred fifty-eight Hellenic constitutions, evaluated them carefully, and framed his conclusions on the basis of ample factual data. Note the famous, dispassionate opening:

Every state is a community of some kind, and every community is established with a view to some good; for mankind always act in order to obtain that which they think good. But, if all communities aim at some good, the state or political community, which is highest of all, and which embraces all the rest, aims at good in a greater degree than any other, and at the highest good.[54]

Aristotle has little respect either for the communism of the *Republic* or the oligarchy of the *Laws,* for both are impracticable in details and, if practiced, would lead to ruinous dissension.[55] Indeed, any state which is excessively one thing or another tends to deteriorate: monarchy becomes despotism, aristocracy becomes oligarchy, timocracy becomes democracy. There is imbalance, and hence a lessening of the general good, both in oligarchy and extreme democracy. "Wherever men rule by reason of their wealth, whether they be few or many, that is an oligarchy, and where the poor rule, that is a democracy." [56] Aristotle is likewise skeptical of an aristocracy. He would agree with Horace that *vixerunt fortes ante Agamemnona,* but it too often happens that a noble stock degenerates "towards the insane type of character, like the descendants of Alcibiades or of the elder Dionysius." [57]

In short, there is no absolutely preferable type of constitution; therefore in his government as in his ethics man should strive for a balanced mixture of various elements. In all states there are rich and poor and merely well-to-do, and since the latter are a majority the constitution should be

---

[53] See Charles Howard McIlwain, *The Growth of Political Thought in the West* (1932), pp. 56-60.
[54] *Pol.*, 1252.
[55] 1261 ff.
[56] 1279-80.
[57] *Rhetorica*, 1390.

built around the mean which they represent: "the middle class is least likely to shrink from rule, or to be over-ambitious for it; both of which are injuries to the state." [58] Without mentioning his old master by name, Aristotle seems to have him in mind when he describes the pernicious effects of Plato's oligarchic despotism:

Again, those who have too much of the goods of fortune, strength, wealth, friends, and the like, are neither willing nor able to submit to authority. The evil begins at home; for when they are boys, by reason of the luxury in which they are brought up, they never learn, even at school, the habit of obedience. On the other hand, the very poor, who are in the opposite extreme, are too degraded. So that the one class cannot obey, and can only rule despotically; the other knows not how to command and must be ruled like slaves. Thus arises a city, not of freemen, but of masters and slaves, the one despising, the other envying; and nothing can be more fatal to friendship and good fellowship in states than this. [59]

It follows, then, that "a city ought to be composed, as far as possible, of equals and similars; and these are generally the middle classes." [60] Aristotle does not fear to extend his humanistic regard for man to the realm of politics; indeed, it is in communal life that man, who is by nature a political animal, finds his necessary fulfillment, for "the end of the state is the good life." [61] When a good life is made politically secure for a majority of the citizens, the best state exists. [62] This means that the most acceptable form of political organization will combine timocracy and democracy: "the mean condition of states is clearly best, for no other is free from faction; and where the middle class is large, there are least likely to be factions and dissensions." [63] When every man, "whoever he is, can act best and live happily" then the state is good. [64]

Thus Aristotle's thinking shapes towards its majestic end. In the vast sweep of activity that toils ever upward, through the interaction of form and matter, man marks merely a stage. A complex organism in a universe ineffably purposeful, it is his function to accommodate and harmonize all the stresses of his divided nature. Neither in nutrition nor sensation does he achieve his entelechy, but in reason. Because he must adjust himself to the moderate and temperate activity necessary to society (for he is a social creature), he employs his practical reason, exemplified by the moral virtues; but his highest function, speculative intellection, operates in the

[58] *Pol.*, 1295.
[59] *Pol.*, 1295.
[60] 1295.
[61] 1280.
[62] 1295.
[63] 1296.
[64] 1324.

realm of pure conceptual thought. Aristotle, like Plato in the *Phaedo,* reveals a professional bias for the *bios theoretikos,* the life of theoretical speculation by which man approaches God's function of thinking on thinking, and with which he moves deifically in the realm of invariables.[65] But such a life, Aristotle has the common sense to realize, "would be too high for man." [66] Happiness, clearly, is an activity that is good in itself, and not one that points to an ulterior good. It is, in short, activity in accordance with virtue, both moral and intellectual; and virtue means the highest coördination of all the disparate functions of man *qua* man.

Aristotle, no less than Socrates and Plato, found permanence and reality in conceptual knowledge. And as a rationalist in the great tradition, he marks the most systematic reaction against Democritean materialism, for, in spite of his insistence on the ontological significance of particulars, his teleology demands the greatest possible reverence for mind. Reason (*nous*) is for him, as for his illustrious predecessors, the governing permanence of the cosmos. His universe is through and through rational. Because Aristotle places man in his proper context at the middle of the *scala naturae,* he is able to formulate an ethics that requires not only the fullest exploitation of man's reason but also the gratification of those lower faculties without which he would cease to be man, and become something else. Emerson says somewhere that religion is a set of obligations originating with God, ethics a set of obligations originating with man. In these terms, at least, Aristotle is the prince of ethicists.

[65] Such pure speculation, it would appear, involves mathematics, metaphysics, and perhaps natural philosophy (*Meta.,* 1005, 1026). The *Ethica Eudemia* more summarily calls it (1249) "the contemplation and service of God." See Ross, *Aristotle,* p. 234.
[66] *Eth. Nich.,* 1117.

# V

## THE ETHICS OF STOICISM

### THE COSMOS

WHEN ARISTOTLE DIED IN 322, a year after his illustrious pupil Alexander the Great, an epoch in Greek philosophy closed. After him, as Mr. Whitehead has said, the effort to account rationally for the universe was abandoned.

Duller men were content with limited accuracy and constructed special sciences: thicker intellects gloried in the notion that the foundations of the world were laid amid unpenetrable fog. They conceived God in their own image, and depicted him with a positive dislike of efforts after understanding beyond assigned methodologies. Satan acquired an intellectual character and fell by reason of an indecent desire to understand his Creator. It was the downfall of Greece.[1]

That slippery time when Greece as a political and intellectual force was succumbing to the Latins of the West and the Semites of the East produced men who, if not titans, were wonderfully symptomatic of reorientation, and whose influence has not yet spent itself. Zeno and Epicurus, both in their young manhood when Aristotle died, are the symbols of decline. That one proved particularly prognostic of the rigidity of Christian ethics and the other of the *Weltschmerz* and weary intellectual satiety of the end of an era indicates the emergence of new coördinates with which man was to adjust himself to the universe about him.

Zeno's arrival at Athens near the end of the fourth century with a cargo of purple was strangely unprophetic of his career in that city. The shaggy Semitic moralist—he must have been shaggy—who was to cast such a shadow across the ancient world was presently attracting pupils to the painted porch (*stoa*) by the very ardor and intensity with which he offered succor to the downtrodden.[2] Like all notable men, he is inconceivable apart from his time. Philosophically, politically, and morally the decayed Athenian city-state was ready to listen to the stranger who promised release from the twin oppressions of fear and desire.[3] That miraculous

---

[1] *Adventures of Ideas*, pp. 132-33.
[2] See Gilbert Murray, *The Stoic Philosophy* (1915), pp. 16 ff., and Henry Dwight Sedgwick, *Marcus Aurelius* (1922), p. 243 on the similarities between Zeno and St. Paul.
[3] See Edwyn Bevan, *Stoics and Sceptics* (1913), p. 28.

quickening of national life that had followed the expulsion of the Persians waned as hastily as it had flared. After Thebes had exhausted herself on Sparta, only Athens was left to challenge the Macedonian. And although Demosthenes could nobly harangue his compatriots, neither he nor they were capable of decisive action after Chaeronea (338). The next three decades merely confirmed the catastrophe. Alexander, the Diadochi, and Demetrius Poliorcetes each in turn denied freedom to those too weary and too impotent to fight for it.

Plato and Aristotle had brought to speculation new conceptual grandeur, but their kind of philosophic thought could provide no solution to the urgent problems of their posterity. As Cicero, who was nothing if not practical, said, a man who read Plato could be impressed and believe; but "when he closed the book, the reasonings seemed to lose their power, and the world of spirits grow pale and unreal." [4] Thinking had to be revamped, and the reception given the new ethical philosophies reveals the popular need for moral guidance and for the solace of dogma. As Zeller has said, Stoic apathy, Epicurean self-contentment, and Skeptic imperturbability were the doctrines which reflected the political and moral impotence of the times.[5] A fragment of Menander, a contemporary of Zeno, sounds what must have been a common note of flippant desperation:

> Think of this lifetime as a festival
> Or visit to a strange city, full of noise,
> Buying and selling, thieving, dicing-stalls
> And joy-parks. If you leave it early, friend,
> Why, think you have gone to find a better inn;
> You have paid your fare and leave no enemies.
> The lingerer tires, loses his fare, grows old,
> And lacks he knows not what: moons round and seeks
> To find an enemy and a plotting world,
> And no smooth passage when, in time, he goes! [6]

But not all men could hide behind the satyr's mask.

Although Zeno wrote on a range of topics almost Aristotelian in scope, it was as a moralist that he impressed the ancient world. It is unfortunate, therefore, that his ethical doctrine has survived only in a few scrappy dicta and in the often sharply critical gossip of Diogenes Laertius. It was Cleanthes (with an alleged production of more than seven hundred books) and then Chrysippus who codified the master's teachings, and put

---

[4] Quoted by William E. H. Lecky, *History of European Morals* (1926), I, 182.

[5] E. Zeller, *The Stoics, Epicureans and Sceptics* (1880), p. 17.

[6] Trans. Gilbert Murray, *The Oxford Book of Greek Verse in Translation* (Oxford: At the Clarendon Press, 1938), p. 527.

into shape the system that Zeno had constructed "hastily, violently, to meet a desperate emergency." [7] Later the lawyers of Rome further developed the creed, particularly in its legalistic implications. But Stoicism has always exerted its profoundest influence as an attitude rather than a philosophic system. The dominant tone of Stoicism is one of dogma. Although the Stoics wrote on logic and natural science, they were primarily moralists and dogmatists, and as such ridiculed by the Skeptics. The Stoics did not seek the amiable virtues of tolerance and suspended judgment. The protean diversity, flexibility, and plasticity of Plato's thought are antipodal to them; historically they owed much to the austerities of those Cynics (notably Antisthenes and Diogenes) who had caricatured Socrates' views into asceticism and obscurantism. [8]

Like other post-Aristotelians, the Stoics were philosophically eclectic. Their physics, derived from Heraclitus, is a materialistic monism that construes all phenomena as body acting upon body. In such a universe, abstractions like Plato's justice are unthinkable, and knowledge (as Hobbes was to argue many centuries later) could rely upon nothing but the data of sensation. [9] Fire, the primal stuff of the universe, is the inexorable God-force that rationally directs the unceasing material changes towards a certain worthy end, for the Stoics conceived the cosmos as essentially dynamic and essentially teleological. "Fluxes and changes perpetually renew the world, just as the unbroken march of time makes ever new the infinity of ages." [10]

Man's knowledge of such a universe is nothing more than the presentation (*phantasia*) of sensory data. Some presentations are so obviously and compellingly true that, as Zeno himself put it, they take hold of us and drag us to assent. [11] Such a certain impression, derived sensuously or from unquestioned premises through logical deduction, is the Stoic *phantasia kataleptikē* whose "compelling force" is the "proper criterion of truth." [12] Zeno, characteristically, could best illustrate the power of our subjective reaction to such true presentations by stretching out his fingers (sensory data), closing his hand (assent), clenching his fist (conceptual knowledge), and finally driving one fist into the other (certain knowledge). Although Skeptics like Arcesilaus and Carneades brilliantly hammered at such a subjective and materialistic epistemology, the Stoics maintained

---

[7] Bevan, p. 32. The great compendium of Stoic texts is Ioannes ab Arnim, *Stoicorum Veterum Fragmenta* (4 vols., 1905-1924).

[8] See Donald R. Dudley, *A History of Cynicism* (1937), pp. 99-103.

[9] Every duty, says Marcus Aurelius (VI.26), is the sum of separate duties.

[10] Marcus Aurelius, VI.15; cf. IV.43, VII.19. See Zeller, p. 173, Windelband, *A History of Philosophy*, p. 187.

[11] Quoted from Sextus Empiricus by Bevan, p. 35.

[12] Diogenes Laertius, p. 279.

that what we know about the world we know solely through sensation. When our knowledge is wrong it is so because we have misinterpreted the data of sense.[13] Since all presentations result from the activity of some external object on the *tabula rasa* of our perceiving apparatus, the ultimate criterion of truth is the necessary agreement of our impressions with nature. Truth is imposed upon us, and our access to it is through a necessary conformity to its source.[14]

In an essentially hylozoic materialism the Stoics saw at work Aristotelian teleology, under the rational direction of the God-force. Stoic "substance" or "something" is the basic corporeality (*arché*) which finds expression in the four categories, reduced from Aristotle's ten, of subject, property, variety, and variety of relationship. These highest universals, the *summa genera,* include all matter, and the inexorable transformations of material things have as their goal the achievement of each thing's proper function through its *physis* or principle of growth: a plant by vegetation, a beast by its animal soul, a man by reason.[15] The dynamic central power —variously called the soul of the world, the reason of the world, destiny, God—imposes order on nature; and conformity to nature (the sympathy of the whole, as later Stoics called it) became the ultimate ethical principle. In a pantheistic universe there could be no evil, and the majestic design of the whole embraced and justified all apparent discrepancies of the parts.

All things come from that one source, from that ruling Reason of the Universe, either under a primary impulse from it or by way of consequence. And therefore the gape of the lion's jaws and poison and all noxious things, such as thorns and mire, are but after-results of the grand and the beautiful. Look not then on these as alien to that which thou dost reverence, but turn thy thoughts to the one source of all things.[16]

The teleological monism of the Stoics made inevitable their emphasis on order, design, and law; for the early Stoics this became the foundation of ethics, for the Roman Stoics the basis of the jurisprudence which they bequeathed to Christendom. If the universe is dynamic process following strictly teleological lines determined by God, then man as a part of the uni-

---

[13] There are four stages of knowledge: sense-perception, memory, experience (a configuration of similar memories), and notions. Man's unique faculty of reason deals wholly with conceptual notions. See Diogenes Laertius, pp. 277 ff.

[14] When combinations or configurations of disparately received impressions occur spontaneously to various persons, the result is the "primary conceptions" which the Stoics held to be the "natural types of truth and virtue, and as such the distinctive possession of rational beings" (Zeller, p. 81).

[15] See Bevan, p. 56; Murray, pp. 32-33.

[16] Marcus Aurelius, VI.36; cf. II.3, V.8, VII.9, XII.26.

verse can find his best function in acknowledging the cosmic order and adapting himself to it. "The perfect happiness of life is when everything is done according to a harmony with the genius of each individual with reference to the will of the universal governor and manager of things." [17] All men, says Cicero, have received reason and law from nature, and the end of life, which is moral worth, is to heed the promptings of our innate sense of law. "For those creatures who have received the gift of reason from Nature have also received right reason, and therefore they have also received the gift of Law, which is right reason applied to command and prohibition. And if they have received Law, they have received Justice also." [18]

Thus the Epicureans are wrong in making pleasure the end of life, and the Skeptics are wrong in making law merely a matter of convention. For virtue is man's proper end, and law is the means by which he attains it.[19] "True law is right reason in agreement with nature; it is of universal application, unchanging and everlasting; it summons to duty by its commands, and averts from wrongdoing by its prohibitions." It transcends senates and jurors, Rome and Athens, past and present. "One eternal and unchanging law will be valid for all nations and all times, and there will be one master and ruler, that is, God, over us all, for he is the author of this law, its promulgator, and its enforcing judge." [20] Thus did the characteristic Greek belief in an orderly cosmos become, in the hands of a Roman lawyer like Cicero, the keystone of Christian morality and jurisprudence for more than a thousand years. For to equate natural law with the providence of God was inevitable.[21] In the first book of his *Consolations* Boethius personifies law and determinism as "stelliferi conditor orbis," and in the fourth God's decrees are called providence—"ipsa illa diuina ratio." This divine reason controls even fate, "a disposition inherent in changeable things, by which Providence connecteth all things in their due order." [22] And Aquinas, so much dominated by a sense of cosmic law and order, reaches back to Cicero and Zeno when he writes about *lex aeterna,* the divine reason of the universe, and *lex naturae,* man's participation in eternal law. "Now among all others, the rational crea-

---

[17] Diogenes Laertius in Bakewell, *Source Book in Ancient Philosophy,* p. 274; cf. Marcus Aurelius, II.9.

[18] Cicero, *De Legibus,* I.12.

[19] Cicero, *De Finibus,* II.14; cf. the eloquent peroration to Torquatus, II.34.

[20] Cicero, *De Re Publica,* III.22. On the history of the concept of natural law see J. Walter Jones, *Historical Introduction to the Theory of Law* (1940), pp. 98 ff. A good short discussion, with particular reference to the concept of natural law in the Renaissance, is in Louis I. Bredvold's "The Naturalism of Donne," *JEGP,* XXII (1923), 477 ff.

[21] See Ernst Troeltsch, *The Social Teachings of the Christian Churches* (1931), I, 143.

[22] I.5, IV.6.

ture is subject to Divine providence in the most excellent way, in so far as it partakes a share of providence, by being provident both for itself and for others. Wherefore it has a share of the Eternal Reason, whereby it has a natural inclination to its proper act and end: and this participation of the eternal law in the rational creature is called the natural law." [23] Man is linked by nature to God, for nature, as Seneca had long before argued, is nothing other than reason.[24]

Such notions of natural law as exemplifying the reason of the universe form the basis of the immemorial argument from design by which the problem of evil is shown to be no problem at all and by which all things proclaim the glory of God. The awful structure and rationality of the cosmos give man the clue to virtuous conduct, which is to understand the design and fit himself into it. Zeno had laid down the axiom that to live virtuously is to live according to nature, "for nature leads to this point." [25] And Cleanthes in his noble hymn, the great literary monument of Greek Stoicism, had voiced the central precept with his singing robes around him: "there is no higher office for a man—nor for a god—than ever rightly singing of universal law." [26]

### THE INDIVIDUAL

The ethical ideal of the Stoics, derived from their pantheistic and deterministic monism, was embodied in the sage or wise man. A creature of incredible moral excellence, he exemplified the Stoic creed of living in accord with nature. Although he was only a dazzling abstraction, like the Buddha and the Hellenized Christ and Nietzsche's *Übermensch,* he has fascinated posterity: the Roman Stoics saw in him, perhaps, the portrait of the ideal man as lawyer: cold, passionless, knowledgeable; and the Renaissance titans, from another perspective, construed the sage as the quintessence of individualism, for Chapman's Bussy and Shakespeare's Brutus, only two among many, are the superb tragic heroes who stand against the whole world and catapult to defeat with plumes unsullied. Nothing better indicates the turn in post-Aristotelian thought than the emergence of the sage as ideal man. As one who has achieved tranquillity, he has transcended humanity and withdrawn from the world to which Aristotle had tried to adjust man. His apathy symbolizes the profound weariness and resignation attending the death agonies of the Hel-

---

[23] *Summa Theologica* ([1920?]-1925), II.1.91.2. Tertullian suggests an analogy between Stoic Fate and the Christian Logos; see B. J. Kidd (ed.), *Documents Illustrative of the History of the Church* (1920-1923), I, 142.

[24] *Ad Lucilium Epistolae Morales,* LXVI.39 ff.

[25] Diogenes Laertius in Bakewell, p. 274.

[26] *Ibid.,* p. 287.

lenic era, and his inhuman elevation is a tacit denial of that sense of harmony and proportion that had made Greek humanism so comely.

The sage's preëminence depends ultimately upon knowledge: his knowledge of the inscrutable and transcendent majesty of universal law, by which all that happens happens of necessity; and his knowledge that he, a unit in the cosmic design, must subordinate himself to the natural course of events. "For to grumble at anything that happens," says Marcus Aurelius, "is a rebellion against nature, in some part of which are bound up the natures of all other things." [27] To the sage, passion, which is the disproportionate reaction to externals, is an acknowledgment of disharmony with nature, and therefore an unmitigated evil. Reason is a proper acceptance of the universe, and when our impressions, through the misconstruing of sensory presentations, are twisted into something alien to nature by an "excess of impulse," we are ruled by passion, whence all our woe.[28] For the "nature of understanding," says Epictetus, is to assent to the true, dissent from the false, and (a late emollient of Greek orthodoxy) to remain aloof from the uncertain.[29] Thus, passion is an error of judgment, a misinterpretation of nature: in Cicero's words, "an agitation of the soul alien from right reason and contrary to nature." [30] Nature is rational, and it is man's highest obligation, as a rational creature, to conform to nature; when he fails to do so, he is irrational and a prey to the vagaries of passion. This disequilibrium between man and nature assumes one or four forms: pleasure, desire, care, and fear. But the ramifications of these cardinal passions are legion. Avarice, for instance, is a wrong judgment of money, fear of future troubles, lust of lawful pleasures. Man may destroy his judgment in many ways, and the valid presentation of a good thing desired rationally may be twisted into monstrous misconceptions which lead to monstrous action.

From this kind of error the sage is free. Thus he exemplifies the Socratic dictum that knowledge is virtue. Living *ex ductu rationis,* he possesses the four cardinal virtues of wisdom, courage, self-control, and justice. He knows the pure and liberal pleasure (*liquidae voluptatis et liberae*) of rational knowledge, by which he achieves tranquillity—of all things, the most to be desired.[31] This involves not, as Plato and Aris-

---

[27] II.16.

[28] See Zeller, p. 244. Nietzsche (*Beyond Good and Evil,* I.9) has a caustic commentary on the Stoic formula: "You desire to *live* 'according to Nature'? Oh, you noble Stoics, what fraud of words! Imagine to yourselves a being like Nature, boundlessly extravagant, boundlessly indifferent, without purpose or consideration, without pity or justice, at once fruitful and barren and uncertain: imagine to yourselves *indifference* as power—how *could* you live in accordance with such indifference?"

[29] *The Discourses,* I.28.          [30] *Tusculan Disputations,* IV.11; cf. Bevan, p. 102.

[31] Cicero, *De Finibus,* I.58; cf. Seneca, *De Tranquillitate Anima,* II.7.

totle had humanistically suggested, the control of passion, but its deracination: the sage transcends those factors of human conduct that make it human. A partial evil is still an evil, and a blemish on the cosmic harmony: *omne enim malum, etiam mediocre, magnum est.*[32]

If you see a man who is unterrified in the midst of dangers, untouched by desires, happy in adversity, peaceful amid the storm, who looks down on men from a higher plane, and views the gods on a footing of equality, will not a feeling of reverence for him steal over you?[33]

The sage has achieved not a synthesis and harmony of the various elements of human nature, passionate and rational, but the utter eradication of all save reason. He has become, in effect, an Eleatic absolute on two legs. For passion is a disease, a sickness in the polity of universal law: *inveterata vita et dura;*[34] and of all things the sage reverences most the miraculous regimen of cosmic law.

The sage's tranquillity does not necessarily consist of pleasures; they are present, if at all, merely as accoutrements to the essentially correct assent he gives the presentations of sense. If possible, he will of course choose the "preferred things" like strength and health, but only if they come to him according to nature (*kata physin*). Agony may be his destiny, but he may refuse to assent to pain as an evil. Or he may scornfully relegate it to the category of indifferent things, and thus choose to negate life through the notorious Stoic expediency of suicide.[35] The important thing, however, is the universal harmony that the sage comprehends; it absorbs all incidental discomforts whatever. And for this reason, distress or pain, his own or another's, should properly not move him at all. "Be not whirled aside; but in every impulse fulfil the claims of justice, and in every impression safeguard certainty."[36] Grief is an "irrational contraction of the soul,"[37] and all error or passion involves irrationality; therefore indulgence in melancholy is not for the sage. Pleasure is not only not an unmitigated good, argues Cleanthes; it may be a positive evil in that it generally implies an outward and passionate striving for external satisfaction.[38]

---

[32] *Tusc. Dis.,* III.22; cf. Zeller, pp. 251 ff.

[33] Seneca, *Epistolae Morales,* XLI.4.

[34] A favorite idea of Cicero's. See *Tusc. Dis.,* bk. IV, *passim; De Fin.,* III.10.

[35] According to Diogenes Laertius (p. 270), Zeno himself established the precedent. "When he was going out of his school, he tripped, and broke one of his toes; and striking the ground with his hand, he repeated the line out of the Niobe: —
I come: why call me so?
And immediately he strangled himself, and so he died."

[36] Marcus Aurelius, IV.22.

[37] Diogenes Laertius in Bakewell, p. 276.

[38] See Zeller, p. 237.

To link pleasure with virtue, thundered the flinty Seneca, is a "vicious procedure which flatters the worst class of men." [39]

What element of evil is there in torture and in the other things which we call hardships? It seems to me that there is this evil,—that the mind sags, and bends, and collapses. But none of these things can happen to the sage; he stands erect under any load. [40]

Cicero's teacher, the famed Posidonius, writhing in torment, exulted through his clenched teeth: "Do your worst, pain, do your worst: you will never compel me to acknowledge that you are an evil." [41]

Since the sage's avoidance of passion is his avenue to moral conduct, he can be moved no more by the aberrations of others than by his own. All fear, anger, vanity, pity, indulgence, sorrow, and compassion are false assents. They must be rigorously repudiated because they imply ignorance of the total scheme of things. Comprehending the great design of nature, the sage will understand rationally the distress of his fellows, but he will never surrender himself to pity. How can he pity pain or misery in another when he would scorn it in himself? He knows the terrifying and sublime interdependence of all parts of the cosmos, and from his lofty vantage he can survey accidental or apparent ills with fortitude. Pain is of no consequence: *si gravis, brevis; si longus, levis.* "Of course you will suffer," agreed Epictetus. "I do not say that you must not even groan aloud. Yet in the centre of your being do not groan." [42]

The impossible elevation of the sage has always repelled those motivated by either humanistic common sense or Christian benevolence. For the sage, *naturae humanae exemplar,* was in all respects an incredible figure. Obviously, few could be sages, and in their moral rigidity the Stoics tacitly despised the mass of mankind: the sage himself is an indictment of the human race. [43] Chrysippus went so far as to make immortality the exclusive reward of the wise man, [44] and Marcus Aurelius, the most ap-

---

[39] *De Vita Beata*, XIII.3.

[40] Seneca, *Epistolae Morales*, LXXI.26.

[41] Quoted by Bevan, p. 29; cf. Boethius, *Consolation*, I.4.

[42] Quoted by Murray, *The Stoic Philosophy*, p. 47. Seneca, in his *De Clementia*, draws a celebrated distinction between clemency and pity: the one an act of judgment, the other of unreasoning emotion. See Lecky, *History of European Morals*, I, 189-90.

[43] See Windelband, p. 169. In the *Moralia* ("Quomodo quis quos in virtute sentiat profectus") Plutarch sharply criticizes the notion of Stoic perfection; but Epictetus, who lived late enough to enjoy the mollified form of Stoicism, has a piece "On Progress or Improvement" (*Discourses*, I.4). See Clement of Alexandria, *Exhortation to the Greeks*, XII.94.

[44] The Stoics' attitude towards religion was in general tolerant. Their system itself was as much religion as philosophy, and although they could not believe in popular theologies they were willing to employ the popular deities as allegorical representatives of cosmic processes. As to immortality, they were divided: Zeno was ambiguous; Cleanthes believed

pealing of the Stoics, admitted that the wise man was daily tried by "the busybody, the thankless, the overbearing, the treacherous, the envious, the unneighborly" [45]—in short, by the vast majority of men who were beneath his contempt. Lucian charmingly demonstrated in his *Hermotimus* the futility of the concept of the incredibly wise man, who in the end turns out to be much like the rest of us. But in its wrathful denial of the errors that afflict most men, Stoicism became, in its ethics at least, little more than a weird blueprint for perfection. Plutarch, especially, attacked the Stoics on this point: they do not discuss the problem of evil, he complained; they merely do not recognize it. The sage, wrapped in his own self-righteousness, blandly ignored the most tearing problems of humanity; he could not allow his tranquillity to be disturbed.[46] Of course, to account for evil in any sort of pantheism has occasioned some of the most diverting mental gymnastics in the history of thought. The Stoics relied wholly on the argument from design, and their position has been of great solace to many a lesser man since. Almost anything, suggests Marcus Aurelius, when viewed properly by a man of "sensibility," turns out to be merely a "pleasing adjunct to the whole." [47] Cleanthes, in his beautiful hymn, refused to budge from the proposition that whatever is, is right, but at least he admitted a feeble disclaimer: "Nothing occurs on earth apart from thee, O Lord, nor at the airy sacred pole nor on the sea, save what the wicked work through lack of reason." [48]

### ROMAN STOICISM: THE NOTION OF LAW

Western Europe has inherited most of its Stoicism from Rome, which found in the severe ethical discipline of the Greek Stoics a set of attitudes peculiarly congenial to a people of empire. Everyone knows of the courtly Seneca, who had the honor to commit suicide at Nero's suggestion; Epictetus, the Phrygian slave; and Marcus Aurelius, one of the most perenni-

---

in immortality for all men; Chrysippus only for the sage. But until the Roman period, most Stoics thought that all souls, as well as the whole universe, would be reabsorbed into the cyclic conflagration that through some cosmic alchemy turned everything into the primal element of fire. See Zeller, ch. XIII; Davidson, *The Stoic Creed*, ch. XI; Lecky, I, 163 ff.; Marcus Aurelius, IV.21, XI.3, XII.31; Martin P. Nilsson, *A History of Greek Religion* (1925), pp. 290-91; Gilbert Murray, *Five Stages of Greek Religion* (1925), pp. 162, 199; Rohde, *Psyche*, p. 500.

[45] I.1.

[46] See Davidson, *The Stoic Creed*, pp. 188 ff., and Zeller, ch. XI, on the modifications of the Stoic doctrines. On Plutarch's attitude towards Stoicism, see T. R. Glover, The *Conflict of Religions in the Early Roman Empire* (1909), pp. 73-4.

[47] III.2; cf. Bakewell, p. 279; Rohde, *Psyche*, p. 513, n. 40.

[48] Bakewell, p. 277; cf. Bevan, p. 54. For a lively discussion of the Stoics' treatment of the problem of evil see B. A. G. Fuller, *A History of Ancient and Medieval Philosophy* (1938), pp. 213 ff.; cf. Davidson, *The Stoic Creed*, pp. 223-27; More, *Platonism*, p. 151.

ally appealing personalities of antiquity. Even the last authentic voice of the classical world, Boethius, found solace in those ideas of cosmic law, intransigent individualism, and resignation that enable him to approach his own end and the end of an era with philosophic detachment. Stoicism in Rome had always been popular, however, although more urbane and less austere than in Greece.[49] The cosmopolitan tolerance that had fashioned the Roman Empire from the *disjecta membra* of the ancient world, accommodating many peoples and many faiths and many religions in one *imperium,* had inevitably wrought a new flexibility in the earlier orthodoxy. By the time of Augustus, Stoicism had ceased to be the fashionable cult of wealthy aristocrats, and was percolating to the masses. Indeed, after Cicero, the incorrigible popularizer, and Cornutus, the friend and teacher of Persius, had spread the doctrine, Stoicism was a rival to the new Christianity—so much so that Nero found it expedient to curb them both. But Hadrian, traditionally alleged to have been the friend of Epictetus, was sympathetic to the creed, and his grandson by adoption was Marcus Aurelius, who persecuted the Christians and in his *Meditations* built one of the noblest monuments of Stoicism.

The Stoic emphasis on individualism and on the inviolability of law were the two factors most appealing to the Romans. Even more than Aristotle, the Stoics gave a unity and integrity to the individual soul (over its temporary states and functions) that could result only in a strong assertion of personality. "You may fetter my leg"—it is Epictetus the slave speaking—"but my will not even Zeus himself can overpower."[50] For the governing faculty of the soul is the organ of assent; through it one controls or surrenders to passion, and thus the individual is made solely responsible for the state of his soul. The Stoic relied upon himself; a citizen of the world of expanding geographical and political limits, he, unlike Plato and Aristotle, could find no ethical or educational corrective in the intensely communal city-state. Stoicism purported to be practical: its ambiguity about the promise of a future world and its insistence on moral conduct here and now reveal its purpose of inducing that rational tran-

[49] In spite of the brilliant and damaging attacks of the Skeptics, the Middle Stoa passed on to a line of illustrious men, though with some modifications, the dogma of the founders. The doctrines of Zeno and Chrysippus were known throughout the Hellenic world. Diogenes of Selucia had been sent by the Athenians to Rome on business of state, and there he successfully mixed politics with philosophical disquisition; Panaetius, the friend of Scipio Africanus and Polybius, spread Stoicism through his contact with aristocratic Romans; and Posidonius, the celebrated teacher of Rhodes, made an influential convert in young Cicero. The standard treatment of the subject is E. Vernon Arnold, *Roman Stoicism* (1911); see also Lecky, *History of European Morals,* I, 177-225, 292-317.

[50] *Discourses,* I.13. But elsewhere (III.12) Epictetus admits that the struggle between a charming young girl and a beginner in philosophy is uneven.

quillity that comes from utter self-control and self-reliance.[51] The ruling faculty of each man imposes a unity on the swarming presentations of sense, and, by granting or withholding assent, it becomes the monitor and symbol of personal integrity. "For nowhere," says the Stoic emperor whose life was a dedication to harassing duty, "can a mind find a retreat more full of peace or more free from care than his own soul." [52] And in the Renaissance, when the world was too much with men, the notion of Stoic self-sufficiency was to prove irresistible to the Faustus-type that, like Bussy D'Ambois, at the end could retreat only to itself and hurl defiance as it went to destruction. It is not strange that Justus Lipsius, a man much buffeted by the changes and chances of his troubled times, found his truest solace neither at Rome nor Geneva, but in his study with Seneca.

A more persistent influence of Stoicism, and one memorialized in literature by Cicero,[53] the great eclectic, has been its reverence for law. The Greeks had deified cosmic law as the principle of rational order regulating the transformations of matter, but the Latins, confronted with enormous problems of jurisprudence and administration, pragmatically developed the concept of law as a tool of empire. Belief in the inviolability of natural law, with its implication of a moral order applicable to all men alike, was adduced as a powerful support of the *jus naturale* from which both Roman and subsequent jurisprudence derived so much of its dignity.[54] Stoicism had risen in a world torn loose from its former allegiance to the individual city-state; and its substitute of a noble cosmopolitanism was predicated on the moral obligation of the individual to acknowledge both his personal integrity (equality under the law) and his cohesion with a larger order, either cosmic or imperial.

Like early Christianity, to which it presents many analogies, Stoicism

[51] See Rohde, *Psyche*, pp. 500-501.

[52] IV.3.

[53] For Cicero's objections to orthodox Stoic ethics, see Heinrich Ritter, *The History of Ancient Philosophy* (1838-1846), IV, 146-47. On the Ciceronian concepts of *jus* and *lex* see Taylor, *Ancient Ideals,* I, 448; cf. William Archibald Dunning, *A History of Political Theories: Ancient and Modern* (1902), pp. 104 ff.; Troeltsch, *The Social Teachings of the Christian Churches,* I, 150 ff.; Ed. Meynial, "Roman Law," *The Legacy of the Middle Ages* (1938), pp. 386 ff. The subject is exhaustively treated in such standard works as R. W. Carlyle and A. J. Carlyle, *A History of Medieval Political Theory in the West* (1903 ff.); Otto Gierke, *Political Theories of the Middle Ages* (1900); Charles H. McIlwain, *The Growth of Political Thought in the West* (1932). As a Stoic, Cicero was characteristically eclectic in an age of syncretism. First attracted (in *De Finibus*) to the Skepticism of Carneades, he progressed in such works as the (now lost) *Hortensius* (which Augustine mentions with admiration) and the *Tusculan Disputations* to a generally Stoic point of view. See J. M. Robertson, *A Short History of Morals* (1920), pp. 144 ff.; W. R. Halliday, *The Pagan Background of Early Christianity* (1925), p. 175. *De Natura Deorum,* a characteristic dialogue, involves a Skeptic (Velleius), a Stoic (Balbus), and a nonsectarian (Cotta).

[54] See Alfred North Whitehead, *Science and the Modern World* (1931), p. 16.

made for the universalization and democratization of individual responsibility. Epictetus the slave and Marcus Aurelius the emperor both insisted on the brotherhood of man, and on each man's significance in the
cosmic order. Why strike a stupid servant in passion, asks Epictetus.
"Slave yourself, will you not bear with your own brother, who has Zeus
for his progenitor, and is like a son from the same seeds and of the same
descent from above?" [55] The world-citizenship that ignored the confused
claims of smaller groups imposed a new spaciousness on political thought,
just as Christianity extended the domain of religious benefits. "There is
one who says *Dear City of Cecrops!* Wilt thou not say *O dear City of
Zeus?*" [56] The Roman Stoics were awed by the grandeur of the concept:
universal reason, apprehended rationally by men, working out its divine
justice on all men alike. The idea of nation, largely neglected by the
Greeks for geographical and political reasons, was shaped by the Romans
into a rationalization whose magnificence they fondly felt to be commen-
surate with the glory of their empire.

It would be hard to overestimate the influence of Stoicism on, first, the
development of Roman jurisprudence and, subsequently, on the medieval
correlation of law with divine providence. If all men, at least all Roman
citizens, are equal—and the very root of Roman political theory is the
concept of popular sovereignty[57]—then the law common to all men is the
origin of the state. "Quid est enim civitas nisi juris societas?" [58] This law
was basic, universal, and eternal, valid for all people everywhere. "Omnes
homines natura aequales sunt." The extension of citizenship implemented this equalitarian jurisprudence until finally, in A.D. 212, Caracalla
conferred the rights of citizenship on all freeborn men throughout the
whole Empire. Zeno himself, according to Plutarch, had argued that "we
should not live in cities and demes, each distinguished by separate rules of
justice, but should regard *all* men as fellow-demesmen and fellow-citi-
zens; and there should be one life and order as of a single flock feeding
together on a common pasture." [59]

---

[55] *Discourses*, I.13.

[56] Marcus Aurelius, IV.23. Seneca considered (*De Vita Beata*, III.3) the height of wisdom
to be the rational observance of law; "ab illa [that is, natural law] non deerrare et ad illius
legem ex exemplumque formari sapienta est."

[57] Thus McIlwain (*The Growth of Political Thought in the West*, p. 122): "In Roman
constitutional theory, therefore, the evidence leaves little doubt that the sovereign power
was regarded as an emanation from the *populus*, and when exercised by a *princeps* or
*imperator*, that this authority was his by delegation of the people." See Carlyle, *A History
of Medieval Political Theory in the West*, I, 9.

[58] Cicero, *De Re Publica*, I.32.

[59] Quoted by Ernest Barker, "The Conception of Empire," *The Legacy of Rome* (1924),
p. 52.

If the Romans had any originality whatever—and it is problematical—
it was for administration. But even so, they found ready at hand in the
Stoicism they borrowed from Greece the germ of the notions of law and
of universality which they employed in ruling their world-state. In *ius
naturale* ("que apud omnes gentes peraeque servantur, divina quadam
providentia constituta, semper firma atque immutabilia permanent"),[60]
*ius gentium* (the laws of contracts and property), and *ius civile* (the law,
written and unwritten, within a state), the Stoic lawyers and jurisconsulists
of the Empire established those basic notions of law which was Rome's
chief legacy to western Europe.

For almost three centuries after Augustine, the Emperor and his Empire provided the coördinates within which men functioned under law.
The deified Emperor symbolized the divinity of law,[61] and his Empire its
universality. When a new kind of divinity and universality was provided
by the rapidly developing Christian Church, it was not too difficult to
transfer emperor-worship and Roman citizenship to their religious equiva-
lents. Constantine, in 312, merely recognized Christianity as an acceptable religion; though nominally a Christian, he remained *Pontifex Maximus* of the old Roman civic religion. But fifty years later Gratian forbade
pagan rites, and Theodosius I, in calling the synod of Constantinople
(381), made it possible for the young Church to destroy the Arian heresy
and thus pursue its development as an organized world-religion with a
universally valid creed.[62]

Thus in the late Empire the Church as well as the state became the
origin and the symbol of law. You are within the Church, not above it,
Ambrose warned Valentinian II.[63] And as the state weakened and almost
died, its nominal rulers welcomed the Church as a new citadel of law—
especially since the law of the Church could be identified with God's
providence.[64] The Church could also provide a theological sanction for
even civil law: coercion and prohibition were made necessary by Adam's
fall. Obedience to law, therefore, became a religious duty, and such inequalities and oppressions as men suffered under a bad ruler were condoned as part of God's plan for the discipline of the race. When Paul
spoke of the "powers that be" he provided the Middle Ages with one of
its most cherished rationalizations. If there be powers, it is man's duty to

---

[60] *Imperatoris Iustiniani Institutionum* (1890), I.2.11.
[61] See A. D. Nock, "Religious Developments from the Close of the Republic to the Death
of Nero," *Cambridge Ancient History*, X (1934), 481 ff.
[62] See Barker in *The Legacy of Rome*, pp. 80-81.
[63] See Carlyle, I, 180 ff.
[64] See McIlwain, pp. 164-66.

submit, for thus God's providence manifests itself. Is not slavery itself, asks Augustine, the punishment for sin? [65]

But to return to Roman concepts of universality. There were also economic factors at work. Since every element of Roman life made for a close social texture it would be disingenuous to divorce the cosmopolitanism of Roman Stoicism from economic considerations. The ancient republican veneration for the patriarchal family merged easily into the typically Roman veneration for the ties and obligations of the state; the triune complexity of the political machine (consuls, patricians, plebs) resulted in marked cultural integration; and Roman state religion, long on formalism and ritual, short on imagination and personal intensity, remains a cogent rebuttal on Erastianism.[66] In the Empire, when Stoicism became a force in Roman life, all these tendencies focused on the concept of an *imperium* whose economic structure was massive. Because the economic consolidation of the Empire made it both convenient and necessary for satellites to annex themselves to the stronger party, Stoicism emerged as ideological apology for a *fait accompli*. It alone of ancient philosophical systems, as Kenneth Burke has pointed out, could provide the "appropriate cooperative slogans" and thus become the official Roman approximation of *Weltbürgertum*.[67] What Mr. Toynbee has called the universal state succeeded the Hellenistic time of troubles to engulf the whole Mediterranean world in the Roman *imperium*.

[65] *The City of God,* XIX.15.

[66] See Taylor, *Ancient Ideals,* I, 389 ff.; cf. Gaston Boissier, *La Religion Romaine d'Auguste aux Antonins* (1884), I, 13; François Picavet, *Esquisse d'une histoire générale et comparée des philosophes médiévales* (1907), pp. 46 ff. (on the religious cast of Roman Stoicism).

[67] *Attitudes towards History* (1937), I, 148. Mr. Burke argues (I, 152) that Stoicism was a form of collectivism based on a noncollectivist system of ownership. "Stoic cosmopolitanism was developed by those who were most concerned with the communicative aspect of the Roman economic integer."

# VI

## THE DECAY OF HUMANISM

THE STOICS, who took themselves very seriously, framed the most imposing, and in a way the most influential, of post-Aristotelian systems. But,
as we have seen, they mainly borrowed their cosmology and achieved an
ethics of salvation only at the expense of the central tradition of Greek
humanism. They demanded simultaneously an inhuman exaltation of the
individual and the deracination of those very qualities most characteristically human, and so they purchased moral excellence at a cost that Aristotle would have thought too high. The contemporary Hellenistic ethical
systems are guilty of a similar unbalance. Epicureanism became superficial, Skepticism nihilistic, and Neoplatonism—in which philosophy finally
crossed the boundary to religion—frankly mystical. To them we must
now turn to see how the tradition of Greek rational humanism at last
played itself out.

### EPICURUS

Epicurus (341-270 B.C.) is clearly symptomatic of the slackening of Greek
thought, even though he echoes, as from afar, those organ notes of the
grand tradition.[1] In a period of decay and dissolution, he, like the Stoics,
was content to leave metaphysics to earlier and better men, for practical
conduct was his main concern.[2] Like Zeno, an unhappy spectator of the
decline of Hellas, he advanced a way of life which, though in certain
points antipodal to the rugged contemporary Stoicism, nevertheless had
a similar impetus, world-weariness, and a similar goal, repose in a crumbling society. Both philosophies, Stoicism and Epicureanism, were nothing if not practical: they made it their chief business to consider man's
well-being, and to suggest ways to achieve it; both, as if in revulsion from

[1] Recently, interest in Epicurus has become wider and more sympathetic. See Norman W.
DeWitt, "The Later *Paideia* of Epicurus," *Transactions and Proceedings of the American
Philological Association*, LXVIII (1937), 326-33; also his "Epicurean Doctrine of Gratitude,"
*American Journal of Philology*, LVIII (1937), 320-28. For recent work on Epicurus see
*The Year's Work in Classical Studies: 1938* (ed. S. G. Owen, 1938), p. 74.

[2] The remark is in general true of all post-Aristotelian thought. The boorish Cynic
Diogenes as well as the graceful Cyrenaic Aristippus both claimed intellectual descent from
Socrates, but both were immediately interested in finding a feasible way of life. See Murray,
*Five Stages of Greek Religion*, pp. 117 ff.

the abstruse, difficult conceptualism of Plato and Aristotle, went back through Socrates to the materialists for their physics; both, in a culture which had lost its cohesion, reflected clearly those individualistic tendencies that would have made Aristotle, dedicated to the concept of organism, avert his eyes in sorrow.[3]

The Epicurean system is uniquely simple.[4] It had a single founder who all alone established the canon, and the doctrine itself, though derivative and often shallow, was in the main unaltered through six centuries of wide popularity. Admired in Rome as early as the middle of the second century, Epicurus' teachings not only attracted a consistently numerous following but, unlike most philosophies, enjoyed the support of a poet of genius. For Lucretius, though a Stoic in temperament, could not swallow Stoic theology. Cicero, who nibbled at whatever Greece had to offer, tells how converts were compelled, with Druidical zeal, to commit to memory the very words of the master.[5] And Epicurus, if we may trust Diogenes Laertius, wrote more than three hundred works without a single citation from anyone else. That the school, in spite of its longevity, was intellectually sterile did not perplex its devotees; for them philosophy did not necessitate the arduous and continuous investigation of truth; its one function was to teach the uses of well-being.

Epicurus himself fostered this attitude of passive acceptance. Because he despised grammar, history, and mathematics, he excluded them from his teaching. *Nullam eruditionem,* says Cicero's Epicurean, *esse duxit, nisi quae beatae vitae disciplinam adjuvaret.*[6] Logic baffled him, and so he neglected it. Consequently, his system, such as it is, falls into the divisions of natural and moral science, prefaced by the elementary logic of the so-called canonic. In this canonic, notoriously the weakest part of his system, Epicurus attempted to establish a test for truth without relying either on formal logic or dialectic.[7] For him as for the Stoics, truth is a matter of sensation: whatever we experience is true.[8] "If you fight against all sensations," he warned, "you will have no standard by which to judge even those of them which you say are false."[9] Notions, or conceptual

---

[3] See Zeller, *Stoics, Epicureans and Sceptics,* pp. 503 ff.

[4] I have drawn mainly on the admirable collection of Epicurean doctrines in Cyril Bailey's *Epicurus: The Extant Writings* (1926). The other ancient authority (apart from the Roman popularizers) is Diogenes Laertius. The always dependable Zeller, pt. III, is a useful secondary source.

[5] *De Fin.,* II.7. According to Diogenes, Epicurus, as he lay dying in his bronze bath, strictly enjoined his disciples to remember his precepts (*Vita Epicuri* in Bailey, p. 151).

[6] *De Fin.,* I.21.

[7] Cicero, *De Fin.,* I.7.

[8] Sextus Empiricus, *Against the Logicians,* VII.203.

[9] "Principal Doctrines," no. 23 (Bailey, p. 101).

reconstructions, do arise, but only through a repetition of the same experience; and opinion is merely a reflection upon notions. Thus Epicurean logic resolves itself into the most unabashed subjectivism.[10]

The physics are most simply described as Democritean.[11] Because Epicurus' system had to exclude mental or formal conceptual values, it posited a complete materialism—which, happily, was ready at hand in the doctrines of atomists. Epicurus reaffirmed their views, if not with originality at least with the prolixity of thirty-seven books.[12] He considered nature as purely mechanistic: there are the atoms and the void, and whatever happens is a result of the fortuitous collision of the minute, indestructible, and corporeal particles of reality. Teleology is scornfully excluded, for, said Lucretius, "not by design did the first-beginnings of things station themselves each in its right place guided by keen intelligence, nor did they bargain sooth to say what motions each should assume."[13] But there is an element of probability: in the ceaseless downward rush of atoms, a slight "swerving" may possibly lead to the creation of indeterminable clusters.

The soul itself is corporeal, of course, and when it dissolves at death, its component atoms are reabsorbed into the vast womb of nature. Hence there is no immortality; there is no hereafter. "Death is nothing to us: for that which is dissolved is without sensation; and that which lacks sensation is nothing to us."[14] There are immortal and perfectly happy gods, it is true, who act in all respects like highly cultivated Greeks; but their plane of existence, in the interstellar realms, is so far above that of ours that it is degrading and absurd to fancy their concerning themselves with human destinies. From them, mortals have nothing to fear, and the oppression of religion is merely another of life's many unnecessary agitations. For thus attempting to uproot a vulgar polytheism Epicurus elicited Lucretius' noble tribute, at the opening of the De Rerum Natura, to that man of Greece who first dared expose the fallacies of religion. In some respects the man of Greece's method was almost psychiatric. By demonstrating, as he thought, the insufficient basis for troublesome fixations, Epicurus was able to render negligible the futile terrors of man. The gods could thus be eliminated as factors in human conduct; death, stripped of

---

[10] See Zeller, pp. 431 ff.

[11] See "Epicurus to Herodotus," Bailey, p. 18 ff., *passim*.

[12] *Vita Epicuri* in Bailey, p. 145.

[13] *On the Nature of Things*, I.1021 ff. One might read natural law into the apparently random aggregations of atoms; the "swerving" seems to suggest something like emergent evolution, and the plotted curve of average atomic clusters. See Whitehead, *Adventures of Ideas*, p. 155, Bailey, *The Greek Atomists and Epicurus*, p. 318.

[14] "Principal Doctrines," no. 2 (Bailey, p. 45).

its spurious accoutrements of uncertainty and horror, could be viewed dis-
passionately; all the hollow fantasies of man, examined in the merciless
white light of materialistic analysis, may at length be expeditiously rejected. The world does not deceive us, Goethe remarks somewhere; we
deceive ourselves.

On this basis of logic and physics, Epicurus is able to construct an ethics
to his own taste. It is, in all truth, little more than a development and re-
finement of the Cyrenaic deification of pleasure. The only unconditioned
evil is pain; the only unconditioned good is pleasure. "Cum praesertim
omne malum dolore definiat, bonum voluptae." [15] Life, therefore, should
revolve itself into an effort to flee the one, to seek the other. But since
pleasure to Epicurus is merely the freedom from pain, an untroubled
mind becomes the *summum bonum*. "The limit of quantity in pleasures
is the removal of all that is painful." [16] Although the celebrated Epicurean
*ataxaria* implies the reëstablished equilibrium resulting from the gratification of desire (for the normal condition of man is good), more organically
it involves the concept of repose—that is, of not having desires so as not
to make well-being depend upon motion after externals. It is thus negativistic. Epicurus, rising at least above the shallow hedonism of the Cyre-
naics, makes pleasure mean the cumulative, long-term repose that comes
from the avoidance of pain.[17] He would not, consequently, urge or even
allow a wild profligacy, or unconditioned surrender to passion, as the
nearest approach to bliss. True well-being depends, instead, on the discrimination and judgment that enables one to choose, in a broad context of
experience, that mode of conduct which insures the greatest ultimate peace
of mind. Intelligence, or rational decision, is the key to happiness, for by
it we may realize that even bodily pain, if conducive to a larger end of
repose, may be borne gracefully. Epicurus regarded as inhuman and unnatural the Stoics' disregard for misery unless motivated by the desire for a
more expansive contentment: happiness is always the exclusive goal of
human conduct. Because mental states are more enduring than bodily
states, being subject to recollection and anticipation, carnal and transitory
desires are beneath the consideration of the wise man; a life of reason is
the surest guide to *ataxaria*.[18]

Happiness is virtue, then, and virtue is happiness. Virtue as a good in
itself is rejected, for when such abstractions as it and beauty and the like

---

[15] Cicero, *Tusc. Dis.*, V.26.

[16] "Principal Doctrines," no. 3 (Bailey, p. 95).

[17] *Vita Epicuri* (Bailey, pp. 169-71). For a telling statement of the attitude (though with
a suggestion of Christian disapprobation), see Browning's *Cleon*.

[18] "Principal Doctrines," no. 20 (Bailey, p. 99); see "Fragments," no. 4 (Bailey, p. 107).

fail to give us pleasure, says Epicurus laconically, *Chairein eateon*—"we must tell them goodbye." [19] The capacities of intelligence, self-control, freedom from fears and prejudices, and release from the bondage of external temporary desires—these are qualities of the wise man, who in his happiness and repose lives as a god on earth.

Thus, though its basis is vastly different, Epicurean ethics have much in common with the Stoics': both demand that the wise man exercise rational control over his passions and desires in order to obtain a more comprehensive well-being. To reduce our physical wants, remarks Epicurus, is to increase our chances of happiness; to minimize as much as possible the urges of passion is to insure our peace of mind. Although he thought that men, as ideal sages, should release themselves "from the prison of affairs and politics," [20] he realized that they have to live in a given social texture; and lest they become incivil beasts, like the Cynics, they must accommodate themselves to the demands of life—honor, sex, friendship— by achieving a proper synthesis of their wants. Not for Epicurus the drastic extirpation of the passions, not the unearthly perfection demanded by the Stoics; instead, by rational, that is, prudential, control in discriminating among the elements of life, we arrive at that repose (or complacency, to echo a harsher opinion) that is the crown of virtue.

However close they were in some points of doctrine, the Stoics and Epicureans differ importantly in conceiving man's role in the universe. The teleological nature of design which the Stoics worshipped can make man only an adjunct to a larger whole; the Epicureans, strongly individualistic, find man's salvation (and the Christian concept is not wholly malapropos) within himself and in his native intelligence, not in conformity to a superimposed pattern. And so Epicureanism, for all its *lacunae,* is a backwater in the surging current of Greek ethical thought; it found philosophic justification for resisting the pressure of externals, and it found that the seeds of man's well-being are innate and internal. Its wry, shallow humanism—so sadly deteriorated from that *paideia* praised by Plato and Aristotle—marks the last weary effort of the pagan world to accept man on his own terms. The triumph of Christianity, if nothing else, shows how feeble the effort was.

### SKEPTICISM

There is a certain comfortable regularity with which the movements of Hellenistic philosophy appeared. Events, intellectual and political, conspired to evoke the clashing dogmatisms of Stoicism and Epicureanism,

---

[19] "Fragments," no. 12 (Bailey, p. 123).
[20] "Fragments" (Vatican Collection), no. 58 (Bailey, p. 115).

which, in turn, made necessary and inevitable the Skepticism of the "Academies." Each movement appeared *seriatim* in the decline of Hellas. It is normal that earlier dogmatic pronouncements on the nature and method of human happiness should, in the rhythm of action and reaction, have elicited a general defamation of dogmatism. The Skeptics entered when the stage was set, the cue given; and their entrance, impressive enough to jolt at least part of the ancient world out of its lethargy of inflexible dogmatism, has never wholly lost its theatrical charm. For with a singleness of purpose worthy of Zeno himself and a dialectical skill (in a man like Carneades) far surpassing that of their adversaries, the Skeptics disqualified as candidates for the *summum bonum* both Stoic conformity and Epicurean hedonism. In a world gone quite mad, systems of such ponderous cocksureness canceled each other out; the Skeptics, therefore, as Diogenes explains curtly, declared all dogmatic philosophers to be fools. A truly wise man, unlike the pompous and incredible sage, found happiness not in blind acceptance of this or that jargon or dogma, but in the voluntary suspension of belief that left the mind detached and free. This was the true *ataxaria*.

Like other post-Aristotelian movements, Skepticism put philosophy into a bondage of utility. A philosophy that failed to consider human happiness realistically and that failed to evolve a *vade mecum* of practical conduct was as the tinkling cymbals which St. Paul has derided. Happiness, the Stoics and Epicureans would have us believe, is a corollary of knowledge. If one *knows* enough in an accredited way (of the scheme of nature or of the rational discrimination of pleasures), an inevitable good will follow. The Skeptics, whose antirationalism is, if not Hellenic, at least understandable, took malicious delight in suggesting that ignorance is bliss. They would deny, explains Diogenes in his capacious way, "the existence of any demonstration, of any test of truth, of any signs, or causes, or motion, or learning, and of anything as intrinsically or naturally good or bad." [21] Only when one foregoes all desire for certain knowledge, and frees himself from the tyranny of that most comic and intolerable passion, can he be happy.

The waxing individualism that emerged from the decay of Greek civic life—so far removed from the man-in-society assumption of Plato and Aristotle—had already revealed itself in both Stoicism and Epicureanism; the Skeptics developed it virtually to the point of solipsism. The whole negativistic and subjective tone of the movement echoes, of course, such earlier spontaneous skepticisms as the Sophists and even the mockingly inquiring Socrates of the dialogues.[22] But the New Academy elevated an

[21] Diogenes Laertius (trans. Yonge), p. 413.   [22] See Bevan, *Stoics and Skeptics*, p. 124.

attitude into a philosophic system: by renouncing all allegiances, by *dogmatically* refusing to support any belief, any opinion, any data, any dogmatism, they pushed to the threshold of common sense that winsome, open-eyed scrutiny of facts so characteristic of the best in Greek thought.[23]

The shadowy Pyrrho of Elis (*ca.* 360-275 B.C.), whom Bury has called the apostle of disillusionment, was a contemporary of the founding fathers of Stoicism. He left no writings, although the Old Academy he headed did establish the major premise of Skepticism: man is incapable of certain knowledge.[24] Sextus Empiricus, to whose indefatigable talent for analyzing rival systems only to reject them we owe so much of our knowledge of ancient thought, puts the matter quite simply:

Skepticism is an ability, or mental attitude, which opposes appearances to judgements in any way whatsoever, with the result that, owing to the equipollence of the objects and reasons thus opposed, we are brought firstly to a state of mental suspense and next to a state of "unperturbedness" or quietude.[25]

From this initial categorical denial of the possibility of knowledge it follows that a suspended judgment is the only recourse of a sensible mind, and that such a suspension can result only in the unshakable and objective peace of mind that preserves the wise man from vexing commitments and bondages. Since neither Socratic conceptual rationality nor sensory data conduce to irrefragable knowledge, a withdrawal from belief is the most certain obligation of man. For every opinion, an opposing opinion; for every affirmation, a negation:[26] Pyrrho and his disciple Timon saw everywhere the principle of *isosthenia* in operation. Because they, like Xenophanes long before, concluded that "there is nothing anywhere but guessing," [27] they could advocate as the surest road to happiness nothing other than a retreat in good order before the conflicting claims of existence. Such a retreat, a refusal on principle to submit to the passion of convictions, was ethically rewarding: the imperturbability accompanying a resolute expulsion of strong allegiances is itself the supreme good. Like the Stoic and Epicurean, the Skeptic hunted the same quarry, though with a different weapon. However various the means of achieving them, the

---

[23] The most copious source of Skeptical doctrine is the work of Sextus Empiricus; Diogenes Laertius provides a characteristically lively account; Zeller (*Stoics, Epicureans and Sceptics*) has an admirable synoptic discussion; Mr. Bevan's little book, already cited, is charming and sympathetic; the ultimate authority, of course, is Victor Brochard's *Les Sceptiques Grecs* (1887).

[24] See Brochard, p. 394.

[25] *Outlines of Pyrrhonism*, I.8.

[26] *Outlines of Pyrrhonism*, I.12.

[27] Quoted by Bevan, p. 121.

apathy, *ataxaria,* and imperturbability of the post-Aristotelian philosophic systems were virtually the same.

Because the Old Academy was coeval with Stoicism (and because Carneades himself was presently to be an extraordinarily critical pupil of Chrysippus) the rigid toploftiness of that school may very likely have inspired the practical, negativistic trend of the Skeptics. With the New Academy, led by Arcesilaus, Skepticism, developing its antirationalistic thesis systematically, expanded into philosophic maturity. Arcesilaus (*ca.* 315-241 B.C.), whose skill in dialectic was considerable and diverting, directed his heaviest attack against Stoic epistemology. (His success in demonstrating the invalidity of the "irresistible impressions" did not, however, induce him to attempt a similar assault on the theories of Plato and Aristotle.) "Arcesilas [*sic*] set on foot his battle," explains the Skeptic in Cicero's *Academica,*

. . . not from obstinacy or desire for victory, as it seems to me at all events, but because of the obscurity of the facts that had led Socrates to a confession of ignorance, as also previously his predecessors Democritus, Anaxagoras, Empedocles, and almost all the old philosophers, who utterly denied all possibility of cognition or perception or knowledge, and maintained that the senses are limited, the mind feeble, the span of life short, and that truth (in Democritus's phrase) is sunk in an abyss, opinion and custom are all-prevailing, no place is left for truth, all things successively are wrapped in darkness.[28]

Arcesilaus found the most convenient basis for action to be neither the unshakable "knowledge" of the Sage nor the opinions of the fool, but the calculated probability of the observant man. For such a man, explains Sextus, right action is merely that which "possesses a reasonable justification." [29]

Carneades, whose quickness of wit, says Cicero, was "almost divine," was the ablest of the Skeptics both in exploiting the fallacies of the dogmatists and in developing the positive theory of probability. Living a century after Arcesilaus, he was in a position historically to make the accumulated data of rival systems the butt of his destructive analysis: he most successfully worked out the latent negativism of Skepticism. Not only did he ceaselessly attack the Stoic claim of knowledge; he turned his clinical eye on the scientific materialism of the atomists which had been warmed over by both the Stoics and the Epicureans. Everything was subjected to his scrutiny and his scorn: logic, theology, divination, ethics, and determinism. But as a constructive thinker he was no less effective. In

I.12.
[29] *Against the Logicians,* I.158. On the theory of probability see Zeller, pp. 534 ff., 553 ff.

developing the theory of probability as a motive for practical conduct, he compelled even the Stoics to modify their crude dualism of good things and bad things to include a third class of "preferred" things. He brought a new plausibility to the doctrine of the "reasonable," in which he, like Arcesilaus, found the most workable subjective ground for action.

Aenesidemus not only formulated the famed "Ten Modes" (or Tropes) to demonstrate the utter impossibility of certain knowledge;[30] he even denounced such of his elder brethren as Carneades for concealing the wolf of dogmatism in the lamb's skin of Skepticism. But the most important of the later Skeptics was Sextus Empiricus. This man of medicine, like Luke the Greek physician, has given us most of our information of ancient Skepticism. If not an original thinker, he was an unconscionably diligent compiler, an arid anthologist whose books are valuable in spite of (or perhaps because of) his complete lack of discrimination. As Brochard remarks drily, he seems to have proposed as his goal to omit nothing.[31] Because the Renaissance learned its historical Skepticism mainly from Sextus, his emphasis on relativism is significant. He stated most overtly the latent insouciance and complacency of his predecessors. Pyrrho, long before, had declared that "there was no such thing as downright truth; but that men did everything in consequence of custom and law. For that nothing was more this than that." [32] If nothing is certain and if any dogmatic conviction is folly, then one's only recourse—apart from plotting the probable, which Sextus tended to distrust—is to conform with disinterest and without vehemence to the workable patterns of conduct one finds at hand. Because one cannot remain completely inactive, he must live "in accordance with the normal rules of life, undogmatically." [33] Indeed, a superficial token reverence for tradition and social usage is as much a sensible man's concern as his constraint of passion. Long before Montaigne, Sextus had concluded that outward conformity was the most commodious and expeditious means to the desired end of peace. "We live in an undogmatic way by following the laws, customs, and natural affections." [34]

Skepticism is an attitude, not a philosophy. As such, it served well the

---

[30] Sextus (*Outlines of Pyrrhonism*, ch. XV) discusses at length not only Aenesidemus' ten modes but also the five additional modes of Agrippa. But all the modes—variety in animals, variety in humans, circumstantial conditions, intermixtures, relativity, etc.—merely formulate systematically the foundations of doubt. See Diogenes Laertius, pp. 409 ff.

[31] *Les Sceptiques Grecs*, p. 321.

[32] Diogenes Laertius, p. 402.

[33] *Outlines of Pyrrhonism*, I.23.

[34] *Ibid.*, I.231; cf. Bevan, p. 146.

needs of the Hellenic world in its death throes. Epictetus conveys the spirit of the whole movement in a single pungent anecdote:

Pyrrho used to say that there is no difference between dying and living; and a man said to him, Why then do you not die? Pyrrho replied, Because there is no difference.[35]

And thus the humanism formulated by Socrates and his disciples flickered and died. Man is no longer the crown of nature, *facile princeps* of all things. He no longer assumes divinity through his innate capacity for rational knowledge. He is merely a sensitive organism whose sensations can tell him nothing of truth or reality or permanence. And to live is therefore as good as to die.

## NEOPLATONISM

When Justinian closed the school at Athens in A.D. 529, forty-four years after the death of Proclus, the last great Neoplatonist, the philosophical tradition of Hellas officially ended. But none the less a faint echo of the great tradition persisted in Neoplatonism as it gradually merged into Christianity. With it, the Socratic rational tradition reached its extremest end and its extinction before it was absorbed into the medieval Christianity upon which Augustine had put his seal. Neoplatonism represents the last half-hearted effort of the ancient world to cope rationally with the irrational world of sensation. For all post-Socratic philosophy, the world of sense had presented problems never treated by the early materialists; indeed, the great body of Greek thought is an attempt to explain and to come to terms with the objective world known through sensation. Even the materialist physics of the Stoics and the Epicureans accompanied an ethics that mainly ignored the demands of man's sensitive soul. And the Platonic tradition, to say nothing of the mystery religions, had been increasingly earth-fleeing.

Neoplatonism, as heir to all Greek philosophy, was inordinately eclectic; in it most earlier idealisms were consolidated. Its regard for the individual is Aristotelian; its intense distrust of empirical knowledge derives from the metaphysics of Plato; its ethics are generally Stoic; even the Skeptics, whom the Neoplatonists so deeply abhorred, contributed negatively to the new syncretism: the attitude that man is of himself capable of nothing, certain of nothing, merged with the prevailing disenchantment with the humanistic tradition, and, together with those mystery religions that re-

[35] *Discourses*, frag. 93. Cf. Sextus Empiricus, *Outlines of Pyrrhonism*, III.24.

pudiated reason altogether, led to the suprarationalism of Neoplatonism.[36]

Neoplatonism climaxed and extinguished the tradition of Greek humanism. In no other system is man regarded so highly, his superiority to nature so vehemently affirmed, his divinity so intensely argued. Conversely, in no other system is the objective world of sense, of which he is a part, so despised. Man's importance and dignity lie not in his material but in his mental being. The emphasis, however, is not on his capacities for conceptual thought or on reason, but—and this is uniquely Neoplatonic—on his suprarational prowess, his divine faculty that lies above reason as reason lies above sensation. Rationalism gives way before mysticism, about which, as is notoriously known, no one has succeeded in being either articulate or rational.

Plotinus[37] himself, a third-century Egyptian who had absorbed all the intellectual legacies of a dying world, erected his system not only on the moribund tradition of Greek humanism but also on the powerful new mystery religions, Christianity and others.[38] The result was an attempted reconciliation of religion with philosophy, and the sheerest kind of transcendentalism. For to Plotinus reality lay wholly within the nameless Being, the One (*to en*), the Infinite. This Being, who alone has real existence as the causality of all other life, is the perfectly good and illimitable Unity which permits no predication.[39] It is without attributes and it is beyond intellection, being, or feeling. It is the beginning and the end of all, the Platonic ideas consolidated and rarefied into one inclusive Form of all things and all forces. And because Neoplatonism is basically an attempt to clarify the relationship between the sensible world and the One, this ineffable Source is made the origin of all created things. Like a powerful light that illumines the surrounding darkness, or like the center of a series of concentric circles fading away into nonentity, the One is related to everything else. All creation is a hierarchy of emanations, each giving origin to the next, and each successively weaker than its parent. Life derives from the One and flows back into it, and thus all created things, insofar as they are illumined by the One, or emanate from it, are in part

[36] See Thomas Whittaker, *The Neo-Platonists: A Study in the History of Hellenism* (1918), ch. V, *passim;* Adolf Harnack, "Neo-Platonism," *The Encyclopaedia Britannica,* 11th ed., XIX, 373.

[37] Plotinus, as we learn from the charming biography of his disciple Porphyry, through his teaching attained an eminently respectable position at Rome. His torturously contrived writings (he much preferred the spoken word), were gathered into fifty-four treatises and then edited into six groups of nine parts each (the *Enneads*) by Porphyry. I shall quote from the translation by Stephan MacKenna.

[38] See Franz V. M. Cumont, *Les Religions Orientales dans le paganisme romain* (2d ed., 1909), pp. 298-99.

[39] See Windelband, *A History of Philosophy,* pp. 235 ff.; *Enneads,* VI.7.38.

divine and therefore good; in its excess of goodness and perfection, its essence overflows the whole sensible universe.[40] Only that which lies without the radius of such emanations is bad, in that it is merely *not;* for it is uncreated, unshaped matter, negative and meaningless.[41]

All nature is ranged in hierarchies about this First Mover (*pronton dynamis*): Being itself, then mind or *nous* (the realm of Forms), and then the objective world. First and nearest is *nous,* the ideal Form that differs from the One in that it is accessible to the human mind. The *nous,* in turn, is linked to the soul, like itself, incorporeal, but bridging the abyss between Form and the world of sense. This soul, unlike the *nous,* is divisible, and so may penetrate and lose itself in the sensible world. If the soul remains an indissoluble essence, it is absorbed into ecstatic contemplation of the *nous;* and if it is dispersed into individual souls it transfers the archetypes of the Ideal into sensibles, thus working formatively on the brute matter of the cosmos. So long as soul thus penetrates and informs matter, the result is good, for it shares divinity and is a shadow of perfection. But as the circles widen and fade away, as the object is illumined less and less by the Source of light and life, matter intrudes itself. Matter is merely that which is unaffected by soul, and thus it is nothing. It is uncreated and immaterial (for soul has not formed it into corporeality), it has no attributes, it is nonbeing. Because it is without Form or idea, it is merely the raw material for the configurations elicited by soul; and because it is without soul, without any influence of the One, it is evil.[42]

From this metaphysics Plotinus evolved an ethic that inevitably abhorred sense and exalted spirit. Lying between the realms of matter and mind (*nous*), man signalizes the union of soul and body; his chief end, therefore, should be to establish a proper relation between the two. In effect, this means that as he approaches pure spirituality he betters himself; as he lives sensuously, he removes himself from the One. By relying on mind, the soul frees itself from corporeality and begins the long ascent to the One.[43] This progress is marked by a graduated series of virtues, each more soulful and less corporeal than the last. The anthropocentric and humanistic tendency of earlier ethics, even Plato's, which attempted to make possible man's well-being as a man, disappears in Plotinus' fear of the world's contagion. He attempts not a harmony of soul and body

---

[40] The metaphor is employed by Plotinus himself (*Enneads,* V.2.1.).

[41] See *Enneads,* III.6.7.

[42] On the Neoplatonic concept of matter see William Ralph Inge, *The Philosophy of Plotinus* (1918), I, 128 ff.

[43] *Enneads,* IV.8.2. (on the imprisonment of soul in body); cf. Edward Motley Pickman, *The Mind of Latin Christendom* (1937), I, 35 ff.; Paul Elmer More, *Hellenistic Philosophies* (1923), p. 187.

but a repudiation of body by soul.[44] The soul turns inward to itself by passing from the civil virtues (decorative but not edifying) to the purifying virtues that free one from the pulls of the flesh and turn one to contemplation and renunciation. The soul, says Plotinus,

> . . . will hold itself above all passions and affections. Necessary pleasures and all the activity of the senses it will employ only for medicament and assuagement lest its work be impeded. Pain it may combat, but, failing the cure, it will bear meekly and ease it by refusing assent to it. All passionate action it will check.[45]

And thus at last man arrives at the divine and suprarational virtues which make possible a mystical union with the One. This is the end of life: the identity of the human soul with its ultimate source, the flowing-back into the reservoir of Being. Neither man's reason nor his volition can induce the mystic union. Plotinus himself, according to Porphyry, achieved the ecstasy of mysticism at least four times, and Porphyry, in his sixty-eighth year, "was once admitted and entered into Union."[46] The mystical experience is the crown of wisdom. "This is the life of gods and of the godlike and blessed among men, liberation from the alien that besets us here, a life taking no pleasure in the things of earth, the passing of solitary to solitary."[47]

Beyond Neoplatonism, the philosophy of aspiration could not go. In its terms, man's link with the divine was potentially so close and factual that he could in effect become God. No higher consummation could be conceived. But this mystical ecstasy was predicated on a metaphysics that literally denied the reality of the objective world. It was the last ingenious but futile protest of the ancient world against the change that threatened permanence; it was the despairing wail of terror: since the world could not be conquered, it could be legislated out of existence. In Plotinus' attempts to rise above the world of sense—he would neither sit for a portrait nor speak of his parents—he extinguished both man's corporeal being and his intelligence. His philosophy, suffusing all existence with the white, blinding light of divinity, abandoned rational analysis for ecstatic and inarticulate annihilation.

[44] See Henry Sidgwick, *Outlines of the History of Ethics for English Readers,* pp. 106-107.
[45] *Enneads,* I.2.5. The Stoic echoes are clear. But on the important matter of suicide Plotinus differed from the Stoics; see *Enneads,* I.9.
[46] Porphyry's *Life,* 24 (McKenna, I, 24). On Plotinian mysticism see Whittaker, *The Neo-Platonists,* ch. VI; More, *Hellenistic Philosophies,* pp. 183 ff. Plotinus himself, who coined the term *ecstasy* (François Picavet, *Esquisse d'une histoire générale et comparée des philosophes médiévales,* p. 51), described the stages of the mystical experience (*Enneads,* V.3.13 ff.).
[47] *Enneads,* VI.9.11.

By the sixth century, Neoplatonism had succumbed to the regnant Christianity which, in a way, it had tried and failed to philosophize. Their rivalry was inevitable, for they contested for the same prize. Both the philosophy and the religion, as Harnack has said, were directed towards the same ethical goal: to liberate the human soul from the bondage of sensuality—a consummation, they agreed, which could be achieved not by man's own efforts but by some supernatural aid, either divine grace or mystic revelation. The testimony of Augustine himself, in the seventh book of the *Confessions,* shows that at least from the fourth century on the bond between the two was close; and his momentous doctrines about God and matter and the nature of evil are all under great debt to the Neoplatonists whom he cites with admiration.

Plotinus and Porphyry were clearly not Christians, but they had probably been influenced by sophisticated Jews like Philo who sought to Hellenize religion, by Christians like Justin and Athenagoras who owed much to the ethical systems of Greece, and by the Gnostics of the second century. With the successors to Plotinus—Iamblicus, Amelius, and Maximus, for instance—the correspondence between Neoplatonism and Christianity was acknowledged, and until the age of Valentinian and Theodosius the Neoplatonists had reason to hope that they might purify the crudities of the new religion into philosophy. But even after Neoplatonism had ceded, in the fifth century, all claims to exist as an independent philosophical system, it continued to exert a profound influence on the mysticism of the Middle Ages through the writings of the Pseudo-Dionysius.

Probably no other man about whom so little is known has had a comparable effect on the intellectual development of Europe. The "Areopagite" (mentioned in Acts XVII:34 as one of the Athenians converted by Saint Paul) was, several centuries after his death, named by the Pseudo-Dionysius as the author of a group of theological tracts that were actually forgeries. The texts themselves, probably composed before the early sixth century, were translated by Erigena in the ninth, after which they gradually became known and reverenced all over Christendom.[48] But the real author and the date and place of composition are still unknown.

In the four tracts and ten letters that have survived—*Concerning the Celestial Hierarchy, Concerning the Ecclesiastical Hierarchy, Concerning Divine Names, Concerning Mystic Theology*—most of the mystic tradi-

[48] As an example of the way in which Dionysius' doctrines were spread note the anonymous fourteenth-century English translation of *De Mystica Theologia,* based on the paraphrase of Vercellensis, itself based on the redaction (from Erigena?) of Johannes Sarracenus. See *The Cloud of Unknowing and Other Treatises by an English Mystic of the Fourteenth Century* (ed. Dom Justin McCann, 2d ed., 1936), pp. 249-83.

tions of antiquity, and notably of Neoplatonism, are synthesized with Christian theology.[49] Dionysius works inside the dogma of the Church— for instance, he preserves the Holy Trinity[50]—but he construes God as the Neoplatonic Monad, the essence of Being which transcends Being, and the source of all that is good and beautiful. "The Good and Beautiful are the cause of all things that are; and all things love and aspire to the Good and Beautiful, which are, indeed, the sole object of their desire." [51] The recurrent theme of the Areopagite is the central importance of God. He is the One Being (*to en*) which transcends predication and comprehension, and therefore we approach Him not through rational knowledge but through the cloud of unknowing, the brilliant darkness of suprarational intuition. The very apex of Being, He transmits being to other things in a hierarchal gradation from Himself, the center, outward. In His love and infinity, God overflows with Being, and to know His perfection is man's highest glory.

You should, in the purposive practice of mystic contemplation, escape the senses and lay aside the guidance of the intellect, leaving behind, indeed, all that belongs to the sensual and the intellectual spheres, escaping alike what is and what is not, and rise upward toward union with Him who is above all knowing and all being. By a continuous and total abandonment of yourself, and withdrawal from all things, relinquishing all and freed from all and thus purified, you will pierce to the region of Divine darkness transcending all essence.[52]

In the Areopagite's beautifully articulated conception of a transcendent triune deity as the ineffable source and center of all being, ranged about Him in descending hierarchies,[53] the Middle Ages found a virtually canonical source for some of its most characteristic and well-loved ideas: the supremacy of God, the derogation of sensibles, the concept of hierarchal order and proportion, the exfoliation of symbol. Through the Pseudo-Dionysius the Middle Ages found a link to the mysticism of antiquity, and

---

[49] Dean Inge is very critical of Dionysius' clumsy welding of Oriental and Western mystic traditions; see his *Christian Mysticism* (1913), pp. 104-22; for a more sympathetic account see Arthur Edward Waite, *Lamps of Western Mysticism* (1923), pp. 134-44.

[50] Thus the *De Mystica Theologia*, I.1 (Migne, *PG*, III, 998): "Trinitas supernaturalis, et supraquam divina et supraquam bona theosophiae Christianorum praeses, dirige nos ad mysticorum oraculorum plus quam indemonstrabile, et plus quam lucens et summum fastigium, etc."

[51] Quoted by Inge, *Christian Mysticism,* p. 106.

[52] Quoted by Sheldon Cheney, *Men Who Have Walked with God* (1945), p. 165.

[53] See, for instance, *De Divinis Nominibus,* IX.2 (Migne, III, 910): "Ac magnus quidem Deus appellatur, secundum sibi propriam magnitudinem, quae magnis omnibus de se communicat, et omni magnitudini extrinsecus superfunditur et supraexpanditur, locum omnem complectens, omnem numerum excedens, omnem transiliens infinitatem, et juxta supraquam plenitudinem suam ac magnificentiam, etc."

until Lorenzo Valla, with his godless scholarship, exposed the forgery, generation after generation read him with reverence. Hugo of St. Victor, Peter Lombard, Bonaventura, Alexander of Hales, Ficino, Pico della Mirandola, John Colet—these are only some of the questing spirits that found solace and inspiration in his work.[54]

[54] The literature of mysticism is immense, but some of the most useful general works are those of Evelyn Underhill—*Mysticism* (1930) and *The Mystic Way: A Psychological Study in Christian Origins* (1913). Edward Ingram Watkin's *Philosophy of Mysticism* (1920) is learned and suggestive, and there are handy compilations of mystical texts in Robert Alfred Vaughan's *Hours with the Mystics* (1856) and Edward Gall's *Mysticism throughout the Ages* (n.d.). For an introduction to the enormous complexity—bibliographical and other— of the Pseudo-Dionysius see Jos. Stiglmayer, "Dionysius the Pseudo-Areopagite," *The Catholic Encyclopaedia* (1907 ff.), V, 13 ff. The bibliographical essay in Cheney (pp. 385 ff.) is also useful, and much more general.

# VII

WHEN STUDYING THE GREEKS one sometimes thinks that they, embarrassingly enough for posterity, had all the really significant ideas first. Mr. Whitehead's *mot* that Western thought is merely a footnote to Plato recognizes the intellectual priority of Hellas, and it is a recognition with which Europe has repeatedly refreshed itself. Our survey of Greek thought, meager and synoptic as it is, may perhaps now be drawn into focus so that the contributions that the Greeks made to the study of man may be summarized and evaluated before we pass on to the Christian view of man.

Greek philosophy, at least until it became almost exclusively ethical following the death of Alexander, was primarily concerned with metaphysics, from which its ethics was derived. The central question that haunted every Greek thinker, until the Stoics and their successors ended original thought on the subject, was the question of being. On the answer to this rested their various ethical systems which together have formed the tradition of rational humanism for Western Europe. The question itself might be most tersely posed thus: what is permanence, and what is change? What is ultimately and absolutely "real" and why? Confronted by the swarming complexity of the universe, the Greeks addressed themselves first to the problem of explaining that complexity and finding within it a substratum of permanence. Once this was done, man's place in the cosmos could be more easily and accurately calculated.

Most pre-Socratic thought concerned itself so exclusively with metaphysics and ontology that it neglected everything else—a neglect that cannot be charged to Plato and Aristotle. That the universe was essentially *material* appeared axiomatic to the Ionian hylozoists; therefore they felt free to conjecture upon the nature of the ultimate matter underlying the transformations so obvious to sense. This conscious search for a monistic principle of explanation is the first significant advance of Greek thinkers on a primitive acceptance of polytheistic pluralism. Incidentally, it adumbrated the first naturalistic view of man, for the Ionians refused to consider him as other than natural, and therefore subject to the same natural processes of coming-to-be and passing-away as all other things.

Concurrently, the mystical Pythagoreans of Magna Graecia were formulating a quasi-religious ethics correlated to a conflicting view of reality as mathematical relationship rather than matter. The connection between the ethical and metaphysical strains of Pythagorean thought is anything but clear to us, with our scanty sources, but even to the ancients it was sufficiently obscure to cause a split in the development of the cult. One, more conservative, branch developed the almost Orphic doctrines of reincarnation, taboo, and general asceticism, while the other became more scientific and mathematical. Plato was powerfully, if sporadically, attracted by this kind of mysticism which chastened the flesh to elevate the spirit, but it remained for Orphism to codify the attitude into dogma. Its full implications were not revealed until the advent of a much more significant and sophisticated mystery religion, Christianity.

Heraclitus and Parmenides, inheriting the materialistic assumptions of the Ionians, each advanced his own banner. One could conclude only that change was the essential of nature or being, the other that being is solely real because it is above change. Already the dualism between permanence and change was making itself felt in conflicting philosophical systems, and the other Pre-Socratics devoted themselves in the main to finding a compromise between the mutually exclusive positions. Empedocles and Anaxagoras arrived at virtually the same armistice: there is a plurality in the way things stand in relation to one another, but there is a permanence and unity in the things themselves. This is essentially the view of the atomists, who developed with uncommon success the materialism suggested by the Ionians. Only the atoms and the void are real, but the configurations of atoms in that void are as bewilderingly devious as the data of sense lead us to think.

Socrates marks a great moment in the history of man's effort to understand. Revolting not only from the materialism of the atomists but also from the skepticism and slippery relativism of the Sophists, he turned the tide of Greek speculation. He succeeded, without writing a word, in substituting for the materialism of Democritus another kind of permanence—mind. And by viewing man in nature, rather than nature alone, he emphasized the ethical and humanistic element that was to become so characteristic of subsequent Greek philosophy. He inaugurated the quest for a "higher" reality which Plato poetically and mystically attained, and which Aristotle, scientist that he was, systematized.

Socrates' preoccupation with mind and its corollary, knowledge, as the permanence standing against change not only denies the atomistic materialism; it denies also the moral relativism that followed the Sophists' refusal to treat metaphysics. If one virtue embraces all qualities and arts and goods, as the early Platonic dialogues argue, that single virtue must be knowledge. The kind of knowledge taught by the Sophists was idiosyncratic and personal and above all practicable, because it had as its object particular things. But Socrates' knowledge was directed towards the permanent, the objective, and the conceptual; and as such it was the monitor regulating the disunity and fluctuations of sensory experience. Socrates shared with Protagoras, however, the belief that knowledge could be taught, and so he harangued the Athenians ceaselessly to seek and to inquire so that they might cultivate that condition of wisdom which stands as a rock against the illusions of opinion and of sensation.

Plato inherited the great problem of permanence and change. Through Socrates' teaching, he was convinced that mind is superior to matter, and that knowledge of the permanent is higher than opinion of the changeable. Socrates, for all his dazzling dialectical skill, had a latent strain of mysticism. The daemon that urged his soul to virtue anticipates Plato's recurrent flight into the empyrean, either of poetry or myth-making. For there are things, as Plato remarks in his seventh epistle, that no man writes down; there are insights and revelations which transcend literary expression. The most significant by-product of this mystical persuasion was Plato's conviction that philosophy is the art of dying, for by it one passes beyond matter and sense. Another was his doctrine that the highest knowledge is of Forms, the archetypes of all material things and the goal of man's most mature intellection.

But in spite of his characteristic deification of mind (which sometimes, as in the *Phaedo,* resulted in an ascetic repudiation of matter) Plato remained a genuine humanist: he dignifies man by insisting that his highest faculty is rational knowledge by which he knows timeless and immutable reality. Plato's supremest belief is in a *ratio,* a rational order exemplified in the realm of Forms and ideas transcendent to the jockeyings of material things, and man, through his innate rational faculty *as man,* may comprehend these Forms. In his practical role as moralist and political philosopher Plato was still the rationalist: the cosmic order, because it is rational, is knowable, and man's knowledge of it, exemplified in his personal and political conduct, will result in the well-being of balance, design, and symmetry. Plato had difficulty in showing how the Forms influenced matter, but he insisted that a knowledge of Forms would insure man's virtue. "That we shall be better and braver and less helpless if we think that we ought to enquire, than we should have been if we indulged in the idle fancy that there was no knowing and no use in seeking to know what we do not know;—that is a theme upon which I am ready to fight, in word and deed, to the utmost of my power."

Aristotle, the last of the great trio, shared Socrates' veneration of rational knowledge and Plato's belief in man's capacity for moral well-being derived from rational knowledge. But he could not accept his teacher's solution to the problem of permanence and change: he could not leave unbridged the chasm between the realm of changeless Forms and the realm of changeable matter. By synthesizing all earlier thought, he provided, as he thought, an essential continuity between the two. Evolving matter strives teleologically towards form; form shapes and rationally informs the flux of matter. A biologist who saw all the manifestations of life ranged from the zoöphytes to the realization of pure form (God), Aristotle was obsessed with the concept of teleological development. Thus, as he thought, he had shown how the conceptual reason of form interacts with matter, and he had maintained the majestic belief that the universe is rational.

Nearly all the metaphysical systems of Hellas were predicated on the dualism of mind and matter, and because the Greeks inherently revered intelligence and knowledge (the properties of mind) both their metaphysics and ethics were rationalistic. Matter changed, but mind, like the Eleatic absolute, had objective and eternal reality. From the crude gnomic utterances of even such materialists as Democritus, through the loftiest pages of Plato, and on to the last mutterings of the dogmatists, Greek ethics tended to fortify man against the delusions of change and to unite him with the permanence of reason. Passions or perturbations of the soul (even if, as the atomists thought, the soul was material) were nothing more than the desires stimulated by material externals—the lust for money, the lust for food, the lust for temporal power, the lust for prodigal sexuality were appetites whose objects were transitory and uncertain. Plato did not legislate matter out of existence, but he did believe it to be a low order of reality, the flickering shadow of transcendent Forms. Aristotle had more regard for matter, but even he imposed upon it a teleology dictated by the superior power of rational form.

Socrates' injection of intelligence into the scheme of nature, and the eventual triumph of his concept of governing mind, gave a new center for man's ethical obligation. If, as all agreed, unstable matter, stimulating man's own passionate material nature, generated those consuming passions that unbalanced and even destroyed its victims, then mind, man's highest natural faculty, should regulate conduct. Reason, the agent of intelligence, became the charioteer in Plato's myth. Reason could not only induce man to that knowledge of ultimate reality; it could, more practi-

cally, discriminate among and police the stimuli of matter and thus lead
to rational conduct.

The Greeks never ignored the fact of man's mixed nature. His complexity was stated systematically in Aristotle's psychology, but Plato too
had been clearly aware of it; and both, though they enthroned reason,
made provision for man's corporeality in their ethics. Like true Greeks,
they never lost sight of the fact that man had to live with himself. As
philosophers they could yearn to transcend sense, or to make God the
apotheosis of pure intelligence, but as moralists they realistically accommodated all parts of man's nature, brutish and deific: thus the uses of
physical beauty in the *Symposium* and thus Aristotle's hierarchal psychology. Man is involved in the teleological movement of the cosmos, and
he has the unique gift of reason whereby he may direct his upward progress towards the realization of form. Human conduct, then, is properly
rational, and should represent the most successful exploitation of all his
faculties under the guidance of reason. To understand his own mor-
phology as well as that of the universe is man's highest function, and
leads to the state of well-being which is virtue.

This is the apogee of humanism—which, for the Greek, was an attitude
and habit of mind rather than a philosophical system or a cult. It informed the art, the religion, and the sophisticated philosophies of Hellas.
That man's complex and stratified nature is revealed in various kinds of
activity; that the intrinsically significant human personality must be regarded as embracing all such subordinate "parts" as reason, desire, will,
and sensation; that a proper balance of these parts is essential to man's
well-being; that virtue is the functioning of man's complicated organism
in its most successful and varied aspects under the domination of reason—
these are some of the great humanistic assumptions revealed in every
product of the Greek mind.[1]

Some echo of Periclean humanism sounds from even the decadence of
Greek thought, but in the main, post-Aristotelian philosophy tended to
discard the metaphysical and ethical optimism of the high period. The
Stoics, Epicureans, and Skeptics could hardly share Plato and Aristotle's
confidence in a rational universe when the world they knew appeared excessively irrational. The Neoplatonists of the early Christian era, on the
other hand, frankly forswore philosophic rationalism for something very
like a redemptionist religion, by which man escaped his carnal nature in
mystic ecstasy. Generally, the dogmatisms of the last period attempted

---

[1] See W. T. Stace, *The Destiny of Western Man* (1942), pp. 63-4; Henry Osborn Taylor,
*The Classical Heritage of the Middle Ages* (1903), pp. 18 ff.

little more than to seize and exploit man's faint hope for limited well-being. Metaphysical long views made way for more pressing ethical problems—for open and shut solutions of the immediate difficulty of subsisting with the least pain in a crumbling world. As T. V. Smith has put it, if men cannot get what they want, there remains the humbler virtue of learning to want what they get. Although this shift of gravity from metaphysics to ethics involved a reversal to Democritean materialism for both Stoics and Epicureans, it did not mean an abandonment of the typical Greek reverence for intelligence and reason. While reverting to a materialist monism, both the great dogmatic systems sustained their belief in the efficacy of man's rational control over the vagaries of sense. But the distrust they harbored against metaphysical rationalism culminated in the nihilism of the Skeptics, who questioned not only the notion that the universe is rational but also that man would have the capacity for rational comprehension even if it were. In their blanket condemnation of knowledge they threw out the baby with the bath water and refused allegiance to matter and sensation as vehemently as to mind and reason. The wheel had come full circle.

None the less, the memory of the great tradition is yet green. By maintaining the primacy of reason, the Greeks were able to formulate the ethics of humanism. Virtue is knowledge: the pronouncement of Socrates not only implied the supremacy of reason; it also made it possible for man, by using the reason which is one of his natural faculties, to attain the good life. Morality, thus, is not a superimposed canon to which men blindly and dutifully conform. The Greeks would not have understood that the fear of Jehovah is the beginning of wisdom. They held virtue to be knowledge, which was every man's innate birthright. Their ethics were immanent. They, who knew so well how to enjoy life, and to express their enjoyment in beauty, revered all of life too highly to deny any part of it. They respected man too much to subordinate him (whose complexity they never ceased to marvel at) to a remote Setebos of a god who decreed right and wrong, and who parceled out pain and pleasure arbitrarily, or in return for services rendered. In their judgment, man was himself his own best master simply by exercising his prerogative of reason. His goal was not "salvation"—the concept of being saved from innate sin was foreign to the Greeks, save the Orphics—and for sin they had no word. Man could live brutishly, enslaved by animal passion and bound to matter; or he could live divinely, satisfying the natural demands of his sensitive soul under the guidance of reason. The chariot of his soul was drawn by all the forces of his intricate nature, but reason, proudly triumphant, was the driver who held in check the plunging beasts.

## PART II

*The Christian View of Man*

# VIII

## THE RELIGIOUS ATTITUDE

### RELIGION AND PHILOSOPHY

THE GREEK PHILOSOPHIC TRADITION, beginning with a naive naturalism, rising to the superbly argued rationalism of the high period, and at last exhausting itself in the ethical patchworks of Zeno, Epicurus, and Pyrrho, had on the whole viewed man benevolently. He was a rational animal quite at home in a universe essentially rational. Plato, the greatest and most supple-minded of the Greeks, entertained many kinds of thought, but his persistent interpretation of the cosmos construed mind or intelligence (*nous*) as the "beginning of motion" and thus the determining factor shaping uncreated matter—inchoate and primordial—toward rational forms.[1] Greek ethics, derived from a rationalistic metaphysics, held the good life to be one of rational fulfillment for man, the microcosm who like the macrocosm had many parts. If he used his innate reason to achieve a just and harmonious balance of his diverse elements he could align himself with that majestic force (*nous*) giving intelligence and form to the whole creation. Ethics, thus, were immanent: man had within him a rational faculty that, allowed to guide the turbulent stresses of his mixed nature, would drive his chariot ever upward.

But latent in the Greek mind, and occasionally emerging on the level of organized thought, was the consciousness, not of man's noble congenital capacities, but of his weakness, his innate depravity, and his shattering inability to control his destiny. This is an attitude very close to religion, which so often trembles beneath the surface of Plato's thought.[2] Homer's plaintive wail long before, that of all creatures that move and breathe on the face of the earth man is the feeblest, voices a melancholy that finds persistent restatement.[3] Plato urged that philosophy was the art of dying, Sophocles mourned man's advent on the planet, and even Aristotle, the prince of rationalists, suggested that it were better never to be born.[4]

---

[1] See *Timaeus*, 48.

[2] Note, for instance, the remark in the *Phaedrus* (244) that the divine gift of "madness" is the "source of the chieftest blessings granted to men," and also the aesthetics of insanity in *Ion* (especially 533-34); cf. *Ody.*, VIII.498.     [3] *Iliad*, XVII.446 ff.

[4] See A. H. Butcher, "The Melancholy of the Greeks," *Some Aspects of the Greek Genius* (1893), pp. 133-76.

Apart from these sporadic literary echoes, however, this attitude of asceticism, rejection, and impotence was formally organized into theology. Orphism, centering about notions of sin, guilt, and vicarious salvation, presents the sharpest contrast to the customary optimistic humanism of the Greeks. In recognizing man's frailty and the world's wickedness, it codified for the Hellenic world an asceticism and an eschatology that, in Christian theology, was to exert incalculable influence on the intellectual development of Europe.

Even at this late date, an adequate definition of religion is unattainable. It remains the supreme symbol of what is perhaps its most fundamental quality, which is mystery. As such, it is to be distinguished from philosophy. Both are modes of reacting to experience, and both rise from the same set of problems.[5] But religion acknowledges the supremacy of forces beyond either man's comprehension or control, and it derives its character from organized belief in that supremacy. Religion formulates man's incapacity for rational explanation: it celebrates and ritualizes his impotence; it sublimates mystery into theology. Philosophy, however, does none of these things—or when it does, as in Neoplatonism, it has become religion. It confronts the data of experience, examines them with ostensible objectivity, and attempts to explain and systematize them.

Whatever religion is, it is not the philosophic attempt to understand the universe. Nearly a century of intense, professional investigation of comparative religions has failed to find the key that will unlock them all.[6] Max Müller, really the founder of the study, thought that at least in primitive religions personification was basic: religion is a faculty which "enables men to apprehend the infinite under different names and under varying disguises."[7] A sophisticated Catholic like Cardinal Newman speaks of the "knowledge of God, of His Will, and of our duties towards Him";[8] a folklorist like Alexander Krappe of "the sum total of beliefs and practices having reference to man's relationship with the Unknown or Unknowable";[9] an artist like Rodin of the mysterious, the unexplained, and the unexplainable. Even the anthropologists fail to agree. The great Edward Tylor insisted on the importance of animism, but Codrington has modified this view to a universal belief in a force called *mana* by the Melanesians, and the eminent Sir James Frazer, in his many books, interpreted

[5] See F. M. Cornford, *From Religion to Philosophy* (1912), *passim*.
[6] For a useful survey of the main theories of religion (with excellent bibliographies) see Horace L. Friess and Herbert W. Schneider, *Religion in Various Cultures* (1932), pp. 3-11.
[7] *Lectures on the Origin and Growth of Religion* (1879), p. 21.
[8] *An Essay in Aid of a Grammar of Assent* (1870), p. 378.
[9] *The Science of Folklore* (1930), p. 310.

religion as man's effort to control by magical practices. Sociologists like Jane Harrison and Émile Durkheim developed the theses that religion is a social force—the codification of mob-emotion and group-ritual; and Sigmund Freud, applying to religion the methods of psychoanalysis, saw it as a neurosis providing an escape mechanism for infantile jealousies, with the rituals and taboos as merely wish-projections. The famous tag of Petronius—*primus in orbe deos fecit timor*—anticipates over the sweep of centuries J. W. Haupt's theory that a general fear (*Weltangst*) is the universal motive behind all religions.

In nearly all these judgments there lurks the element of mystery, and the cognate element of fear. Primitive man, as anthropologists since Tylor have repeated, is surrounded by forces so devastatingly beyond his strength that his only reaction can be one of humility or resignation. He formalizes his abjection before the unknown, and in place of a principle of explanation he establishes ritually his own impotence. He imposes upon himself a set of obligations to signalize his inferiority and dependence, and thus, perhaps, to channelize or attenuate the potentially destructive energies of the unfathomable.[10]

A closely allied phenomenon is primitive man's fundamental urge to invest inanimate nature with animate qualities. The inexorable dualism that forces itself on even the most unreflecting—life and death, day and night, body and breath, dreams and waking—shows primitive man not only that he leads a double life, but also that the same ambivalence characterizes external nature.[11] All experience, as Heraclitus poetically recognized, is a grand dialectic. And so man interprets his environment in dualistic terms, extending his own mystifying dualism of body and spirit, corporeal and incorporeal, to his physical surroundings. Such an anthropomorphic transference means that nature is invested with a set of usually deplorable human attributes: rancor, vengeance, scorn, and misuse of power. This is the ultimate pathetic fallacy, and it has resulted, in virtually all primitive cultures, in the manufacture of "deities" who reflect their creators' own most lamentable characteristics. It is Browning's Caliban plucking off the crab's pincers and Torquemada's compelling the reluctant to conversion. This animism is what Hume long ago ironically recognized as the "universal tendency among mankind to conceive all beings like themselves."

Thus man dramatizes his impotence and projects life into those elements

[10] See Kenneth Burke, *Attitudes towards History*, I, 56, n.

[11] See Tylor, *Primitive Culture* (1874), I, 499 ff.; cf. Frank Byron Jevons, *An Introduction to the History of Religions* (1911), pp. 11 ff. For a critique of Tylor's animism, see R. H. Lowie, *Primitive Religion* (1924), pp. xiii ff., 106 ff. See Ruth Benedict, "Religion" and Franz Boas, "Mythology and Folklore" in the very useful *General Anthropology* (1938).

of nature which baffle and threaten him. Such terrifying and dimly under-stood phenomena as a flood, the loss of a warrior by a falling boulder, the birth of a child, although they affect men drastically, are not subject to comprehension or control. Whereas the Ionian naturalists assigned natu-ral causes capable of natural explanation, the ordinary man (primitive or otherwise) would ordinarily posit the existence of animate forces which exert arbitrary direction on the course of events. Such forces, or spirits, or *mana,* however, might possibly be bargained with. For if they exhibit human qualities (e.g. of cruelty or revenge), perhaps they may be swayed by appeals to their pride, mercy, or even sex. (When the ancient Latins were uncertain of the *numen* in a strange place, they provided for all con-tingencies with the prophylactic tag, *Si deus si dea, sive mas sive femina.*) Knowing the nature of the gods, man might therefore anticipate their reaction, and, by studied and ritualized obeisance, might palliate, mollify, and flatter his gods into a favorable attitude. By sly contrivances puny man could domesticate his masters. Such contrivances are the self-imposed denials and obligations which man assumes. The manmade symbols of abnegation or taboos—extending from human sacrifice and flagellation to the observance of such dietary restrictions as Lent—are thought to be efficacious: by a present deprivation man may avert future evils, and by dramatizing his inferiority establish a proper relation with the mysterious forces that dominate his life. All organized religions, in their rites and ceremonies, embody this basic notion of subservience before a superior power, and of placating that power to insure future well-being.

It would appear, therefore, that even a tentative definition of religion must accommodate the cognate concepts of animism and taboo. Tylor's as a "belief in spiritual things" [12] is less satisfactory than Frazer's: "a propitiation or conciliation of powers superior to man which are believed to direct and control the course of nature and of human life." [13] Whatever degree of sophistication a religion may have reached—animism which sees soul in every stick and stone, polytheism which refines and synthesizes an earlier animism, or monotheism which simplifies all the forces of nature into one dominant power—one can usually detect the twin ideas of spirituality and propitiation.[14]

Long before Xenophanes appeared to mock them, the early Hellenes

[12] I, 424.

[13] *The Golden Bough: A Study in Magic and Religion* (1931), p. 50. Note two famous definitions from antiquity: Cicero's (*De Nat. Deo.,* II.28) and Lactantius' (*Institutes,* IV.28).

[14] See Sir James George Frazer, *The Worship of Nature* (1926), I, 6 ff.; cf. Salomon Reinach, *Orpheus* (1930), pp. 1-27, an opinionated but readable discussion.

had enjoyed a strenuous animism. When Wordsworth spoke of the lively Grecian who could find a commodious place for every god he was recording a sober fact that one forgets when reading Aristotle. Herodotus could with certainty trace the Greek pantheon no further than Homer and Hesiod,[15] but Andrew Lang and many others have uncovered an animism behind the literary monuments of those quasi-religious poets.[16] Their religion is brazenly anthropomorphic. The all-too-human deities who gambol about Olympus—itself like nothing so much as an expensive summer resort[17]—are relatively late syntheses reflecting the Greeks' own intense humanism. They are energetic creatures, fond of doing and of living; not a one of them symbolizes the fact of pain, and resignation and asceticism are unknown to them. They take a lively interest in things on earth,[18] and are, by turns, jealous,[19] vindictive, and indulgent towards the earth-creatures below.

But since Sir Arthur Evans has so brilliantly revealed a Cretan civilization flourishing millennia before Homer, we have somewhat lengthened the perspective of Herodotus. It is becoming ever plainer that behind literary history there extends a dark backwards in which lie embedded some aboriginal attitudes of man toward deity. What we know as organized belief or theology can be best understood by referring it to such beginnings.[20] One of the residues of such primitive attitudes in Hellenic culture was the Orphism that after the sixth century exerted so pervasive an influence on the Greeks. As Miss Harrison has shown in her famed *Prolegomena,* Greek animism had to pass through several preparatory stages before it could achieve the ethical and theological sophistication of Orphism. While the Homeric Olympian rituals (which were mainly civic functions) used the formulary *do ut des,* seasonal rites like the Anthesteria, Thargelia, and Thesmophoria substituted placation for confraternity with the gods: *do ut abeas.* Their rituals symbolized purgation and the removal of natural evil, and their matrix was one of elaborate purification. After due precaution and ritual cleansing, the suppliant

---

[15] II.53.

[16] See Andrew Lang, *Myth, Ritual, and Religion* (1887), I, 255 ff.

[17] *Ody.,* VI.43 ff.

[18] Note, *inter alia,* the plague of Apollo (*Iliad,* I.43 ff.) and the theme of the propitiation of the gods when Achilles woos the wind with sacrifice to light the pyre of Patroclus (*Iliad,* XXIII.193 ff.).

[19] See Thucydides, VII.77. On the theme of the jealousy of the gods (which plays so large a part in Greek drama) see J. A. K. Thomson, *Irony* (1927), 8 ff. and *passim.*

[20] Frazer, for instance, in *The Fear of the Dead in Primitive Religions* (1933), p. 4, has isolated the belief in immortality as universal and primal. Great religions, like Christianity or Buddhism or Islam, merely articulate the aboriginal beliefs. And without them the "towering structure of theology would topple over and crash to the ground.".

could handle the *sacra* which, having deific properties, assured the worshipper deific power and influence. Towering behind every such rite, like a gigantic cliff, was the unquestioned verity of sympathetic magic. In Orphism, too, converge and become systematic the immemorial beliefs in purification, magic, and ritual salvation.

Dionysus was a chthonic god of Crete who in that mysterious and remote culture had been known and worshipped under several names—Phanes and Zagreus among others.[21] After Ouranos had wrested the universe from the Titans, Zeus begat upon Rhea his dread daughter Koré-Persephone, who in turn bore to her father the lusty infant Dionysus. But when Zeus enthroned the youth as the new ruler of the cosmos, he aroused the wrath of the resuscitated Titans. They, perhaps urged by the jealous Hera, enticed the young god with a mirror and tore him to pieces as he played with it. Apollo assembled the scattered remnants at Delphi, but Athene brought the heart to Zeus. He devoured it, and then upon the comely Semele once again sired Dionysus, triumphant in death. For their crime the Titans were demolished with a thunderbolt, but from their cinders rose a wholly new race of men. These novel creatures inherited from the Titans the taint of inherited crime, and were thus congenitally evil; but from Dionysus, whose flesh the Titans had tasted, they derived a divine and holy spark.

This myth, involving the notions of sin, death, and resurrection, was in its various forms basic to the various Dionysiac cults of the ancient world. In Crete, where his worship seems to have begun, he was celebrated under different names and with different symbols of affinity (such as serpents and bulls' horns), but the ritual was stylized. On a lonely mountaintop, at night and in the light of flickering torches, the devotees—mainly women —would gather to the strange, unearthly music of flutes, drums, and cymbals. Beginning with shrill cries and twitching movements, they would soon be dancing—not sedately, but with fantastic and orgiastic abandon. The women, streaming their loose-fitting *bassarai* made of fox skins, and waving live snakes or wearing horns on their heads, would surrender themselves to the frenzied movements of the dance until, completely swept away in hysteria, they would bear down on a beast (usually a bull) chosen as their victim, and with ecstasy tear it to pieces and devour its bloody flesh.

The key to this ritual was ecstasy: literally, the celebrant's stepping out

---

[21] Syncretism was already at work. Dionysus was *polynomous,* known by many names. See Cicero, *De Nat. Deo.,* III.23; Rohde, *Psyche,* p. 256; W. K. C. Guthrie, *Orpheus and Greek Religion* (1935), pp. 41, 110. Dionysus is not an Olympian deity in Homer, and indeed appears importantly only once (*Iliad,* VI.129 ff.).

of her old life into a new, the purposeful removal of the soul from its body, and its ultimate identification (by a ritual eating of the god-symbol) with the source of power. If all religions have as their aim union with god, a merging of weakness with strength, then the Dionysiac *ekstasis* achieved it in the most forthright way. By partaking of the flesh of the god—for Dionysus, in trying to escape the Titans, had transformed himself into a bull, in which shape his pursuers slew him—the believers became gods themselves. The Dionysiac frenzy thus induced *enthusiasmos*, by which the god entered into and possessed the celebrant. "O glad, glad on the mountains," sing Euripides' bacchae,

> To swoon in the race outworn,
> When the holy fawn-skin clings,
> And all else sweeps away,
> To the joy of red quick fountains,
> The blood of the hill-goat torn,
> The glory of wild-beast ravenings,
> Where the hill-tops catch the day;
> To the Phrygian, Lydian, mountains!
> 'Tis Bromios [i.e. Dionysus] leads the way.[22]

The body, evil because of its Titanic stain, was severed from the soul whose goodness derived from Dionysus himself.

Transferred from Crete, and with Orpheus as its prophet, the Dionysiac cult became something more than Bacchic orgies. It became a relatively sophisticated mystery religion, very like the mystical cults of the Pythagoreans, and centering about a rigid dualism of body and soul, elaborate ritual purifications, and eschatological promises of salvation. Orpheus, whatever his origins or historicity, by the sixth century symbolized to the Greeks the primordial notions of purification and of symbiotic union with a suffering and resurrected god.[23] He himself was obviously not a god,

---

[22] *The Bacchae*, 133 ff. (*The Complete Greek Drama*, II, 231). See Rohde, pp. 257 ff. For an interesting discussion of comparable elements in the religion of the American Plains Indians see Ruth Benedict, *Patterns of Culture* (1934), pp. 82 ff.

[23] Orpheus was perhaps originally a god of darkness, but about the tenth century he became localized in the legend known to western Europe through Virgil and Ovid. The most famed of the pre-Homeric poets, Orpheus, son of Oeagrus and Calliope, was a Thracian contemporary of the Argonauts whom he accompanied to Colchis. So skilful was he that Apollo presented him the lyre with which he could charm both beasts and rocks. Orpheus married the nymph Eurydice, at whose death he was so much grieved that he followed her to Hades, where with his art he won her back. But because he turned to look upon his wife as he was leading her earthward, Proserpine snatched her back again.

> Iti omnis
> effusus labor atque immitis rupta tyranni
> foedera, terque fragor stagnis auditas Avernis.

but a cultural hero who could claim affinity with a god. Slain in a Bacchic rite, and like Dionysus dismembered by the frenzied women, he became a mediator between god and man, and the possessor of those secrets that would make men divine.[24] The god of Orphism was Dionysus, its ritual was a refined Bacchic rite whose theme was ecstasy. The pattern is much like that of other mystery religions of antiquity based on the ritualized identification of the initiate with a dying god: Dionysus suggests Adonis, Osiris, and Christ; Orpheus, such a prophet and mediator as Mithra and the Hellenized Logos of Christianity.[25]

The details of Orphic ritual are maddeningly obscure, mainly because the initiates were sworn with terrifying oaths to secrecy. But as Plutarch observed, initiation (*teleisthai*) and death (*teleutan*) are cognate.[26] The initiate, like the god whose union he seeks with sympathetic magic, must die and be born again; and the ritual, therefore, dramatized the symbolic death of the candidate and his rebirth or spiritual conversion. Presumably, most initiatory rites included the three stages of preparation and probation, initiation and communion, and finally blessedness and salvation.[27] But to reconstruct the actual—and probably very theatrically impressive—ceremonies is now impossible. The Eleusinian mysteries seem to have been divided into three parts: things enacted (*dromena*), things shown (*deiknumena,* the *sacra* and statues?), and things said (*legomena*).[28] The Orphic rites were no doubt similarly elaborate.

Orpheus was thereafter so disconsolate that he scorned the women of Thrace; they, perhaps in their Bacchic orgy, fell upon him and tore him, like the sacred bull, into bloody fragments. The muses, however, gathered his limbs and buried them at the foot of Olympus; his head, thrown into the Hebrus, rolled down to the sea and finally came to rest at Lesbos. There too his lyre was carried.

> His gory visage down the stream was sent,
> Down the swift *Hebrus* to the *Lesbian* shore.

[24] See Euripides' beautiful chorus beginning "What else is Wisdom," *Bacchae*, 887 ff. (*The Complete Greek Drama*, II, 260).

[25] On the Oriental influences in Orphism see Arnold Joseph Toynbee, *A Study of History* (1934 ff.), V, 84 ff.; cf. V, 434-35.

[26] See W. R. Halliday, *The Pagan Background of Early Christianity* (1925), p. 243; E. Hatch, *Influence of Greek Ideas and Usages upon the Christian Church* (1898), p. 289; Vittorio D. Macchioro, *From Orpheus to Paul* (1930), pp. 76 ff.

[27] See S. Angus, *The Mystery-Religions and Christianity* (1925), pp. 76 ff.

[28] See F. M. Cornford, "Mystery Religions and Pre-Socratic Philosophy," *The Cambridge Ancient History*, IV, 528. The celebrated eleventh book of Apuleius' *Metamorphoses* is the *locus classicus* of mystery initiation. Sketchy and enigmatic as the account is, it is probably as accurate a record of a mystery ritual as we shall ever possess. The hero, currently in the form of an ass, is urged by Isis to undergo initiation into her cult to achieve complete restoration. He agrees, and then surrenders himself to a long preparatory regimen. Living in the sacred precincts of the shrine for several days, he is constantly exhorted by the officials of the cult who attempt to achieve a proper emotional and psychological attitude in the candidate. At last, with elaborate baths and purificatory ceremonies, he enters the last ten-

The Orphic initiate—for that matter, the initiate of any of the ancient mystery religions—was a creature set apart, blandly certain of his superiority to the unwashed. For the Greek, mystery initiation tended to loosen civic and family ties, but it strengthened enormously the individual awareness of sin and of salvation.[29] Even the skeptical Euripides and the mocking Aristophanes assume unwonted reverence before this fact. Not only was the initiate a marked man in this life—he of course was dedicated to ritual purity in the form of such taboos as a meatless diet, avoidance of woollen clothing, refusal to kill flesh (all based on the principle of transmigration)[30]—but he also had the glorious assurance of future bliss. The eschatological promise was the supreme fact of the cult. At death the initiate would present himself for judgment before Minos, Aeacus, and Rhadamanthus (those dread monitors of Plato's great Orphic myths)[31] to be committed to eternal beatitude while the souls of the unworthy and uninitiated will be condemned to yet another term of imprisonment in a body.[32]

Before the spiritual revival of the sixth century, the Greeks had little conception of an afterlife. Homer's Patroclus is a pallid vestige of his former virile self, a half-man; Socrates before his judges echoes an earlier attitude when he is agnostically noncommittal about immortality; another world is not even mentioned in Pericles' funeral oration.[33] The Orphic hope of blissful immortality perhaps explains the burgeoning of the cult in the sixth century. Together with such initiatory rites as the Eleusinian mysteries (which employed the myth of the lost Proserpine and thus sug-

day novitiate of strict dietary and physical taboos. The actual ritual of initiation is, naturally, not described, save in these veiled words: "I drew nigh to the confines of death, and having trodden the threshold of Proserpine, I was borne through all the elements and returned to earth again; I saw the sun gleaming with bright splendor at dead of night; I approached the gods above the gods below, and worshipped them face to face." For analyses of this passage see Halliday, pp. 256 ff.; Arthur Darby Nock, *Conversion; The Old and the New in Religion from Alexander the Great to Augustine of Hippo* (1933), ch. IX. Clement of Alexandria, arguing for the new Christianity, audaciously undertakes to lay bare the rival mysteries: "I will tell openly the secret things, and will not shrink from speaking of what you are not ashamed to worship." But his *exposé*, even so, is not very revealing. See the *Exhortation to the Greeks*, II.13 ff.

[29] See Cornford in *The Cambridge Ancient History*, IV, 535.

[30] On the Pythagorean and Orphic correspondences, see Robin, *Greek Thought and the Origin of the Scientific Spirit*, pp. 53, 68.

[31] *Gorgias*, 533 ff.; *Phaedo*, 112 ff. Plato may have been an initiate, for his thought is drenched with Orphic notions—or are they Pythagorean? He sometimes alludes to the rites as if he were an initiate, but he is invariably careful to reveal nothing.

[32] The Orphic "heaven" consists of curiously mundane joys of feasting, drinking, and urbane conversation among disembodied souls. It offers the sharpest contrast to the desolation of Homeric and Hesiodic eschatology. The *katabasis* in the eleventh book of the *Odyssey* has been construed by some, however, to show Orphic interpolations. See Macchioro, pp. 37 ff.

[33] See Rohde, *Psyche*, ch. I; Nock, *Conversion*, p. 28.

gests affiliations with the innumerable fertility rites of primitive cultures) it made enchanting if extravagant promises to the Greeks discontented with the sterile civic pomp of the Olympian religion. "Blessed among men upon the earth," rings out the hymn to Demeter, is he who has insured in future bliss; "but he that is uninitiate in the rites and has no part in them has never an equal lot in the cold place of darkness." [34] The Dionysiac ecstasy introduced a new concept of immortality to the *bakchos* who found union with god. By developing such indigenous Grecian elements as the primitive cults of the dead [35] and the mantic-cathartic rites of purification it reached far dack to dim, aboriginal, and truly popular beliefs. And when, in the process of sophistication, Orphism evolved a prophet like Orpheus, a theology, and a sacred literature,[36] it became a cult of genuine appeal.[37]

Such a development coincided with what Mr. Gilbert Murray, in a famous phrase, has called the failure of nerve.[38] For Homer's vigorous, earthy, and positive acceptance of life Orphism substituted notions of sin, remorse, and suffering. In the main, Greek philosophy affirmed man's dignity and innate excellence. It was in the widest sense of the word

[34] F. M. Cornford, *Greek Religious Thought* (1923), p. 51. Euripides' *Bacchae* is filled with allusions to the eschatological promise. "Life is such a little thing," the chorus chants (l. 400; *The Complete Greek Drama*, II, 240). And Dionysus tells Pentheus, about to bind him, not to violate the sacred things, "I having vision and ye blind" (l. 242; II, 245).

[35] See Rohde, ch. V; Clifford Herschel Moore, *The Religious Thought of the Greeks* (1916), pp. 44 ff.

[36] The literature has mainly disappeared, but it must have been extensive. The Neoplatonists apparently knew the "Rhapsodic Theogony," a poem of perhaps twenty-four books which was the compilation of many earlier Orphic scriptures. See Cornford in *The Cambridge Ancient History*, IV, 536. Also there are the famous gold plates excavated in 1879-1880 from the necropolis at Thurii in southern Sicily and later elsewhere throughout the Hellenic world (Petelia, Crete, and even Rome). These thin grave-tablets, rolled in amulets and buried with the initiates, bear crudely scratched formularies and prayers that, however cryptic and enigmatic, are our most valid source of Orphic dogma. From them may be derived a fairly homogeneous theogony and eschatology—even a geography of the other world. The literature on the gold plates is vast. Gilbert Murray's translation appears as an appendix in Jane Harrison's *Prolegomena to the Study of the Greek Religion* (1903), pp. 659 ff. See Guthrie, *Orpheus and Greek Religion*, pp. 171 ff.; Cornford, *Greek Religious Thought*, pp. 60 ff.; Macchioro, pp. 109 ff.; Arthur Bernard Cook, *Zeus: A Study in Ancient Religion* (1914-1940), III, 419, n. 3.

[37] Jaeger (*Paideia*, I, 164), almost alone, tends to discount the influence of Orphism. But many have found strong Orphic traces in pre-Socratic philosophy, especially in Heraclitus and the Pythagoreans. See Macchioro, pp. 169-76; Guthrie, pp. 216 ff.; Cornford, *From Religion to Philosophy*, pp. 183 ff.; Moore, *Religious Thought of the Greeks*, pp. 60 ff. Plato, at least in the *Phaedo*, sometimes sounds like an initiate. See *Cratylus*, 400; *Phaedo*, 69 ff.; *Phaedrus, passim*; Republic, 364; the doctrine of recollection in the *Meno*; the myth of the Pamphylian Er in the *Republic*. Aristotle, it is needless to say, was not impressed: "What is given us in the form of mythical sophistry is not worth the attention of a serious thinker" (quoted by Guthrie, p. 71).

[38] *Five Stages of Greek Religion*, ch. IV.

humanistic. But Orphism proclaimed his weakness and congenital depravity, erecting a myth to explain the evils of his fleshly nature and an eschatology to escape them. It made man's "salvation" inorganic—a matter of ritual purification and of currying favor with a superior and inexplicable power, rather than of developing rationally his proudly human faculties. Greek history is a story of the progressive disenchantment with the world and the flesh, and the crumbling institutions of the golden age. And Orphism, or something like it, was inevitable, for it gave theological sanction to despair and rejection. It formally derogated this world and this life; through ritual purity and initiation it promised such bliss and security as men yearned for. By acknowledging man's weakness and fleeing from it to a power vicariously attained in deity, it offered solace and salvation for the hard bondage of the flesh.

# IX

## THE CHRISTIAN FRAME OF REFERENCE

### CERTUM EST, QUIA IMPOSSIBILE EST

THE INTRICATE POLYPHONY OF HISTORY is not at all like the homophony of thesis-ridden books about history. But that certain motifs are basic and recurrent in human thought seems indisputable. Because the kind of thinking that Orphism represents is not confined to Greeks of a certain period, our survey of the Orphic attitude should serve as the first one-finger statement of a theme that Christianity was to develop gigantically. Christianity is a phenomenon—or set of counterpointed phenomena—that in its origins, alliances, and repercussions was implicated with many strands of ancient thought. It passed through intricate phases of increasing complexity and sophistication: from the primitivism of the early synoptic gospels, through the Hellenizing of Paul and the author of the fourth gospel,[1] through the era of the powerful heresies of the Gnostics and the Donatists and the Arians, through the dogmatism of the Nicene fathers and of Augustine, through the bureaucratization of Gregory the Great, through the mysticism of Erigena and the Victorines, through the rationalism of Aquinas and the Schoolmen, and so on to the Renaissance and the Reformation. Its history is the intellectual and emotional history of western Europe. But its original and persistent impulse has much in common with the Orphic subordination of man to deity and with the Orphic hope of heaven.

It should be remembered, however, that Orphism was but one of hundreds of mystery cults that appeared in the Hellenistic East and simultaneously in the Rome of the late Republic and the Empire. From India to Britain the mystery religions were fermenting like yeast, bewitching tens and hundreds of thousands with the promise of vicarious atonement —even of personal immortality—and with the magic of their rituals. Cybele, the Great Mother, had been imported to Rome from Phrygia as early as 204 B.C.[2] In her orgiastic worship, centered about her beloved Attis who

---

[1] For an interesting challenge to the common notion that John is late and Hellenistic see Erwin R. Goodenough, "John a Primitive Gospel," *Journal of Biblical Literature*, LXIV (1945), 145-82.

[2] See Cyril Bailey, "Religion and Philosophy," *The Legacy of Rome*, pp. 259 ff.;

died and was raised again, the celebrants received initiates by bathing them in the blood of a sacrificial bull, thus cleansing them of sin and assuring them a new life. "Dea magna," sings Catullus in his *Atys,*

> dea Cybella, dea domina Dindymi,
> procul a mea tuus sit furor omnis, era, domo:
> alios age incitatos, alios age rabidos.

It was more than eighteen centuries before a gentle Englishman named Cowper was to write "There is a fountain filled with blood," yet the rites of the Magna Mater and of the Mithraic taurobolium were old when Marcus Aurelius was a boy. If Christ had not conquered the Roman Empire, Renan once said, Mithras would have. His cult began in Persia, was brought by Pompey's soldiers from Cappadocia, and presently spread as far as the Danube and Britain. Mithras, son of Ahura-Mazda, was the militant *soter* (his worship was strong among the Roman legions) who struggled against Ahriman, the prince of darkness. He slew the great bull whose blood, in the ritual of the cult, purified the initiates. His worship was presumably directed by an organized clergy who presided at ceremonies where consecrated bread and wine were passed on the seventh day of each week.[3]

When Lucretius wrote his great *De Rerum Natura* on the thesis "tantum religio potuit suadere malorum" he could not have been unmindful of the mystery cults swirling through the Mediterranean world. In Syria, Tammuz, the risen god, was worshipped with ecstatic rites; in Greece, Dionysius; in Egypt (and later throughout the known world), Isis and his risen spouse Osiris. Though each was different, they all exercised the same appeal. A divine mediator (Dionysius, Mithras, Christ) interceded with God for sinful man; the symbols of fertility quickly merged with those of mother love and eternal tenderness; for Demeter, Cybele, Iris, and later Mary, the mother of Jesus, all knew suffering and the death of their beloved; the rituals of communion with the god and the splendor of initiatory purification promised a holiness and a divinely sanctioned security against the world, even against death, hitherto unattainable by sinful man. There is little wonder that Minucius Felix, in the second century, could record in his *Octavius* of the mysteries of the East that "haec tamen Aegyptia quondam nunc et sacra Romana sunt." [4]

---

M. Rostovtzeff, *Rome, A History of the Ancient World,* II (1927), 66; A. D. Nock, "Religious Developments from the Close of the Republic to the Death of Nero," *Cambridge Ancient History,* X (1934), 508; Theodor Mommsen, *The History of Rome* (1874), III, 522 ff.

[3] On the influence of Mithraism see De Burgh, *The Legacy of the Ancient World,* pp. 282 ff.

[4] *Octavius,* ch. XXIII. As the exciting research of scholars like Frazer and Cumont shows,

The actual influence of Orphism on Christianity is one of those moot questions that elicit massive erudition from specialists. Orphism has been called "the harbinger of the Mystery-Religions and Christianity in the West, and its success regarded as the first prominence of the long dominance of Oriental religious thought in the Mediterranean world."[5] But those who think of Christianity as *sui generis* refuse to pollute their faith by admitting correspondences to its early rivals. The early fathers, for instance, were accustomed to the accusation that theirs was merely one more pestiferous mystery cult, and they were accustomed to denying it. On this point, even so tolerant and Hellenistic a man as Origen was vehement: what was remotely godlike about that "madman Dionysius"?[6] Justin Martyr, more blandly, described the Dionysiac myth as the contrivance of demons to vex the true believer.[7] And Paul himself, well aware of the syncretism of burgeoning mystery cults, thundered: "Whom therefore ye ignorantly worship, him I declare unto you."[8] By implication, at least, he confesses to a similarity in kind between pagan and Christian mysteries. Clement of Alexandria, although contemptuous of all rival cults, employs the terminology that characterizes them all: "O truly sacred mysteries! O pure light! In the blaze of the torches I have a vision of heaven and of God. I become holy by initiation."[9] Even after Christianity had conquered its rivals, when Augustine preached without scriptural authority a probationary existence wherein fire purifies the soul, he drew copiously from Orphic and Virgilian lore.[10]

the mystery cults, and their interdependence, are a fascinating but difficult subject. For a good short discussion, with bibliographical leads, see Will Durant, *Caesar and Christ* (1944), pp. 522 ff.—a much better book than some of its more sober and pretentious rivals.

[5] Angus, *The Mystery-Religions and Christianity*, p. 150; cf. Jevons, *An Introduction to the History of Religions*, p. 328.

[6] *Contra Celsum*, III.23; cf. IV. 15-17; V.49.

[7] *The First Apology*, ch. XXXIII.

[8] Paul commonly employs such mystery-terms as *teleios* and *mysterion*. See G. W. Butterworth's "Appendix on the Greek Mysteries" affixed to *Clement of Alexandria* (LCL, 1919), p. 389; cf. Halliday, *The Pagan Background of Early Christianity*, pp. 5 ff., 315. Employment of Orphic terms may have been merely a literary fad—as in Seneca (*Epis.*, LXXIX.12) and Cicero (*De Leg.*, II.14).

[9] *Exhortation to the Greeks*, XII.92.

[10] On such a perplexed question I can merely suggest some of the more interesting discussions: Franz V. M. Cumont, *Les Religions Orientales dans le paganisme romain* (1909), p. 106; Nock, *Conversion*, pp. 203 ff.; Albert Schweitzer, *Paul and His Interpreters: A Critical History* (1912), ch. VII (with a good bibliography); Hatch, *Influence of Greek Ideas and Usages upon the Christian Church*, pp. 283 ff.; Edward Carpenter, *Pagan & Christian Creeds* (1920), pp. 243 ff.; Angus, *The Mystery-Religions and Christianity*, *passim* (an excellent survey). Some scholars make much of the correspondences in details. For instance, Macchioro (*From Orpheus to Paul*, ch. IX) exhausts the analogy of the Orphic Zagreus and the Pauline Christ (cf. Origen, *Contra Celsum*, I.18; Reinach, *Orpheus*, p. 215). Others take comfort in the art of the catacombs, in which the figure of Orpheus charming the beasts blends into the

Certain similarities inevitably suggest themselves, in spite of the disclaimers of the apologists. Both Orpheus and Christ are suffering godmen who died and were reborn; both erected—or their disciples erected, for Christ at least was much more eager to deliver his message than to establish a church—an organized religion that necessitated a theology of ever-increasing complexity; both theologies are predicated on a belief in the intrinsic evil of matter and flesh, and a conviction of man's innate sinfulness; both religions employ such analogous rituals as the sympathetic magic of eating the god (the Bacchic orgy of *omophagia* and the Christian communion) and of submitting to certain taboos; both promise release from guilt through the vicarious suffering of a god; both promise to the true believer a personal immortality of the soul, freed from the corrosion of the flesh and from all temporal and spatial limitations whatever. Perhaps one did evolve independent of the other, but both center about a common set of attitudes.

All the evidence points to syncretism. Any given moment of history is the past hurtling through the present into the future. The dynamics are unceasing, and no society or no era is ever stabilized except in the pages of a book. Even so, the stability invariably represents a false simplification. The transition from the Hellenic to the Roman Imperial world was for antiquity a time of kaleidoscopic dissolutions and reconstructions. The death agony of the old culture was long and agonized, and the failure of nerve that gripped the whole eastern Mediterranean was, after Actium, endemic. The great god Pan lay long a-dying, and everywhere men grasped at the straws of whatever faith would solace them most. Mystery religions appeared, coalesced, and dissolved apart again, all trying frantically to improve man's sorry lot by repudiating the world, and to find a solace in eternity for the political, intellectual, and moral chaos so horribly near at hand. If man could not save himself and slough off his sense of sin, he might enjoy vicarious salvation and atonement through this or that redeemer. The quest of Justin Martyr is symbolic: he sought comfort from a Stoic, then from an Aristotelian, then a Pythagorean, then a Platonist—only to fall at last gratefully into the bosom of the Christian church.[11] The time was ripe for a philosophy like Skepticism, and for those

symbol of Christ as the good shepherd (see Guthrie, *Orpheus and Greek Religion*, p. 264). The famous Berlin amulet, showing a crucified man over the legend ORPHEOC BAKKIKOC, has been interpreted as clear evidence of the syncretism of Orpheus with Christ. (Guthrie, pp. 265 ff., has a full discussion and bibliography.) But it, like the Ruthwell Cross or the Frank's Casket, so dear tö ʾAnglo-Saxon scholars, seems to have become a malignant riddle for the savants.

[11] See the *Dialogus cum Tryphone Judeo* in Migne, *PG*, VI, 471 ff.; cf. Tertullian, *Apology*, ch. XXXII (Gwatkin, *Selections*, p. 115).

mystery cults that repudiated the turbulence of this uncertain world for the promise of static perfection in another one. Out of the welter of the innumerable mystery religions produced by this attitude, Christianity— *exitiabilis supersititio*, in the famous phrase of Tactitus—emerged and triumphed.[12]

### THE METAMORPHOSIS OF JESUS

To explain how an unpretentious morality like that preached by Jesus in the hills above Galilee developed into the church of Gregory the Great is, if one has a taste for theology, a fascinating but endless task. Eighteen centuries of piety and two of intense secular scholarship[13] have failed to reconstruct the whole story; and, barring the hypothesis of a divinely nurtured growth, it is unlikely that we shall ever account completely for the expansion and triumph of an obscure Semitic mystery cult which conquered not only its rival cults, but also the Roman Empire. However, certain gross and obvious stages of mutation may be cited. It is easy to see that Jesus meant one thing to the plain blunt man who wrote the second Gospel and something very different to the Hellenistic author of the fourth. It is easy to see that Paul, in his pastoral letters, further complicated the Christology and theology that in his salad days he had sought to exterminate. It is easy to see that a highly sophisticated and philosophical mind like Origen's, at the end of the second century, read a new kind of metaphysics into the residuum of faith, and that the Nicene disputants were eruditely concerned about questions that never occurred to Jesus.

But these men are beacons of change: they signify the fact of mutation rather than explain its course. Happily, it is no part of our business to make the attempt at explanation. We have merely to know that during the first four centuries of our era a practical ethics based on notions of reciprocal love became, progressively, a redemptionist mystery cult, and

---

[12] On the pervasive influence of Orphic lore see Salomon Reinach, *Cultes, mythes et religions* (1905-1906), I, 313. Rome, during the Empire, was of course notoriously susceptible to Eastern mystery cults, and especially to Mithraism. See Nock, *Conversion*, pp. 41 ff.; Boissier, *La Religion Romaine*, I, 380 ff.; Lucretius, V.1194; Guthrie, *Orpheus and Greek Religion*, pp. 18-19. An old, but still fascinating, account is Cumont's standard *Les Religions Orientales dans le paganisme romain* (1909). See Adolf Harnack, *The Mission and Expansion of Christianity* (1908), I, 290 ff.

[13] To follow the history of the "higher criticism"—which has meant the attack, since the eighteenth century, on the historicity of Christ and the divinely sanctioned validity of Christianity—would take a book. Hermann Reimarus (who died in 1768) opened the question for scholarship, and the erudition that has flooded Europe since has kept it open. Gotthold Lessing, Heinrich Paulus, David Strauss, Ferdinand Baur, and Ernest Rénan are merely a few of the more notorious *bêtes noires* who disturbed the tranquillity of our grandfathers. They seemed to agree that the hypothesis of a divine Christ and a divinely inspired Bible stands up under neither rational analysis nor close textual criticism.

gradually the dominant religion of the whole Mediterranean world. In the course of this incredibly intricate evolution, what began as attitude became dogma; what began as a group of like-minded followers of a certain itinerant Galilean moralist became the Holy Catholic Church. But before the Church could be secure it had to evolve its dogma and to enthrone attitude and opinion as divine revelation. Thus it made effective and even obligatory the views of man and his relation to the universe that were to dominate the Middle Ages.

Jesus himself was neither a theologian nor a metaphysician. A man of intense piety and reverence for the religion of his race, he insisted that his business was to preach the Kingdom of God. By precept and example he taught the virtues of simple piety, of love for all mankind and for God, of an ineffable veneration for the human soul.[14] He wished, as he said repeatedly, that the reign of God might be acknowledged in the hearts of men, so that the cherished prophecies of Judaism might be at least metaphorically fulfilled: "And the Lord shall be king over all the earth: in that day shall there be one Lord, and his name one."[15] This consummation would come, Jesus believed, when man loved God with all his strength and heart, and his neighbor as himself.[16] Although Jesus was of course aware of the Messianic expectations of his downtrodden people[17]— thy Kingdom come, he taught the faithful to pray—he was extremely chary of claiming divine sanction for his mission. Similarly, he was chary of identifying himself as other than the Son of Man, an ambiguity that could mean either a human being or (as used in Daniel) the Messiah.[18] At least during his early mission, Jesus held that the Messianic kingdom would not be temporal, or even very glorious by the standards of the world. It would be the universal incidence of charity, and the rule of love in every man's heart.

Later, however, he came to believe—and thus incurred the hatred of the Pharisees who brought him to death—that he himself was if not a political Messiah at least the agent of God to herald His kingdom on

---

[14] The similarities between Socrates and Jesus did not go unnoticed even by the early Church. See, for instance, Justin Martyr, *Second Apology,* ch. X.

[15] Zechariah, XIV:9. For some of the famous millennial promises of the Old Testament see Isaiah, IX:6 ff.; Micah, V:2; Ezekiel, XXXIV:23.

[16] Mark, VII:29-31. And yet Jesus condoned many of the social ills of his time. He applauded the good servant who doubled—was it by usury?—the money of his master (Luke, XIX:11 ff.); he blandly accepted the fact that the poor we shall have always; he was untroubled, as the Church has always been untroubled, by the fact of slavery (Matthew, XXIV: 46).

[17] See, *inter alia,* Mark, IX:2-7; Luke, X:23-24; Matthew, VII:21.

[18] On the implications of this troublesome term see Cecil John Cadoux, *The Historic Mission of Jesus* (n.d.), pp. 90 ff.

earth. At Caesarea Philippi, before he went down to Jerusalem and to agony, he asked his disciples what men thought of him. Some said he was John the Baptist, some Elias, some Jeremiah, they reported. But Peter "answered and said, Thou art the Christ, the Son of the living God." And for his opinion Jesus told him that he was blessed, for he must have had a divine revelation.[19] As he entered Jerusalem the Pharisees warned him to rebuke those who hailed him a king, but, by now apparently convinced of the divinity which he had earlier explicitly denied, he answered that even if the people were silent "the stones would immediately cry out."[20] Whatever Jesus actually was, he was bound over by the Sanhedrin to the Roman civil authority as a political revolutionist, and for this he died a felon's death. "King of the Jews" was the mocking label he bore as he hung on the cross.

Immediately after the crucifixion the process of deification began in earnest. Jesus' disciples, who had fled to the north when their master was slain, returned to Jerusalem. Claiming to have seen the risen lord and to have received the promise of his millennial appearance, they confidently awaited the arrival of their Messiah who would fulfill the prophets and establish the kingdom of God. Such teaching as the faithful did was in Jerusalem, and confined to Jews who could share their millennial expectations.[21] But as time passed and the longed-for second coming was postponed, they went further afield to preach salvation and spread their eschatological hopes.[22] In so doing, they acted, as they believed, with divine sanction. They had been promised by their risen lord that the Holy Ghost would presently descend upon them, after which they were to take the gospel to Judea, Samaria, and the uttermost parts of the earth.[23] When, therefore, at Pentecost they heard the mighty wind and saw the cloven tongues like as of fire playing about their heads, their mandate was clear.[24] The Apostolic mission had received its divine impetus, and as the persecutions of the Sanhedrin became more severe the faithful scattered abroad and "went every where preaching the word."[25]

[19] Matthew, XVI:13 ff. There is a slightly different account of the matter in Mark, VIII:27 ff. Here, as elsewhere, Mark is probably nearer the truth; it is not unlikely that the passage in Matthew is a much later interpolation, for it contains a celebrated and frequently cited franchise for the Roman Church.

[20] Luke, XIX:40.

[21] Luke, XXIV:52.

[22] See Henry Melvill Gwatkin, *Early Church History to A.D. 313* (1912), I, 59 ff.; Albert Henry Newman, *A Manual of Church History* (1901-1903), I, 83 ff.; Arthur Cushman McGiffert, *A History of Christianity in the Apostolic Age* (1899), pp. 48 ff.

[23] Acts, I:8; cf. Matt., XVIII:18-20; Luke, XXIV:47-48; John, XX:21-23.

[24] Acts, II:1 ff.　　[25] Acts, VIII:4.

It was in the first generation following the crucifixion that the concept of Jesus underwent its drastic transformation from the master of a group of Jewish moralists, to the Jewish Messiah, to the deity of a world-wide redemptionist cult. The Messiah (*Christos* in Greek) became the Lord (*Kyrios,* a common mystery term), and at last the Savior (*Soter*). Thus Jesus came to be identified by the gentiles, even in terminology, as a typical mystery deity. There was, as always, a strongly conservative party among his followers who resisted the semantic and geographical extension; they believed that the message of the Messiah's coming should be carried only to the circumcised and that in Jesus the promises of Judaism were at long last fulfilled. For some ten years these tories, led by Jesus' brother James, stayed at Jerusalem and rigorously observed the Law while awaiting the second coming of their racial Messiah. But the liberals like Peter and Stephen were living and preaching dangerously. Stephen was stoned by the Sanhedrin, Peter flogged, and all of their persuasion were preaching a radical and international gospel of Jesus as the savior of the whole world. When the Jews at Jerusalem finally revolted against Rome in A.D. 66, the Christians spread abroad, too much engrossed in their mission to dally in local politics. Hencefore Jew and Christian were to mean different things.[26] The Apostles and disciples went everywhere—Philip to Samaria, John to Ephesus, Peter to Syria, and yet further, Paul as far as Rome. Intent on democratizing salvation, they sang the new song of salvation, and following the Roman roads throughout the Empire, they began to spread the cult that was, in the great systole and disastole of events, to conquer even Rome itself.[27]

Paul, whose influence on the aggrandizement of the Church and the development of its theology is virtually incalculable, construed his religion as one of divine revelation. On the road to Damascus, probably in the very year of the crucifixion, he was flooded and illumined by the

[26] See Louis Duchesne, *Early History of the Christian Church* (1909-1924), I, 85 ff.

[27] Paul's first mission began perhaps in A.D. 45; when he died (perhaps with Peter at Rome) about 64, it was in the Neronian persecution that itself showed how far a left-wing Jewish cult had spread. Such documents as Justin's *Apology* (*ca.* 150) and Origen's *Contra Celsum* (*ca.* 284) reveal the Church in the process of a growth that called forth the Decian persecutions (250), ostensibly inaugurated because the Christians failed to rally to the cause of Rome against the barbarians. The Valerian terror came only six years later, but in 261 Gallienus issued the first edict of toleration. After the persecution under Diocletian (303-11)—the last and greatest organized assault on the expanding Church—it was clearer than ever that, as Tertullian said, the blood of martyrs was the seed of the Church. Constantine's vision at the Mulvian Bridge may have turned him to the Church, or perhaps it was his own appraisal of the drift of events; at any rate the Edict of Milan (313) in effect proclaimed the defeat of paganism. And the Council of Nicaea (325), which Constantine himself convoked, inaugurated the theocratic Middle Ages.

knowledge that the Lord Jesus Christ, whose faithful he had been persecuting, was the divine Son of God—the image of the deity, the creator of the world, and the head of the Church. The nature and function of Christ, as Paul describes them in his Epistle to the Colossians, are of the first magnitude: his nature is divine and his function is to redeem sinful man through his incarnation and his death on the cross. For Paul's theology was essentially of the cross. As he said, unless the resurrection occurred, his hope of heaven was nothing. Though subordinate to "the invisible God," Jesus is the savior of the race; and to believe in his divinity and the mystery of his resurrection is to achieve union with deity and thus salvation. The absolutely necessary faith in this mystery—and so Paul specifically names it[28]—is symbolized by the ritual initiation of baptism and preserved by partaking of the Eucharist. The consequences will be not only an immortality of bliss but a temporal life of love, humility, and purity. Not to believe, on the other hand, is death and eternal punishment for the sin which all mortals must pay for either directly or vicariously through the suffering and resurrected God. For the saved, however, as the long triumphal paean in Galatians shows, there is a new life and a new hope: man finds vicarious absolution for his sins against God in the incarnation and death of the God-man and the promise of eternal bliss in his resurrection.

Though Paul, to an extraordinary degree, was both a man of vision and a man of action, he was haunted by the *malaise* of his era. Living, as he thought, in the very dregs of time, he was convinced of the world's decay and of the hopelessness of all secular striving. Like so many of his age he sustained himself with the expectation of the speedy end of the world, and his millennial hope was the cry of a desperate man: "but this I say, brethren, the time is short." [29] Therefore, like Zeno before him, he constructed a system of frantic urgency—one in which the role of salvation was intensified and democratized as a bulwark against the wrath to come.

A Pharisee, "a Hebrew of Hebrews," trained by Gamaliel and strong in the patient faith of his people, Paul built his early career on his reverence for the Jewish Law: thus his scornful repudiation of the Messianic claims advanced by the disciples of Jesus. But after his conversion he realized that his legalism was barren and that through the Law he had died in the Law.[30] By the intensity of his mystical conversion on the road to Damascus his reverence for the Law was absorbed into his burn-

[28] Eph., III:3 ff.
[29] I Cor., VII:29.
[30] Gal., II:19.

ing personal experience of deity; and, retiring to Arabia,[31] he permitted himself time to think out the significance of his revelation.[32] His conclusion, of immense importance to the expansion of the Church, was that the function of the Judaistic Law, though from God and therefore holy, was merely preparatory. It protected the Jews from error so that when Jesus came to fulfill its promises they might receive him. "Wherefore the law was our schoolmaster to bring us unto Christ, that we might be justified by faith."[33] But mere obedience to Law yielded to faith, for through the faith accessible to everyone salvation was at hand. Thus through Paul's extension of the franchise of salvation, Christianity became a universal redemptionist religion and not a Jewish cult. "There is neither Jew nor Greek, there is neither bond nor free, there is neither male nor female: for ye are all one in Christ Jesus."[34] Like the empires of Alexander and of Augustus, like the brotherhood of man preached by the Stoics, Paul's Christianity transcended religious or racial limitations.

Thus Paul implemented the genuine ethical democracy preached by Jesus. He struck a new note in mystery religions, and the far-flung communities he established or ministered to were tokens of the universality of Christianity. All men became the heirs of Christ and, under proper conditions of faith and ritual atonement, candidates for salvation. But the view of man that Paul developed theologically and spread about the Mediterranean world was neither new nor optimistic: it embodied the familiar Oriental notions of the sinfulness of the flesh and the depravity of the race, and it rang all the changes on the desperate urgency of man's plight.[35] Like Augustine, his spiritual heir, Paul was dominated by the need for atonement. Every great revival of Pauline theology through fifteen centuries has occurred when men were most acutely aware that the world was too much with them and that they were the chief of sinners. Man, inherently evil through the defection of his first parent, is alien from God in a world of iniquity. Wracked by

[31] On this very obscure phase of Paul's career see McGiffert, *A History of Christianity in the Apostolic Age*, p. 161.

[32] Gal., III:6 ff.

[33] Gal., III:24.

[34] Gal., III:28. The Gnostics of the second century split with the main stream of Christian development on the role of Law. Vehemently gentile, they repudiated the Law as evil, the work of a lesser deity, and inimical to Christianity; they divorced the Old Testament from the New. Oddly enough, Justin Martyr, one of the first to denounce Gnostic Christology, also tends to reject the whole Judaistic conception of the Law. The bulk of his famous *Dialogue with Trypho* is given over to establishing the proposition that Christ both fulfilled and invalidated the old Law. "There are," he makes the Christian convert say (ch. XXX), "many righteous men who have performed none of these legal ceremonies, and yet are witnessed by God Himself."

[35] See Hastings Rashdall, *The Idea of Atonement in Christian Theology* (1919), pp. 83 ff.

the lusts of his carnal nature, heir to affliction, capable of nothing by himself, he is, without the grace of God and the vicarious atonement of Christ, the outcast of creation. "O wretched man that I am! who shall deliver me from the body of this death?"

This attitude is of course antipodal to the humanistic assumption of man's native worth and dignity. To the Greeks, such "salvation" as man requires he can find within himself by exercising rational self-control. Aristotle does not call for a redeemer because he feels no need of redemption and is obsessed by no sense of sin. The world as he viewed it was essentially good (that is, rational and orderly), and if man exploited his inherent rationality he might come to very comfortable terms with it. But not Paul. For all his Roman citizenship he was a Jew, lashed by the Jew's remorse and desolation, the Jew's excruciating sense of sin, of God's omnipotence, of man's frailty. "There is none righteous, no, not one." [36] The mighty Epistle to the Romans is a long threnody for fallen man and a hymn of hope for better things. In Paul's view, the human race, deserted by God, is writhing under the miseries of its own creation, and his burning rhetoric plays like lightning over the dismal scene:

Being filled with all unrighteousness, fornication, wickedness, covetousness, maliciousness; full of envy, murder, debate, deceit, malignity; whisperers, backbiters, haters of God, despiteful, proud, boasters, inventors of evil things, disobedient to parents, without understanding, covenantbreakers, without natural affection, implacable, unmerciful: Who knowing the judgment of God, that they which commit such things are worthy of death, not only do the same, but have pleasure in them that do them.[37]

Is it any wonder, then, that God should turn away His face? And is it not the most divine mystery that He should take pity on sinful man and snatch him from the jaws of his own destruction? For by the grace of God and the sacrifice of His Son, man who was dead in sin has been made quick again. "For by grace are ye saved through faith; and that not of yourselves: it is the gift of God." [38]

### THE SEED OF SALVATION

Although the growth of the Church during its first century was slow, it was steady.[39] Its gradual expansion against the opposition of rival mystery cults—and against the enmity of those Romans (like Caecilus in Minucius Felix' *Octavius*) who feared it as a pestiferous rival of the

---

[36] Romans, III:10.
[37] Romans, II:29-32.
[38] Eph., II:8.
[39] For a classical account see Harnack, *The Mission and Expansion of Christianity*, I, 319 ff.

Empire—must be at least partially attributable to the tremendous achievement of Paul and the Apostles in democratizing salvation. Paul's insistence on the wretched condition of man was correlated with his ecstatic promise of a new life through Christ. In making the solace of eternal bliss available to all he touched on the deepest fears and deepest aspirations of all the downtrodden of his age.

Moreover, we must not forget the original note of optimism in the teachings of Jesus. The master himself was dominated by the ethical principle of love for all mankind, and even Lucian, who ridiculed all religions, acknowledged with amazement the tenderness and benevolence of those curious Christians. The synoptic gospels (and especially Mark's, the oldest) deal little with ritual and theology: the theme is an ethic of reciprocal love for everyone, and the recurrent metaphors are those of God the father, man the child, Christ the good shepherd. Whereas Paul himself, a haughty man, a Jew, a Roman citizen, carried his message of redemption up and down the world, rival faiths and rival philosophies, as Origen was to point out contemptuously, scorned the mass of mankind as fools and inferiors.[40] Clement of Alexandria, at the opening of the third century, exulted in the thesis that, after Pentecost, had inspired the Apostles to their prodigious achievements: "For nothing stands in the way of him who earnestly desires to come to the knowledge of God, not want of instruction, not penury, not obscurity, not poverty." [41] In *Octavius,* the charming second-century dialogue of Minucius Felix, the defense of Christianity is not in terms of theology or Christology; there is no mention of Christ, of Pauline doctrine, of the Trinity, but there is a winsome pride in the ethos and universal charity of Christian life. "We think scorn of the high-brow philosophers, corrupters of youth, adulterers, and tyrants, for ever disclaiming against their own pet vices. As for us, the wisdom we display lies not in outward dress, but in the mind; we do not preach great things, but we live them; our boast is that we have won what they with the utmost strain have sought, yet could not find." [42]

For the original and positive ethical basis for Christianity was love. Christ was, by the standards of the Nicene disputants or of Augustine,

---

[40] The snobbery of the Stoic sage was, of course, notorious, but Judaism was also fiercely exclusive, as we see in Paul's agonized questions concerning the importance of Law. Jehovah, it is promised, will limit his favors to his chosen people: "Ye shall be unto me a kingdom of priests, and a holy nation" (Exodus, XIX:5-6). Plato's liking for aristocracy was strengthened by what he saw of democracy. See the *Republic,* 470; W. W. Tarn, "Alexander the Great and the Unity of Mankind," *Proceedings of the British Academy,* XI (1933), 124 ff.; Arnold, *Roman Stoicism,* pp. 4-5; Origen, *Contra Celsum,* VII.60; Ernest Sihler, *From Augustus to Augustine* (1923), p. 20.

[41] *Exhortation to the Greeks,* X.83.

[42] Minucius Felix, ch. XXXVIII.

not a theologian, but he knew what they sometimes forgot: the infinite importance of the human soul. Socrates, in his own way, had known it too, but his disciples had not been fired with missionary zeal; they had attenuated and rarefied his message to the Athenians into a lofty philosophical rationalism far beyond the comprehension of most men. The early Christians, however, had a clear mandate from their master to carry the glad and simple tidings to the whole world. Until they succumbed to the exigencies of theology, dogma, and ecclesiastical administration they brought a new ethics and a new hope to the ancient world: God is love. The soul is holy, able to know God, and therefore of ultimate significance. Love, as it is interpreted in the fourth Gospel, is the primary fact of the universe which clarifies the relation between God and man. As God loves us, so must we love Him and each other.

Christ preached love not only as the ethical propulsion for all conduct, human and divine, but also as the essential fact of religious experience, for by love we achieve union with God. In his last years, Plato talked more and more of God—the *Laws,* for instance, might be called, among other things, an essay in theology—but he interpreted God as consummate rationality, to be approached by man through rational knowledge. Jesus approaches his God through love. "I in them, and thou in me, that they may be made perfect in one." A corollary of primary significance to this doctrine of love is the increased importance of the individual, whence derives all the humanitarianism and benevolence of Christianity. Although Christ's teaching was, as he believed, based on Judaism, it emphasized personal holiness and minimized ritual.[43] His was a gospel of self-sanctification. What matters it to a man if he gains the whole world and loses his own soul? The kingdom of God is within. The very essence of primitive Christianity was its *inwardness.* Other religions, said Lactantius, are merely rites "pertaining to the fingers only"; but Christianity demands "a good mind, a pure breast, an innocent life."[44] Clement of Alexandria rings all the changes on this theme of optimistic individualism. It is the nature of man, "as man, to be in close fellowship with God." Man is "made for the contemplation of heaven, and is in truth a heavenly plant, to come to the knowledge of God."[45]

Although this kind of individualism was hardly new—the Stoics had been preaching it for two centuries—it roused the keenest antagonism

---

[43] See Troeltsch, *The Social Teachings of the Christian Churches,* I, 52 ff.; Lewis Mumford, *The Condition of Man* (1944), pp. 52 ff.

[44] *Divine Institutes,* V.20. Note Athanasius' account of the influence of Christianity on both the individual and society, *De Incarnatione Verbi,* 51 ff.

[45] *Exhortation to the Greeks,* X.80; cf. X.82.

from formalists like the conservative Pharisees and Sadducees. And when, in the fullness of time, the new cult was compelled to erect barriers of dogma and bureaucracy, the ethical individualism of Jesus was ruthlessly subordinated to ecclesiastical solidarity. However, even in the relatively sophisticated theology of the fourth Gospel (A.D. 100-140?) something of the original emphasis on individualism remains, though in the Hellenistic doctrine of the Logos. Out of his incalculable love for man, God contrived the Logos, the divine mediator between Him and His creatures. Like Plato's *demiurgos,* linking the realms of ideas and matter, the Christian Logos unites man with God.[46] In a recurrent Johannine metaphor, it is the light that reveals a knowledge of God.[47] The inwardness and ethical elevation of Christianity, no less than its democratic regard for the individual, results from this divine illumination. Upon the proposition that the kingdom of God is within, the whole structure of Christian optimism is reared.[48]

Thus, by and large, Christianity possessed all the requisites of success. In response to a widely felt sense of sin and need for redemption it both emphasized (and theologically explained) man's depravity and afforded him an elaborate eschatological promise. In response to a general dissatisfaction with the rational humanism of the Greek tradition it elevated the mysteries of faith and vicarious atonement over the less spectacular pleasures of rational self-sufficiency. To a world rapt in the dream of Alexander and in the universality of the Roman Empire, it made salvation international and truly democratic. To a world sunk in despair, says Clement with more piety than accuracy, the new light of God, "with a swiftness beyond parallel," "shone forth upon the earth and filled the whole world with the seed of salvation." [49] The victory was not easy; Christians met at worst with organized persecution, at best with slander. Athenagoras reports that the brethren were commonly charged with

[46] On the theological development of the doctrine of the Logos—which by the time of the Council of Nicaea (325) was to pose a crucial problem—see Origen, *De Principiis,* II.6.3; Augustine, *The Enchiridion,* ch. XXXIII ff. Augustine (*The Confessions,* VII.9.13 ff.) is careful to deny any correlation between the Platonic and the Christian Logos, but the suggestion of Neoplatonism is unmistakable. Elsewhere (*The City of God,* VIII.5) Augustine admits that "no philosophers come nearer to us than the [Neo-] Platonists." On the Greek conception of the Logos, see Moore, *The Religious Thought of the Greeks,* p. 319; Murray, *Five Stages of Greek Religion,* pp. 185-88; Elsee, *Neoplatonism in Relation to Christianity,* pp. 34 ff.

[47] John, I:9, III:19-21, V:35, etc.

[48] See Sidgwick, *Outlines of the History of Ethics,* pp. 117 ff. For an erudite discussion of the implementation of the doctrine of love in the early Church see Harnack, *The Mission and Expansion of Christianity,* I, 147 ff.; cf. John Herman Randall, Jr., *The Making of the Modern Mind* (1926), pp. 42 ff.

[49] *Exhortation to the Greeks,* X.85-86.

atheism, Thyestean feasts, and Oedipodean intercourse.[50] Minucius Felix' Caecilius denounces the cult for cannibalism, obscene initiatory rites, adultery, and incest ("inpudentibus tenebris nexus infandaᴖ cupiditatis involvunt per incertum sortis").[51] But the Christians, notable no less for the purity of their lives than for their proselytism, pursued their faith with the sobriety and calm assurance of heaven that shines through every page of Justin Martyr's *Apology*. And thus, explains Eusebius, "by the power and assistance of Heaven the saving word began to flood the whole world with light like the rays of the sun. . . . In every city and village arose churches crowded with thousands of men, like a teeming threshing floor." [52]

Tertullian's quiet pronouncement is no doubt adequate: "We are a body knit together as such by a common religious profession, by unity of discipline, and by the bond of a common hope." [53] That common hope could be everyone's. Universalism was in the *Zeitgeist*. With the decline of the old city-state and the decay of narrow loyalties, many had prophesied hastening ills.[54] But the turbulence of Greece was succeeded by the majesty of Rome. The new cosmopolitanism was reflected as clearly in the extension of the Empire as in the extension of the Church. Celsus recognized a leveling tendency in the new faith, and scorned the allegiance to a religious rather than a political unity. But Origen, his great opponent, could only pity those bound by local mores. His horizons stretched beyond nations. Like Tertullian, he recognized only one commonwealth—the world.[55]

### THE REJECTION OF PAGANISM

About the turn of the fifth century, long after the Holy Spirit had descended on the Apostles at Pentecost, Jerome looked about him and acknowledged a momentous fact of history: "The Roman world is falling: yet we hold up our heads instead of bowing them." [56] From the very beginning of the Christian era the faithful had been aware of the chasm separating them from the pagan mores and institutions of the unsaved. Although they rendered unto Caesar the things that

[50] Kidd, *Documents Illustrative of the History of the Church*, I, 108.

[51] *Octavius*, ch. X.

[52] *The Ecclesiastical History*, II.3.

[53] *Apologeticus*, ch. XXXIX.

[54] See Halliday, *The Pagan Background of Early Christianity*, pp. 237 ff.; Nock, *Conversion*, pp. 99 ff.

[55] On some of the Stoic influences at work see Léontine Zanta, *La Renaissance du stoïcisme au XVIᵉ siècle* (1914), pp. 99 ff.; for Origen's universalism see *Contra Celsum*, V.35 ff.; cf. Angus, *The Mystery-Religions and Christianity*, pp. 283 ff.

[56] *Letters*, no. LX.

were Caesar's, they lived for eternity. They rejoiced in their salvation, and viewed the world about them with objectivity if not contempt. The sharp dichotomy of Augustine's twin cities emerged gradually, but the cleavage was in most Christians' minds from the beginning. As the cult increased in numbers and evolved a church, it more and more assumed the functions that Augustus had hoped would eternally belong to the Roman Empire. It developed new principles of cohesion and order, giving a unity to the Mediterranean world that, in spite of the efforts of men like Constantine and Theodosius, was fracturing.[57] This transformation—the great theme of Gibbon's *Decline and Fall*—marked the passage from classical antiquity to the Middle Ages.

So gradual and significant a change can be neither traced accurately nor described adequately. The world was not pagan one day, and Christian the next. Christianity extended far back before the birth of Christ for some of its basic attitudes, and paganism exerted an educational and disciplinary influence on Christianity for centuries after the Roman Empire faded away. But if a compendious explanation is wanted—even though it it is a false simplification—it might be this: in the Christian world God usurped the place man had occupied in the pagan world. An anthropocentric universe was replaced by a theocentric universe, humanism by theocracy, knowledge by faith, explanation by mystery, the state by the church.

The dynamics of history are never precipitate. It is easy to see the difference between the first century A.D. and the ninth, more difficult to see the difference between the first and the fifth, and very difficult to see the difference between the first and the second. Boniface VIII or Bonaventura were obviously aware of their distance, chronologically and emotionally, from classical antiquity, but apologists like Justin Martyr and Minucius Felix were still powerfully attracted to a past that had not yet spent its force. One of the most charming remains of an otherwise not very charming century is the *Octavius* of Minucius Felix, a third-century Christian. The arguments that Octavius uses against the polytheistic paganism of his friend Caecilius, as they walk along the Tiber from Rome to Ostia, reveal the strength of both views of life, and attest, if unintentionally, to the lingering appeal of Hellenism.[58] Gnostics like Valentinus and Marcion, and Montonists like Tertullian, broke sharply with the traditions of humanism; but men like Clement and Origen, both cultivated Alexandrians, were not reluctant to salvage some of the good things of antiquity.

[57] This is the thesis, brilliantly developed, of Charles N. Cochrane's *Christianity and Classical Culture: A Study of Thought and Action from Augustus to Augustine* (1940).
[58] See Mumford, *The Condition of Man*, pp. 77-79.

Historically, Christianity had been syncretistic,[59] and some of the more urbane apologists found it hard to sever themselves from a rich past. For instance, a famous ethical treatise like Ambrose's *De Officiis Ministrorum,* which is closely modeled on Cicero's *De Officiis,* shows the continuing power of pagan, and particularly Stoic, morality. The ethical elevation of the patriarchs, in Ambrose's judgment, reflects merely the discipline of the four cardinal virtues of prudence, justice, courage, and temperance.[60] More notoriously, Origen was so congenial to paganism that, in the opinion of a less yielding posterity, he approached heresy. One of the recurrent themes of Jerome's letters is his distrust of Origen's liberalism—a distrust that Augustine turned into something very like hatred.[61] After all, what could be done with a dangerous radical who preached that the kingdom of God will some day end, that after the resurrection our bodies will be corruptible, that we should pray to God and not to Christ?[62] But Lactantius, not yet hardened by dogma, undertook to oppose the Stoics—not because they were pagan, but because their ethics was so severe and inhumane. Passions should not be extirpated, he argues; they should be channelized: fear is holy and not evil when it is the fear of God.[63]

After the Council of Nicaea, however, this willingness to learn from antiquity largely disappears. Augustine, a man of learning and in his younger days a teacher of rhetoric, was vastly indebted to Neoplatonism; yet as a Christian he could only condemn it. Between Christian and pagan he drew a sharp line; to him, sheep were one thing, and goats another. As for those heathen philosophers who believe

that the sovereign good and evil are to be found in this life, and have placed it either in the soul or the body, or in both, or, to speak more explicitly, either in pleasure [Epicurean?] or in virtue [Stoic?], or in both [Aristotle?]; in repose or in virtue, or in both; in pleasure and repose, or in virtue, or in all combined; in the primary objects of nature, or in virtue, or in both,—all these have, with a marvellous shallowness, sought to find their blessedness in this life and in themselves.

Christians are quite otherwise. They look to their happiness in a future life which pagan philosophers refuse to believe in "because they do not

[59] Newman, in the celebrated fifth chapter of *An Essay on the Development of Christian Doctrine* (1845) cites the syncretistic and assimilative genius of Christianity as proof of its validity.

[60] I.24. See Henry Osborn Taylor, *The Classical Heritage of the Middle Ages,* pp. 75 ff.; Cochrane, *Christianity and Classical Culture,* pp. 373-74. Note Jerome's discussion of passion, *Against the Pelagians,* II.6.

[61] See *The City of God,* XI.23.

[62] A catalogue of sins drawn up by Jerome, *Letters,* no. XCII.

[63] *Epitome of the Divine Institutes,* ch. LXIV.

see it, and attempt to fabricate for themselves a happiness in this life, based upon a virtue which is as deceitful as it is proud." [64] The tradition of classical humanism was thus anathema: a virtue with reference to man and to this life was supplanted by a faith with reference to a transcendent deity and to a hope of heaven. Lactantius, the Christian Cicero whose death perhaps coincided with the Council of Nicaea, appeared to his more severe brethren doctrinally inexact and perhaps even heretical, but even so he was able to formulate man's new spiritual coördinates with classical terseness:

> The world was made by God, that men might be born; again men are born, that they may acknowledge God as a Father, in whom is wisdom; they acknowledge Him, that they may worship Him, in whom is justice; they worship Him, that they may receive the reward of immortality; they receive immortality, that they may serve God forever. So you see how closely connected the first are with the middle, and the middle with the last.[65]

Such a fundamental reversal of the humanistic view of man and of the universe is reflected in many ways and is articulated more clearly as we approach Augustine. His sweeping condemnation of the *civitas terrena,* his great symbol for paganism, climaxes four centuries of Christian obscurantism. Paul, on the Hill of Mars, had inveighed against the illusions of paganism; his posterity delighted in developing the theme. Tertullian denounced all philosophers as *haereticorum patriarchae philosophae;*[66] Lactantius, the classical stylist, banished Homer because "he was able to give us no information relating to the truth, for he wrote of human rather than divine things";[67] Ambrose scorned the cosmology and astronomy of the presumptuous heathen because they obviously had not "climbed up into the heavens, nor measured the sky, nor examined the universe with their eyes";[68] Jerome, an educated man whose letters show all the tricks of classical rhetoric and who was not above quoting Virgil on occasion, wrote off Latin literature in a single famous sentence: "How can Horace go with the psalter, Virgil with the Gospels, Cicero with the apostle?" [69]

[64] *The City of God,* XIX.4.

[65] *Epitome of the Divine Institutes,* ch. LXIX.

[66] *De Anima,* ch. III.

[67] *Divine Institutes,* I.5.

[68] *On Belief in the Resurrection,* II.86; cf. *Duties of the Clergy,* II.2.

[69] *Letters,* no. XXII. Hellenic Alexandrians like Clement and Origen were sufficiently liberal to admit the trivium and quadrivium (grammar, dialectic, rhetoric, geometry, arithmetic, astronomy, and music) as useful preparation for theology. But most of their successors were less tolerant. Some monastic arbiters, like Isadore of Seville, flatly condemned the reading of any pagan author without special permission. See Taylor, *Classical Heritage,* pp. 44 ff.

But not only were the graces and appurtenances of paganism contemptuously rejected. The humanistic view of life was rightly held by the more profound fathers to be antithetical to what Clement hails as the new song. It had to be destroyed, root and branch. The folly of philosophy is axiomatic to Lactantius: "knowledge cannot come from the understanding, nor be apprehended by thought; because to have knowledge in oneself as a peculiar property does not belong to man, but to God." [70] Augustine admits that some philosophers, "by God's help," approached truth—but only to sink back into impotence. They are betrayed by human infirmity and fall again into error. "And this was ordered by divine providence, that their pride might be restrained, and that by their example it might be pointed out that it is humility which has access to the highest regions." [71] Augustine, the most philosophical of the fathers, poured the most scorn upon philosophy. On the discords of the various pagan systems—288 by Varro's count—he rails with sublime invective; for whereas shallow-witted philosophers continually seek truth, Christians rest easy in the certainty that they have attained it.[72] And by the time Augustine was solidifying dogma and his great contemporary, Jerome, was translating the Vulgate, they had cause to view the extinction of paganism with a satisfaction that on occasion was vainglorious. In the preface to his translation of Galatians Jerome asks, without waiting for the answer:

How few are there who now read Aristotle? How many are there who know the books, or even the name of Plato? You may find here and there a few old men, who have nothing else to do, who study them in a corner. But the whole world speaks the language of our Christian peasants and fishermen. The whole world re-echoes their words.[73]

Two centuries earlier, Clement had thought it necessary in his *Exhortation to the Greeks* to warn the unsaved of the "absurd pretensions" of godless sanctuaries, mouths of caverns full of jugglery, the Thesprotian caldron, the Cirrhaean tripod, the Dodonian copper.[74] Jerome, however, could view the *fait accompli* and exult. "Even in Rome itself paganism is left in solitude." The old temples are inhabited only by the owls, and

---

[70] *Divine Institutes*, III.3. The whole of bk. III is relevant, "Of the False Wisdom of Philosophers." Similarly, Hippolytus, by legend a converted Roman soldier, examined and rejected most of the religions of antiquity; his *Refutation of All Heresies* contains much useful information on forgotten faiths like Gnosticism.

[71] *The City of God*, II.7.

[72] *The City of God*, XVIII.41; cf. XIX.1 ff.

[73] *The Principal Works*, p. 498.

[74] II.10.

the very standards of the soldiers are emblazoned with the sign of the Cross.[75]

During the first four centuries, then, the articulate Christians were trying to rid themselves of every taint of paganism.[76] There must have been something of a guilt-complex to account for the vehemence of their denials: some, at least, must have been aware of their indebtedness to the mystery cults and to the ascetic tradition of Greek philosophy. Clement, for instance, was drawn to Plato[77] and, unconsciously, to the redemptionist cults, and in lashing out against them he condemned the species rather than the genus. How could anyone, he cries, give "credence to worthless legends, imagining brute beasts to be enchanted by music, while the bright face of truth seems alone to strike you as deceptive?"[78] Augustine rationalized the good things of antiquity with characteristic agility. Both Plato and Jeremiah, he points out, were in Egypt at the same time, and the prophets obviously antedated Pythagoras; therefore the ascetic and mystic strain of Greek thought, meager as it is, is clearly derivative from the Lord's anointed. To think otherwise is a "thing which it is the height of folly to believe."[79] Actually, the fathers were justified in seeing the tradition of classical humanism as the archheresy, and their tactics in combating it as necessary to their strategy of elevating God and reducing man.

Against the Greek belief in a rational universe subject to man's rational knowledge they therefore erected the edifice of Christian faith—faith in an inscrutable deity who mysteriously and arbitrarily sustains the universe and all in it, and whose omniscience and omnipotence make blasphemous any effort towards rational comprehension. When Newman, setting himself against the aggressive intellect of his impious age, declared that "it is not a necessary mark of a true religion that it is rational in the common sense of the word,"[80] he was in the main tradition of Christian

---

[75] *Letters,* no. CVII; cf. nos. XIV, LVIII.

[76] Perhaps a few more references would be in order. See Colossians, II:8; Origen, *Contra Celsum,* I.12; Clement of Alexandria in Gwatkin, *Selections,* p. 107, and, for Tertullian, pp. 119-21; Burke, *Attitudes toward History,* I, 156. The influence of Greek philosophy on early hexaemeral literature is discussed by F. E. Robbins, *The Hexaemreal Literature: A Study of the Greek and Latin Commentaries on Genesis* (1912), pp. 1-23.

[77] *Exhortation to the Greeks,* V.59.

[78] *Exhortation to the Greeks,* I.2. Note Cumont's generalization (*Les Religions Orientales,* pp. 194-95) on the syncretism of mystery cults: "Il est de l'essence du paganisme que la nature d'une divinité d'elargit en même temps que la quantité de ses fidèles augmente."

[79] *On Christian Doctrine,* II.28.43; cf, II.40.60, on the uses of pagan philosophy. Eusebius (*The Ecclesiastical History,* VI.18) tells of the pious use he made of his pagan education. See Gibbon, *Decline and Fall,* II, 312 ff.

[80] Charles Frederick Harrold (ed.), *A Newman Treasury* (1943), p. 321.

apologetics. The mighty doctrines of the incarnation and the resurrection symbolized mysteries that dwarfed man's understanding, and therefore the role of faith in the development of Christianity was inevitably enormous. "I do not require a reason from Christ," said Ambrose. "If I am convinced by reason I reject faith." [81] Faith, indeed, is the debt we owe for vicarious salvation, the suspension of disbelief by which man humbles himself before God. "Pay first that which you owe, that you may be in a position to ask for what you have hoped." [82] To seek to understand the mysteries of God is the mark of the unsaved, and to know nothing in opposition to the rule of faith, says Tertullian, "is to know all things." [83] On this assumption Augustine constructed his epistemology: the highest wisdom is the knowledge of God, but it comes to man, the passive recipient, only by the grace of divine illumination. "For there are innumerable questions the solution of which is not to be demanded before we believe, lest life be finished by us in disbelief." [84]

*Gnosis* (knowledge), the central concept of Greek thought, informed both metaphysics and ethics. For it, Christianity substituted *pistis* (faith), implying that the nature of a sovereign God—and the concept suggests something not unlike Oriental despotism[85]—lay far beyond the feeble comprehension of man, who, though the child of God, had in seeking knowledge disobeyed God and thus was sunk into bottomless iniquity. For the Greek ideal of rational and organic well-being Christianity advanced the notion of organic depravity and thus the eschatological promise of a "salvation" not earned but gratuitously bestowed. (It was when Paul spoke of eschatology that the men of Athens, who had hitherto listened to him respectfully, rose against him, so alien was the idea.) Man needed only faith, for God's grace and Christ's sufferings absolved his sins. "God forbid," breathes Augustine fervently, that any man should by his own efforts save himself.[86] For the Greeks, rectitude and morality were themselves merely aspects of knowledge; for Augustine, the only knowledge lawful for man was the "goodness of the Creator." [87] All else lay "beyond the pale of the Church of Christ." [88]

The fact that Christianity so quickly became a redemptionist cult made

[81] *On Belief in the Resurrection*, II.89.
[82] *Concerning Repentance*, II.9.
[83] *On Prescription against Heretics*, ch. XVI.
[84] *The Letters*, no. CII.
[85] See Boas, *The Major Traditions of European Philosophy*, pp. 116 ff.
[86] *The Enchiridion*, ch. XXX.
[87] *The Enchiridion*, ch. IX.
[88] *On Christian Doctrine*, II.39.58. On superimposed (theological) ethics, see Robertson, *A Short History of Morals*, ch. II, *passim*.

this emphasis on faith inevitable. Conversely, it made inevitable the detestation of pride, the bumptious reliance on one's own strength. The theocratic tradition of Judaism, with which Christ had regarded himself in essential agreement, had posited legalistic and ritualistic subjection before a God whose decrees were immutable and unquestionable. "Therefore thou shalt love the Lord thy God, and keep his charge, and his statutes, and his judgments, and his commandments, alway." [89] Mount Sinai symbolized much to the mind of Israel, and Christ himself insisted that he had come to fulfill the prophets, not destroy them. The Jewish theocracy, functioning through a code divinely revealed, had construed morality as law sanctioned by divinity and involving reward and punishment. Its ethics was superimposed, and the levitical formalism of the Deuteronomic Code demanded a rigid conformity to ritual and authority. With the expansion of the Christian Church this concept, though somewhat mollified by Christ himself, was developed as a necessary condition for ecclesiastical dominance. The good life was one of faith in God and of unquestioning obedience to his divinely appointed agents.

Celsus, that plaintive pagan voice crying out against the Christians, had said that those strange folk "do not examine, but believe." [90] And to the searching mind of Greece this was the most lamentable of follies. The fact of revelation implicitly denied the validity of reason, and explicitly demanded an act of faith. The sacrificial salvation on which was built the theology and eschatology of Christianity transcended, as the best minds of the Church insisted, all rational explanation. Even Aquinas, the most rational of theologians, was to boast that such a mystery as the Trinity mocked man's effort to understand and thus proved the glory of God.

[89] Deut., XI:1. See George Foot Moore, *History of Religions* (1914-1920), II, 13 ff. for a lucid account of Judaism.
[90] Origen, *Contra Celsum*, I.9.

# X

## THE WINDS OF DOCTRINE

### THE ONTOLOGY OF GOD

THE SHAPING OF CHRISTIAN DOCTRINE toward the massive formulation of the Nicene Creed in the fourth century is a history of lost causes. The disputes and rival heresies that racked a burgeoning religion—the form of the sacraments, the date of Easter, the date of the second coming, the celibacy of the clergy, the ecstatic prophecies of Montanism[1]—have long since had a merely antiquarian interest, but in the second and third centuries they were (or seemed to be) of crucial significance. We are not concerned, however, with the development of doctrine; we are concerned with the ways in which the new faith affected man's view of himself and his relation to the universe. In those terms, the cardinal problem of the early Church was what we shall call the ontology of God. Simply posed, the question was this: what is the nature of God and what is His relation to the world of sensibles?

The difficulty of defining God and explaining the mechanics of his operation arose very early. The Apostles could and did construe Jesus either as the Jewish Messiah or, with Paul, as a subordinate deity—the Son of God whose divinely sanctioned mission was to atone for the sins of the world. But within a couple of generations after the crucifixion, the Church, an expanding organization, began to feel the need of uniform doctrine; in trying to achieve uniformity it fractured here on one point of theology, there on another. If Jesus was the Messiah, then his religion was racial and not universal; if he was a subordinate deity, doing the will of his superior, then polytheism became inevitable; if he was actually God, *verus Deus,* then how could he become a man and die? The problem of Christology is seen, of course, in the Canon itself. Perhaps even before Paul's death, the unknown author of the Epistle to the Hebrews was radically revising the correlation between the Messianic promise of Judaism and the universal salvation of Christianity. In this Epistle Christ is seen as transcending the prophets of the Law: he is the "Apostle and

---

[1] For discussions of the organization of early Christian communities, the growth of the clergy, the development of the sacraments, etc., see McGiffert, *A History of Christianity in the Apostolic Age,* pp. 506 ff.; Gwatkin, *Early Church History,* I, 248 ff.

High Priest of our profession," [2] the son but not the minister of God, and the founder of a new religion whose central mystery is vicarious salvation and whose key is faith—"the substance of things hoped for, the evidence of things not seen." [3] In the Hellenistic fourth Gospel, written perhaps a generation later, Christ becomes the Logos—the incarnate deity who, unlike the Jesus of the second Gospel, had received his mandate directly from God his Father and therefore claimed divinity. "I and my Father are one." [4] Although the Christ of the fourth Gospel is lesser than the Father (he says that his function is to do the will of God) he insists that faith in Him is essential to salvation.[5] His eschatological promise is clear: whoever believes in Him "hath everlasting life." [6] Whereas both Matthew and Mark quote the dying Jesus as crying, with human poignancy, "My God, my God, why hast thou forsaken me?" John sees the crucifixion as the consummation of a deific plan: hence the apopemptic "It is accomplished." [7]

Without tracing in detail the evolution of Christian theology during its first century we may see how in the so-called Apostles' Creed, the monument of the second-century Church, there had been achieved a compendium of generally accepted principles. Tentative statement though it is, it is a formulation of eschatological hopes rather than metaphysical subtlety. It shows how far along the road of dogma the Church had come, and how remote it was from Jesus, the son of Joseph and Mary, who had taught his simple morality among the Galilean hills.

I believe in God the Father Almighty: Maker of heaven and earth.

And in Jesus Christ his only (begotten) Son our Lord; who was conceived by the Holy Ghost, born of the Virgin Mary; suffered under Pontius Pilate, was crucified, dead, and buried; he descended into hell; the third day he rose from the dead; he ascended into heaven; and sitteth at the right hand of God the Father Almighty; from thence he shall come to judge the quick and the dead.

I believe in the Holy Ghost; the holy catholic Church; the communion of saints; the forgiveness of sins; the resurrection of the body; and the life everlasting. Amen.[8]

[2] III:1.
[3] XI:1.
[4] John, X:30.
[5] VI:38.
[6] VI:47.
[7] See Moore, *History of Religions,* II, 140.
[8] I quote from the eighth-century received form in Philip Schaff, *The Creeds of Christendom* (1882), II, 45. The Apostles' Creed is not the work of one man or even the product of a single century. It seems to have taken shape gradually and in various forms, but it represents the dogmas generally held by the Western Church during the ante-Nicene era. Of course, there is a vast literature on its evolution. A convenient account is that of Edgar C. S. Gibson, *The Three Creeds* (1912), pp. 39-111.

It became clear, however, as Christianity drew to itself more converts—and more articulate, sophisticated converts—that the implications of this creed required clarification. As the Church was extended, both geographically and intellectually, the old Semitic acceptance of a theocratic universe had to be modified to satisfy the metaphysical demands of those (like Origen and Clement, for instance) who had been nurtured in the tradition of Greek philosophy. Although this philosophy was moribund, the Platonic quest for absolutes had not been forgotten, and a simple anthropomorphism was no longer acceptable to cultivated and erudite theologians. Thus the importance of the ontology of God. If He was—as generally believed—permanent, absolute, perfect, then how precisely could he have any connection with the world of men and affairs, so lamentably impermanent, relative, and imperfect? Justin Martyr, about the middle of the second century, had defined God as "that which always maintains the same nature, and in the same manner, and is the cause of all other things." [9] But to determine in just what way God is the cause of all other things, or how he can traffic with the realm of sensibles so antithetical to the divine nature, posed a very great problem. It was the old problem of permanence and change, of Plato's Forms and their influence on particulars. How could the Church link God to man, infinity to the finite, without falling into the pit of polytheism or jeopardizing the absolute perfection of deity?

To work out the theological and metaphysical solution of this problem required the best efforts of the best minds in the early Church. Inevitably, the solution derived largely from (or evolved simultaneously with) Neoplatonism: only by construing the universe as a series of emanations from the absolute Being could God be saved in His infinity or the world explained as having any correlation with God. Augustine states the issue with his characteristic vigor:

We need a Mediator who, being united to us here below by the mortality of His body, should at the same time be able to afford us truly divine help in cleansing and liberating us by means of the immortal righteousness of His spirit, whereby He remained heavenly while here upon earth. [10]

In Christian theology, only thus could the immemorial dualism of permanence and change be bridged: by converting Jesus into a mediator, at once God and man, and thus a participant in both divinity and temporality. [11] Through him, God was brought to earth without ceasing to be

[9] *Dialogue with Trypho,* ch. III.
[10] *The City of God,* IX.17.
[11] See Duchesne, *Early History of the Christian Church,* II, 101.

God. The fourth Gospel marks one step in the evolution of this concept, and the Nicene Creed, by establishing the dogma of a triune God, marks its official culmination.

## GNOSTICISM

Before the dogma of the incarnate Christ was achieved, battles were lost even if campaigns were won. The Trinitarian victory was fiercely contested before the Church finally overcame the widespread reluctance to construe God in human terms. The tenacity of the great Gnostic heresies shows how dearly held was the notion of a monotheistic God utterly alien from the evil of the world and the flesh; and such heresies as Monarchianism show the fantastic ingenuity expended in maintaining the unity of God. The Monarchians—unitarians who had never heard of New England—sought to prove the absolute divinity of both God and Christ by their doctrine of the modes or aspects of deity. As Father, God is the creator of the world, but as Son He assumes another mode to become its savior. By their opponents the Monarchians were dubbed "patripassians," for they thought of God as hanging on the cross.[12]

It was the various kinds of Gnosticism, however, that most clearly marked the opposition to a Trinitarian theology. Gnosticism, one of the most fantastically complicated phenomena of church history, was more a set of attitudes than a religion. Although it existed before Christianity, having its roots far back in the ascetic dualisms of India and Persia, it took many forms and evolved many theologies, for it was inherently syncretistic. The ease with which it assimilated to its own uses this deity or that, adapting itself to dozens of mystery cults, in large measure accounts for its serpentine history. Also, it accounts for the fact that Gnostics fastened themselves to the early Church and exploited its theology and Christology for their purposes. That Gnosticism was quickly held a threat to the apostolic Church is apparent by the violence of the attacks it suffered. Justin Martyr, Irenaeus, Tertullian, Hippolytus—to name only the most famous and the most articulate of its opponents—wrote against it with learning, vehemence, and, above all, prolixity. Indeed, since its own apparently extensive literature has disappeared, what knowledge we have of Gnosticism comes mainly from its enemies.[13]

[12] See Wilhelm Moeller, *History of the Christian Church: A.D. 1-600* (1912), pp. 223-231.

[13] There are discussions of Gnosticism in all the standard church histories. The following articles (and especially Arendzen's) provide both useful surveys and bibliographical guides: E. F. Scott, "Gnosticism," Hasting's *Encyclopaedia of Religion and Ethics*, VI, 231 ff.; J. P. Arendzen, "Gnosticism," *The Catholic Encyclopaedia*, VI, 582 ff.; Wilhelm Bosset, "Gnosticism," *The Encyclopaedia Britannica* (11th ed.), XII, 152 ff. See G. R. S. Mead, *Fragments of a Faith Forgotten* (1906), pp. 136 ff.

The attitudes subsuming all the hybrid Gnostic theologies were in clear opposition to the development of Trinitarian Christianity. To apparently all Gnostics, of whatever color or local variety, the implacable dualism between spirit and matter, good and evil, was the primary fact of experience. As in Zoroastrianism and later in Manichaeism (both of them probably related to Gnosticism), the opposition between the principles of good and evil was unceasing and universal; the world was a monument to evil. The pessimism resulting from this view was profound: man, as a corporeal creature, is the symbol of iniquity, and the end of his existence should be to escape the pollution of his carnal nature. The means of escape, it is superfluous to add, are not within his own power: he can only hope to elicit the aid of this or that God-sent savior and thus, transcending the flesh, return to the father-spirit of good. Since God is immutably and absolutely good, He is obviously cut off from all intercourse with the material realm that is a cosmic stain.

This dualism, with its corollary of pessimism, is common to all mystery religions. The Orphics and Paul of Tarsus, *mutatis mutandis,* reveal a cognate attitude. Also, like other mystery religions, Gnosticism demands a redemptionist theology. But here the similarity, at least with Christianity, ends. The secret of salvation with the Christians was faith, but with the Gnostics it was knowledge (*gnosis*).

The *gnosis* that gave the Gnostics their generic name was obviously not the kind of knowledge that Plato and Aristotle celebrated. In a religion of revelation and redemption, *gnosis* could only be the knowledge necessary for salvation; and this, in Gnostic doctrine, was the always exclusive and usually occult knowledge of formulae, initiatory rituals, and even magical incantations. By such knowledge one could escape the general damnation of the flesh. Thus a certain Gnostic teacher named Menander claimed, according to Irenaeus,[14] to possess a certain kind of knowledge by whose magic one could "overcome those very angels that made the world; for his disciples obtain their *resurrection* by being baptized into him, and can die no more, but remain in the possession of immortal youth." Hence all the mumbo-jumbo and mystic paraphernalia of Gnostic worship, and the cross-fertilization of many strains of magico-mystical Oriental thought. With their various brands of indispensable knowledge the Gnostics became snobbish ritualists;[15] they alone, they boasted, knew

---

[14] *Irenaeus against Heresies,* I.23.5.

[15] Renan (*Marc-Aurèle et la fin du monde antique,* 1881, p. 115) makes a characteristically ironical comment on the Gnostic teachers: "Affectant une plus haute culture intellectuelle et des moeurs moins rigides, ils trouvaient une clientèle assurée dans les classes riches, qui éprouvaient le désir de se distinguer de d'échapper à la discipline commune, faite pour des pauvres."

the secret rites which could release man from the bane of corporeal existence.

Even the redemption sought by the Gnostics was not, like Paul's, a personal redemption resulting in a pure life and a spiritual rebirth. Rather, it was cosmic: the whole creation must be saved from sin, and the material universe must revert, somehow, to the purity of spirit. Although each Gnostic sect advanced its own brand of *gnosis* and took solace in its own ritual, they all writhed under the consciousness of material evil. "This utter pessimism, bemoaning the existence of the whole universe as a corruption and a calamity, with a feverish craving to be freed from the body of this death and a mad hope that, if we only knew, we could by some mystic words undo the cursed spell of this existence—this is the foundation of all Gnostic thought." [16]

The problem of the ontology of God becomes crucial with such Alexandrian Christian Gnostics as Basilides (fl. 117) and Valentinus (fl. 160). Specifically, they were very hard put to it to accommodate in their views of God and the world any notion of the incarnate Christ. Could God become man without foregoing divinity? Could there be any interaction of the twin cosmic forces of good and evil? Hippolytus denounces Valentinus as a Pythagorean and a Platonist, and Basilides as an Aristotelian,[17] but actually they were Oriental mystics wrestling with the problem of an incarnate god. Basilides represents something very like Persian dualism. He reduces the whole universe to the antagonistic principles of light and darkness (*vide* the Zoroastrian Ormuzd and Ahriman) continually striving for mastery. God, the parent of light, has animated the heavens with 365 spirits and has surrounded Himself with the seven mystic hypostases of *nous, logos, phronesis, sophia,* and the like. From these—not from a theocratic God—the world of sense accidentally derives.[18]

Valentinus, a much more cultivated thinker, exercises his wits to explain how such a world has come about and how Christ, the savior, can condescend to traffic with it.[19] His God is virtually a Neoplatonic absolute at the apex of a transcendent pantheistic universe. From this ineffable and of course incorporeal Being there proceed, by emanation of His goodness, the lesser hierarchies of spirituality. The jargon itself is spectacular.

There is a certain Dyad (two-fold being), who is inexpressible by any name, of whom one part should be called Arrhetus (unspeakable), and the other Sige

---

[16] Arendzen, "Gnosticism," *The Catholic Encyclopaedia*, VI, 593.
[17] *The Refutation of All Heresies*, VII.2.
[18] See *Irenaeus against Heresies*, I.24; cf. Hippolytus, VII.2 ff.
[19] See F. Legge, *Forerunners and Rivals of Christianity* (1915), II, 83 ff.

(silence). But of this Dyad a second was produced, one part of whom he [Valentinus] names Pater, and the other Alethia. From this Tetrad, again, rose Logos and Zoe, Anthropos and Ecclesia. These constitute the primary Ogdoad.[20]

In spite of all these brave translunary creatures emanating from one another we are still far from the realm of matter. So traditional and so rigid was Valentinus' dualism and so intense his hatred of corporeality that he could explain the creation of matter only by hypostatizing a cosmic accident. For the world resulted not from the emanation of the Dyad (God), but through the fall of a lesser spiritual creature. Like Lucifer, a fallen angel brought all our woe. The primary hypostases, high in the scale of emanations and therefore close to the source of being, gave birth to the lesser Aeons, which themselves are noumenal, immaterial, and supersensible. One of the lesser of these, *Sophia* (wisdom), conceived an unholy desire to know the Godhead, and for her presumption—like the presumption of the primal man in eating of the tree of wisdom—she was expelled from the *pleroma* (the totality of all the spiritual agencies emanating from God).

From this angelic fall, then, are derived the world and its inherent evil hopelessly cut off from God. Fear, grief, and wickedness, the attributes of *Sophia* after her disaster, became by transference the attributes of the corporeal creation.[21] From this deplorable state of affairs, however, Valentinus was able to take some comfort by explaining how man and the world of sense might return to the holiness of the pleroma. Two of the greater Aeons, *Nous* and *Alethia,* mate to produce two sibling Aeons, Christ and the Holy Ghost. (The sexual machinery of Gnosticism is very elaborate.) These two restore some sort of order to the pleroma rent asunder by *Sophia's* defection, after which all the Aeons together hatch out Jesus Soter, the *Logos* or cosmic redeemer. It was this great savior who descended into the body of the historical Jesus at his birth. But—and this is indicative of the Gnostic aversion to the notion of incarnate deity—the Logos remained a God uncontaminated by the flesh: he merely used the person of Jesus as a vehicle for his divine mission.[22]

---

[20] *Irenaeus against Heresies,* I.11; cf. Hippolytus, V.24 ff. See Mead, *Fragments of a Faith Forgotten,* pp. 294 ff.

[21] The actual creation of the world, explains Irenaeus (I.5, cf. II.19) was the work of the Demiurge, "the Father and God of everything outside the Pleroma, being the creator of all animal and material substance."

[22] One of the most famed of the Gnostics (if he was a Gnostic) was Marcion, who labored to divorce Christianity from Judaism. The Docetic heresy which he fostered, and which the Church so frantically opposed, held that Christ was a phantasm, a God whose substance was celestial even though he was apparent to the gross organs of sense. See Duchesne, I, 133 ff.

The perplexities of Gnostic mythology—and we have sketched only one of dozens—would seem to reveal nothing but the infinite mythopoeic faculty of certain types of mentality. Actually, however, these absurdities were merely the verbalizations of a widely held set of attitudes. Such Gnostics as Valentinus were significant in the evolution of Catholic dogma. As repositories of Oriental mysticism, a decayed Hellenic tradition, and the emerging Neoplatonism of Alexandria, they indicate the lengths to which men of the second century could go in sterilizing the concept of God. The crucial problem of the early Church was to reconcile monotheism, with its corollary dualism of spirit and matter, and the deity of Christ, a God-man. And although the Gnostics were repudiated by a Church that wished to preserve God as God and yet make Him the incarnate savior of the world, they serve historically to show how powerfully contested was the idea that a God would pollute himself by becoming a man.

### THE INCARNATE GOD

Alexandria, and not Rome, was the center of Christian thought in the second and third centuries. The metropolis of Hellenistic culture, it was there that all schools of thought met and mingled. There Philo Judaeus, who died about the same time as Paul, had tried to reconcile Greek philosophy with the Jewish Law; there the Gnostics had spun out their endless systems; there Plotinus, in the third century, was to formulate Neoplatonism; and there, in the great catechetical school of Clement and Origen, Apostolic Christianity underwent its decisive impact with Greek philosophy.

Origen (ca. 185—ca. 254) wrote, if legend is true, six thousand books; he produced the greatest apology of Christianity in his *Contra Celsum;* he inaugurated allegorical interpretations of the Scriptures; he wrote endless commentaries on the Bible; and, in his *De Principiis,* he formulated the first systematic theology of his religion. In spite of the opposition he encountered, both during his life and for centuries after his death, he contributed powerfully to the development of Catholic dogma. He brought philosophical awareness to the early Church, and his conception of the ontology of God attained the status of dogma at the Council of Nicaea.

Origen did not have a very original mind, but he was a man of great erudition and a powerful synthesizer. In developing the doctrine of the Logos that was at once God and man he drew on nearly a thousand years of philosophical speculation. Heraclitus, in the sixth century, had identified cosmic reason as the logos that maintains *dikē* and relationship between all the parts of the universe[23]—a suggestion not welcomed by his posterity that demanded a sharp dualism between the noumenal and the phenomenal. Anaxagoras, for instance, had argued that reason (*nous*) transcended the world of sense and was independent of it; and Plato, developing this dualism majestically, clearly separated the realm of Forms from the realm of sensibles. But Plato was never beguiled by the virtue of consistency. In a famous passage of the *Timaeus*[24] he gave full rein to his mythopoeic bent by suggesting the existence of a world-soul—"a third and intermediate kind of essence" that, participating in both the absolute and the sensible, constitutes "a mean between the indivisible, and the divisible and material." This facile and casual solution of the problem of permanence and change, supported by Plato's prestige, has enjoyed a very frisky life to our own day. In the opinion of Mr. Whitehead, Pluto's suggestion was "his most unfortunate essay in mythology. The World-Soul, as an emanation, has been the parent of puerile metaphysics, which only obscures the ultimate question of the relation of reality as permanent with reality as fluent." [25]

Its weaknesses, however, have not hindered its popularity. The Stoics adopted and developed the idea, predicating some sort of active intellect as permeating all the changes of a teleological universe, and simultaneously the notion appeared in late Judaistic thought. Since the earlier anthropomorphic God of Moses and Joshua had retired an incalculable distance from the world, He was thought of as still somehow related to it by the divine Word, itself almost a creative principle. "By the word of the Lord were the heavens made; and all the host of them by the breath of his mouth." [26] Philo of Alexandria gave the doctrine of the Logos an importance it has never lost. Although he of course repudiated Stoic materialism, he conveniently transferred the Logos to a Platonic absolute (the Hebraic God) that creatively shapes the world of matter to its own divine ideas.[27] Through the Logos God expresses His divine attributes in action; indeed, in Philo's view, the Logos assumes almost the status of a secondary god, the agent of the supreme deity and also the means by which man is able to rise above his corruptible flesh.

It is apparent that this concept was supremely convenient to the evolving Christology of the Church: with Philo we are very close to the fourth Gospel which he so profoundly influenced. "Believest thou not that I am

---

[23] See Windelband, *A History of Philosophy*, pp. 36-37.

[24] 34-35; cf. *Timaeus*, 28 ff.

[25] *Adventures of Ideas*, p. 166.

[26] Psalms, XXXIII:6; cf. Isaiah, LV.11; Prov. VIII.22.

[27] See "On the Creation of the World," ch. V-VI (*The Works of Philo Judaeus*, Bohn Library, I, 5 ff.).

in the Father, and the Father in me? the words that I speak unto you I speak not of myself: but the Father that dwelleth in me, he doeth the works." [28] The epistles to the Ephesians and Colossians (and of course to the Hebrews) mark the early formulations of this doctrine, but when John specifically identifies the historical Jesus with the divine Logos, Philo's abstract theory or principle of explanation becomes personified. In John, the Word becomes flesh and assumes its redemptive function as part of the divine scheme for the salvation of a sinful world. This was the view that, during the second and third centuries, became a common-place; [29] but it was Origen who developed it philosophically and system-atically.

In Origen's theology Christ is the Logos generated of the essence (*ousia*) of the Father. But because begotten—only the Father is eternal—He is a derivative God, divinely good but with the reflected goodness of His creator. [30] "Wherefore we have always held that God is the Father of His only begotten Son, who was indeed born of Him, and derives from Him what He is, but without any beginning." [31] Following His own generation, this Logos in turn generated the Holy Spirit, by which lower rational souls are taught to know God. [32] At length, however, and at the Father's behest, He descended to earth to enter the undefiled body of Jesus: thus Christ, the *theanthropos* (god-man) appeared to perform the function of redemption. And this is the ultimate mystery, as Origen candidly points out:

. . . how that mighty power of divine majesty, that very Word of the Father, and that very wisdom of God, in which were created all things, visible and invisible, can be believed to have existed within the limits of that man who appeared in Judea; nay, that the Wisdom of God can have entered the womb of a woman, and have been born an infant, and have uttered wailings like the cries of little children! [33]

From this dilemma "the narrowness of the human understanding can find no outlet." In Jesus Christ we see a man when we look at a God, and a God rising from the grave when we expect the crucified man to rest in the awful eternity of death. He is a creature in whom both natures, hu-

---

[28] John, XIV:10; cf. X:38; XVII:21, 23; XV:27; V:19.
[29] See, for example, Hippolytus, *Refutation of All Heresies*, X.29.
[30] Also a very popular view, and a popular metaphor. Thus Tertullian (in Kidd, *Documents*, I, 142): God produced Christ as the sun produces rays of light. Therefore that "which hath come from God is God, and the son of God, and both are one."
[31] *De Principiis*, I.2.2.
[32] I.3.1 ff.
[33] II.6.2.

man and divine, are composite. "To utter these things in human ears," confesses Origen, "or to explain them in words, far surpasses the powers either of our rank, or of our intellect and language." [34] But Origen explains them nonetheless. The fact is that the Logos merely used the body of Jesus without undergoing its bodily death, for divinity, being spiritual, cannot know passion. The God-man was born when the pure and incorruptible soul assumed a body; this soul was the intermediary between Christ and Jesus, "it being impossible for the nature of God to intermingle with a body without an intermediate instrument." [35]

Origen's theology met wide opposition, and for obvious reasons.[36] By subordinating the Son to the Father, and the Holy Ghost to the Son, he collided squarely with what was to be the Nicene dogma of the eternal equality of the three members of the Trinity; moreover, by rarefying his eschatology until he refused to admit the resurrection of the body, or the existence of an actual hell, he enraged those who conceived (vulgarly, as Origen thought) of the afterlife in material terms. Nonetheless, he made a lasting impression on Christian doctrine. Although the concept of the Logos was not original with him, and although he shared the theory of emanations with the hated Gnostics, he succeeded in giving to Christian theology a pervasive Neoplatonic cast that from the Nicene disputants, from Augustine, from Dionysius the Areopagite, from Erigena was to receive restatement and rejuvenation throughout the Middle Ages.

### THE COUNCIL OF NICAEA

Although the significance of the Council of Nicaea was not lost on its delegates, it is unlikely that they comprehended the magnitude of their achievement. A man would have needed a keen sense of history to realize the importance of the principles there laid down. And yet, with the comfortable perspective of fifteen centuries we can now see that the decisions made there have determined the course of Christian theology to our own day. If one finds solace in sharp lines and clear contours, he could find a no more convenient event than the Council of Nicaea for the close of pagan antiquity and the opening of the Middle Ages: the dogma there promulgated not only determined the question that had been harassing the Church for centuries, it also determined the intellectual and emotional frame of reference within which medieval man was to function.

The occasion for Constantine's calling together, in A.D. 325, some 318 bishops at Nicaea, in what is now northern Asia Minor, was a dramatic

---

[34] II.6.2.
[35] II.6.3.
[36] See Duchesne, III, 27 ff.

flaring of the dispute that had been smoldering almost since the crucifixion. Some seven years earlier a certain Arius, a priest of Baucalis in
Egypt, had made bold to declare that it was blasphemous to consider
Christ, the Logos, as coequal with God. For one thing, since he was begotten by the Father, it was patently absurd to think of them as coeternal,
and for another, if he was created (as God was not) it must have been
from nothing and not from the divine substance of God. Further, the
Holy Ghost, generated by the Logos, was similarly inferior to the Logos,
as the Logos was to God. As conceived by his implacable enemy Athanasius, Arius' position was clearly heretical:

God was not always a Father, but there was a time when God was not a Father.
The Word of God [i.e. the Logos] was not always, but originally from things that
were not; for God that is, has made him that was not, of that which was not;
wherefore there was a time when He was not; for the Son is a creature and a
work. Neither is He like in essence to the Father; neither is He the true and
natural Word of the Father; neither is He His true Wisdom. . . . Wherefore He
is by nature subject to change and variation, as are all rational creatures.[37]

In short, by denying the divinity of Christ Arius had cut the Gordion
knot of accommodating more than one God in a monotheistic religion.

This was an open attack—the last and greatest, as it happened—on the
old question: what is the nature of God, and what is His relationship to
the world? It was the last significant effort in the western Church to
establish a complete monotheism with an ineffable and transcendent God
acting on the realm of matter only through a subordinate and mediating
Logos. And although it preserved God as a veritable Platonic absolute,
it reduced Christ to the level of temporality and change.[38]

These wicked views of Arius were shocking enough for his bishop,
Alexander, to rebuke him sharply. But when Arius persisted in his
blasphemy, and even gained converts among the clergy, Alexander called
a council of Egyptian bishops which promptly outlawed the rebels. The
question was too grave to be thus dismissed, however. Arius continued
to expound his theology and, worse, to draw followers, until presently the
whole eastern Mediterranean was in turmoil. To those comfortably accustomed to the traditional view of a divine Christ, the Arians were condemned as "lawless men, enemies of Christ, teaching an apostasy which
one may justly suspect and designate as a forerunner of the Antichrist." [39]

[37] Athanasius, *Depositio Arii*, ch. II.
[38] On the Arian heresy see Duchesne, II, 100 ff.; Moeller, *History of the Christian Church:
A.D. 1-600*, pp. 382 ff. A celebrated book by a celebrity is John Henry Newman's *The
Arians of the Fourth Century* (1833). A standard study is H. M. Gwatkin's *Studies of
Arianism* (2d ed., 1900).
[39] Athanasius, *Depositio Arii*, ch. I.

Many others, however, both laymen and clergy, were drawn to support Arius' doctrine. Presently it became clear to Constantine—sole emperor, now that Licinius was disposed of—that the dispute might throw into religious chaos an empire that he had just succeeded in restoring to political tranquillity.

Therefore he called the famous council, making it very plain in his letter to both Alexander and Arius that he wished a speedy compromise of what was at best a trivial question. "For as long as you continue to contend about these small and very insignificant questions"—and this indicates the profundity of Constantine's interest in Christianity—"it is not fitting that so large a portion of God's people should be under the direction of your judgment." To "wrangle together" over trifles, he went on like a man whose patience was sorely tested, "is vulgar, and rather characteristic of childish ignorance, than consistent with the wisdom of priests and men of sense." [40] When the delegates—mainly from the East, but a few from the West—assembled in the hall of an imperial palace, the meetings were opened by the emperor himself, the better to "restore to health the system of the world" which Constantine feared was about to shatter on a negligible point of theology. [41]

As the acrimonious debates showed during the three months the council was sitting, however, the issue was not negligible. To determine the "consubstantiality" (*homoousia*) as opposed to the mere "similarity" (*homoiousia*) of Christ to the Father was the problem, and if Arius prevailed in declaring that Christ was not God the very foundation of the Church might crack and in its fall destroy the Empire. Never before or since, probably, has so much depended on construing a single letter in a single word. Arius, lean, austere, and melancholy, defended his views with a vehemence that was excelled only by Athanasius, the archdeacon whom Alexander had prudently brought along to conduct the persecution. If we may believe Socrates, the fifth-century church historian, the merits of the case were quickly apparent, and the council, "having scarcely patience to endure the hearing" of Arius' "abominable blasphemies," cast its vote against him. [42] When the delegates prepared to formulate their conclusions dogmatically, only the two bishops of Marmorica Ptolemais found, with Arius, that it was impossible to subscribe to a Trinitarian theology. For such intransigence the council anathemized

---

[40] Eusebius, *Life of Constantine*, II.71.

[41] *Ibid.*, II.65. For discussions of the council see Charles Joseph Hefele, *A History of the Christian Councils* (1894-1896), I, 262 ff.; Adolf Harnack, *Lehrbuch der Dogmengeschichte* (1888-1890), II, 224 ff.; Archibald Robertson (ed.), Athanasius' *Select Writings and Letters*, pp. xiii ff.

[42] Kidd, *Documents*, II, 10.

them and Arius, and Constantine, the secular arm, obligingly exiled them to Illyria. Further, Constantine, hoping at last for peace, ordered all the works of Arius burnt and all persons found possessing them executed. The Nicene Creed then promulgated, the delegates were entertained lavishly by the emperor with a banquet and went their ways rejoicing.[43] And why not? asks Athanasius, whose side had won. "For what does that Council lack, that anyone should seek to innovate? It is full of piety, beloved; and has filled the whole world with it. Indians have acknowledged it, and all Christians of other barbarous nations." [44]

This is a pardonable exaggeration, for, as Athanasius' own frantic exertions following the council show, the Nicene Creed did not end all controversy.[45] But it did provide a core of dogma around which a unified Church might be erected. Although Gibbon, with typical cynicism, names as a by-product of the council the "spirit of discord and inconstancy, which, in the course of a few years, erected eighteen different models of religion," [46] the Nicene Creed was the most significant formulation of dogma of the early Church.[47] For the western Church it prescribed faith in one God the Father as the absolute sum of all perfections, thus preserving the divine essence as a metaphysical absolute with no defilement. Furthermore, it confirmed the divinity of one Lord Jesus Christ—a Neoplatonic emanation of the Absolute but nonetheless His coequal in divinity: "Filium Dei unigenitum, et ex Patre natum ante omnia saecula, Lumen de Lumine, Deum verum de Deo vero, genitum, non factum, consubstantialem Patri." Through Christ as Logos all things were made, and by Christ as mediator, who became man without ceasing to be God, the divine atonement was wrought for the whole human race. Finally, the third member of the Trinity was declared to be the Holy Ghost, the giver of life who proceeds from the Father and the Son[48] but

[43] See Charles Norris Cochrane, *Christianity and Classical Culture* (1940), pp. 210 ff.—an extremely able account, to which I am much indebted.

[44] *Ad Afros Epistola Synodica*, ch. II.

[45] Before he died, Constantine recalled Arius from exile (330), and—such are the hazards of theological disputes—Athanasius (who had succeeded to the see of his patron Alexander) was exiled to Trèves in 335. The old hostility continued, even though Arianism ceased to be a threat to the Church. Athanasius, for instance, could not resist repeating some scandalous gossip about the death of Arius: God destroyed him, without benefit of communion or before he could return to the faith he had desecrated, as he was answering the "necessities of nature." And, Athanasius adds (*Ad Episcopos Aegypti,* ch. XIX), when Constantine learned this he was "struck with wonder" to find him thus convicted of perjury. On the persistence of the Arian heresy see George Park Fisher, *History of Christian Doctrine* (1909), pp. 139 ff.

[46] *The Decline and Fall of the Roman Empire,* II, 319.

[47] For the text and variants see Schaff, *The Creeds of Christendom,* I, 24-29.

[48] This "from the Son" is the notorious *Filioque* clause, an addition made at the third Council of Toledo (589) and subsequently incorporated into the Nicene Creed.

is properly worshipped and glorified together with them (*simul adoratur et conglorificatur*). Having thus stated the nature and functions of the triune God, the Creed quickly summarized the remaining articles of faith:

[Credo in] et unum, sanctam, catholicam et apostolicam ecclesiam. Confiteor unum baptisma in remissionem peccatorum; et expecto resurrectionem mortuorum, et vitam venturi saeculi. Amen.

Thus, three centuries after the crucifixion, the main lines of Christian doctrine were officially laid down. The deification of Christ was now complete, and the mystery elements preached by Paul were now codified into dogma. By the early fourth century, the unpretentious morality of the Sermon on the Mount was hopelessly outmoded. After Nicaea, a Christian was a devotee of a trinitarian mystery religion who had declared his faith in the annunciation, the passion of Christ, the resurrection, and the last judgment. He had undergone such initiatory rites as baptism and communion, and he looked forward to an eternity of bliss as the reward of his Christian life. "When Christianity came to be defined in these terms," Lewis Mumford has said, "it should have been apparent that Jesus of Nazareth was the first heretic." [49]

Indeed, even in the fourth century there were those who had to swallow their objections. Basil, for instance, admitted that the Trinitarian dogma was both incomprehensible and a contradiction in terms—but only in human terms, he adds quickly, "yet not therefore a contradiction in fact; unless indeed anyone will say that human words can express in one formula, or human thought express in one idea, the unknown and infinite God." [50] Athanasius, who knew what miracles uniformity of faith might achieve in an expanding Church, never faltered in his defense of the Creed. Forty years after the Council of Nicaea he was still urging its advantages:

In this faith, O Augustus, it is necessary that all should abide, since it is divine and apostolic, and that no one should disturb it by subtleties and logomachies, as the Arian fanatics have done, who say that the Son of God is from nothing, and that once He was not, and that He is created, and made, and changeable. [51]

Doctrinal considerations apart, the Council of Nicaea marks a significant moment in the intellectual history of Europe. It rang down the

[49] *The Condition of Man*, p. 75; cf. Hatch, *Influence of Greek Ideas and Usages upon the Christian Church*, p. 1.
[50] Quoted in Athanasius, *Select Writings*, p. 366, n. 1.
[51] Kidd, *Documents*, II, 80.

curtain with a certain theatrical flourish on a concept of nature and knowledge that had dominated pagan antiquity for nearly a thousand years. After Nicaea, it was no longer possible for Christian Europe to maintain, as the Greeks had generally maintained, the existence of two radically different kinds of reality and two kinds of knowledge available to man about them. At Nicaea there perished the Platonic notion that the realm of intelligibles (or ideas, absolutes, Forms) constituted the attainable object of rational knowledge, while the realm of sensibles constituted the object of subjective opinion.[52] No longer was it possible to believe as a Christian that rational knowledge of the highest reality was available to man through his innate rational faculty. By the doctrine of a trinitarian deity—God as the absolute, the Son as the *ratio* and mediator who links the absolute to the sensible, the Holy Ghost as the principle of divine energy and movement through which the Logos manipulates the realm of sensibles —the Church in effect abolished the dualism of two kinds of being. It legislated out of existence the concept of a rational reality discernible to reason, and substituted the single receptacle of faith. By the supreme paradox of three gods in one, of a Christ that was begotten by the Father and yet had always existed, of a God who was also man without ceasing to be God, the Nicene Creed put all experience beyond the scope of man's comprehension. Before the mystery of the Trinity, as even Aquinas was to confess, man's reason fluttered and failed.

By definition, Christ the God-man annihilated man's proudest possession, his capacity for rational knowledge. Christ as mediator relieved man of responsibility for his conduct. The Socratic dictum was overturned, and virtue was made faith. Through the Logos, God contrives salvation for sinful man, and man's only part in the transaction is to pay the debt of faith to a deity whose workings he could never understand. If you cannot understand, Augustine was to say a century later, believe in order that you may understand. For man and nature lay prostrate before an inscrutable God. As the Nicene Creed states unequivocally, from the workings of the deity are derived the structure and the operation of the sensible world: the *unus Deus* is the creator *coeli et terrae, visibilium et invisibilium*. To understand either himself or the world around him man must presume to understand a God who transcends human comprehension. And thus, as Cochrane has said, the Nicene Creed substituted for the classical approach to God through nature the Christian approach to nature through God.[53] Both the exaltation of God and the subordination of man

---

[52] See the *Timaeus*, 37-38 for a statement of this dualism.
[53] *Christianity and Classical Culture*, p. 237.

were achieved at the Council of Nicaea. Although it took Christendom a couple of generations to produce Augustine, who would mercilessly exploit the degradation of man for which the Nicene Creed provided the theoretical basis, the council inaugurated the theocratic Middle Ages. The era of a thousand years of faith began.

# XI

## AUGUSTINE AND THE MEDIEVAL VIEW OF MAN

### THE GLORY OF GOD

IF PAUL LAID THE FOUNDATION for Christianity in Europe, Augustine, Bishop of Hippo (354-430) sketched the lines that its massive structure was to take in the Middle Ages. Like all great men, Augustine could not have been born at a more appropriate time. He appeared as the spokesman for his faith at the chaotic end of the fourth century, when the values and institutions that had given coherence to the world for a thousand years were fracturing and crumbling. More than any other man of his time, he was the architect of the Christian culture that rose from the ruins of paganism.

The son of a pagan father and a Christian mother, an expensively educated teacher of classical rhetoric,[1] a high-blooded libertine, Augustine responded, during his young manhood, to the most fashionable intellectual and emotional currents of his time. Like the seeker of truth in Justin Martyr's *Dialogue with Trypho,* he passed from one allegiance to another. After a youth that combined, conventionally, education and dissipation, he was drawn to the rigors and the pageantry of Manicheism; from that he passed to an urbane philosophical skepticism, and from that to the solace of Christianity. His progress was symptomatic of an age of flight, when all men were seeking desperately a sanctuary in the midst of political, military, and intellectual anarchy. Augustine's thinking was shaped by the traditions of Latin oratory and his theology by Neoplatonism; he was more than a link between paganism and Christianity. Inheriting the

[1] The relations of Augustine, and of his age, to the intellectual heritage of antiquity have been learnedly treated by Henri-Irénée Marrou, *Saint Augustin et la fin de la culture antique* (1938). He poses (p. 390) the central problem very sharply: "Le christianisme avait été amené à prendre conscience de son opposition radicale à la civilisation grécolatine au fin de laquelle il se developpait. Mais s'il était évident qu'il fallait la condamner dans son ensemble, cette condamnation devait-elle porter sur tous ses éléments pris chacun à chacun? Et spécialement du point de vue de la culture, fallait-il renoncer à ses techniques scholaires, littéraires, scientifiques, philosophiques, oublier tout ce que contenaient ses livres, tout ce qu'enseignaient ses maîtres, et la seule Bible en main, repartir de zéro?" In spite of his denunciation of the moral and political pollution of pagan in the second book of *The City of God,* Augustine (and his great contemporary Jerome) owed more to his classical education than he would perhaps care to admit.

dogma of the early Church, he made it his career to develop theologically its implications that were to dominate men's thinking for six centuries. He formulated the medieval view of man and his relation to God.

This view, in its broadest terms, was constructed upon two cognate assumptions: the perfection of God and the imperfection of man. These notions were, of course, original neither with Augustine nor with his Church; but Augustine was a man of titanic intellect and titanic passion, and he articulated them with unrivaled force. To understand his influence on posterity we have merely to read the so-called Athanasian Creed which, within a century of his death, appeared as the monument to his theology. That "rigid system of Christianity"—which according to Gibbon "has been entertained, with public applause, and secret reluctance" [2] by the Catholic Church to our day—was not challenged by a genius comparable to Augustine until the appearance of Aquinas in the thirteenth century.

The tone of the Athanasian Creed is dogmatic and damnatory; its theology is proudly reared on the assumption of man's depravity and God's omnipotence; its strength derives from the fact of a single powerful Church; its dogma dictates belief in the great mysteries of the Trinity, the incarnation, the resurrection.

Whosoever will be saved [the famous *quicunque vult* phrase]:[3] before all things it is necessary that he hold the Catholic Faith: Which Faith except every one do keep whole and undefiled: without doubt he shall perish everlastingly. And the Catholic Faith is this: That we worship one God in Trinity, and Trinity in Unity. . . . Furthermore it is necessary to everlasting salvation: that he also believe rightly the Incarnation of our Lord Jesus Christ. . . . Perfect God: and perfect Man, of a reasonable soul and human flesh subsisting. . . . Who although he be God and Man; yet he is not two, but one Christ. . . . Who suffered for our salvation: descended into hell: rose again the third day from the dead. . . . At whose coming all men shall rise again with their bodies; And shall give account for their own works. And they that have done good shall go into life everlasting: and they that have done evil, into everlasting fire. This is the Catholic Faith: which except a man believe faithfully, he cannot be saved.[4]

From the second Gospel to the Apostles' Creed, then to the Nicene Creed, then to the Athanasian Creed the Church had made its stately progress. In the three great creeds the sword of faith had been forged for the Middle Ages. Because Augustine so truly represented his Church and impressed his personality so strongly upon its development he is the symbol

[2] III, 377.
[3] See Gibson, *The Three Creeds*, pp. 195 ff.
[4] Schaff, *The Creeds of Christendom*, II, 66 ff.

*par excellence* of the medieval mind. To understand some of his basic convictions is, in a sketch like this, a useful way to understand the centuries of men whose thinking he influenced.

The emotional progress which Augustine has described in the *Confessions* represented a search for the proper symbols in which he might express the two most passionate drives of his passionate nature: his adoration for the immaterial and the absolute, his detestation for the relative and the material. His problem was the problem that has beset all philosophers trying to adjudicate the relation of permanence and change, but he wrought his solution with a mind essentially religious rather than philosophic. That he fell so easily and so early into the crude dualism of the Manichees shows the direction of his thought: he wished to construe positive good and positive evil in the sharpest terms possible, and to give them dramatic personification. A decade later, however, it was the materialism of Manicheism that repelled him.[5] How, he then asked himself, could the good be other than immaterial? Could permanence and excellence be other than suprasensible? In Neoplatonism he found a more commodious system—a monism that elevated the good into a transcendent, nonphysical absolute and that legislated the evil of matter quite out of existence. It was in Christianity, however, that Augustine's search ended. It had all the advantages and none of the disadvantages of Neoplatonism: it deified the absolute into God; by equating matter with evil it despised both as the deprivation of being; and with an elaborate theology and eschatology it made evil man wholly dependent on God for his release from the bondage of the flesh.[6] Augustine could not rest in a Platonic dualism of Form and sensibles; he had to buttress and dramatize his convictions with the religious equipage of divinity, mystery, worship, and sin.

When, at Milan in 386, Augustine underwent his conversion, it was with the theatrical finality of Paul on the road to Damascus. As he flung himself down beneath the fig tree, crying "How long, Lord? Wilt Thou be angry for ever?" he heard the child's voice chanting "Take up and read; take up and read." And hastening to the Scriptures he opened them at random to read the words of Paul: "Not in rioting and drunkenness, not in chambering and wantonness, not in strife and envying; but put ye on the Lord Jesus Christ, and make not provision for the flesh, to fulfil the lusts thereof." In that moment he knew, as Paul had known, that all the

[5] *Conf.*, III.7 ff.
[6] See *De Gratia de Libero Arbitrio,* II.12.17; cf. Maurice de Wulf, *History of Medieval Philosophy* (1925-1926), I, 119.

gloom of doubt vanished away.[7] The long struggle between the two wills
—*illa carnalis* and *illa spiritualis*—was resolved. The intensity of this conversion—it was, of course, the ecstasy of mysticism—served not only as a
fitting climax to Augustine's passionate search for the absolute; it determined, as his subsequent writings were to show, the boundaries of his
*Weltanschauung:* the ineffable power of God, and the hideous evil of
the world, the flesh, the unsaved man.

The implications of this view are seen at once in Augustine's epistemology. It had been the great effort of Greek philosophy to analyze experience into terms of permanence and change, and to show what kind
of knowledge man might have of them. But the Nicene Creed and the
establishment of Trinitarian Christianity, by dislocating the classic dualism, had annihilated the pretentions of man's rational knowledge. Augustine's mystical apprehension of God proved to him, as it were, the
futility of seeking a rational comprehension of the absolute. As if to complete the degradation of man's proud cognitive faculty he made the highest
knowledge (the awareness of God) a matter of divine illumination. This
kind of knowledge comes to man, if it comes at all, only if God wills it:
man is the sponge who passively absorbs the revealed vision which God
grants him, not the consciously seeking rational agent who attains knowledge by his own efforts at comprehension. "Noli foras ire; in te ipsum
redi: in interiore hominen habitat veritas." Long before Descartes, Augustine stated the proposition that consciousness—specifically the consciousness of doubt, which had been so piercingly apparent to Augustine
—is the surest proof of man's identity.[8] He constructed his epistemology,
therefore, around the two irreducible factors of knowledge: the knower
and the thing known. But by making one the passive recipient of knowledge, the other the active source and object of knowledge, he undermined
the pagan foundations of pagan humanism. He relieved man of the
responsibility of achieving knowledge other than by waiting for it and
wishing for it. The Neoplatonic principle of illumination (and Augustine constantly employs the metaphor) replaces that of rational investigation. Since God, the only valid object of knowledge, is ineffably beyond
the scope of man's understanding, He can be comprehended, if at all,
only by revealing Himself to man. Piety replaces wisdom, faith replaces
comprehension, revelation replaces investigation.[9]

---

[7] *Conf.*, VIII.12.28-29; cf. Pierre de Labriolle, *History and Literature of Christianity*
(1925), pp. 401 ff.

[8] See *De Beata Vita*, ch. VII; *De Trinitate*, X.14; cf. Windelband, *History of Philosophy*,
pp. 277 ff.

[9] See *The Enchiridion*, III.2; *Conf.*, VI.5, XII.15.20.

As God is the source and object of all knowledge, he is the Neoplatonic absolute of being, goodness, and power. In the mighty *City of God,* the product of his last years, Augustine gave a definitive statement to the theocentric interpretation of experience which shaped medieval thought. In the face of the barbarian invasions which had overrun even Rome itself, Augustine gathered his resources of learning, piety, and rhetoric to declare the fact of a theocratic universe—one created and directed by the inscrutable will of God, for Whose purposes all events move to their appointed ends and Whose glory all creation conspires to demonstrate. Incidentally, *The City of God* is Augustine's theodicy, both his answer to the problem of evil and his affirmation of an omnipotent deity by whose will even the wicked world and sinful man are put to glorious uses.

It must have been very early in his career on this planet that man recognized the primary and inexorable fact of life: that the processes of birth, life, and death involve an appalling amount of suffering. Although primitive men have always very forthrightly attributed the evil in the world to their malicious deities, their more sophisticated brethren have had more difficulty in reconciling the existence of evil with the concept of an omnipotent and benevolent God. For Christians, particularly, the question of God's responsibility for the deplorable affairs of this planet has always been urgent. *Si deus bonus est, unde malum?* In spite of the popularity of the Stoic argument from design—that in a teleological universe all apparent evil is actual good in the cosmic plan—Hume's statement of the dilemma is still pertinent: "Epicurus's old questions are yet unanswered. Is he [God] willing to prevent evil, but not able? Then he is impotent. Is he both able and willing? Whence then is evil?" [10]

The Greeks had resolved the problem of evil into terms of permanence and change. In general, their position was that matter, which is unstable, is evil; that reason, which enjoys an Eleatic permanence, is good. Evil is not a creation of man's perverted will but merely a characteristic of matter. [11] Following Parmenides, they had consistently held matter in opprobrium as the very antithesis of reason, Idea, Form, conceptual reality. [12] In Neoplatonism, an earth-fleeing philosophy, the derogation of matter had reached its apex—and it was from Neoplatonism that Augustine learned most about the perfection of pure insubstantial being, about the wickedness (that is, the nonentity) of matter. "For in Matter," said Plotinus, "we have no mere absence of means of strength; it is utter

[10] Quoted by Carl Becker, *The Heavenly City of the Eighteenth-Century Philosophers* (1932), p. 68.

[11] See Reinhold Niebuhr, *The Nature and Destiny of Man* (1941), I, 246.

[12] See Werner Jaeger, *Aristotle,* ch. VIII *passim.*

destitution—of sense, of virtue, of beauty, of pattern, of Ideal principle, of quality. This is surely ugliness, utter disgracefulness, unredeemed evil." [13]

This view of matter resolves a dualism into a monism: evil, that is, matter, becomes of no consequence metaphysically because it has no existence. Anything that can rightly be said to exist exists by participating in the very source and center of being; and whatever does not has no existence. Matter, unillumined by being, is uncreated, and its evil is of deprivation and deficiency. Nothing was easier, therefore, than for Augustine to substitute *God* for *being*: God is exonerated, and the palpable evil of the world is such not because He is impotent to banish it but because He does not flood it with His goodness. Evil is, consequently, nothing more than the absence of good (*privatio boni*); conversely, if things *are*, they in some measure participate in the excellence of their creator.

All which is corrupted is deprived of good. But if they be deprived of all good, they will cease to be. For if they be, and cannot be at all corrupted, they will become better, because they shall remain incorruptibly. And what more monstrous than to assert that those things which have lost all their goodness are made better? Therefore, if they shall be deprived of all good, they shall no longer be. So long, therefore, as they are, they are good; therefore whatsoever is, is good. That evil, then, which I sought whence it was, is not any substance; for were it a substance, it would be good. For either it would be an incorruptible substance, and so a chief good, or a corruptible substance, which unless it were good it could not be corrupted. I perceived, therefore, and it was made clear to me, that Thou didst make all things good, nor is there any substance at all that was not made by Thee; and because all that Thou hast made are not equal, therefore all things are; because individually they are good, and altogether very good, because our God made all things very good. [14]

Whether or not one can follow the sinuous logic of this argument, he can see its intention and its implication: God has created the universe and it is altogether very good. This conviction, as developed so gigantically in *The City of God,* provided an answer for all of Augustine's problems. Given the transcendent and absolute goodness of God, and the potential goodness of all His creation, the world—wicked though it be—becomes the theatre wherein is enacted the majestic working out of God's purposes.

It is true that wicked men do many things contrary to God's will; but so great is His wisdom and power, that all things which seem adverse to His purpose do still tend towards those just and good ends and issues which He Himself has foreknown. [15]

---

[13] *Enneads,* II.4.16.

[14] *Conf.,* VII.11.18.

[15] *The City of God,* XXII.2.

There is evil, of course: one cannot confuse the heavenly and the earthly cities. But the evil is not of God's creation, for that is unthinkable; it is of man's perverted will, and thus becomes the object of God's ameliorating providence. As Origen, another Neoplatonist, had long before said, "it is the mind of each individual which is the cause of the evil which arises in him, and this evil in the abstract." [16] *Omnes nihil aliud quam voluntas sunt.* Thus it was from the exercise of his will, directed away from God and towards the glorification of himself, that Adam sinned and polluted all his race. Where God is not, evil is; and although God employs it for His own deific purposes, He cannot be held responsible for its origin.

The sins of men and angels do nothing to impede the "great works of the Lord which accomplish His will." For He who by His providence and omnipotence distributes to every one his own portion, is able to make good use not only of the good, but also of the wicked.[17]

Thus Augustine gradually centered upon his conception of a theocratic universe. It was a universe demonstrably filled with evil and stained by the wicked fruits of man's perverted will, but none the less a universe established and controlled for His own inscrutable ends by God. With far more conviction than Alexander Pope, Augustine could say, Whatever is, is right.

Accordingly, two cities have been formed by two loves: the earthly by the love of self, even to the contempt of God; the heavenly by the love of God, even to the contempt of self. The former, in a word, glories in itself, the latter in the Lord. For the one seeks glory from men; but the greatest glory of the other is God, the witness of conscience. The one lifts up its head in its own glory; the other says to its God, "Thou art my Glory, and the lifter up of mine head." . . . The one delights in its own strength, represented in the persons of its rulers; the other says to its God, "I will love Thee, O Lord, my strength." . . . But in the other city there is no human wisdom, but only godliness, which offers due worship to the true God, and looks for its reward in the society of the saints, of holy angels as well as holy men, "that God may be all in all."[18]

### THE INFAMY OF MAN

Augustine's conception of a theocentric universe was one of his legacies to the Middle Ages. Another was his atrabiliar view of the human race.

---

[16] *De Principiis,* II.10.15.
[17] *The City of God,* XIV.27; cf. XIV.3 and Athanasius, *Contra Gentes,* I.3.7: man's wickedness is not substantial, but the result of a perverted free choice.
[18] *The City of God,* XIV.28.

The two were complementary, for like all theists Augustine was compelled to find a scapegoat to bear the guilt of the world's evil. It was inevitable that the doctrine of original sin, or something very like it, should be employed in fixing the responsibility on man. Cardinal Newman, who so often reminds one of Augustine, has stated admirably in his *Apologia* the generic problem that must have confronted Augustine:

*If* there be a God, *since* there is a God, the human race is implicated in some terrible aboriginal calamity. It is out of joint with the purposes of its creator. This is a fact, a fact as true as the fact of its existence; and thus the doctrine of what is theologically called original sin becomes to me almost as certain as that the world exists and as the existence of God.

Just as Augustine loved God, he hated man. What became a doctrine began as an attitude, for do not all doctrines represent merely the effort to verbalize and rationalize that which is held emotionally? In the passionate heaving of his Latin we catch something of Augustine's violence when he contemplated the human race.

Quid amor ipse tot rerum uanarum adque noxiarum et ex hoc mordaces curae, perturbationes, maerores, formidines, insana gaudia, discordiae, lites, bella, insidiae, iracundiae, inimicitiae, fallacia, adulatio, fraus, furtum, rapina, perfidia, superbia, ambitio, inuidentia, homocidia, parricidia, crudelitas, saeuitia, nequitia, luxuria, petulantia, impudentia, impudicitia, fornicationes, adulteria. . . . Verum haec hominum sunt malorum, ab illa tamen erroris et peruersi amoris radice uenientia, cum qua omnis filius Adam nascitur.[19]

The theological justification for this wrathful rejection of the race occupied much of Augustine's life, but his labor was not in vain. He established a view of humanity that was official during the Middle Ages, and that, after Calvin's restatement, has not yet run its course in the modern world.

Augustine's detestation of his kind seems to have begun in his revulsion from the brutal fact of man's carnal nature and his carnal desires. By his own perhaps highly colored confession a shameless profligate in his youth, he was both tortured and mastered by sex. Here, as elsewhere, he is Paul's spiritual heir. Although the Greeks had shared a general distrust of matter, it was as the object of uncertain knowledge; otherwise they adjusted themselves quite comfortably to the facts of life. The body and its physical well-being were legitimate objects of concern, as the ethics of humanism make clear. It remained for the mystery religions and Neoplatonism, in their flight from the world, to view man's physical equip-

[19] *The City of God*, XXII.22.

ment and needs with abhorrence. The asceticism that was directly counter to pagan humanism became, inevitably, a part of Jesus' teaching. Although he enjoyed himself in a perfectly human way at the marriage feast in Cana, he insisted that man should deny himself. When tempted by Satan, he renounced the world and the flesh—a renunciation that in his later ministry was developed into the paradox that a man must lose his life to save it. The Pauline development of this pronouncement has never lost its influence: it is to Paul's good offices that we mainly owe the long career of asceticism in the Christian tradition, for between the soul and the body he never compromised. Adopting the common mystery religion notion that the soul, itself incorporeal, is subject to spiritual influences, he peopled the universe with forces that assaulted and battered the soul through its weaker vessel, the body.[20] Refining the crude demonology of evil forces rampant in the cause of evil, he consolidated them all in the concept of sin. Sin is the villain of the Pauline drama. It thwarts the human personality, for by seducing the body it destroys the soul.

Paul feared and was fascinated by sex as ardently as he desired redemption. Sex was of the body, and in the body "dwelleth no good thing." The doctrine is hammered relentlessly. "For to be carnally minded is death; but to be spiritually minded is life and peace." Those who live by the flesh "cannot please God." Salvation depends on necessary faith, and faith on the presence of the Holy Ghost, the mystical indwelling force accessible to the soul.[21] The sonorous rhetoric of the epistle to the Galatians is clear and damning:

This I say then, Walk in the Spirit, and ye shall not fulfil the lust of the flesh. For the flesh lusteth against the Spirit, and the Spirit against the flesh: and these are contrary the one to the other: so that ye cannot do the things that ye would.[22]

Everywhere there are Augustinian analogies. Listen to the agonized *Confessions:*

But I, miserable young man, supremely miserable even in the very outset of my youth, had entreated chastity of Thee, and said, "Grant me chastity and continency, but not yet." For I was afraid lest Thou shouldest hear me soon, and soon deliver me from the disease of concupiscence, which I desired to have satisfied rather than extinguished.[23]

[20] See Harnack, *The Mission and Expansion of Christianity,* I, 31 ff.
[21] See Romans, VIII:2; Galatians, V:16-17; cf. Augustine, *Conf.,* VIII.11.
[22] V:16-17; cf. Romans, VI and VIII *passim.*
[23] VIII.7.17.

There is something rather pathetic in the way in which Augustine, old and gnarled in his struggles as a militant Christian, tortured himself so persistently with the problem of sex. "Is not the life of man upon earth a temptation, and that without intermission?" [24] Long after he had put aside his concubine and renounced the flesh-pots he continued to wonder why God had not taken other means of perpetuating the race. "Who does not know what passes between husband and wife that children may be born?" [25] Although he tried hard to tolerate the necessity of conjugal love, his assent, like Paul's, was grudging: he would concur with Jerome's terse decree that virginity is wheat, wedlock barley, and fornication cow-dung.[26] Before the advent of Christ, Augustine decided, marriage was obviously necessary "for the purpose of begetting a people [that is, the Jews] for God." But since, the duty "has ceased to be indispensable," there being quite enough sinners at large already for "spiritual regeneration, from whatever quarter they derive their natural birth." [27] And as for heaven, there sex will be no problem. There will be males and females, but "the female members shall remain adapted not to the old uses, but to a new beauty, which, so far from provoking lust, now extinct, shall excite praise to the wisdom and clemency of God, who both made what was not and delivered from corruption what He made." [28]

In short, Augustine found symbolized in man's bodily function his generic corruption. Perhaps much of the emotional fervor of his religion derived from the sublimation of his own passionate sexual nature.[29] Even his religious imagery is erotic: Continency appears as a nubile woman, "not barren, but a fruitful mother of children of joys, by Thee, O Lord, her Husband." [30] Because Augustine's God in an incorporeal absolute, the

[24] *Conf.,* X.30.39.
[25] *The City of God,* XIV.18.
[26] *Letters,* no. XLVIII; cf. *Against Jovinianus,* I.7.
[27] *Of Marriage and Concupiscence,* I.14.
[28] *The City of God,* XXII.17. Another pretty problem (*ibid.,* XIV.23-24) was that without Adam's fall there would have been no sexuality, and thus sin was necessary that the race might fall into lust and thus ultimately propagate the saints. This argument is obviously absurd, says Augustine, for we must believe that the genitals, like all members obedient to the will, could "have discharged the function of generation, though lust, the award of disobedience, had been wanting." If Adam had not fallen, then there would have been no struggle between an impotent will and lust as now, and "the field of generation should have been sown by the organ created for this purpose, as the earth is sown by hand."
[29] Thus Werner Achelis, *Die Deutung Augustins* (1921), pp. 15-16: "Dem anzutretender Nachweis sei kurz vorausgeschicht, dass die in den Konfessionen berührten sexuellen Verhältnisse, besonders aber die mehrjährigen Konkubinate, die in theologischen Lehrbüchern, wie in den kurzen Einleitungen zu Augustin, als Unzucht schlimmster Art dargestellt zu werden pflegen, in Wirklichkeit für die damalige Zeit nicht das geringste Anstössige besassen." [30] *Conf.,* VIII.12.27.

chastity which He expressly commands[31] insures that a good Christian will deny the flesh.[32] This fierce asceticism was, probably, the earliest and most dramatic aspect of Augustine's general attack on man's inherent depravity; but on the emotional attitude it suggests he built a theological edifice as vast and complicated as a medieval cathedral. The poignancy of his struggle to conquer the flesh became the poignancy of his dark, sin-ridden theology by which he completed his glorification of God and his indictment of man.

In this matter as in so many others, however, Augustine reflects the attitudes of his age. Obviously there was an intense personal element in his preoccupation with sex, but in the last days of the Empire there was apparent a general strategy of retreat (as Lewis Mumford has called it) from all things of this life and this earth. One of the most dramatic manifestations of this cultural movement was monasticism: it was an institutionalized expression of man's loathing for what was proper to man, a denial of what modern vitalists have taught us to worship as the Life Force. "What, indeed," asks Gregory the Great (who had his own troubles in getting monks to remember their vows) "is a monk's state of life but a despising of the world?"[33]

The aversion from the obvious and deplorable fact of sex was one of the fundamental motives in the monastic movement. The emotional quality of Christian asceticism is nowhere seen more clearly than in the letters of Jerome. Sitting alone in a parching desert, he remembered the pleasures of Rome; filthy from not bathing, clothed in rags, emaciated and ill, surrounded by beasts and scorpions, he thought of shapely virgins and the fire of his lust would almost consume him.

Helpless, I cast myself at the feet of Jesus, I watered them with my tears, I wiped them with my hair: and then I subdued my rebellious body with weeks of abstinence.

And—as he thought—he won his struggle against life. His oratory was the mountain and the cliff, and at last the angelic hosts would come and sing of his victory over the sinful flesh.[34]

The cult of chastity to which Jerome was a convert had impeccable sponsors. Did not Paul condone matrimony only with reluctance, and had not Origen castrated himself?[35] As Gibbon has said, "It was with

---

[31] *Conf.* X.30.40.

[32] *Conf.*, X.23.32. See Edward Motley Pickman, *The Mind of Latin Christendom* (1937), I, 67 ff.

[33] *Selected Epistles*, XII.24.          [34] *Letters*, no. XXII.

[35] Origen's voluntary castration was, in the judgment of Eusebius (*Ecclesiastical History*, VI.8) an indiscretion that "gave abundant proof of an immature and youthful mind."

the utmost difficulty that ancient Rome could support the institution of six vestals; but the primitive church was filled with a great number of persons of either sex, who had devoted themselves to the profession of professional chastity." [36]

But it was not only the denial of the flesh that the early ascetics demanded: even reason, as a human faculty, was suspect. Whatever was human was vile. Inevitably, then, the development of monasticism embodied the principle of symbolic suicide. From the time of St. Anthony, who for twenty years secluded himself in a cave to nourish his spirit and chastise his body, devout persons had assumed a set of rigorous taboos through which they hoped to slough off their earthly part.[37] The *regula* of Pachomius and then of Saint Basil, in the fourth century, formulated the ascetic doctrine for the Eastern Church; in the West the movement was consummated by the administrative and executive ability of Saint Benedict. And although during the Middle Ages the monasteries were a refuge from a turbulent world, and maintained, after their fashion, the tradition of literacy, the monks were essentially negativists.[38] In spite of the elaborate nomenclature of a "father" God and his children, and of holy men as fathers ministering to their spiritual children, the monks persisted in denying the indispensable force necessary for the perpetuation of life on the planet. From the beginning, the monastic movement expressed a profound *contemptu mundi*. Contemplation and retreat excused the ascetic from the necessity of moral conduct. The vows of poverty, chastity, and obedience in effect denied three of man's main obligations—to his physical welfare, to his family, and to his political group. As a repudiation of all secular and social responsibilities, monasticism was the Church's answer to the humanism of Greece.[39]

But the Church had to evolve a theological sanction for its degradation

---

[36] *The Decline and Fall of the Roman Empire*, I, 550; cf. III, 520, for Gibbon's general evaluation of the monastic movement.

[37] See Ernst Troeltsch, *The Social Teaching of the Christian Churches* (1931), I, 102 ff., 237 ff.

[38] By the ninth century, monasticism had become venal and corrupt, and an institution shamelessly used for political purposes. Hence the great reforms. In 910 Berno established the House of Cluny, and in 1003 Peter Damian reformed the Augustinian order. Notably ascetic and severe, as if in reaction to the laxity of the older orders, were the Carthusians (established in 1086) and the Cistercians (established in 1098). For a learned and charming essay on the corruption and scandals of late medieval monasticism see G. G. Coulton, "The Monastic Legend," *Ten Medieval Studies* (1930), pp. 1-29; cf. "The Truth about the Monasteries," *ibid.*, pp. 84-107.

[39] See Kenneth Burke, *Attitudes towards History*, I, 67, n.; I, 90 ff. For a defense of monasticism on this point see Adolf Harnack, *Monasticism* (1913), p. 13; cf. Herbert B. Workman, *The Evolution of the Monastic Creed* (1913), pp. 29 ff.

of the whole human race. Orphism had accounted for man's natural depravity as the stain of his Titanic ancestors; similarly, Christianity employed the adamic myth of Judaism. In the seventeenth century, when theology had once more become the subject of speculation, Robert Burton gave a pointed explanation of the melancholic doctrine of original sin: Adam's disobedience had led to "that general corruption of mankind, as from a fountain flowed all bad inclinations, and actual transgressions, which cause our several calamities inflicted upon us for our sins." [40] Man is the child of Adam, said Bossuet more curtly: "that is his crime." Since the Old Testament had attached no doctrinal significance to the Adamic myth, Paul's development of its implications derived chiefly from hints in rabbinical and apocalyptic literature. But with Paul, as four centuries later with Augustine, the impulse for theological explanation came mainly from a sense of sin;[41] they both generalized for the human race from their own self-indictments. Paul's epistles soon acquired divine sanction, of course, and on the basis of his ejaculatory theology Augustine erected his massive doctrine of original sin.

Its premises are clear enough in Paul: "wherefore, as by one man sin entered into the world, and death by sin; and so death passed upon all men, for that all have sinned." [42] Man, inherently depraved, can hope for salvation only through the vicarious atonement of Christ and through the faith which is possible only by the gift of grace. "That as sin hath reigned unto death, even so might grace reign through righteousness unto eternal life by Jesus Christ our Lord." [43] Fathers like Justin Martyr, Origen, and Tertullian had failed to exploit Paul's theory, but Augustine gloried in its implications. Superbly ambivalent, it possessed every advantage: it glorified God while it degraded man; it put squarely on man's shoulders the responsibility for evil, and it revealed yet another facet of God's perfection by dramatizing his attribute of compassion. In Augustine's development, the doctrines of original sin and grace are mutually dependent: without man's sin there would be no occasion for grace, and without grace the whole human race would be hopelessly lost. For to Augustine, Adam was a kind of Platonic *eidos*—the Form of all humanity—and thus every man's share in Adam's sin became unarguable. Adam's guilt provided a dramatic justification for the damnation of all his posterity.[44] Moreover, Adam's sin was precisely that most heinous in the sight

---

[40] *The Anatomy of Melancholy* (Bohn's Standard Library, 1896), I, 150.

[41] Romans, VII:17, 21; cf. McGiffert, *Christianity in the Apostolic Age,* pp. 123 ff.

[42] Romans, V:12; cf. I Corin., XV:22.

[43] Romans, V:21. On the alleged Orphic correspondences see Macchioro, *From Orpheus to Paul,* pp. 191 ff.; Reinach, *Orpheus,* p. 88.

[44] See Boas, *The Major Traditions of European Philosophy,* p. 117.

of God: it was the sin of disobedience, which by nature violated the omniscience and omnipotence of God, and, as it were, presumed to elevate
man as a rival to God. Obedience, as Augustine made clear, is "the
mother and guardian of all the virtues in the reasonable creature, which
was so created that submission is advantageous to it, while the fulfilment
of its own will in preference to the Creator's is destruction."[45] Thus
Adam, setting against the will of God the fulfillment of his own will,
chose the disobedience that brought to him and all his race damnation.

The two cardinal facts of man's relation to God are, then, suggested
by the two mighty doctrines of original sin and of divine grace. Man has
sinned, and sinned of his own free will; therefore his responsibility is
complete and his punishment is merited. But God in His infinite mercy
has turned evil to good, as is His wont: by pouring the gift of grace,
totally undeserved, on sinful man, and by appointing His Son as the redeemer of the race, He has snatched man from the fire of his own destruction. Between them, these two doctrines symbolize the gap between
the humanistic and the Christian views of man. In one, he is a potentially
good creature, a rational animal capable of high knowledge and autonomous well-being. In the other, he is the fallen creature enveloped in
aboriginal sin against God Himself, impotent to save himself from the ruin
which is his generic mark, and dependent for succor on the unmerited
compassion of an outraged deity. His clearest sign is his depravity; his
greatest need is for redemption.[46]

Augustine's radical departure from the humanistic tradition is apparent
in his substitution of will for reason in his hierarchy of value. As the
Trinitarian dogma of Nicaea had announced, the Christian ethic was to
deify mystery and to chasten man's presumptuous claim of rational knowledge—a program with which Augustine was in complete agreement. For
him, will, not reason, is the dominant force in the universe, and God
Himself, the sum of all absolutes, is the absolute will. Like man, He is
a creature of will, but His will is *ipso facto* for good while man's is ordinarily for evil.[47] What God wills must be good because He wills it,

---

[45] *The City of God*, XIV.12.
[46] On the element of redemption in Augustinian theology see Rashdall, *The Idea of
Atonement in Christian Theology*, pp. 330 ff.; cf. Toynbee, "The Sense of Sin," *A Study
of History*, V, 442 ff.
[47] Augustine's insistence on the role of will finds expression in his rejection of Stoic apathy.
He urges not the suppression of passion—for that would be a denial of life—but the effort
to direct the will (stirred by appetite) towards proper objects. "In our ethics," he says
(*The City of God*, IX.5), "we do not so much inquire whether a pious soul is angry, as
why he is angry." After all, Christ was righteously indignant when he drove the money-
lenders from the temple. If the will is proper, the resulting passions "will be not merely
blameless, but even praiseworthy" (*The City of God*, XIV.6). Citizens of the City of God

not because it is rational: sovereignty supplants intelligence. In Greek thought, virtue is a form of knowledge; the universe is essentially rational and man may, by knowing it rationally, live the good life. Man's true sovereignty is to act rationally. But with the triumph of Christianity this interpretation of experience wavered and fell. The universe became the creation of an inscrutable and suprarational deity who desired not comprehension but worship. His preëminence depended not on the sovereignty of His reason, but on the sovereignty of His power.[48]

It is this glorification of will that makes possible the doctrine of original sin. Man is evil because he willed to disobey God; he may attain unmerited redemption because God wills to give him grace—not, as Augustine insists, because it is rational.

And the kingdom of death so reigned over men, that the deserved penalty of sin would have hurled all headlong even into the second death, of which there is no end, had not the undeserved grace of God saved some therefrom.[49]

Adam sinned when he was free to choose either good (obedience) or evil (disobedience), but "not without reward if he willed the former, and not without punishment if he willed the latter."[50] The essential fact is, however, that his sin was an error of will, not judgment. Because he of course had freedom of choice—otherwise "both punishment and reward would be unjust"[51]—his evil was "not a substance, but a perversion of the will, bent aside from Thee, O God, the Supreme Substance, towards these lower things, and casting out its bowels, and swelling outwardly."[52]

If, then, it is by a perversion of his indisputably free will that man has sinned, it is by the exercise of God's will that he may be saved from the consequences of sin. The gift of grace is the supreme example of God's sovereignty. Without it man is lost, but with it he attains faith, and through faith, salvation. "The spirit of grace, therefore, causes us to have faith, in order that through faith we may, on praying for it, obtain the ability to do what we are commanded."[53] Thus, the fact that it is impossible for man to obey God's will without grace demonstrates, to Augustine's entire satisfaction, the weakness and depravity of the race.

may with propriety "both fear and desire, and grieve and rejoice"—fear divine wrath, desire eternal life, grieve for sinners, rejoice at the hope of salvation (*The City of God*, XIV.9).

[48] See Boas, *The Major Traditions of European Philosophy*, p. 120.
[49] *The City of God*, XIV.1.
[50] *The Enchiridion*, ch. CV; cf. ch. XXXII.
[51] *De Gratia et Libero Arbitrio*, II.1.3.
[52] *Conf.*, VII.16.22.
[53] *De Gratia et Libero Arbitrio*, ch. XXVIII.

His weakness thus proved, man may then "resort to the Saviour, by whose healing the will may be able to do what in its feebleness it found impossible." [54]

As if to dramatize the absolute sovereignty of God's will Augustine developed from a few phrases of Paul's the doctrine of predestination. Although Adam sinned from the perverted use of his free will, God willed that he should do so. Adam's only freedom was freedom to choose evil, and by his sin the free will of all later men is preordained to evil. Adam alone enjoyed a genuine alternative, but even it was merely theoretical since God had eliminated the possibility of a good choice. That Adam had free will despite God's foreknowledge of the event is, as Augustine admits, a "question of such obscurity that I can neither bring it home to the intelligence of other people, or understand it myself." [55] But its very mystery commends it: because it baffles human intelligence, it is divine.

Now, against the sacrilegious and impious darings of reason, we assert both that God knows all things before they come to pass, and that we do by our free will whatever we know and feel to be done by us only because we will it. [56]

By this mental gymnastic, Augustine is able both to place full responsibility for sin on man and to preserve unimpaired God's sovereign control over the course of events. From the beginning of time each act in the cosmic drama had been willed by God: Adam's sin, God's mercy, and man's redemption. But to demonstrate beyond question the sovereignty of God and the impotence of man, Augustine insists on the fact of election. Certain chosen spirits are elected for salvation, others for damnation. Nothing could be more arbitrary and deific. Since the whole race is sunk in sin, it is an act of magnificent sovereignty for God to name some—no less polluted by original sin than the others—as the objects of irresistible grace. But Paul himself was Augustine's authority. Had not he spoken of that happy "remnant" saved by the "election of grace?" [57]

Will any man dare to say that God did not foreknow those to whom He would give to believe, or whom He would give to His Son, that of them He should lose none? And certainly, if He foreknew these things, He as certainly foreknew His own kindness, wherewith He condescends to deliver us. This is the predestination of the saints—nothing else; to wit, the foreknowledge and the preparation of God's

---

[54] *The Letters*, no. CXLV.
[55] *On the Soul and Its Origin*, IV.16.
[56] *The City of God*, V.9.
[57] Romans, II:5; cf. I Peter, I:2.

kindness, whereby they are most certainly delivered, whoever they are that are delivered.[58]

The Greeks had accepted the notion of fate (*nemesis*) and had erected a great dramatic literature around it, but for them fate was the inexorable working out of cause and effect; it proved the fact of a rational moral order in the universe. Augustine preserved the idea of *nemesis,* along with the Stoic idea of providence, but he called it predestination and he made it the suprarational manifestation of God's inscrutable will. In a theocentric universe it could scarcely be otherwise.

The triumph of Augustinian theology was marked by its victorious encounter with the Pelagian heresy. When Pelagius came out of the north to maintain, against the Bishop of Hippo, the inherent dignity of man and to exonerate the race from Adam's guilt, Augustine girded his loins for the last and greatest of his doctrinal wars. He had fought the Manicheans, he had fought the Donatists, and in his last years he hurled all his titanic energies against the "most fatal dogma" that man is innately good; that he rationally exercises his free will upon genuine alternatives; that each man is responsible only for his own sins, and not for the Adamic sin of the race. But Pelagius was no unworthy opponent. "What blind folly!" he exclaims in a letter of A.D. 414:

What rash profanity. We make the God of knowledge guilty of twofold ignorance: of not knowing what He has made [i.e. sinful man], and of not knowing what He has commanded. As if, in forgetfulness of human frailty, which He made, He had laid upon men commandments which they could not bear; and at the same time (oh, the shame of it!) we ascribe unrighteousness to the Just One, and cruelty to the Holy One, first by complaining that He has commanded something impossible, and next by thinking that a man will be condemned by Him for things that he could not help; so that (sacrilegious it is even to hint it), God seems to have been seeking not so much our salvation as our punishment.[59]

But Augustine's atrabiliar and theocratic theology prevailed against all such objections. As Jerome, his great contemporary put it, if man's will were free, as Pelagius said, then man would not need God, would not pray. For the Pelagians need no external help: "away with fasting, away with every form of self-restraint." [60] Although Jerome grants the diffi-

[58] Kidd, *Documents,* II, 244-45. Cf. *On the Predestination of the Saints,* ch. XI: "Many hear the word of truth; but some believe, while others contradict. Therefore the former will to believe; the latter do not will. . . . But since in some the will is prepared by the Lord, in others it is not prepared, we must assuredly be able to distinguish what comes from God's mercy, and what from his judgment."

[59] Kidd, *Documents,* II, 161-62; on the Pelagian heresy see Duchesne, II, 143 ff.

[60] *Letters,* no. CXXXIII.

culties of reconciling Augustinian free will with original sin, he sweeps them aside. To seek to limit the inscrutable ways of God by criteria of human reason is to fall "in a deep abyss of blasphemy." [61] It was this enthronement of faith that was to dominate the Middle Ages. At the Council of Orange (529) the Augustinian triumph over Pelagius was made official. "Whoever asserts that the transgression of Adam" injured merely himself and not his posterity, or denies that both the body and soul of all men are irrevocably stained with sin, "wrongs God and contradicts the Apostle." [62] The twenty-five articles of Augustinian theology decreed by the bishops at Orange were confirmed by Boniface II in 530, and the sway of Augustine over the medieval Church was acknowledged.

GOD AND MAN

In order to justify the title of this chapter it now remains to indicate some of Augustine's influence on the medieval Church. It is of course an absurd simplification to say that only Augustine shaped the medieval Christian view of man. The seven centuries between him and Aquinas produced Erigena and Abelard, Bonaventura and the Victorines, Gregory the Great and Charlemagne. But by and large, the attitudes around which the medieval Church erected its dogma and its institutions were the attitudes that Augustine, at the opening of the Middle Ages, had most passionately defended. Mr. Whitehead has spoken of the "fundamental assumptions" unconsciously held by men of various schools of thought in a given epoch.[63] It is the thesis of this chapter that some of the most important assumptions of this sort current between the sixth and the twelfth centuries had been most powerfully formulated by Augustine. Certainly, the influence of no single man was greater than that exerted by the Bishop of Hippo. As Paschasius Radbert, speaking for the ninth century, said, *Augustinum quem contradicere fas non est.*[64]

Reduced to their simplest terms, the two fundamental assumptions derived from Augustine that formed the warp and woof of medieval thought were 1) the assumption of man's weakness and 2) the assumption of God's omnipotence. Upon the first was built the institution of the Holy Catholic Church as the indispensable agent of salvation; upon the

[61] Jerome, *Against the Pelagians*, bk. II.

[62] Kidd, *Documents*, II, 334; cf. Romans, V:12. The Pelagian heresy had been formally condemned at Carthage in 412, at Ephesus in 431. See Henry Hart Milman, *History of Latin Christianity* (1883), I, 142, 163-64.

[63] *Science and the Modern World*, p. 71.

[64] Quoted by Reginald Lane Poole, *Illustrations of the History of Medieval Thought* (1884), p. 49, n. 23; cf. John Neville Figgis, *The Political Aspects of S. Augustine's 'City of God'* (1921), pp. 81 ff.

second was built the notion of a theocentric (and theocratic) universe in which everything existed for the fulfillment of God's will. We must now examine their implications in some detail.

It might be thought that Augustine's epistemology would lead to a highly individualistic kind of religion. The intuitive and suprarational apprehension of deity which he himself enjoyed was, however, not the kind of religious experience that he was permitted to recommend for others. It is one of the paradoxes of history that Augustine, having attained his revelation on such intimate and personal terms, should devote the rest of his life and all his genius towards strengthening institutional Christianity. He made it his career to formulate the doctrine of the Western Church; instead of becoming one of the great mystics he became one of the great organizers of prescriptive and compulsory Christianity. A mighty disputant who would crush heresy as he would a scorpion, he recognized the necessity of formulating the uniform creed which a powerful Church demanded. In each of his great campaigns he strove to make salvation a matter of uniformity of doctrine, not of personal intuition. In spite of all the latent individualism of his epistemology, the effect of his labors was to make individualism virtually impossible during the Middle Ages.

The reason for this shift of the basis of religious experience was the fact of man's weakness and sin. As Seneca had long before suggested,[65] man had originally been good, and the clearest proof that he is no longer so is the existence of coercive laws and institutions. This notion, translated into terms of Christian theology and developed by Augustine, was dominant throughout the Middle Ages and beyond. The fifth-century Athenians had recognized the distinction between nature (*physis*) and convention (*nomos*), but most of them had maintained, against the Skeptics, that law was natural, not conventional, just as reason is natural. Augustine, however, shifted the emphasis: man in a state of nature (that is, without grace) is incorrigibly bad, having fallen from his pristine virtue; therefore the existence of conventional institutions (like the Church, like the state) is necessary, both as a result of sin and a remedy for sin.[66] The Church and the state, in a theocratic universe, could only be construed as coercive institutions made necessary by the universal depravity resulting from man's fall. Consequently, obedience to such divinely sanctioned institutions became man's duty. There are powers that be, Paul had said; and if there are, the medieval Church inferred,

[65] *Epis.*, XC.4 ff.
[66] See Carlyle, *A History of Medieval Political Theory in the West*, V, 441 ff.

they exist to work out God's purposes. Therefore, man's role is submission. If there are inequalities and injustices, if there are masters and slaves, we can only accept them as factors in God's program for the regeneration of the human race.[67] The enormity of man's offense against God justifies whatever apparent miseries and superimposed authorities he is compelled to submit to.

To achieve salvation, then, the individual surrenders to the Church all his religious prerogatives. Faith, the key to Augustine's thought, means a willing suspension of individualism. *Ex fide vivimus, ambulamus per fidem.* If we cannot understand the mystery of the Trinity, we can—and must—accept it none the less. Contemplation and devotion and submission are man's highest functions, for the baleful effort to investigate, to question, to come to conclusions on the basis of human reason is both useless and impious. Man can know only what God chooses to reveal to him, and His Church is the sole channel and repository of revelation. In the ninth and tenth centuries, intellection for its own sake virtually disappeared, at least in the monasteries where literate men gathered. In the celebration of the holy offices and the sacraments a candidate for the City of God might very well fill his waking hours with the institutionalized devotion of matins, lauds, prime, terce, sext, nones, vespers, and complines. For the brethren it was these holy duties, for the laymen it was the prescribed and uncritical acceptance of the creeds and the observance of the sacraments wherein lay salvation. If the highly organized Church dreamed of by Augustine and wrought by Gregory the Great was, as it claimed, a redemptive agency, then it was imperative that it hold the exclusive franchise for redemption. Salvation is made possible only through the gift of grace and the faith in the vicarious atonement of Christ, of course; but these requisites were in the keeping of the Church, and therefore an unquestioning acceptance of its creeds and a faithful observance of its sacraments could insure the bounty of salvation.

When the Church institutionalized faith, it institutionalized ethics. Whereas heresy had been unknown in the ancient world, the medieval man could not live save in a context of authority and conformity, both political and ecclesiastical. Thus not only the categorical seven deadly sins, but also the juridical distinction between "deadly" and "venial" sins, and the twofold morality: one for the layman, the other for the cleric. This has been dismissed by Wundt, with characteristic bluntness, as ethically worthless, but it gave to medieval society its shape and cohesion. The theocratic intent and the development of ecclesiastical juris-

---

[67] *The City of God,* XIX.15.

prudence in the medieval Church made not only possible but inevitable prescribed penances for sin. Morality, thus, became largely a matter of legality.

The notion of the exclusive franchise of the Catholic Church in mediating between God and man was of course not original with Augustine. Lactantius had held that an Arian, a Valentinian, or a Novation was actually not even a Christian, because the Catholic Church alone "retains true worship";[68] Ambrose thought that the Catholic Church enjoyed the absolute monopoly of absolving sin.[69] Such opinions were common in the fourth century after the council of Nicaea had demonstrated the need for a centralized and standardized source of ecclesiastical authority. In this matter, as in so many others, Augustine absorbed and restated the main currents of doctrinal developments. Dominated as he was by the concept of the Church and its sacraments as representing the mystical body of Christ, he was fully aware of the need for uniformity of belief. In its present state, he remarks in a letter, the Church, because it is "so constituted as to enclose much chaff and many tares, bears with many things." But he yearned and worked for uniformity: that which is not warranted by the Bible, by the great councils, or by the "practices of the universal Church" he thought should unquestionably "be abolished without hesitation."[70] Thus it was natural that he should maintain, against the Donatist heresy, the objectivity and universal validity of the sacraments. Even though a priest be unworthy, if he represents the Holy Church, the sacraments which he administers will be efficacious. The symbolic value of the rite is unimpaired by the celebrant; the sanctity of the form, as prescribed and administered by the Church, transcends all other questions.

Return then, O ye transgressors, to a right mind, and do not seek to weigh the sacraments of God by considerations of the characters and deeds of men. For the sacraments are holy through Him to whom they belong; but when taken in hand worthily, they bring reward; when unworthily, judgment.[71]

If Augustine laid the doctrinal foundation for a universal Church, it was Gregory the Great (540?-604) who by his administrative genius went far towards achieving one. Not for nothing was Gregory a devoted student of the great bishop's works. Because Augustine himself obviously had more interest in the heavenly city than in the earthly city, he tended

[68] *Divine Institutes*, IV.30.
[69] *Concerning Repentance*, I.3.
[70] *The Letters*, no. LV.
[71] Kidd, *Documents*, II, 229.

to neglect secular law and the immediate problems of organization in favor of the future commonwealth of the saved. For him, the cultivation of the soul was more important than either political or ecclesiastical administration.[72] He had, therefore, largely ignored the secular on the assumption that this earth is transitory and trivial, not to say evil. But as Mr. Whitehead has pointed out, the Church could not persist in maintaining its early asceticism and obscurantism. "The obstinate survival of the present world was upsetting the unworldly tactics of the early Christians."[73] It was Gregory, coming to the papacy in 590 after winning success as both a secular and ecclesiastical administrator, who set about to consolidate the organization of the rather sprawling Church. In establishing the medieval papacy and suggesting the limits to which it might aspire, he made possible the theocracy of the Middle Ages.

Gregory made his Church an instrument of political and economic power. He appointed agents to supervise the collection of fees due the Patrimony of St. Peter; and from the papal holdings in Italy, Gaul, Dalmatia, and Africa he garnered the revenues that made him a great landlord. His training as a secular legalist and administrator, as well as his patrician birth, fitted him to hope that he might centralize in the Church all the power and authority for which men yearned after the old configurations of political power had dissolved. In developing the concept of papal sovereignty, both spiritual and temporal, Gregory gave meaning to the medieval view that though the state was independent of the Church, it needed the sanction of the Church. To trace the history of this idea would be to write a history of medieval Europe. Thus, after the lapse of centuries, John of Salisbury argues in his *Policraticus* that secular laws are valid only if they imitate the sacred canon,[74] and that monarchy can claim authority only if it is a reflection of the majesty of God as revealed by the Roman Church.[75] And in spite of the misfortunes of John's patron, Thomas à Becket, we must remember the time when Henry IV was humbled in the snow at Canossa before Gregory VII, when Innocent III was the most powerful prince in Europe, when Dante wrote his *De Monarchia* (anachronistic though it was at the time), and when the Canon Law as summarized by Gregory IX in 1234 became the model of jurisprudence.[76] Some of the fruits of Gregory's work are seen in perhaps the most notorious pronouncement of the medieval papacy,

---

[72] See Dunning, *A History of Political Theories*, pp. 156-58.

[73] *Adventures of Ideas*, p. 103.

[74] See Carlyle, *A History of Medieval Political Theory*, IV, 332, n. 3.

[75] IV.7. Note John's analysis of the functions of a prince (IV.7) and of a soldier (VI.9).

[76] See Gabriel Le Bras, "Canon Law," *The Legacy of the Middle Ages* (1938), pp. 321 ff.

the *Unum Sanctum* of Boniface VIII: "we declare, we say, we define and pronounce to every human creature it is absolutely necessary to salvation to be subject to the Roman pontiff." A man who could speak thus and command an international audience could reasonably enough claim the right to name and depose kings, or to make himself the arbiter of secular law.

Gregory was no Innocent III, but it was his dream to make the Roman Church preëminent. To this end its economic aggrandizement, its political development, its unification of doctrine and ritual, its claim as the sacrosanct agent of God all contributed.[77] His zeal in this endeavor is apparent in the famous *Regulae Pastoralis* (which Alfred the Great caused to be translated into Anglo-Saxon), but it is in the streams of letters that the man is seen most clearly. His words to some bishops (in choosing whom he was extremely careful) set the tone of his labors: "we are constrained by the care of the government which we have undertaken to extend vigilantly the solicitude of our office, and to instruct the minds of our brethren by addresses of admonition, that no wrongful presumption may avail to deceive the ignorant nor any dissimulation to excuse those who know."[78] He followed this principle rigorously.

To Augustine, prior of the Coelian Hill monastery, whom he had sent to England as part of his elaborate missionary program, he writes at length answering questions on administration and canon law.[79] To one Gulfaris, ardent in winning Istrian schismatics back to the Church, he urges all possible "zeal for the unity of our holy faith" so that as many as possible may be lured "from the error of their schism into the bosom of the Mother Church."[80] He claims it is the height of impiety and ignorance for those who ignore his anathema to think they can "loose the binding of the holy Church."[81] As he explains elsewhere, "if (which God forbid) we neglect ecclesiastical solicitude and vigour, indolence destroys discipline, and certainly harm will be done to the souls of the faithful."[82] Writing to the aged Janarius, Bishop of Baralis, he quotes scripture to the effect that one should revere one's elders, and thereupon immediately berates the old reprobate. Were he not so gentle a pontiff, warns Gregory, "we should smite thee with a definitive curse." As it is, Janarius is lucky to escape with only a reprimand, but his companions

[77] On Gregory's view of his office see F. Homes Dudden, *Gregory the Great* (1905), I, 225 ff.; for his view of the Church, II, 405 ff.
[78] *Selected Epistles*, IX.68.
[79] XII.64.
[80] IX.93.
[81] XI.45.
[82] IX.41.

in evil—he had unjustly seized some land and plowed it on the sabbath —are to be excommunicated for two months. And if it happens again, "we no longer spare either thy simplicity or thy old age." [83]

The most notorious example of Gregory's papal solicitude, however, is probably his letter to Desiderius, Bishop of Gaul. His sin had been to show an inordinate interest in the teaching of grammar, and Gregory finds it hard to mention the matter "without shame" for it is "execrable for such a thing to be related of a priest." He can only hope that the gossip is untrue, in which event "we shall give thanks to our God, who has not permitted your heart to be stained with the blasphemous praises of the abominable." [84] If, as Ernest Renan thought, Christianity had in the second and third centuries sucked "comme un vampire la société antique," [85] what must we say of Gregory's efforts in behalf of education in the sixth? But the medieval Church extended its functions and achieved its importance on the premise that Augustine's view of man was accurate. Its strength lay in its unique function of mediating between man and God, and it undertook to do for man what he could never do for himself. It was, as Dante was to boast at the end of the Middle Ages, Christ's "Spouse and Secretary," [86] and it was as essential to salvation as was the Bible.[87] As a redemptive agency it was indispensable to man; therefore it could legitimately exact its tribute of faith and submission.

The second fundamental assumption which Augustine bequeathed the Middle Ages was that of a theocentric and theocratic universe. All "natures" whatever, he declares in his great monument to God's providence, exhibit rank and species and "a kind of internal harmony." Therefore they are "certainly good." Even things without "everlasting being" by their very inconstancy demonstrate God's design: "they tend in the divine providence to that end which is embraced in the general scheme of the government of the universe." [88] Even wretched men, who without grace know neither peace nor the sense of order from which peace comes, prove the fact of providence. "Inasmuch as they are deservedly and justly miserable, they are by their very misery connected with order. They are not, indeed, conjoined with the blessed, but they are disjoined from them by the law of order." [89]

This principle of order is one of the most persistent notions in the his-

[83] IX.1.
[84] XII.54.
[85] Marc-Aurèle, p. 589.
[86] Convivio, II.6.
[87] Paradiso, V.76-78.
[88] The City of God, XII.5.
[89] The City of God, XIX.13.

tory of thought. Although the Greeks had tended to correlate it with the essential rationality of the universe, and the men of the Enlightenment with the scientific mechanism of the universe, the Middle Ages, following Augustine, could interpret it only as the corollary of God's omnipotence and omniscience. A century before Augustine, Lactantius, the Christian Cicero, had tried to find God's benevolent providence in the fall of every sparrow: "and in how wonderful, how divine a manner" did God contrive man's nostrils—"so that the very cavity of the nose should not deform the beauty of the face!—which would certainly have been the case if one single aperture only were open." [90] Eight hundred years later John of Salisbury adorns the same moral.

Indeed the wisdom and goodness of God, in which originate all things, are with perfect truth called nature, and nothing works contrary to this because nothing annuls the purpose of God or interferes with those causes which have existed from eternity in the mind of him who in his understanding has made the heavens.[91]

One could assemble hundreds of such opinions, but these from Lactantius and John of Salisbury are typical of the frame of mind which finds its greatest medieval statement in Augustine's *City of God*. If God is, as Augustine says, a sovereign manipulating events as a chess player his pawns, then all history becomes theology, all the data of experience the manifestations of God's will. In the Christian epic of the creation, the fall, and the redemption, the universe is the stage for the mighty drama of salvation.[92] Just as God caused Alaric to sack Rome, so He contrives all events to manifest His providence and thus glorify Himself.[93]

The implications of this assumption were worked out with infinite precision in the Middle Ages. It determined man's view of himself and his place in the universe. Ptolemaic astronomy, to name a classic example, was employed by generations of theologians to show how God revealed His providence in the ordering of celestial bodies. The earth, to these men, was the center of a series of concentric circles stretching up to God; and man as ruler of the earth was the focus of the whole creation, the protagonist on the cosmic stage.[94] The seven planets, Dante explains

---

[90] *On the Workmanship of God*, ch. X.

[91] *Frivolities of Courtiers and Footprints of Philosophers: Being a Translation of the First, Second, and Third Books and Selections from the Seventh and Eighth Books of the Policraticus of John of Salisbury* (1938), II.12 (p. 73).

[92] See Randall, *The Making of the Modern Mind*, pp. 17 ff.

[93] A vestige of this approach to history is apparent in the work of a contemporary Catholic apologist like Christopher Dawson. See his analysis of Augustine's age in *A Monument to Augustine* (1930), p. 16.

[94] For a famous statement of this view see Aquinas, *Summa Theologica*, I.68.4.

gravely, correspond to the seven sciences of the trivium and the quadrivium; the eighth to natural science and metaphysics; the ninth to moral
science; the tenth to the divine science of theology.[95] It is here, in the
tenth sphere, the unmoving empyrean, that the apex of creation is
reached: there resides the "highest Godhead who alone completely beholds Himself." [96] Long before Dante the Pseudo-Dionysius had constructed his mystical Neoplatonic treatises on the assumption that all
things not only receive their existence from God but also tend to return
to God—a state of affairs making for miraculous unity and coherence.[97]
Just as the divine order is revealed in the celestial hierarchy of nine kinds
of angelic beings in three groups—ranging upward from the angels and
archangels to the cherubim and seraphim[98]—similarly the same kind of
order is discernible in the divine institution of the Church: there the
stratification of the clergy and the interdependence of the sacraments
reveal God's plan for the administration of the world.[99]

Even in a piece of hack writing like Honorius Augustadunesis' *De
Imagine Mundi* one sees how few questions were left for the medieval
man to worry about: the world is as it is because God has arranged it
so, and while man's knowledge of God's ways is perhaps cloudy, he may
repose in the certainty that God's ways are best. For instance, Honorius'
geography in the first book is, not to put too fine a point on it, a little
sketchy, but it carries the tone of finality. He knows where hell is ("in
medio terrae") [100] and he knows all he needs to about the planets: "hae
immensa celeritate firmamenti, ab oriente in occidentum rapiuntur." [101]
Honorius' universe may have bewildered him, but it never terrified him,
for he knew that it was one organic whole under the direct supervision
of God, and that therefore all was well and orderly. We should not
worry about our inability to understand all of God's ways and purposes,
warns Dante; "We should rather marvel greatly if at any time the process by which the eternal counsels are fulfilled is so manifest as to be
discerned by our reason." [102]

[95] *Convivio*, II.14.
[96] *Convivio*, II.4.
[97] *De Divinis Nominibus*, IV.14 (Migne, *PG*, III, 711).
[98] *De Coelesti Hierarchia*, VI.2 (Migne, *PG*, III, 200 ff.). Dante's account of the
celestial hierarchy in the *Convivio* is slightly different from that in the *Paradiso* (XXVIII.
130 ff.). The earlier is derived from Gregory the Great, the latter from the Pseudo-Dionysius. See Karl Vossler, *Medieval Culture* (1929), I, 60, n. 1.
[99] *De Ecclesiastica Hierarchia, passim* (Migne, *PG*, II, 369 ff.).
[100] Migne, *PL*, CLXXII, 133. An Anglo-French redaction of the early thirteenth century
has been edited by William Hilliard Trethewey as *A Critical Edition of La Petite Philosophy*
(1939). See pp. liii for a discussion of authorship and contents.
[101] Migne, *PL*, CLXXII, 138.
[102] *Convivio*, IV.4.

Modern historians have perhaps romanticized the medieval synthesis made possible only by the assumption of a theocratic universe. Our age is urbanized, industrialized, and emotionally unsure; therefore many besides Henry Adams have yearned for the pastoral simplicity of the medieval man—even though the simplicity derived from a ruthlessly theocratic culture based on an economy of barter. But even though each man must use his own salt on Adams' reconstruction of the thirteenth century, it is hard to ignore the symmetry of Chartres, of the *Summa*, of the *Divine Comedy*,[103] of the feudal system, of the Ptolemaic cosmology. Everywhere one senses the unquestioned belief in order, structure, hierarchy.

The universal use of symbol, for instance, implied a confidence in the organic unity and design of a theocentric universe: without architectural correspondence and the sure relationship of the part to the whole, symbolism is impossible.[104] Happily, medieval man was sure he knew enough about the universe—the book of nature was the common metaphor—to read it as a symbol: the physical world had its uses, if only one could see the symbolic correspondences between it and the spiritual. As Dante put it in his famous letter of dedication to Can Grande, "of things which exist some so exist as to have absolute being in themselves; others so exist as to have a being dependent on something else, by some kind of relation." [105] To explore such relations was the main business of the medieval artist, and as Dante and the artisans of Chartres show, when thought is symbolic, art is usually allegorical. A poem or a cathedral, no less than the visible world, must be made to serve as the token of a spiritual truth. God Himself had sanctioned the method; as M. Mâle has said, He of course created the world *in principio,* but as a thought in the divine mind; this thought was realized *in verbo* through the Son, who expressed the thought in the thing.

Le monde peut donc se définir: 'Une idée de Dieu réalisée par le Verbe.' S'il en est ainsi, tout être cache une pensée divine. Le monde est un livre immense, écrit de la main de Dieu, où chaque être est un mot plein de sens.[106]

In short, then, everything must stand for something else; every truth must point to some higher truth. As Vincent de Beauvais' *Miroir de la Nature* or Erigena's *De Divisione Naturae* show, the universe is intri-

[103] On which see Vossler, II, 210-14.

[104] See J. Huizinga, *The Waning of the Middle Ages* (1927), p. 187; Mumford, *The Condition of Man,* p. 138.

[105] Ep. X.5.

[106] *L'Art Religieux du XIIIᵉ Siècle en France* (1923), p. 29.

cate, but it is orderly in its accent from matter to spirit. The end of wisdom, therefore, is not facts *qua* facts, but facts as pointers to a higher order of being. Just as there are four meanings in the Scriptures—the literal, allegorical, moral, and anagogical—there are meanings in the facts of nature.[107] Things have "form" and things have "nature," says Hugo of St. Victor, from which follows a great truth:

Ex quo constat quod omnes artes naturales divinae scientiae famulantur; et inferior sapientia recte ordinata ad superiorem conducit. Sub eo igitur sensu qui est in significatione vocum ad res, continetur historia; cui famulantur tres scientiae sicut dictum est, id est grammatica, dialectica, rhetorica. Sub eo autem sensu qui est in significatione rerum ad facta mystica, continetur allegoria. Et sub eo sensu qui est in significatione rerum ad facienda mystica, continetur tropologia; et his duobus famulantur arithmetica, musica, geometria, astronomia et physica. Super haec ante omnia divinum illud est ad quod ducit divine Scriptura sive in allegoria, sive in tropologia; quorum alterum (quod in allegoria est) rectam fidem, alterum (quod in tropologia est) informat bonam operationem: in quibus constat cognitio veritatis et amor virtutis: et haec est vera reparatio hominis.[108]

Thus all human arts and knowledges, properly construed, *subserviunt divinae sapientiae*. When one believes, as Hugo did, that

the spirit was created for God's sake, the body for the spirit's sake, and the whole world for the body's sake, so that the spirit might be subject to God, the body to the spirit, and the world to the body,[109]

then obviously the grand strategy of human knowledge is clear. *Inferior sapientia recte ordinata ad superiorem conducit*. In the theocratic universe bequeathed by Augustine to the Middle Ages, there was a place for everything and everything was in its place. All that remained for man was to determine the symbolic correspondences between higher and lower forms of reality, and thus to glory in God's infinite wisdom revealed in so orderly a universe.[110]

[107] On the fourfold interpretation of the Bible see Dante, *Convivio*, II.i; Ep. X.6 ff.; cf. Vossler, *Medieval Culture*, I, 131-32. For one example among thousands, note the sermons of Saint Bernard—for instance, Sermon VIII, "On the Saviour as a Fount of Grace," *Life and Works* (1889-1896), III, 403 ff.; cf. Sermon XLVII, "Of the Threefold Flowers," *ibid.*, IV, 287 ff.

[108] *De Sacramentis*, "Prologus," cap. VI (Migne, *PL*, CLXXVI, 185).

[109] Quoted by Henry Osborn Taylor, *The Medieval Mind* (1911), II, 91. For a famous Thomistic statement of a similar point of view, see the *Summa*, I.108; cf. Étienne Gilson, *The Philosophy of St. Thomas Aquinas* (1929), pp. 351 ff.

[110] For an interesting study of a very complicated subject see H. Flanders Dunbar, *Symbolism in Medieval Thought and Its Consummation in the Divine Comedy* (1929), *passim*.

# XII

## AUGURIES OF CHANGE

To MEDIEVALISTS NO TERM IS MORE ANNOYING than "the dark ages," and no writer so glib as the historian who bleats of man's "emancipation" in the dawn of a Burckhardtian Renaissance. Such an attitude is warranted: to dismiss with the opprobrious epithets "Scholastic" or "theological" the centuries between Augustine and Petrarch may indicate a writer's scale of values, but it does not explain very much about the Middle Ages. We may smile at the distortion of pagan culture in such a popular medieval textbook as Martianus Capella's *De Nuptiis Philologiae et Mercurii,* laden as it is with allegory, personification, didacticism; but we should also remember Boethius and Erigena, the School of Chartres and Abelard.

The Italian Renaissance was something more than an instantaneous translation from superstition to rationality, from hair-shirts to Lorenzo de' Medici. Voltaire said that religion began when the first fool met the first knave, but only a Voltaire (who often wrote superficial history but knew as well as the next man how to ride a thesis hard) could say of the "priest-ridden," "sottish" thirteenth century that with it we pass "de l'ignorance sauvage à l'ignorance scholastique."[1] Although only a Catholic apologist would insist that the Church invariably used its towering influence for sweetness and light, only a zealous Darwinian like Huxley (with all his strength and all his limitation) would paint medieval thought as black as he did in his *Science and Education.*

Although medieval values were, as I have tried to show, generally Augustinian, and although the five centuries following Augustine were generally unproductive of original thought, there were stirrings of development. There was even a certain degree of literacy. John of Salisbury, the best-read man of his time, displays in the *Metalogicus* and the *Policraticus* not only erudition, but a highly urbane literary taste. Moreover, for a cleric of the twelfth century, and for a man remembered as a powerful advocate of the theocratic state, he sometimes sounds uncomfortably modern.[2] He would have found much to talk about with

[1] *Essai sur les Moeurs,* ch. XLV.

[2] For instance, John discusses (*Metalogicus,* VII.20) a list of things which a wise man may legitimately doubt; cf. Poole, *Illustrations of the History of Medieval Thought,* pp. 222 ff.

Erasmus, and Aquinas would have been welcomed at Plato's symposium. In this chapter, then, I shall try to indicate some of the ways in which men's thinking was being reshaped. In the history of thought there are rarely any new problems—merely new efforts to answer old problems. The late Middle Ages made such efforts, and thus announced, under the very nose of an autocratic Church and within the framework of Scholastic thought, some leitmotifs that in the Renaissance were going to thunder forth *fortissimo*.

REALISM AND NOMINALISM

The notorious controversy over universals may serve to remind us that towards the close of the Middle Ages—that is, in the eleventh and twelfth centuries—thoughtful men were trying to evaluate experience in something other than Augustinian terms. As an effort to determine philosophically the metaphysics of Christian faith, the problem of universals was formulated for the Middle Ages by Boethius' influential translation of Porphyry's *Introduction to the Categories of Aristotle*. Although the issue was to become hopelessly muddled in the wrangling of the Schoolmen, it was of primary importance in posing a basic question: do genera and species exist in nature (*subsistentia*) or are they mere abstractions (*nuda intellecta*)?

From this question Porphyry derived (without solving) a set of riddles that was to tax the best minds of the eleventh and twelfth centuries. Do genera and species exist independently or as projections of our intellection? If they exist in nature apart from us, are they corporeal? Do they exist as objects of sense, or have they an identity divorced from sensibles? [3] That is, are universals merely intellectual abstractions which we verbalize from our experience of particulars, or do they have an existence (as Plato, the most uncompromising of realists, had urged) [4] apart from the objects of the sensible universe? The old problem of permanence and change was thus restated in the jargon of the Schoolmen: do universals exist *ante rem, in rem,* or *post rem*? Abelard, early in the twelfth century, when the controversy was at its height, posed the question very clearly:

[3] Boethius, *Commentary on the Isogoge of Porphyry*, I.10 (Richard McKeon, *Selections from Medieval Philosophers*, 1929-1930, I, 218-19); cf. Etienne Gilson, *La Philosophie au Moyen Age* (1930), p. 27.

[4] Even though the early Middle Ages knew no Greek, it had learned its Platonism from Augustine, and realism constituted orthodoxy—as Roscellinus and Berengarius of Tours were to find out. Even' as late as the twelfth century, before the triumph of Aristotle in the thirteenth, Plato's name had, as Martin Grabman has said (*Die Geschichte de scholastischen Methode*, 1909-1911, II, 65), "im grossen und ganzen einen besseren Klang als der des Stagiriten."

Whether genera and species subsist, that is, signify something truly existent, or are placed in the understanding alone etc., that is, are located in empty opinion without the thing, like the following words, chimera and goat-stag which do not give rise to a rational understanding.[5]

The whole question, stripped of its verbiage, was that of the relation of our intellectual concepts to things existing outside our intellect.[6]

To understand the importance of these questions we must remember the theology of Augustine. He had insisted that when Adam fell, all men fell; when Christ suffered for the sins of the world, all men found atonement; when the Holy Catholic Church spoke, it spoke for all individual churches. Clearly he was suggesting, through myth rather than philosophic concepts, something very like Platonic Ideas, that is, universals, in the symbols of Adam, redeemed humanity, and the Church.[7] When the Scholastic effort was made to identify faith and reason, some of the cardinal doctrines of Christendom—original sin and the Church as a mystical redemptive agency—were forced into the light of philosophic scrutiny through the problem of universals. Thus, perhaps without knowing it, Augustine adumbrated the characteristic realism of the Middle Ages: the conviction that universals have an existence apart from and transcendent to the individual objects of sense. Had Augustine lived in the eleventh century he would unquestionably have called himself a realist and would have argued—with what vehemence we may imagine —that universals exist *ante rem*.

In the work of John Scotus Erigena, surely the most arresting thinker of the ninth century, it is possible to find the seeds of what was later to be called realism. Erigena was no slavish Augustinian (his *De Divina Praedestinatione* would not have pleased the Bishop of Hippo) [8] but belonging as he did to the tradition of Augustine's Christian Platonism he was an incipient realist. In his great *De Divisione Naturae* Erigena analyzed all nature into four categories of being: that which creates and is not created, that which is created and creates, that which is created and does not create, that which is neither created nor creates. As the Neoplatonic translator of the Pseudo-Dionysius, Erigena inevitably identified the first class with God, at once the origin and the goal of all things and the fountain of being that floods the universe. The second

[5] *The Glosses of Peter Abailard on Porphyry* in McKeon, I, 250.

[6] See Maurice de Wulf, "Nominalism, Realism, Conceptualism," *The Catholic Encyclopaedia*, XI, 90.

[7] If a universal was, as Albert the Great defined it, "that which, although it is in one, is naturally apt to be in many" (quoted by McKeon, II, 503) then the Holy Catholic Church was truly a universal which subsumed the reality of any particular church.

[8] See Johann Eduard Erdmann, *A History of Philosophy* (1891), I, 293-94.

and third classes include all being other than God; the second is made up of ideas and archetypes which are the divine will according to which things are formed, and the third is made up of all created individual things patterned after the divine plan. Such things have no independent existence, for they exist only in God and manifest his will. Because each thing is a theophany, a *divina apparitio,* the universal man, for instance, is "a certain intellectual idea formed eternally in the divine mind," [9] and the individual man derives his reality from the universal *humanitas.* The fourth class of nature is, obviously, Neoplatonic nonentity, uncreated matter that reflects nothing of the divine essence.[10]

Such a majestic interpretation of nature is hardly original with Erigena—its germs are in Plotinus[11]—but for the ninth century it represents an intellectually sophisticated attempt to express the medieval principle of theocratic order. Erigena saw the universe as a series of hierarchies, one class stretching up to another in a rational arrangement of the less inclusive surmounted by the more inclusive, until the all-inclusive is attained in God. As the *natura naturans* transcending *natura naturata,* God not only contains all things, he originates all things; and the universal ideas (perhaps the eighteenth century would call them natural laws) which flow from the being of God in turn confer being on the particulars of the sensible universe. One implication of this doctrine is pantheism (for which Erigena was formally condemned at the Council of Sens in 1225): God is the supreme universal that includes all particulars, and the Neoplatonic Eternal Word, as the exemplar of all lower forms of creation, is what two centuries later would be called a *universalia ante rem.*[12] Another implication, dear to the medieval mind, is that matter has less reality than incorporeal forms, for God, the source of all being, is pure form.

The incipient realism of Erigena's thought proved to be extremely congenial to the Middle Ages, but late in the eleventh century it was challenged by Roscellinus. The theological battle which he waged was something more than Scholastic hair-splitting, for in arguing that reality lay not in universals but in the individual objects of sense he was suggesting (without actually advocating) an antispiritual, secular interpreta-

---

[9] McKeon, I, 117.

[10] See Poole, *Illustrations of the History of Medieval Thought,* pp. 64 ff.

[11] See Arthur Cushman McGiffert, *A History of Christian Thought,* II (1933), pp. 171 ff.; Gilson, *La Philosophie au Moyen Age,* pp. 11-26.

[12] Like all pantheists, Erigena is hard put to it to account for evil. If the whole universe is, in varying degrees, a manifestation of the divine mind, how can evil exist? It exists, Erigena argues, from the individual's will misinterpreting and distorting experience; the only hell which an advanced theologian like Erigena will admit to is the hell of a sinful will.

tion of experience. As M. Gilson has said, for the realist humanity is a reality; for the nominalist, there is nothing real but man.[13] Any philosophy which places first importance on the particular, concrete objects of sense, and which in effect abolishes the distinction between sensation and intellectual concepts,[14] is inimical to theology as Augustine understood it. Perhaps M. de Wulf is right in saying that a genuine nominalist, like Hobbes or Spencer, would have been virtually impossible in the Middle Ages. Whatever his proper label—and we know him mainly through the indignant criticism of his opponents—Roscellinus' views were considered dangerous. What else could be thought of a man who suggested that only particular objects of sense are real, and that a universal is merely a convenient abstraction by which man classifies experience—in Anselm's famous critique of Roscellinus' errors, a *flatus vocis?* Like most men who challenge the favorite assumptions of their age, Roscellinus was made to pay the price for his nonconformity. He was found guilty of heresy and compelled to retract, while Anselm of Canterbury and William of Champeaux proceeded to develop realism so inordinately that they made some sort of nominalist reaction inevitable. William maintained, for example, that since the universal substance is entirely and essentially present in each particular, the particular differ not in essence but in the variety of their accidents. The person and genius of Socrates, consequently, are merely individual accidents of the substance (that is, the universal) *humanitas.*[15]

It was Abelard (1074-1142) who achieved a compromise between the warring factions by suggesting a metaphysics much closer to Aristotle than to the Platonism of the extreme realists. By his conceptualism (or moderate realism) Abelard acknowledged that we do entertain abstract concepts, but he was chary in saying that they actually correspond to realities outside our mind. A universal word (for instance, *man*) may be predicated of many particulars, a particular word (for instance, *Socrates*) of only one,[16] and therefore *Socrates* has a more real and tangible referent than *man.* Nonetheless, the universal word acquires at least a conceptual reality when predicated of all objects possessing it (*quod de pluribus natum est praedicari*). In spite of his vacillation, Abelard apparently rejected both the *ante rem* formula of the realists and the *post rem* formula of the nominalists: for him, *universalia sunt in rebus,* and

---

[13] *La Philosophie au Moyen Age,* p. 39.

[14] The high-priest of nominalism, William of Ockham, did in fact emphatically deny the distinction; see *The Seven Quodlibeta,* quodlibet I, question 13 (McKeon, II, 360).

[15] See Andrew Seth Pringle-Pattison, "Scholasticism," *The Encyclopaedia Britannica* (11th ed.), XXIV, 350.

[16] *The Glosses of Peter Abailard on Porphyry* in McKeon, I, 232.

therefore species and genera *non nisi per individua subsistere habent*.[17] It would be too easy to accept Abelard's characteristic boast that "by most potent reasoning" he compelled his old realist teacher, William of Champeaux, "first to alter his former opinion on the subject of universals, and finally to abandon it altogether." [18] But we must regard the popularity of his conceptualism—both Aquinas and his adversary Duns Scotus were on the whole content with it—as the thin opening wedge of a new way of evaluating experience.

If Abelard's *via media* did not close the controversy—his pupil John of Salisbury lists nine contemporary theories on the problem of universals[19]—it did provide a generally satisfactory compromise until the final victory of nominalism. This victory came with the revival of extreme nominalism by the English Franciscan, William of Ockham (d. 1349?) at the very end of the Scholastic period. Ockham consummated Abelard's effort to assert the reality of the particular objects of sense, and with him, on the eve of the Renaissance, the medieval reverence for abstractions and distrust of sensibles received the Scholastic *coup de grâce*. It may have been that the intention of Ockham's nominalist skepticism was to discredit the claims of a rational, Thomistic theology, and thus to strengthen an authoritarian Church. But in maintaining, against the realists, that "the object of sense and the object of understanding are absolutely the same," [20] Ockham was much nearer the Renaissance than the Middle Ages. Actually, the rapid spread of nominalism following Ockham shows how much he reflected the new interest of the Renaissance in the concrete thing rather than the medieval universal. The doctors of the Sorbonne, the paladins of conservatism and reaction, put Ockham's works under a ban as early as 1339, but none the less his views were taught by men like Albert of Saxony and Johannes Buridanus. And after the late fourteenth century nominalism was freely and fashionably expounded, even by Gerson, the chancellor of the University of Paris.[21]

Abélard, then, was anticipating the progress of thought, and his importance lies not only in theological disputation but also in his affirmation of a rational individualism. The reason he so profoundly shocked his contemporaries, and has so persistently charmed posterity was his own in-

---

[17] See Erdmann, *A History of Philosophy,* I, 319.

[18] *Historia Calamitatum,* ch. II.

[19] *Metalogicus,* II.17.

[20] *The Seven Quodlibeta,* quodlibet I, question 13 (McKeon, II, 360). Note also Ockham's argument that abstractive knowledge (as opposed to intuitive knowledge by which a thing is known directly) "abstracts from experience," quodlibet I, question 5 (McKeon, II, 369).

[21] See Erdmann, I, 514 ff.

dividualism in a century that distrusted individualism. As a contemporary of Cellini he would have been less conspicuous, but his *Historia Calamitatum* is a remarkable performance for the early twelfth century. It is not surprising that Abelard, unlike William of Champeaux, has become a subject for romance. Discontented with the prevailing theology of Augustinian Platonism, he turned his interest towards the objects of sense; moreover, he revived an almost Pelagian defense of human nature.

As a theologian, Abelard could chop logic with the most abstruse of his peers: his *Sic et Non* does not make for very breezy reading today, but it was of great importance in establishing Scholastic methodology. Between it and the great *Summae* that followed it there is a clear connection, for Abelard's effort to make theology rational represented Scholasticism at its best.[22] In his *Ethics,* however, he is centuries removed from his time. He there insists on man's moral freedom and moral responsibility: the virtue of an act depends upon its motive, and thus Abelard's morals, like his metaphysics, are built around his regard for the subjective and the individual. He introduced the first new note in ethical theory since Augustine. Man does not inherit Adam's guilt, merely his punishment; and although anyone is a potential candidate for damnation, he may, by exerting his God-given reason in avoiding the weaknesses of the flesh, attain a good life. Man achieves virtuous conduct not solely through the divine gift of grace, but also by regulating his actions rationally. Sin consists "not in desiring a woman, but in consent to the desire, and not the wish for whoredom, but the consent to the wish is damnation." [23] For Abelard, no prescribed index of sins will suffice; it is not the act that is sinful, but the intention. "God considers not the action, but the spirit of the action. It is the intention, not the deed wherein the merit or praise of the doer consists. Often, indeed, the same action is done from different motives: for justice's sake by one man, for an evil reason by another." [24]

Living when he did, and thinking as he did, Abelard was doomed to the calamities he has recorded. By asserting that particulars, the things of this world, have a substantial reality of their own, that man's chief moral weapon is his rational intellect, that God Himself is supremely

---

[22] "A doctrine is not believed because God has said it," wrote Abelard, "but because we are convinced by reason that it is so." See Poole, *Illustrations of the History of Medieval Thought,* p. 153. On the influence of the *Sic et Non* on Scholasticism see Grabman, *Die Geschichte der scholastischen Methode,* II, 213 ff.

[23] *Ethics,* ch. III.

[24] *Ethics,* ch. III; cf. McGiffert, *A History of Christian Thought,* II, 216-17; Gilson, *La Philosophie au Moyen Age,* pp. 75 ff.

rational, Abelard had come far along the road from Augustine to Aquinas. But at the Council of Sens, Abelard, the man of intellect, quailed before Bernard, the man of mystic love who thought it impious to construct syllogisms about the Trinity. When Abelard sweats blood to make a Christian out of Plato, said Bernard, he merely proves himself a pagan.[25] And indeed, the antinomies of the *Sic et Non* would seem to a man like Bernard merely a canceling out of one authority with another, and thus, in effect, a skeptical attack upon all authority. At the Council piety and rationalism confronted each other in the persons of the two most notable ecclesiastics of the century, and piety prevailed. Christendom was not yet ready for the synthesis of faith and reason which Aquinas wrought.

### THE NATURAL THEOLOGY OF AQUINAS

Joseph Glanville said that Aquinas was but Aristotle sainted. Nonetheless, it was ignorant of Macaulay to sneer at Aquinas for his indebtedness.[26] Aquinas must be seen as the finest flower of Scholasticism, the movement that attempted to find a rational basis for Christian faith. By sundering the realms of faith and knowledge—and thus by the consequent destruction of man's confidence in his own intellect—Augustine had made it the function of intelligence merely to demonstrate the truth of a revealed knowledge acquired by faith.[27] It was Aquinas' achievement to restore man to his once-cherished self-respect in his proper intellect. He made it his task to reconcile faith and rational knowledge and thus, ultimately, to revise the Augustinian estimate of human nature.

Attacking the problem systematically, as was his wont, Aquinas found the Platonic-Augustinian dualism of body and soul highly vulnerable. Each individual, he argued, receives from God an active intellect which can be understood only as the Aristotelian form of the body. When Aristotle had called the active intellect separable, he had left dangling the tantalizing question of its immortality. Augustine, with characteristic Platonism, had reserved the active intellect as the exclusive attribute of God's divine illumination: the individual believer could only bask in its reflection, and gratefully pay the debt of faith for the miracle of his salvation. Averroes (1126-1198), going directly to the text of Aristotle, held that the universal active intellect (which, incidentally, he located in

[25] See McKeon, I, 207.

[26] See A. E. Taylor "St. Thomas Aquinas as a Philosopher," *Philosophical Studies* (1934), pp. 226, 233 ff.; on the influence of Aristotle after the twelfth century see Grabman, II, 64 ff.

[27] See Carl Becker, *The Heavenly City of the Eighteenth-Century Philosophers* (1932), p. 7.

the sphere of the moon) made knowledge possible by its operation on the private passive intellects of men. But Aquinas studied Aristotle by day and meditated him by night, and concluded that if the active intellect were the same for all men, personal immortality was impossible.[28] Thus he found a powerful theological motive for reaffirming man's innate rationality: each man possesses an active intellect by which he may know God.

Like Aristotle, Aquinas insisted that the origin of all knowledge, even of those things above sense, lies in sensory cognition: "intellectus circa proprium objectum semper verus est." [29] Man's mind, "the very essence of his soul," [30] has two levels of apprehension: 1) passion includes both the irascible appetite shown by the lower animals for power and the concupiscible appetite for what seems to be agreeable; 2) the will, operating on the data supplied it by the passions, elevates man to the sphere of rational intellection; it does not (Stoically) suppress and eradicate passions, but it does provide a proper *habitus* in utilizing them for knowledge.[31] Together, the passion and the will constitute the "intellectual substance" which is the form of the body.[32]

Each thing must fulfill its function, Aquinas repeats after Aristotle: the acorn to grow into a tree, the axe to cut. Because a man is a rational creature endowed with an active intellect, it is his function to know. As Dante, who had learned so much from Aquinas, was to put it: when it is said that man lives, "it must be understood that man uses his reason, which is especially his life and the actuality of his noblest part." [33] Man's ultimate happiness, says Aquinas, consists not in externalities, or even in such goods of the soul as Aristotle's intellectual virtues; it consists in the "contemplation of truth." And thus the rational knowledge of God becomes the object of all his intellection by leading him to the "most per-

[28] *Summa Theologica*, I.79. For a statement of the Aristotelian position see C. R. S. Harris, *Duns Scotus* (1927), II, 300 ff.

[29] Quoted by M. Ramsay in *A Garland for John Donne* (1931), p. 106.

[30] St. Thomas Aquinas, *Selected Writings* (Everyman Library, 1939), p. 177. Reason and intellect "cannot be distinct powers of the soul" (*Summa*, I.79.8).

[31] *Summa*, I.81.2; cf. Richard B. Baker, *The Thomistic Theory of the Passions and the Influence upon the Will* (1941), pp. 137 ff. Aquinas, no more than any other Catholic, of course did not abandon Augustinian theology. He acknowledges (as quoted by Baker, p. 140, n. 2) that man's passions, in spite of the gift of grace, are tainted by Adam's fall: "Semper remanet colluctatio carnis contra spiritum, etiam post moralem virtutem."

[32] "Since the human soul's act of intelligence needs powers, namely imagination and sense which operate through corporeal organs, this by itself shows that the soul is naturally united to the body in order to complete the human species" (*Summa Contra Gentiles*, II.lxviii; cf. *Summa Theologica*, I.75, *passim*).

[33] *Convivio*, II.8; cf. III.15: "So that if reason is perfect, our essence is perfect to such a degree that a man, so far as he is a man, sees every desire brought to an end in her and so is blest."

fect, the most sublime, the most profitable, the most delightful" of wisdom. God is the teleological goal of man's function.[34]

Given a rational creature like man, precisely how may he know God rationally? Aquinas' answer to this question fills many volumes of the most sophisticated theology ever written, but we may at least suggest the lines his answer took. He began—very significantly, for he was seeking a *natural* theology—with the universe as it appeared to man. Through the things man experiences in the world about him, he is led to know God. For instance, he observes change everywhere: winter into summer, wood into ash, youth into age, life into death. Man may react three ways to this obvious fact of life. He may, like Heraclitus, posit change as an ultimate reality; he may refer each change to some prior change, and thus lose himself in the dark backwards of infinity; or he may, like Aquinas, and Aristotle before him, postulate the existence of a prime and unmoved mover, itself not subject to change but the source of all change whatever.

Similarly, the obvious fact of causation leads Aquinas to interpret God as the uncaused cause of everything. The role of contingency in the universe is enormous: things seem to happen in a possible but certainly not a necessary way; a man may be killed by a falling boulder, but he need not be if he move but a foot. So again Aquinas postulates a necessary being, itself not contingent but the cause of contingency in all other things. The universe everywhere reveals the fact of degrees of excellence, of Aristotelian hierarchies of higher and lower. This fact, too, says Aquinas, points inexorably to the perfection that is God. An imperfect being implies the notion of a perfect being who brings the wheel full circle and in himself completes all the imperfection of the visible universe. Finally, the world presents to man the spectacle of incalculable order and harmony. That a man might walk, he has legs; that a bird might fly, it has wings; that a wolf might stalk its prey, it has a highly refined capacity for smelling.

Now we see that in the world things of different natures accord in one order, not seldom or fortuitously, but always or for the most part. Therefore it follows that there is *someone by whose providence the world is governed*. And this we call God.[35]

[34] *Summa Contra Gentiles*, I.iii. Dante, of course, shares this view. Anything that obstructs man's primary function of rational knowledge is a serious sin, and liable to far more severe punishment than a mere sin of sense, like Paolo's and Francesca's. Note the remark in *De Monarchia* (I.4) that the proper function of man is to utilize his intellect to its fullest capacity, either in speculation or in rational conduct.

[35] *Summa Contra Gentiles*, II.xiii. See C. C. J. Webb, *Studies in the History of Natural Theology* (1915), pp. 233 ff.

Charles Darwin was himself not unaware of the teleological drive of the universe; but what he calls natural selection and adaptability, Aquinas, like Erigena, calls the manifestations of a rational deity.[36]

In these ways, then, by observing the world around him and interpreting it through his innate capacity for reason, man fulfills his function in the ultimate knowledge of God. This is a triumphant rationalism, and it marks the apex of the Scholastic attempt to unite reason and faith. But even Aquinas, *facile princeps* of rational theologians, sets a limit to man's proper scope of intellection. Like John of Salisbury—like all the Schoolmen, in fact—he was reluctant to make a complete identification of reason and faith. As John had said, certain truths must be known by faith alone. "These, though reason may not impel, must be a concession to piety. That belief should be accorded sacraments where reason fails is but what Christ has deserved of us by his many benefits and great miracles." [37] Aquinas admits that reason is inadequate for the soul that craves the highest and holiest union with deity. The "natural light of the understanding" is "of finite power; whereof it can reach to a certain fixed point." [38] Stretching beyond rational knowledge lies the empyrean of God's unfathomable perfection. This, transcending knowledge and all man's power, can be approached only through faith. Just as man's finite reason is incapable of realizing "that God is three and one"—the Council of Nicaea had done its work well—so it is incapable of reaching the heart of the mystery, of leading man to a mystic union with God Himself.[39] Tocco, his biographer, tells that Aquinas passed scarcely a day "without being rapt out of his senses." [40] His habit of perfection was predicated on the fact of mystical ecstasy, and the man who more than any other tried to philosophize religion confessed that the central mystery remains ineffable and suprarational.[41]

[36] There is a very clear statement of this natural theology in the *Summa Contra Gentiles*, II.xiii; cf. Gilson, *La Philosophie au Moyen Age*, pp. 178 ff.

[37] *Policraticus*, VII.7 (Pike trans., p. 237).

[38] *Summa Theologica*, II.2.8; cf. Gilson, *The Philosophy of St. Thomas Aquinas*, p. 357.

[39] *Summa Contra Gentiles*, I.iii; cf. I.v.

[40] Quoted by Martin Cyril D'Arcy, *Thomas Aquinas* (1933), p. 52.

[41] Hence the remark that rational knowledge is to faith as a handmaid to her mistress (*Summa Contra Gentiles*, II.xiv), and that "some supernatural knowledge is necessary" (*Summa Theologica*, II.2.3). Dante, whose *Divine Comedy* is the only peer of the astonishing symmetry of the *Summa*, here as so often echoes Aquinas. He is made (*matto*) who thinks by human reason to fathom the mystery of the Trinity. For the *Inferno* and the *Purgatorio*, Virgil (i.e. human reason) and Beatrice (i.e. natural theology) are competent guides, but they finally give way to St. Bernard, the great mystic who leads Dante to the Vision of the Rose. In the presence of the Virgin and the blinding light of the Godhead flaming amid the soldiery of heaven (*la milizia santa*) rational knowledge is consumed in the ecstasy of mystical union. See *Purg.*, III.34 ff.; *Par.*, XXXI.1-3, 134 ff.; *Par.*, XXXIII. 142 ff.; cf. Taylor, *The Medieval Mind*, II, 538 ff.

Aquinas' resolution of the Augustinian dualism of body and soul made, inexorably, for a new unity. The architectonic splendor of the *Summa* is itself a monument to the order of his system and to the Aristotelian teleology that informs it.[42] For Aquinas, every fact of nature is organically related to the total pattern of the great design. Thus the body, so cordially detested by a Neoplatonist like Augustine, is viewed by Aquinas as merely an instrument of the soul. Even the sexual organs have their proper "end," and "that which is the end of any natural thing, cannot be evil in itself: since that which is according to nature, is directed to an end by divine providence."[43] God is rational, and rationally orders the universe with regard "not only to the species, but also to the individual" —which delicate and double obligation He codifies into natural law.[44]

As a rationalist awed by the theocratic design of the universe, Aquinas puts a very high estimate on law. It is the ordinance of reason (*rationis ordinatio*) promulgated by one in authority for the common good. This definition is broad enough to include not only the *lex aeterna* through which the universe is governed by God's providence, but also natural law; by which man, as a rational creature, participates in the eternal law to distinguish good from evil; human law, the rational application of the principles of natural law to terrestrial matters; and divine law, the revelation of God's truth by which the defects of human reason are supplemented).[45]

In spite of the majestic legality of the universe, there remains for Aquinas, as for any theist, the problem of evil. In fact, by arguing the existence of God from the degrees of imperfection in lower creatures he tacitly acknowledges that nature is by definition other than wholly good. In explaining the dilemma of a perfect God and an imperfect world, however, Aquinas is no more successful than others who have tackled the problem. He suggests that nature is as it is because God, in creating it, employed imperfect materials. Again, that if imperfection did not exist, certain good things contingent upon the fact of imperfection would cease to be. Both explanations are as unsatisfactory as Aquinas' doctrine that man's evil is the result of his own free will, which Aquinas, like Augustine, tries desperately to reconcile with the supreme fact of God's omnipotence. But the theme of the *Summa* is not these theological chestnuts:

---

[42] See D'Arcy, pp. 63 ff., 143 ff.          [43] *Summa Contra Gentiles*, III.cxxvi.

[44] *Summa Contra Gentiles*, III.cxxiii, cxiv.

[45] See the *Summa Theologica*, II.1.90. For discussions of Aquinas' conception of law see Carlyle, *A History of Medieval Political Theory*, V, 37 ff.; Dunning, *A History of Political Theories: Ancient and Medieval*, pp. 192 ff.; McIlwain, *The Growth of Political Thought in the West*, pp. 326 ff.

it is the glory of God. All the vast and marvelous symmetry of the cosmos —biological, political, astronomical, ecclesiastical—points to the same sublime fact: a rational, benevolent God creates and controls the universe to fulfill His awful purpose.[46]

In spite of the success of Thomism, its movement towards a rational, natural religion made powerful enemies. To a Franciscan like Duns Scotus (1265-1308), the work of his great Dominican rival constituted a libel on God's power. Aquinas believed that the intellect (the *supremus motor*) was superior to the will because it sought *verum* and not *bonum*, and that in both God and man the will was a faculty to implement the dictates of reason.[47] Duns Scotus thought that such a view placed impious limits on God's omnipotence and denied the Augustinian doctrine of the freedom of the will. In both God and man, he argued, the will must be sovereign or there will be no freedom. No object of intellection, "nec in universali, nec particulari," can compel the will's assent.[48] For if God's will is rationally circumscribed, then God is limited, and this is unthinkable. "Voluntas divina nihil aliud respicit necessario pro objecto ab essentia sua."[49] Against the presumptions of a rational theology, Duns Scotus was intent on restating the Augustinian sovereignty of a suprarational God. Therefore, he argued, God's will must be primary and autonomous, contingent on nothing save itself.

He construes the will as the *emperans intellectui*: what God wills is good not because it is rational, but because He wills it. God's will, not His reason, is the *summa lex*, and it is man's function to submit to it rather than to debase it by underpinning it with criteria of human reason. This generally Augustinian theology[50] was, of course, a conscious reaction to Thomistic rationalism, but it was more: it was the definitive Scholastic statement of a concept profoundly counter to the whole movement of Scholasticism, that is, the synthesis of reason and faith. And, in a more secular form and more secular terminology, it was to be one of the battle cries of the Renaissance. In the self-determinism of Machiavelli's prince, in the voluntarism of Calvin's terrifying God, in the autonomous individualism of Marlowe's Faustus, even in the "will of the majority" of

---

[46] *Summa Contra Gentiles*, II.ii-iii is a compendious statement of the theology expanded in the *Summa Theologica*.

[47] For Dante's statement of this Thomistic position see *Par.*, XXVIII.109 ff.

[48] See C. R. S. Harris, *Duns Scotus*, I, 177 ff., II, 299 ff.; cf. Bernard Landry, *Duns Scot* (1922), pp. 219 ff.; S. H. Mellone, "Scholasticism," Hasting's *Encyclopaedia of Religion and Ethics*, XI, 239 ff.

[49] Quoted by Harris, p. 184, n. 1.

[50] On the relationship between Augustine and Duns Scotus see Landry, pp. 192-93.

democratic theorists Thomistic rationalism was to be repeatedly challenged.[51]

But this is to anticipate. For the Middle Ages Aquinas wrought the crown of a rational theology which justified the ways of God to man. Without detracting from the glory of God—a more fervent faith than his is inconceivable—he rescued man from the slough of impotence and depravity where he had been flung by Augustine. His rational justification of man's rational nature seemed at long last to unite the realms of faith and reason. Saint Paul joined hands with Aristotle. Descartes' taunt against those excesses of Scholasticism that parodied Aristotle—that to contest Aristotle was an attack upon faith—signalized the success of Aquinas' work. His regard for human dignity, his defense of sensory cognition, his efforts to construct a theology natural to man, his rehabilitation of man's self-confidence all mark the climax of the Middle Ages—and the beginning of the Renaissance. For the Thomistic synthesis not only brought Scholastic thought to its highest expression; it also contained the seeds of the scientific rationalism that was to undermine the authority of the Holy Catholic Church whose saint Aquinas has become.[52]

[51] The texts of Duns Scotus are hard to come by, although there is an excerpt from the *Oxford Commentary* in McKeon, II, 313 ff. For general discussion see de Wulf, *History of Medieval Philosophy*, II, 69 ff.; Windelband, *A History of Philosophy*, pp. 328 ff.; Erdmann, *History of Philosophy*, I, 485 ff.; Boas, *The Major Traditions of European Philosophy*, p. 147. Wilhelm Dilthey (*Weltanschauung und Analyse des Menschen Seit Renaissance und Reformation*, 1923, pp. 8 ff.) has speculated interestingly on the derivation of "eines souveränen höchsten Willen" from the concept of the Roman Imperium.

[52] On the triumph of Thomistic Aristotelianism see Werner Jaeger, *Humanism and Theology*, p. 68, n. 7 (good bibliography); Gilson, *The Philosophy of St. Thomas Aquinas*, pp. 13 ff.; Fortunat Strowski, *Montaigne* (1931), p. 123; Charles Homer Haskins, *The Renaissance of the Twelfth Century* (1933), pp. 341 ff. (bibliography, pp. 366 ff.).

## PART III

# The Renaissance View of Man

# XIII

## VIS INERTIAE IN THE RENAISSANCE

### THE POINT OF VIEW

BECAUSE THE RENAISSANCE CAN MEAN almost anything one wants to make it mean, the mutation of critical opinion about it is an instructive lesson in historical interpretation. The oscillation of opinion from, say, Voltaire to Burckhardt and Symonds teaches us that any appraisal of an epoch is only relatively "true" and that each historian reads into an epoch either what he wants to find there or what his own intellectual climate has conditioned him to find there. Voltaire now seems ludicrously wrong to us, and even though we can still admire Burckhardt we are compelled to modify Symonds' rapture.

Therefore, it is well to be humble in supporting any principle of explanation for so complicated an epoch as the Renaissance—especially when that principle is as elliptical as the one to be advanced in the following chapters. For I shall maintain that in its basic view of man the Renaissance preserved the continuity of medieval and pagan thought, and that, although this view was inevitably a synthesis, it derived its characteristic optimism from those Christian and pagan assumptions that had underlain nearly two thousand years of European thinking.

This is to ignore such crucial developments as the new science and sixteenth-century skepticism, both factors tending to disrupt the traditional view of man. Ultimately they would require a complete revaluation both of man and of the universe of which he had for so long fancied himself the crowning glory. But such a revaluation belongs to the seventeenth century—a genuine turning-point in the history of thought and a far more significant break from the Renaissance than the Renaissance had been from the Middle Ages. Copernicus, Bruno, Bacon, Montaigne of the great *Apology,* and Shakespeare of the tragedies reflect those nascent attitudes presently to fructify in the seventeenth century, but like all geniuses they were both of their time and ahead of their time. Although they are unthinkable out of their historical context, they either anticipate later developments or announce the fracture of the values still unquestioned by their lesser contemporaries. The history of their ideas belongs more properly to the century of Galileo and Locke than to that of Calvin and Spenser.

Thus, even at the acknowledged cost of making a false simplification, I shall emphasize the positive and traditional rather than the negative and *avant-garde* aspects of the epoch between Petrarch and Milton. They were positive because they synthesized and reaffirmed for the last time those values of two thousand years that had enabled man to view himself with attitudes ranging from sober approval to fierce pride. And the new currents of thought were negative because they were, when developed, going to make it impossible for man to persist in his old assumptions; after the seventeenth century a thinking man either had to forego his complacency or find shockingly new grounds for maintaining it.

### THE CONSERVATIVE REVOLUTIONISTS

Henry Adams, who never gave up his efforts to understand the movements of history, speaks of the *vis inertiae* operative in human affairs no less than in mechanics. It is a suggestive concept in trying to account for the conservatism of much Renaissance thought:

The dictionary said that inertia was a property of matter, by which matter tends, when at rest, to remain so, and, when in motion, to move on in a straight line. Finding that his [i.e. Adams'] mind refused to imagine itself at rest or in a straight line, he was forced, as usual, to let it imagine something else; and since the question concerned the mind, and not matter, he decided from personal experience that his mind was never at rest, but moved—when normal—about something it called a motive, and never moved without motives to move it. So long as these motives were habitual, and their attraction regular, the consequent result might, for convenience, be called movement of inertia, to distinguish it from movement caused by newer or higher attraction; but the greater the bulk to move, the greater must be the force to accelerate or deflect it.[1]

The bulk of inherited thought in the Renaissance was immense, and the habitual motives and regular attraction derived from the Middle Ages gave a massive, inexorable movement to nearly three centuries of intense intellectual activity. Indeed, the principle of inertia is discernible even in those areas of Renaissance thought which have traditionally been accounted most rebellious: those men who revolted most noisily from the Scholastic tradition were rarely revolutionary enough to demand a dislocation of the assumptions that had made Scholasticism possible. And in the subject that concerns us here—man's estimation of himself—the sixteenth-century anti-Scholastics coasted along quite comfortably on the

---

[1] *The Education of Henry Adams* (1931), p. 441.

same bland assumptions that had cheered the labors of Peter Lombard and Aquinas.

In the notorious disregard with which most men of the Renaissance viewed the Scholastic tradition we would expect to find, if anywhere, clear proof that these were what Bacon proudly called new men—scornful of the values of the past and intent on formulating different and better values for a roseate future. The mounting dissatisfaction with Scholasticism is, indeed, one of the most recurrent motifs of sixteenth-century thought. Ranging through the whole spectrum of discontent, from cautious disapproval to outright vilification, anti-Scholasticism was a stock attitude. It was a point of departure for metaphysicians like Telesio and Bruno (even though they stayed within the terminology of the tradition they attacked), for educators like Vives and Ramus, for the more advanced theologians, for the humanists (otherwise monuments of conservatism), for barking satirists like Rabelais, for professional prophets like Bacon. In this reaction against an obsolescent tradition, the sixteenth century found a focus for discontent and reform.

Or so it thought. Actually, however, the iconoclasm of these anti-Scholastics did not constitute a fundamental break with the past in evaluating the factors of human dignity. It was an effort either to return to an elder purity (*vide* Copernicus on Ptolemy, Pomponazzi on Aristotle, Erasmus on Saint Jerome), or to restudy and revise the apparatus for ascertaining truth (*vide* Bacon's inductive method); but it can hardly be called a search for new objects of knowledge—that had to wait for the seventeenth century. The revolt against Scholasticism indicates that men were becoming impatient with the manifest corruptions of a methodology, but not that they were compelled toward a radical reconstruction of their view of the world and the "truth" they might know about it. If Scholasticism meant anything, it was that a rational God was the author of a rational universe, and that both were legitimate objects of man's rational knowledge. The prevailing optimism of the sixteenth century required no revision of this set of assumptions; indeed, such assumptions made such optimism possible.

One of the beauties of Scholasticism was its extreme adaptability in expressing those assumptions for the Middle Ages. Thus, even though it was primarily a methodology for exploiting *a priori* truths, it suggests the direction of all medieval Christian thought: that basic urge to reconcile reason and faith that culminated in Thomistic rationalism.[2] The mental gymnastics of Abélard's *Sic et Non,* of the intricate polyphony of Aquinas' *Summa,* of what Bacon called the vermiculate questions of post-Scotist

[2] See Martin Grabman, *Die Geschichte der scholastischen Methode, passim.*

thought fell into disfavor, as all things always do, in a later and more "advanced" age. But it is significant that the Schoolmen were condemned for their method rather than for the truth which they sought to establish by their method, or for the assumptions which made that kind of truth possible.

The Scholastic system was predicated on a foundation of Christian dogma whose articles it undertook to ratify by rational inquiry and speculation. Aquinas consistently maintained that philosophy was only the handmaid of theology, but he made a gigantic effort to house both mistress and maid in the same temple of faith. Even though such mystics as Anselm, Bernard, and the Victorines lay outside the Scholastic tradition, the tradition stretched back to Erigena whose translation of the Pseudo-Dionysius informed all subsequent medieval mysticism. And without Erigena could men like Peter Lombard, Albertus Magnus, Aquinas, and Duns Scotus have perfected the system that was Christian, rational, Aristotelian, and dialectic? When Peter Lombard wrote his famous *Sentences,* toward the middle of the twelfth century, he crowned the efforts of his predecessors and provided a model for his successors. He not only established the question and answer form of exposition, but he established the canon of topics and problems legitimate for speculation: God and His attributes, God in relation to the world, God in relation to man, the Church and its institutions. To select a scriptural text, break it down into propositions, subject each to syllogistic argument in the form of questions and answers, and thus finally ascertain the "truth" compatible with the Bible, the Church, and the Fathers may have seemed a paltry method to Bacon, but to Aquinas it was sublime. And Aquinas has not come down to us as a man of paltry intellect.

But no system ever gains universal assent. As early as the twelfth century John of Salisbury, one of the most learned and intelligent men of his age and himself a product of Scholastic training, found cause to resent the aridities of Scholastic logic. When he revisited his old school at Saint Geneviève he listened to the masters haggling over the same old problems —and as fruitlessly as ever.

And thus experience taught me a manifest conclusion, that, whereas dialectic furthers other studies, so if it remain by itself it lies bloodless and barren, nor does it quicken the soul to yield fruit of philosophy, except the same conceive from elsewhere.[3]

But four centuries later, what had been audacious for John had become conventional: by then scarcely a first-rate thinker other than the Spaniard

[3] Quoted by Poole, *Illustrations of the History of Medieval Thought,* p. 212.

Francisco Suarez seriously defended the Scholastic methodology. The Church, astutely steered by the Jesuits, after the Council of Trent took what it hoped was an invulnerable position behind Thomism. In the great outer world, meanwhile, the Reformers were successfully preaching a revived Augustinian theology and those secular thinkers whom Bacon hailed as the new men were virtually unanimous in rejecting, with various degrees of rancor, the Scholastic path to truth.

To seek a new path to truth, however, is not to seek a new truth. Even in the most vigorous opponents of Scholasticism we find little evidence that the sixteenth century had formulated any real grounds for rejecting the Scholastic assumptions. Copernicus, we must remember, did not know that he was making Galileo and Hobbes possible; he fondly believed he was strengthening the foundations of rational faith in a theocratic universe. As even a cursory sampling of sixteenth-century anti-Scholastic opinion will show, it occurred to few men that Aquinas, though clearly outmoded in his methodology, had been wrong in his assumption that man's proudest possession was his capacity for genuine knowledge. And since this assumption lay at the very center of Renaissance optimism, we must expect to find no real iconoclasm until the new science of the seventeenth century undermined this assumption. The Christian humanists of the Renaissance—the last and greatest of whom was Milton—were contemptuous of the old kind of knowledge, but they never doubted that a better kind was within man's reach. If they had, they would have been neither Christians nor humanists, and therefore all their objections to Scholasticism are, in the last analysis, superficial.

In denouncing Scholasticism, the modernists perhaps thought they were flogging a dead horse. And yet the very persistence of their attacks indicates the vitality of the old tradition—a vitality not really sapped until men like Newton and Locke, at the end of the seventeenth century, successfully advanced a new interpretation of the universe and of the kind of knowledge man might have of it. As early as 1516 Erasmus wrote to Henry Bullock that thirty years before nothing was taught at Cambridge but the dictates of Aristotle and the questions of Scotus. "In process of time," he adds gratefully, "Good Letters were introduced; the study of Mathematics was added, and a new or at least a renovated Aristotle. Then came some acquaintance with Greek, and with many authors, whose very names were unknown to the best scholars of a former time." [4] A year later we find him writing to Capito from Louvain of his enemies among the Sorbonne conservatives—Schoolmen, of course: "They are

[4] *The Epistles* (ed. Francis Morgan Nichols), no. 441 (II, 331).

already condemned here, and at Cambridge they are banished." [5] Nearly three generations later Gabriel Harvey reported from Cambridge that "Aristotles Organon is nighhand as litle redd as Dunses Quodlibet," [6] and at the turn of the sixteenth century Francis Bacon gleefully trained his cannon on what he thought was a dying enemy. But Bacon was incorrigibly optimistic, as the comment of Dr. Donne of St. Paul's indicates: "the Schooles have made so many Divisions, and sub-divisions, and re-divisions, and post-divisions of Ignorance, that there goes as much learning to understand ignorance, as knowledg." [7]

And so on through the seventeenth century. Bishop Hall was sure that "God cannot endure a logician"; [8] John Stradling praised the Neo-Stoical Lipsius because he is "none of those subtle sophisticall ianglers, that place philosophie in the quirks and quiddities of crabbed questions"; [9] and Sir Thomas Browne rejoiced to demonstrate how "imperfect" ancient (that is, Scholastic) learning had been. [10] In his *New Discourse upon Method* Descartes worked hard to discredit the *a priori* abstractions of the Schoolmen, but he himself slipped into the same kind of error. Descartes, however, at least recognized the problem of refuting the Schoolmen, and scientists like Boyle and Newton advanced a genuine alternative to their methodology. Boyle argued that the "uninstructive" terms and concepts of the Schoolmen "do neither oblige nor conduct a man to deeper searches into the structure of things." [11]

But by Boyle's time, the strategy of victory over the old dispensation was clear: it was the search into the structure of things for which mathematics was both the tool and the symbol. The spectacular successes of experimental science, and the holy name of Newton, confirmed the victory; moreover, they accounted for the shift in tone from the querulous plaints of the humanists to the sublime self-satisfaction of the new scientists. Cowley held it axiomatic "that we must not content our selves with that Inheritance of Knowledge which is left us by the labour and bounty of our Ancestors, but seek to improve those very grounds, and add to them new and greater Purchases." [12] And Sprat, the historian of the

[5] *Ibid.*, no. 706 (III, 180).

[6] *Letter-Book* (Camden Society Publications, 1884), p. 182.

[7] *LXXX Sermons* (1640), no. 29, p. 287.

[8] *Meditations and Vows* in *Anglicanism* (ed. Paul Elmer More and Frank Leslie Cross, 1935), p. 220.

[9] Lipsius, *Tvvo Bookes of Constancie,* "The Epistle to the Reader," p. 68.

[10] See Basil Willey, *The Seventeenth Century Background* (1934), p. 53.

[11] *The Christian Virtuoso* in *Anglicanism*, p. 235. For a full account of seventeenth-century anti-Scholasticism see Richard Foster Jones, *Ancients and Moderns* (1936), *passim* and esp. pp. 124 ff.

[12] "A Proposition for the Advancement of Learning," *The Essays and Other Prose Writings* (ed. Alfred B. Gough, 1915), pp. 26-27.

Royal Society, called the faithful to arms against "powerful and barbarous Foes, that have not been fully subdued almost these six thousand Years, *Ignorance* and *false Opinion*."[13] This was the triumphant attitude versified by Dryden,[14] among many others, and sanctified by Newton. The truth of Cowley's dictum was becoming ever clearer: "Our Reasoning Faculty as well as Fancy, does but Dream, when it is not guided by sensible Objects."[15] Mass, gravity, and cohesion, Newton intoned, are not "occult qualities, supposed to result from the specific forms of things; they are general laws of nature, by which the things themselves are formed."[16] From this to Richard Bentley's deistic proposition, in italics, that God *"always acts geometrically"* is but a step;[17] and thus we arrive at the climate of opinion that nurtured Locke, Toland, Collins, Tindal, and Chubb. From this vantage it was easy for a trivial popularizer of Newton to dismiss Scholasticism as "a Chaos of vain and useless Disputes, a Chain of unintelligible Definitions, a blind Zeal for wrangling, and a still blinder devotion for Aristotle."[18]

But this is to look far ahead. The sixteenth century had no such foundation of mathematical positivism for rejecting the Schoolmen, and therefore the basis for its discontent is more trifling and more cautious. The humanists, for instance, raised the charge, very heinous to them, of bad Latinity and obtuse writing. From Paris young Erasmus wrote to Thomas Grey that his Scholastic professors

assert that the mysteries of this science [that is, theology] cannot be comprehended by one who has any commerce at all with the Muses or with the Graces. If you have touched good letters, you must unlearn what you have learnt; if you have drunk of Helicon, you must get rid of the draught.[19]

Because Erasmus made incessant warfare on the illiteracy of the Schoolmen it was only just that Thomas Starkey praised him as a "most famuse dyuyne" who had wrought miracles in the reformation of university

---

[13] *The History of the Royal Society of London* (1734), II.ii (p. 57); cf. "A Model of their whole Design," II.v (pp. 61-62).

[14] See, for instance, "To My Honor'd Friend Dr. Charleton."

[15] "A Proposition for the Advancement of Learning," *The Essays and Other Prose Writings*, p. 27.

[16] See E. A. Burtt, *The Metaphysical Foundations of Modern Physical Science* (1925), p. 219. The most compendious statement of Newton's religio-philosophical views is in the "General Scolium" in the *Mathematical Principles of Natural Philosophy* (ed. Florian Cajori, 1934), esp. p. 546.

[17] For Bentley's Newtonian and deistic arguments see the second Boyle sermon, *Works* (1838), and esp. III, 38, 42-44, 92.

[18] Francesco Algarotti, *Sir Isaac Newton's Philosophy Explain'd for the Use of the Ladies* (1739), I, 26.

[19] *The Epistles*, no. 59 (I, 144).

training and in the instruction of the clergy.[20] But Erasmus, though a born propagandist for "good letters," had neither a very original nor a very philosophical mind. Properly, in his role as prince of humanists he had no stomach for those who would assail man's traditional dignity formulated in traditional terms; as we shall see when we come to examine his theology, he refused to renounce any of those venerable assumptions that made a rational, optimistic Christianity possible. And so from him we should expect a no more searching analysis of Scholasticism than urbane contempt for its literary *gaucherie*.

Touched as many of them were with Neoplatonic mysticism, the humanists were emotionally incapable of the rigors of a rational theology expressed syllogistically. John Colet, a man of great piety and learning, wished to learn nothing from the Schoolmen. If we may believe Erasmus, he thought they were "stupid and dull and anything but clever. For they cavil about different sentences and words, now to gnaw at this and now at that, and to dissect everything bit by bit, seemed to him to be the mark of a poor and barren mind."[21] Luther's humanistic ally Melanchthon shared this view. "Good heavens!" he exclaimed of John Major, a famed Scottish Scholastic. "What wagon loads of trifling! What pages he fills with disputes whether there can be horseness without a horse, and whether the sea was salt when God made it."[22] Erasmus' own criticism was more expressly literary. Because most of the Schoolmen were lamentably uninformed about "more ancient and elegant literature" they exhausted their minds with a "dry and biting subtlety." As a result, "theology, the queen of all science—so richly adorned by ancient eloquence—they strip of all her beauty by their incongruous, mean, and disgusting style."[23] In the *Colloquies* and throughout those thousands of most elegantly turned letters Erasmus returns repeatedly to the attack. His Folly, an audacious wench, makes almost indecent fun of the Schoolmen, and in graver style the *Enchiridion* suggests that the good life is one of unselfish service to Christ the Prince, not one of syllogistic argumentation.

Even the philosophical opponents of Scholasticism, however, though more daring than the humanists, were unable to rise completely above the inherited formulas of thought. Notorious scoundrels like Pomponazzi and Telesio—both detested by their cautious contemporaries as devils with cloven feet—were not nearly so revolutionary as they perhaps seemed

[20] *England in the Reign of King Henry the Eighth. A Dialogue between Cardinal Pole and Thomas Lupset, Lecturer in Rhetoric* (EETS, Ex. Ser., XII, 1871), p. 210.

[21] Quoted by Frederic Seebohm, *The Oxford Reformers* (1896), p. 103.

[22] See Preserved Smith, *Erasmus* (1923), p. 23.

[23] Quoted by Seebohm, p. 129.

to themselves. They were both agitated by the same questions that had teased the Schoolmen, and although they came to rather heterodox conclusions they were content to die in the bosom of Mother Church—even though She herself had forcibly suggested it might be to their advantage to do so. The result of Pomponazzi's labors was a reinterpretation, but not a rejection, of Aristotelian psychology; the result of Telesio's was a further development of post-Scotist voluntarism.

Pietro Pomponazzi (1462-1525) was the most notable of those dissenters to the accretions and distortions that Greek philosophy had suffered at the hands of Scholastic commentators. The unflattering reception accorded his *De Immortalitate Animi* (1516) reflects the basic timidity of the sixteenth century. It was one thing for the Aristotelians of northern Italy to haggle with the Platonic academies of the south,[24] but it was quite another for impious left-wingers like Ermolao Barbaro and Pomponazzi to break the rules and question the immortality of the soul. Even the orthodox Averroists of Padua, led by Nicoletto Vernias and Alessandro Achillini dared not impugn the Thomistic identification of the Christian immortal soul with the Aristotelian active intellect. But after a scrupulous study of the *De Anima*, Pomponazzi came to the unholy conclusion that no less a personage than Aquinas had been guilty of misinterpreting Aristotle. He maintained, following Alexander of Aphrodisias, that because form is unthinkable apart from matter, the soul must perish with the body whose form it is;[25] and furthermore that ethics should consequently be the practice of virtue for its own sake rather than the calculation of celestial punishment or reward. "Praemium essentiale virtutis est ipsomet virtus quae hominem felicem facit."

For his pains in trying to reconstruct properly, as he thought, the actual doctrine of Aristotle, Pomponazzi became one of the most manifest villains in Christendom. The Averroists were his enemies because he had gone back through Averroes to Aristotle; the Church and the Schoolmen were outraged because his quest for truth had jeopardized their exclusive monopoly—the manipulation of divine largesse. And yet Pomponazzi had done nothing to impugn the cardinal tenet of man's belief in his native dignity, which was his capacity for rational conduct; indeed, he had established ethics on an almost Hellenically rational basis. Like Machiavelli, however, he became one of the devils incarnate to the pious of the sixteenth century, and thus he was driven to the ultimate ignoble

---

[24] See John Herman Randall, Jr., "The Development of Scientific Method in the School of Padua," *JHI*, I (1940), 177-206; cf. Henri Busson, *Les Sources et le développement du rationalisme dans la littérature française de la renaissance* (1922), pp. 29-63.

[25] See Andrew Halliday Douglas, *The Philosophy and Psychology of Pietro Pomponazzi* (1910), pp. 98 ff.; cf. John Owen, *The Skeptics of the Italian Renaissance* (1908), pp. 184 ff.

irony: after his book had been burned and he himself had been made liable to the secular arm of the Church, he rationalized his position by the paltry doctrine of the double truth. What he could support as a secular philosopher he could only despise as a Christian. As a thinker he could accommodate the most intolerable heresies, but as the unworthy object of God's grace he accepted *in toto* the dogma essential for salvation. Nothing better reveals the *vis inertiae* of the sixteenth century. Duns Scotus had forced the first wedge in the Thomistic synthesis of reason and faith by elevating God's will over God's reason; William of Occam had enlarged the fissure; and finally a man of Pomponazzi's intelligence was compelled to hide behind the paradox that divorced reason and faith. In 1512 the Lateran Council sanctified the paradox by fiat:

> As what is true can never contradict what is true, we determine that every proposition which is contrary to the truth of the revealed faith is entirely false.[26]

(Although the Church has never encouraged fideism, some of its best minds—Pascal's, for instance—have finally turned to it in desperation.)

The career of Bernadino Telesio (1509-1588) is a similar essay in cautious speculation checked by outraged orthodoxy. Pomponazzi had dared to scrutinize Scholastic psychology, but Telesio, in his *De Rerum Natura* (1563?) ventured on to metaphysics. His reward too, it is almost useless to add, was to have his work placed on the Index. Like many men before and since, Telesio was dissatisfied with Scholastic conceptualism, and so he tried to find a substitute for the derivation of ecclesiastically proper deductions from *a priori* assumptions. Although his empiricism—*non ratione sed sensu*—faintly anticipates Locke's, his age, unlike Locke's, was horrified by an effort to reconstruct epistemology.

Telesio argued that universals are merely the names we humans (who cannot detect minute differences) give to things that more or less resemble each other. But such concepts should not be mistaken for reality. Because those who have hitherto investigated the world have never troubled to look about them carefully ("at nequaquam inspexisse videntur")[27] they have failed to realize that the two basic facts of nature are heat and cold: the one expands, the other contracts, and between them they produce everything in nature.[28] And thus for Telesio matter assumes an almost vitalistic function, so that he eventually arrived at some-

---

[26] See Louis I. Bredvold, "The Religious Thought of Donne in Relation to Medieval and Later Traditions," *Studies in Shakespeare, Milton, and Donne* (University of Michigan Publications: Language and Literature, no. I, 1925), p. 207.

[27] *De Rerum Natura* (ed. Vincenzo Spampanato 1910-1923), "Proemium" to bk. I (I, 6).

[28] *Ibid.*, I.vi (I, 24 ff.).

thing very like the Scotist will to displace the Aristotelian and Thomistic principle of reason as the teleological force of the universe. Telesio even ascribed sentiency to matter; mentality becomes a property of matter, and the soul itself, the sacrum of the Christian tradition, must have a material existence. Man himself is the best example of thinking matter. But again the irony: although Telesio's metaphysics was, at least in its implications, terrifyingly heterodox, he was prudent enough to inject a pious disclaimer by declaring his faith in man's immortal soul bequeathed him by God— "ut sacrosancta Ecclesia docet."

Animam, a Deo optimo maximo creatam et singulis hominibus infusam, universo quidem singulorum corpori, at spiritui praecipue, ut propriam formam inditam esse; itaque substantiam quae in homine ratiocinatur, non unam simplicemque esse sed ex anima a Deo creata et e spiritu e semine educto compositam esse; et facultatem ignotas rerum conditiones ex earum similitudine, quae in ente penitus noto conspectae sunt, cognoscendi, non ratiocinandi intelligendique sed existimandi vel commemorandi potius appellandam esse.[29]

There were others in the sixteenth century who learned to their cost what it meant to challenge those values that had served western Europe for a millennium. Petrus Ramus (1515-1572) made it his career to challenge Aristotelian logic—and he was butchered on St. Bartholomew's eve.[30] Giordano Bruno, whom history has dramatized as the Martyr of the Renaissance, stayed fairly close to the methodology of the Schoolmen, but he dared to explore the implications of the Copernican astronomy.

The excellency of God is magnify'd, and the grandeur of his Empire made manifest; he's not glorify'd in one but in numberless Suns, not in one Earth or in one World, but in ten hundred Thousand, in infinite Globes. . . . By this science we are loosen'd from the chains of a most narrow dungeon, and set at liberty to rove in a most august empire; we are remov'd from conceited boundaries and poverty, to the innumerable riches of an infinite space.[31]

Andreas Osiander had thought it prudent to explain that the *De Revolutionibus,* published (1543) as his friend Copernicus lay a-dying, was

---

[29] *Ibid.,* VIII.xv (III, 131).

[30] In England, and especially at Cambridge, Ramus was well-known. Christopher Marlowe, himself a Cambridge man, in *The Massacre at Paris* (ll. 390 ff.) shows the Guise about to kill Ramus because, as he explains, he had had a "smack in all" and yet had got to the bottom of nothing—in addition to which he had mocked the Organon. Ramus, preparing to die manfully, defies him:

> I knew the Organon to be confusde,
> And I reduc'd it into better forme.

See Frank P. Graves, *Peter Ramus and the Educational Reformation of the Sixteenth Century* (1912); Roy W. Battenhouse, *Marlowe's Tamburlaine* (1941), pp. 26-29.

[31] *Innumberable Worlds* as translated by John Toland, *Miscellaneous Works* (1747), I, 347.

merely hypothetical and therefore not heretical, but Bruno entertained no such reservations. He admitted that his beliefs "may be indirectly opposed to truth according to the faith," [32] and thus the travesty of his trial before the Venetian Inquisition: he was denied an advocate; he was made to establish, if he could, his own innocence of heresy; he was not told the names of his accusers; he was held incommunicado for seven years between his trial and his fiery execution; he was not permitted to cross-examine the witnesses; his prosecutors were his judges.[33] Pomponazzi and Telesio[34] had managed by hook and crook to die in bed, but Bruno, who had encountered hostility all over Europe on his wanderings, was finally delivered over to the Roman butcher in the Campo dei Fiori.

For us, however, Francis Bacon remains the just, mighty, and eloquent spokesman for the revolt against Scholasticism. In those great purple passages of the *Advancement* and the *Novum Organum* (audacious title) he developed most of the heresies of the sixteenth century. Like Telesio he would substitute empiricism for the flatulent *a priori* assumptions of the Schoolmen, but also like Telesio he was unable to free himself from those shackles which he thought to have broken: the Baconian "forms" have all the dignity of a Scholastic abstraction, just as Telesio's principle of heat is uncommonly like Aristotle's efficient cause, so dear to all Schoolmen. Bacon's brazen call to arms is still stirring, of course. He would establish a new methodology for a complete reëxamination of nature, and he would destroy those idols of the tribe which made thought fruitless. For when the mind of man merely works on itself, rather than on things, "it is endless, and brings forth indeed cobwebs of learning, admirable for the fineness of thread and work, but of no substance or profit." [35] And as for syllogistic argument, the crowning glory of Scho-

[32] Cited from the records of the trial by William Boulting, *Giordano Bruno: His Life, Thought, and Martyrdom* (1914), p. 268; cf. I. Frith, *Life of Giordano Bruno the Nolan* (1887), pp. 278 ff.

[33] See Boulting, *Bruno*, p. 280.

[34] For a history of Telesio's reputation and influence see Neil Van Deusen, *Telesio: The First of the Moderns* (1932), pp. 6 ff. A convenient short discussion is the same author's "Place of Telesio in the History of Philosophy, *Philosophical Review*, XLIV (1935), 417-34; cf. Henry Osborn Taylor, *Thought and Expression in the Sixteenth Century* (1920), II, 347-48; Boas, *The Major Traditions of European Philosophy*, pp. 168 ff.

[35] *Advancement of Learning*, bk. I (*Works*, 1857 ff., VI, 122). The Schoolmen have been called many names by many people, but never with more enthusiasm than by Bacon: "Surely, like as many substances in nature which are solid do putrefy and corrupt into worms, so it is the property of good and sound knowledge to putrefy and dissolve into a number of subtile, idle, unwholesome, and (as I may term them) vermiculate questions, which have indeed a kind of quickness and life of spirit, but no soundness or matter or goodness of quality. This kind of degenerate learning did chiefly reign amongst the schoolmen; who having sharp and strong wits, and abundance of leisure, and small variety of reading; but their wits being shut up in the cells of a few authors (chiefly Aristotle their

lasticism, it was worthless and unproductive of new truth: beginning always with an acknowledged truth, it merely proved or disproved what was already known and was therefore incapable of determining the status of a doubtful proposition. It was "contentious and well nigh useless." [36]

And so on through many brave and boastful pages. Yet when we at last arrive at Bacon's own methodology, we find that he was both ignorant and contemptuous of mathematics (the most powerful tool of modern man), and, unlike Bruno, unaware of the implications of Copernican astronomy.[37] He promised to reconstruct human knowledge from the "very foundations" [38] and like Columbus to discover a brave new world [39] —and yet he was at heart a metaphysical realist who, like the Schoolmen, believed in the existence of a basic reality behind the sensibles of observations. This abstract reality he called form, and he made it the ultimate object of his search through nature.

For the Form of a nature is such, that given the Form the nature infallibly follows. Therefore it is always present when the nature is present, and universally implies it, and is constantly inherent in it.[40]

These forms seem to have meant various things to Bacon—sometimes the *cause* of things, like Aristotle's formal cause, and sometimes natural law ("the investigation, discovery, and explanation" of which "is the foundation as well of knowledge as of operation")[41]—but his quest for them was like nothing so much as the Schoolmen's quest for abstract essences subsuming all particulars.

Of a given nature to discover the form, or true specific difference, or nature-engendering nature, or source of emanation (for these are the terms which come nearest to a description of the thing), is the work and aim of Human Knowledge.[42]

dictator) as their persons were shut up in the cells of monasteries and colleges; and knowing little history, either of nature or time; did out of no great quantity of matter, and infinite agitation of wit, spin out unto us those laborious webs of learning which are extant in their books." See *Advancement of Learning*, bk. I (*Works*, VI, 121-22); cf. *Novum Organum*, I.xliii (*Works*, VIII, 78).

[36] *Novum Organum*, I.54 (*Works*, VIII, 84),

[37] See *De Augmentis*, III.4 (*Works*, VIII, 488): "all the labour is spent in mathematical observations and demonstrations. Such demonstrations however only show how all these things [i.e. astronomical phenomena] may be ingeniously made out and disentangled, not how they may truly subsist in nature; and indicate the apparent motions only, and a system of machinery arbitrarily devised and arranged to produce them,—not the very causes and truth of things." Hobbes too was mathematically illiterate, but he at least made a valiant if futile effort to learn geometry.

[38] *Novum Organum*, I.31 (*Works*, VIII, 74).

[39] *Ibid.*, I.92 (*Works*, VIII, 129).

[40] *Ibid.*, II.4 (*Works*, VIII, 170).

[41] *Ibid.*, II.2 (*Works*, VIII, 168).

[42] *Ibid.*, II.1 (*Works*, VIII, 167).

Even though this is very odd doctrine for a man commonly hailed as one of the beacons of modern thought, we should not minimize Bacon's achievement because of his quaint metaphysics. About the time when the Catholic Church, finding new strength in the Counter Reformation, was restating its authoritarian prerogatives—not only does faith exclude all doubt, declared the Council of Trent; it excludes even "the desire of subjecting its truth to demonstration" [43]—Bacon articulated the cardinal principle of modern man's quest for knowledge: that *a priori* conclusions are worthless. Thus, as Mr. Douglas Bush has said, if Bacon had not existed it would have been necessary to invent him.[44] And yet we should realize that Bacon himself was not free of certain *a priori* assumptions. Compared to genuinely original thinkers like Leonardo[45] and Galileo[46]— men who actually had a vision of the new world announced by Bacon— Bacon seems cautious and cumbersome even in the inductive method [47] for which he was worshipped by later English scientists.

Perhaps Cowley was right when he hailed Bacon as the Moses who led erring humanity forth from the "Deserts of but small Extent" to the boundless expanse of scientific knowledge;[48] perhaps the virtuosi of the late seventeenth century were no more than just when they suggested that the best preface for a history of the Royal Society of London would be the works of King James' Lord Chancellor.[49] But also they perhaps lacked the perspective to evaluate Bacon's importance properly. Today we may see that with both his intellectual bravado and his fundamental if less apparent allegiance to inherited ways of thought Bacon was a

[43] Quoted by Preserved Smith, *The Age of the Reformation* (1920), p. 625.

[44] "Two Roads to Truth: Science and Religion in the Early Seventeenth Century," *ELH*, VIII (1941), 86.

[45] This is not the place to discuss Leonardo, but for terse statements of his genuinely empirical habit of thought see his jottings in *The Literary Works* (ed. Jean Paul Richter, 1939), art. 837 (II, 101), art. 1147 (II, 239), art. 1148A (II, 239), art. 1182 (II, 245).

[46] Galileo, far more than Bacon, was the man who closed the era opened by the Council of Nicaea. Even a cursory reading of *Two New Sciences* will show his complete reliance on mathematics, a tool which he, unlike Bacon, used with spectacular success in his experiments. See J. J. Fahie, "The Scientific Work of Galileo," *Studies in the History and Method of Science* (ed. Charles Singer, 1921), 278-80 on Galileo's anticipations of Newton. See also H. T. Pledge, *Science Since 1500* (1939), pp. 60-61; A. Wolf, *A History of Science Technology, and Philosophy in the 16th & 17th Centuries* (1935), p. 29; Burtt, *The Metaphysical Foundations of Modern Physical Science*, p. 64; P. P. Weiner, "The Tradition behind Galileo's Methodology," *Osiris*, I (1930), 732-46.

[47] For Bacon's analysis of induction see the *Novum Organum*, II.10 (*Works*, VIII, 178-79), and for an example—his elaborate investigation of heat—see *ibid.*, II.11 (*Works*, 179 ff.). Note his use of Scholastic terminology ("essence" and "quiddity") in his conclusion, *ibid.*, II.16 (*Works*, II, 205).

[48] "To the Royal Society" in Sprat, *The History of the Royal Society of London*, sig. Al[v] ff.

[49] See Sprat, pp. 35-36.

typical man of the late Renaissance. Like his predecessors of the sixteenth century and like his mighty contemporary Donne,[50] he was at best a transitional figure who knew that he was dissatisfied with the past even though he was unable to forget the accumulated traditions of two thousand years. His failure to formulate a genuinely new interpretation of experience was the failure of his century. And although neither Bacon nor the Renaissance can hardly be charged with intellectual sterility, it is increasingly evident that we must qualify our ancestors' rapture over the Renaissance man's newfound freedom. The synthesis of faith and reason which found expression in Scholasticism was obviously fracturing in the sixteenth century, but Bacon, no less than Pomponazzi and Telesio, shows that one may vocally repudiate a tradition without entirely losing his subservience to it. Although articulate and high-toned contempt for Scholasticism was a fashion followed by the very best people in the sixteenth century, it was hard to forget those assumptions of a theocratic God, of an orderly universe, of a rational man created only a little lower than the angels, that had made Scholasticism possible.

### TOWARD A DEFINITION OF THE RENAISSANCE

If there is an inference to be drawn from our survey of sixteenth-century anti-Scholasticism it is that the fabled emancipation of that period was less thorough than was once believed. Therefore the late nineteenth-century—which is to say Burckhardt's—conception of the Renaissance needs radical revision.

Burckhardt viewed the Renaissance as a spontaneous creation, a glorious epoch formed by the "genius" of the Italian people and their dazzling urban culture of the *quattrocento*. Notoriously unsympathetic to philosophy, Burckhardt began his studies as a critic of art; throughout *The Civilization of the Renaissance in Italy* he conceives of *Kultur* as some transcendent spiritual reality finding expression in the works of magnificent artisans. His acute aesthetic judgments are everywhere interlarded with such phrases as *Entwicklung des Individuums* and *die Entdeckung des Menschens und der Welt*. The close of the thirteenth century, thus, "began to swarm with individuality; the ban laid on human personality was dissolved; and a thousand figures meet us each in its own special

---

[50] The *Anniversaries* are a monument to Donne's skepticism and naturalism, but they preceded the Augustinianism, anti-intellectualism, and mysticism of the massive sermons. See M. Ramsay, *Les Doctrines Médiévales chez Donne* (1924); Louis I. Bredvold, "The Religious Thought of Donne in Relation to Medieval and Later Traditions," *Studies in Shakespeare, Milton, and Donne* (University of Michigan Publications: Language and Literature, no. I, 1925), pp. 193-232; Charles Monroe Coffin, *John Donne and the New Philosophy* (1937); F. M. Maloney, *John Donne, His Flight from Medievalism* (1944).

shape and dress." [51] Together with the state and religion, *Kultur* is one of the three forces that coalesce to produce notable individuals. One finishes Burckhardt's book—as readable as a novel—with the notion that the era inaugurated by Petrarch was *sui generis:* a golden age when Giotto and Lorenzo, Valla and Cellini, walked the shining Italian earth like the gods they were.[52]

After nearly a century, however, the individualism of Burckhardt, like that of Carlyle, appears as perhaps distorted hero-worship.[53] To most of us, history seems more than a succession of great men, like beads on a string. We think—or like to think that we think—in terms of texture, continuity, relatedness. For better or worse, our view of history is anthropological, and we try to reconstruct an era so that we may know the factors—religious, economic, social, artistic, whatever—that underlay the assumptions, the prejudices, and the achievements of the average man. (Inevitably, however, it is to the extraordinary, or at least the articulate, man to whom we must always turn for our knowledge of his era.) [54] It is more profitable to consider Shakespeare as a playwright following certain traditions and trying (successfully, as it happened) to please a public with certain tastes than to bow our heads before the genius that transcends analysis. Ideas, patterns of thought and emotion, and institutions that embody them all have their natural histories, and it is the business of the historian to plot them. Even though we remember certain ages for their great products, any age transcends its spokesmen. Few of us can any longer believe history to be merely the lengthened shadow of great men. Taine's thesis has served as a useful antidote to those who would portray the past in only one dimension.

The Renaissance is singularly complex in that its tensions and stresses produced such gigantic spokesmen. They tend to enchant us, so that we sometimes fail to think of them as men at all. We simplify and per-

<hr/>

[51] *The Civilization of the Renaissance in Italy* (trans. S. G. C. Middlemore, n.d.), p. 70. For a cognate view in a history standard a generation ago, see Edward Maslin Hulme, *The Renaissance* (1914), pp. 59 ff. In William Butler Yeats' *Autobiography* (1938) there is an interesting comparison of portraits by Strozzi and Sargent that echoes a Burckhardtian and Pre-Raphaelite youth; see *The Autobiography* (1938), p. 248.

[52] See Robert Herndon Fife, "The Renaissance in a Changing World," *Germanic Review*, IX (1934), 73-95, for a very able critique of Burckhardt; cf. Roland H. Bainton, "Changing Ideas and Ideals in the Sixteenth Century," *Journal of Modern History*, VIII (1936), 417-43; Louis B. Wright, "Introduction to a Survey of Renaissance Studies," *MLQ*, II (1941), 355-63.

[53] See Norman Nelson, "Individualism as a Criterion of the Renaissance," *JEGP*, XXXII (1933), 316-34. For a pair of old studies suggesting either that the Middle Ages were more than Voltaire had suspected or that the Middle Ages extended longer into the Renaissance than Burckhardt would have dreamed, see S. R. Maitland, *The Dark Ages* (1844) and Vernon Lee, *Euphorion* (1899).

[54] But, for an exception, note Louis B. Wright's extremely interesting *Middle-Class Culture in Elizabethan England* (1935).

sonify the density of the era in titans like Rabelais and Cesare Borgia, but actually the movement of thought between Petrarch and Milton was anything but simple. The more we study those centuries, the less tenable becomes the notion of a sharply delimited Utopia, bounded on one end by the ignorance of the Middle Ages, on the other by the cold materialism of modern science—a Utopia through which stalked transcendent geniuses whose genius, like God's will, was contingent on nothing but itself.

Viewed properly as an era of transition, like any other era, the Renaissance extends itself fore and aft. But especially aft. The centuries between Charlemagne and Aquinas were, it is true, the summit of the age of faith and of theology, but none the less they witnessed the development of an intensely secular interest in the things of this world. The pilgrimages and crusades may have been pious in intention, but from them men learned quite as much about the terrestrial city as they did about the propagation of the faith. The development of the Courts of Love, based on a curious blending of Mariolatry and the coarsest sexuality, gave men and women a new point of reference and a new object of devotion.[55] What a wonderful thing is love, sings Andreas Capellanus, "which makes a man shine with so many virtues and teaches everyone, no matter who he is, so many good traits of character." [56] It might be Castiglione talking. The charm-

---

[55] See J. Huizinga, *The Waning of the Middle Ages* (1927), pp. 76 ff., 288 ff.

[56] *The Art of Courtly Love* (trans. John Jay Parry, 1941), p. 31. That Andreas and his patroness, Marie of Champagne, represent a point of view considerably closer to *The Ladies' Home Journal* than to Augustine is shown pretty clearly in the thirty-one rules of love (pp. 184-86). The twin themes of erotic and religious piety are interestingly woven together in a poem which Sir Thomas More translated from Pico ("The Twelve Properties of Conditions of a Love," *The English Works of Sir Thomas More*, I, 1931, 389-94). Pico ironically inverts the tenets prescribed by men like Andreas by showing God as the object of the lover's passion. Thus his parody of the "property" "To languish ever, and ever to burn in the desire of his love":

> Diversely passioned is the lover's heart:
> Now pleasant hope, now dread and grievous fear,
> Now perfect bliss, now bitter sorrow smart;
> And whether his love be with him or elsewhere,
> Oft from his eye there falleth many a tear,—
> For very joy, when they together be;
> When they be sundered, for adversity.

> Like affections feeleth eke the breast
> Of God's lover in prayer and meditation:
> When that his love liketh in him rest
> With inward gladness of pleasant contemplation,
> Out break the tears for joy and delectation;
> And when his love list eft to part him fro,
> Out break the tears again for pain and woe.

ing freshness and naivete of *Aucassin et Nicolette* consummate beautifully the secular tone of dozens of lyrics like

> Lydia, bella puella candida
> Qua bene supras lac et lilium
> Album, quae simul rosam subidam
> Aut expolitum ebur Indicum,
> Pande, puella, pande capillulos
> Flavos, lucentes, et aurum nitidum . . .[57]

It is not surprising, perhaps, that even the medieval poet luxuriates erotically in this kind of sensuousness, but it is surprising when we find men
of genuine piety like Saint Francis and Saint Bernard luxuriating in a
similar contemplation of the birds and the flowers or in the physical details of the Passion. Bernard's almost erotic preoccupation with the Virgin powerfully influenced the Mariolatry of the late Middle Ages.[58] For
these men, the bleeding Christ was quite as appealing as the philosophical
abstraction of the Logos had been to the Nicene disputants.

This gradual shift in the objects of attention and the quality of emotion toward these objects is reflected in the formal, philosophic thought
of the late Middle Ages. For this reason, among others, it has been argued
that what we have called the Renaissance began in the twelfth century.[59]
Such scholars as Dilthey, Gentile, and Cassirer have shown that the more
we know about the late Middle Ages, the more shadowy becomes the line
between them and the Renaissance. The Nominalism which was so
hotly contested by medieval conservatives acquires new significance if
it is traced through to its historical consequence in the skeptical natural-

---

[57] *An Anthology of Medieval Latin* (ed. Stephen Gaselle, 1925), pp. 68-69.

[58] See Theodore Spencer, *Death and Elizabethan Tragedy* (1936), pp. 16-17. For a specimen of the sensuous elements in Bernard's religious emotion see Sermon XLIII, "How
Meditation of the Sufferings and the Passion of Jesus Christ Enables the Bride . . . to Pass
. . . through the Prosperity and the Adversity of this World," *Life and Works of Saint
Bernard*, IV, 266 ff.

[59] See Charles Homer Haskins, *The Renaissance of the Twelfth Century* (1933). For an
orthodox Catholic attack on the Burckhardtian thesis, see Gerald Groveland Walsh, S.J.,
*Medieval Humanism* (1942). For another approach to the problem of redating the Renaissance see John Herman Randall, Jr., "The Development of Scientific Method in the School of
Padua," *JHI*, I (1940), 178-79, 182. In many of his books Etienne Gilson has urged a re-
examination of the traditional distinction between the Middle Ages and the Renaissance, as
has the eminent Ernst Cassirer in such works as his *Erkenntnisproblem* and *Individuum und
Kosmos*. For an excellent discussion of the problem see Paul Oskar Kristeller and John
Herman Randall, Jr., "The Study of the Philosophies of the Renaissance," *JHI*, II (1941),
449-96. The bibliography in this article may be supplemented by those in the *Journal of
Philosophy*, vols. XXXI (1934)-XXXIV (1937), in Friedrich Ueberweg's *Grundriss der
Geschichte der Philosophie der Neuzeit* (11th ed., 1914), vol. III, and in the *Dictionary of
Philosophy and Psychology* (ed. James Mark Baldwin, 3 vols., 1901-1905), vol. III.

ism of the late Renaissance.[60] If a new regard for individualism and a new realism are the keys to the Renaissance, one should not overlook medieval mystics like Bonaventura or Francis of Assisi, who gloried in the common and the low; or painters like the brothers van Eyck, who in their canvasses show a scrupulous zeal for realistic detail; or philosophers like Abélard and Aquinas, who made cognitive knowledge the basis of a rational theology. And there remains, to defy chronological classification, the vague but tantalizing Franciscan of the thirteenth century, Roger Bacon. His approach to the problem of knowledge—*sine experimentia nihil sufficientur sciri potest*—would have horrified Augustine, but it would have seemed axiomatic to Leonardo and Galileo. One might argue, of course, that Roger Bacon was so far ahead of his time that he spent a large part of his adult life in prison. But what happened to Bruno? to Galileo? to Campanella? to Vanini?

The old catchwords are convenient but inadequate. Michelet's dictum that the Renaissance meant the rediscovery by man of himself and his world is enticing:

*Un monde d'humanité commence, de sympathie universelle.* L'homme est enfin le frère du monde . . . C'est là le vrai sens de la Renaissance: tendresse, bonté pour las nature.[61]

But the quality of Saint Francis' emotion and *tendresse* makes that of his successors thin and almost academic. If emancipation from the shackles of medieval orthodoxy is the central motif of the Renaissance, one should remember that the Church remained potent until the eighteenth century: Calvin, Rabelais, and Loyola rubbed elbows in the same classroom; and as Toffanin has reminded us, heterodoxy was not unknown in the Middle Ages. Both Luther and Calvin read Augustine with loving care, and the humanism of Ficino and Erasmus had its roots deep in the Carolingian revival.

In short, Matthew Arnold's talk about the uprising and reinstatement of man's intellectual impulses and of Hellenism needs a good deal of qualification. As Huizinga has said, the *quattrocento* may seem for all the world like a new age until, at the very end, Savonarola shows how close it lay to the Middle Ages; Petrarch might argue with Augustine to justify the life of sensation, yet he wrote thousands of words on such

---

[60] For a bibliography of this topic see Louis I. Bredvold, "The Religious Thought of Donne in Relation to Medieval and Later Traditions," *Studies in Shakespeare, Milton, and Donne* (University of Michigan Publications: Language and Literature, no. I, 1925), p. 204, n. 32.

[61] *Histoire de France,* VII.xvii.

edifying themes as *de contemptu mundi* and *de vita solitaria*.[62] Petrarch is traditionally called one of the first modern men, yet emotionally he lies closer to Augustine than to Galileo; even his subjectivism is strikingly Augustinian; and he was convinced, as many notables of the Renaissance were, that man, a guest in a strange house on this earth, has as his primary obligation the knowledge of God—*aeterna sapienta per qua ex qua in qua omnia*. Thomas More wavered between a Carthusian monastery and the secular rewards of politics, and even Pico, the golden youth, at last turned from the world to endure flagellation for the Passion of Christ and for "cleansing of his old offenses." [63]

The following pages will, I hope, confirm the thesis that the Renaissance marks no radical new departure in man's habits of viewing himself and the world about him. From the fourteenth to the seventeenth century was a time of febrile activity, intellectual and otherwise, but much of it was traditional, and even when it was new it could not quite disengage itself from the patterns of thought and emotion that had been inherited from the Middle Ages. Of course, there were notable developments: the contemporary of Petrarch cannot be mistaken for the contemporary of Shakespeare, but both would have a great deal in common. Although John Donne often reminds us of Augustine, he, like Milton could have seen Galileo and Hobbes face to face.

Let us turn, then, to those elements of Renaissance thought which drew upon two thousand years of pagan and Christian tradition to reaffirm the belief in the dignity of man.

[62] See *The Waning of the Middle Ages*, pp. 297 ff. Citation could be endless, but for a specimen of Petrarch's lingering medievalism see the *Secret* (trans. William H. Draper, 1911), p. 32, on death; cf. p. 50 for an attack on the dignity of man; pp. 131-32 on love; pp. 166 ff. on human glory. It is significant that in the *Secret* the dialogues between Augustine and Petrarch always end in Augustine's carrying his point.

[63] So records Pico's nephew in the pious biography which Sir Thomas More translated; see *The English Works of Sir Thomas More*, I, 356. For an interesting discussion of some of the problems raised in this chapter see Dana Durand, Hans Baron, Ernst Cassier, *et al.*, "Originality and Continuity of the Renaissance, *JHI*, IV (1943), 1-74.

# XIV

## THE BEST OF ALL POSSIBLE WORLDS

### THE PRINCIPLE OF ORDER

THE RENAISSANCE MAN was one of many legacies, but of them all perhaps the strongest was his optimism. Its strength was reinforced, for it came to him both from the rational theology of the late Middle Ages and from the massive humanistic tradition of pagan antiquity which the learned were rediscovering. In both these traditions man was construed as the glory of the universe. Renaissance optimism was predicated upon a sense of security, the felt existence of order, pattern, and sequence; and because the roots of the Renaissance extended so far back into the Middle Ages, it was to the Middle Ages that the Renaissance was indebted for that principle of order by which man could view his world as the manifestation of an omniscient and omnipotent God and himself as that God's special creation.

Cardinal Bembo's paean in the fourth book of *The Courtier* illustrates the optimism derived from the two mighty traditions of Christianity and paganism:

Beholde the state of this great Inginn of the world, which God created for the helth and preservation of every thing that was made. The heaven rounde besett with so many heavenly lightes: and in the middle, the Earth invironed wyth the Elementes, and uphelde wyth the verye waight of it selfe: the sonn, that compassinge about giveth light to the wholl, and in winter season draweth to the lowermost signe, afterward by litle and litle climeth again to the other part: the Moone, that of him taketh her light, accordinge as she draweth nigh, or goith farther from him: and the other five sterres, that diversly keepe the very same course. These thinges emong them selves have such force by the knitting together of an order so necessarilye framed, that with altering them any one jott, they shoulde be all lewsed, and the worlde would decaye. They have also suche beawtie and comelinesse, that all the wittes men have, can not imagin a more beawtifull matter. Thinke nowe of the shape of man, which may be called a litle world: in whom every percell of his body is seene to be necessarily framed by art and not by happ, and then the fourme all together most beawtifull, so that it were a harde matter to judge, whether the members, as the eyes, the nose, the mouth, the eares, the armes, the breast and in like maner the other partes: give eyether more profit to the countenance and the rest of the body, or comelinesse. The like may be said of all other livinge creatures. ... Beeside other thinges therfore, it giveth a great praise to the world, in saiynge that it is beawtifull. It is praised, in saiynge, the beawtifull heaven, beawtifull earth, beawtifull sea, beawtifull rivers, beawtifull wooddes, trees, gardeines, beawtifull Cities, beawtifull Churches, houses, armies. In conclusion this comelye and holye beawtie is a wonderous settinge out of everie thinge.[1]

For nearly two centuries after Petrarch, man's delight in this spectacle was sublime. Natural philosophy demonstrated the abundance and intricate ordering of physical nature, moral philosophy the existence of natural law (that "certaine knowledge and judgement of good and euill" engraved on all men's hearts),[2] and theology the revelation of a rational deity in control of a rational universe. True, this world and this life are but stages on the road to heaven, but they were contrived for man's employment and pleasure. "Thys ys certayn and sure,—that man by nature fere excellyth in dygnyte al other creaturys in erthe, where he ys by the hye proudydence of God set to gouerne and rule."[3] Upon this cheerful assumption man not only governed and ruled; he also learned to know the goodness of God, for spread out for his edification lay two unimpeachable scriptures—the book of nature ("that universal and publick Manuscript")[4] and the Holy Bible.

> The World's a Booke in *Folio*, printed all
> With God's great Workes in Letters Capitall:
> Each Creature is a Page, and each affect,
> A faire Caracter, void of all defect.[5]

This being so, even the grimmest Protestants could only conclude that it is man's duty to acknowledge "with heart & tong" that all goodness comes from God, whose divinity is mirrored in His Creation.[6]

Man himself—a "creature made of God after his owne image, iust, good and right by nature"[7]—could take a double delight in the physical world: the great design of the universe served as the text for God's provi-

---

[1] Baldassare Castiglione, *The Book of the Courtier* (ed. Walter Raleigh, 1900), pp. 349-50.

[2] Thomas Beard, *The Theatre of Gods Ivdgements* (1631), p. 9; cf. Pierre de La Primaudaye, *The French Academie* (1618), p. 433 (a mammoth compilation of Renaissance knowledge and piety that, after its translation from the French in 1577, was widely admired and frequently reprinted in England).

[3] Starkey, *England in the Reign of King Henry the Eighth*, pp. 11-12.

[4] Sir Thomas Browne, *The Religio Medici & Other Writings* (Everyman's Library, 1931), pp. 18-19.

[5] Guillaume Du Bartas, *Deuine Weekes & Workes* (1605), p. 7.

[6] Jan van der Noot, *A Theatre for Voluptuous Worldlings*, 1569 (Scholars' Facsimiles & Reprints, n.d.), sig. Dviiir. Note Calvin's elaborate development of this thesis (*The Institution of Christian Religion* (trans. Thomas Norton, 1561), I.v: "That the knowledge of God doeth shiningly appeare in the makyng of the world and in the continual gouernement thereof."

[7] *The French Academie*, p. 5.

dence and power, and its aesthetic surface provided a boundless subject for artistic creation. Guillaume Du Bartas, whose piety far exceeds his art, rejoiced that his muse was "trayned in true Religion," for God Himself was among other things a "good Artizan." [8] Sir Thomas Browne merely changed the diction to suit the times when he praised God as a "skilful Geometrician." [9] Neither had Galileo's knowledge of mechanics, but they exercised their piety by thinking of God as the master mechanic. This *Weltbaumeister*, as Dilthey has called Him, had merely to reveal the marvels of a perfectly designed universe to instruct man in proper piety. The Middles Ages and the Renaissance knew very little about the physical universe, but what they knew was extremely useful: there were many deists who lacked only the mechanistic and scientific bases of deism.[10]

Just as the existence of natural law (which "ys euer one, in al cuntreys fyrme and stabul, and neuer for the time varyth") [11] pointed to the eternal moral structure of the universe, its physical marvels could only demonstrate the glory of the God who created them. As an artisan, William Caxton was in the vanguard of the Renaissance; as a thinker he made no effort to break any patterns. Yet the tight little cosmology he paints in the *Mirrour of the World* is as close to the tenth century as to many of Copernicus' contemporaries. God made the world, explains Caxton,

alle round, lyke as in a pelette the whiche is al round; and he made the heuen al rounde whiche enuyronneth and goth round aboute the earthe on alle parties hooly without ony defaulte, alle in lyke wise as the shelle of an egge that enuyronneth the white al aboute.[12]

Spenser, the Christian, the Neoplatonist, and the artist, joins the swelling chorus with Calvin, who has not impressed posterity as an essentially optimistic person. The poet's

> Then looke, who list thy gazefull eyes to feed
> With sight of that is faire, looke on the frame
> Of this wyde universe[13]

[8] *Deuine Weekes*, p. 238.

[9] *Religio Medici*, p. 18.

[10] See Louis I. Bredvold, "Deism before Lord Herbert," *Papers of the Michigan Academy of Science Arts and Letters*, IV (1925), 431-42.

[11] Starkey, *England in the Reign of King Henry the Eighth*, pp. 15-16.

[12] *Mirrour of the World* (ed. Oliver H. Prior, EETS, Ex. Ser., vol. CX, 1913), pp. 48-49. Lambertus Danaeus (whose *Wonderfull Woorkmanship of the World* had been Englished in 1578) was as orthodox in his cosmology as Du Bartas; see George Wesley Whiting, *Milton's Literary Milieu* (1939), pp. 6 ff.

[13] "An Hymne of Heavenly Beautie," ll. 29-31.

restates the theologian's belief that one needs only to regard "ce beau chef d'oeuvre du monde universe en sa longeur et largeur, qu'on ne soit, par maniere de dire, tout esbouy d'abondance infinie de lumiere." [14] And so on, far into the eighteenth century, by which time Newtonian science had been welcomed to reinforce the argument from design which had cheered the Stoics, Augustine, Aquinas, which yet cheers a few hardy people even today.

Augustine, when the Roman world was falling apart, had established for Christendom the notion of a theocratic universe designed to manifest the will of God; Aquinas, at the end of the Middle Ages, had shown the universe to exemplify rationally the divine reason. The Renaissance joyfully wrote variations on both themes. In the great book of nature, says La Primaudaye, man can read the majesty of God, for all the creatures in it are "like so many preachers and general witnesses of the glory of their Creator." [15] In considering the world from top to bottom Phillippe de Mornay, the French Protestant whose piety was admired by Sir Philip Sidney, could find nothing, "either so great or so small, which leadeth us not step by step into a God-head." [16] Such evidence was not only a prop to the faithful; it was a refutation of the atheists. Even Francis Bacon, by no means a saint of the Church, "had rather believe all the fables in the Legend, and the Talmud, and the Alcoran, than that this universal frame is without a mind." [17] For more cautious thinkers it was a theme hallowed by tradition, boundless in its implications.

Come thither then thou Atheist whosoeuer thou art; set on worke this noble sence [of sight] thoroughly to view, this excellent and perfect workemanship of God, this huge masse which containeth all things. Lift up thy sight up on high from whence thou hast taken thy beginning. Behold the throne of Maiestie. [18]

When Sir Thomas Browne, a professed conservative in religion, praised

---

[14] *Institution de la Religion Chrestienne,* 1541 (ed. Abel Lefranc, Henri Chatelain, Jacques Pannier, 2 vols., 1911), I, 10; cf. Donne, *Fifty Sermons* (1649), no. 36, p. 325.

[15] *The French Academie,* p. 635.

[16] *A Work Concerning the Trunesse of Christian Religion,* 1581 (trans. Arthur Golding, 1617), p. 3. Golding used the partial translation left by Sir Philip Sidney, and Sidney's sister, the Countess of Pembroke, translated Mornay's *Discours de la Vie et de la Mort,* a work of considerable Protestant severity. Thomas Heywood, in one of the dullest poems ever to attain the dignity of print, employed both prose and verse to show how a contemplation of the universe should reconstruct atheists and "bring them to the way" (*The Hierarchies of the Blessed Angells,* 1635, p. 5). The whole of the first book ("The Seraphim") is one long argument from design which is supplemented by a prose addendum (pp. 31-52; cf. pp. 193 ff.).

[17] "Of Atheism," *Works,* XII, 131.

[18] Andreas Laurentius, *A Discourse on the Preservation of the Sight: of Melancholike Diseases; of Rheumes, and of Old Age,* 1599 (Shakespeare Association Facsimiles, no. 15, 1938), p. 14.

the "theology of the Heavens," he echoed Copernicus, the prophet of new things. The first book of *De Revolutionibus,* which was to shatter man's immemorial tranquillity, reveals a characteristically medieval attitude toward the universe as the symbol of theocracy. The sky is a "visible God," the sun a beautiful temple: all nature shows the existence of teleological, animistic forces working toward the harmony of the whole, and the whole to be crowned by a benevolent and omniscient God.[19]

We find, therefore, under this orderly arrangement, a wonderful symmetry in the universe, and a definite relation of harmony in the motion and magnitude of the orbs, of a kind it is not possible to obtain in any other way.[20]

Pico della Mirandola, who loved learning only less than he loved God, obviously knew nothing of the new astronomy, yet he voiced his theocratic optimism in similar terms.

Iam summus Pater architectus deus: hanc quam videmus mundanam domum diuinitatis templum augustissimum archane legibus sapientiae fabrefecerat.[21]

He, like so many of his contemporaries, could only bow in reverence before that divine providence by which all things are held in delicate adjustment of means to ends.[22]

### THE SANCTITY OF DUE DEGREE

Renaissance man's optimistic interpretation of the book of nature was strengthened by the long habit of thinking in terms of hierarchies. The principle of order found its mythology in those nice gradations that marked upper from lower in both heaven and earth: in the hierarchies of the blessed angels and the hierarchies of the Roman Catholic Church, in animate and inanimate creation. Western Europe for a thousand years had been obligated to the Alexandrian Neoplatonists for setting in motion this habit of thought. The changes rung on the schematization of the Pseudo-Areopagite merely show how settled the habit had be-

[19] See Edgar Zilsel, "Copernicus and Mechanics," *JHI,* I (1940), 113-1.

[20] *De Revolutionibus,* I.10 (*Cambridge Readings in the Literature of Science,* 1928, p. 13). Note the remark of Rheticus, Copernicus' disciple in *Three Copernican Treatises* (ed. Edward Rosen, 1939), pp. 132, 143; cf. Burtt, *The Metaphysical Foundations of Modern Physical Science,* p. 47.

[21] "Oratio quam elegantissime de Hominis celsitudine & dignitate," *Opera* (1557), fol. 55ᵛ. Excerpts from the "Oratio" have been translated into English as "Of the Dignity of Man" by Elizabeth Livermore Forbes, *JHI,* III (1942), 347-54. There is an Italian translation in Giovanni Semprini, *La Filosofia di Pico della Mirandola* (1936), pp. 223 ff.

[22] Citation here could be endless. But note Du Bartas' ludicrously detailed catalogue of man's equipment (*Deuine Weekes,* Sixth Day, First Week), a passage dwarfed by the much more elaborate effort in the second book of *The French Academie.'*

come, and it was inevitable that it should at last receive the sanction of both Aquinas and Dante.[23] But behind the Neoplatonists lay greater men. As Mr. Lovejoy has shown,[24] both Platonic dualism and the Aristotelian device of systematizing observation had taught the ancients to use categories and pigeonholes in interpreting experience. By the time of the Renaissance the great chain of being was a principle of explanation known to every educated man, and no doubt to many who were unable to read.

Inevitably, the traditional reliance on hierarchies made it possible to assign man a lofty place in the scheme of things. His niche was secure, certainly a little lower than the angels but just as certainly much higher than the brute beasts. Since the universe was static, with all things immutably fixed in their divinely appointed places, a recognition of man's obvious superiority to other creatures was merely a religious function. To read the book of nature is to know the importance of due degree, and thus we may see how, says Raymond de Sebond (the victim of Montaigne's merciless irony),

beginning with creatures of the lower grade and mounting up from the first step and lower scale of nature, we gradually arrived at the genuine apprehension and knowledge of God, supremely mighty, supremely wise and supremely good. So that the creatures have led us and raised us by an ascent and staircase admirably devised to God the Creator of all things, considered as the one supreme principle and Father and Creator of all things.[25]

Given the proper working-conditions, a man might develop this theme endlessly. In the Renaissance, men like Sebond and Du Bartas and La Primaudaye did so. They constructed hierarchies within hierarchies: not only is one class above another, but within classes there are degrees. Fire is the highest element, the lion is the best beast, the oak is the best tree, gold is the best metal, *ad infinitum*. All nature thus reveals the order, symmetry, and due degree ordained by God.

The habit of thought exemplified by Sebond inevitably made for the

---

[23] See *Par.*, canto xxviii; cf. Spenser, "The Teares of the Muses," ll. 506 ff. A short but suggestive discussion of Neoplatonic hierarchies in the Renaissance is in E. M. W. Tillyard, *The Elizabethan World Picture* (1944), pp. 37-38.

[24] *The Great Chain of Being* (1936).

[25] Quoted by Clement C. J. Webb, *Studies in the History of Natural Theology*, p. 305. These are Sebond's categories: 1) the inanimate realm of elements and minerals; 2) the vegetative realm (subdivided to account for creatures having touch but not movement or memory, those having memory and movement but not hearing, and those having all sensory faculties); 3) man, whose faculty of reason makes him emperor of the earth; 4) angels; and 5) God, the apex and author of all creation. Sebond's *Theologia Naturalis*, written about the middle of the fifteenth century, was translated by Montaigne in 1569.

acceptance and celebration of things as they are. Long before Pope wrote his *Essay on Man*, Du Bartas had argued that God has arranged matters thus and so, and for man to transgress the limits divinely sanctioned is impious.[26] To aspire to change the pattern, to question the equilibrium of nature, or even to rise in the world (before capitalism and Protestantism had rationalized as a religious duty that which the Elizabethan moralists had condemned as vaulting ambition), could only be accounted sinful. Spenser's Sir Artegall,[27] it will be remembered, came upon a "mighty gyant" who with "an huge great paire of ballance" was attempting some cosmic leveling. He wished to restore what the sea had stolen from the land, the fire from the air, "and all things would reduce unto equality." Of course, the "vulgar," seduced by the hope of "uncontrolled freedome," flocked about him, but Artegall was compelled to read him a very stern lecture on his impiety. "All change is perillous," and things should be left as they are.

> They live, they die, like as He God doth ordaine,
> Ne ever any asketh reason why.
> The hils doe not the lowly dales disdaine;
> The dales doe not the lofty hils envy.
> He maketh kings to sit in soveraity;
> He maketh subjects to their powre obay;
> He pulleth downe, He setteth up on hy;
> He gives to this, from that He takes away:
> For all we have is His: what He list doe, He may.

If this is true—that it is true no traditionalist dared doubt—then the vexed question of accounting for evil evaporates. It should suffice "Christian modestie," says La Primaudaye,

to beleeue that there is one onely, soueraigne, diuine, and vniuersall prouidence, reaching and extending it selfe ouer all, which gouerneth and worketh by numbers, weight, and measure in all generally and particularly.[28]

Thus, in the theocratic tradition, sin is nothing less than the deliberate transgression of God's commandments, and evil is the name that man gives to what seems bad merely because he cannot, or will not, admit that God's providence goes beyond his comprehension. That man should sin at all is preposterous, for he has merely to follow the Bible and the uni-

---

[26] *Deuine Weekes*, p. 13.
[27] *The Faerie Queene*, V.ii.30 ff.
[28] *The French Academie*, pp. 880-81.

versal natural law implanted in his heart. But when he does sin, God's
retributive justice is sure: either the sinner is tortured by his own re-
morseful passions or he is punished by tyrants who (even if they are
respectable infidels like Attila or Tamburlaine) are divinely contrived
as scourges of God.[29] All of which proves that man's temporal misfortunes are evil only for himself and for the nonce: their teleological significance and eventual benefits are hidden in God's inscrutable providence.

The Middle Ages, as we know from Chaucer's Monk and from Lyd-
gate's lugubrious *Fall of Princes,* had interpreted tragedy as the *exempla*
of fickle Fortune's catapulting men from "heigh degree" to "hir adver-
sitee." The extensive mirror literature of the sixteenth century, most notably represented by *A Mirror for Magistrates,* continued this tradition.[30]
Inevitably, the notion emerged that the apparently irresponsible whirling
of Fortune's wheel was identical with the providence of God. As Calvin
explained,

the chaunces as well of prosperitie as of aduersitie the reason of the fleshe doeth
ascrybe to fortune. But whosoeuer is taught by the mouth of Chryst, that all the
heares of hys hed are numbered, will seke for a cause further of, and wyll fyrmelye
beleue that all chaunces are gouerned by the secrete councell of God.[31]

The wicked are, of course, punished justly: they have sinned against
God, and their misfortunes should furnish a text for the faithful. But
even a good man thrown into adversity may take solace in reflecting
on God's inscrutable ways. In his hot youth, Sir Walter Raleigh had

[29] See Calvin's elaborate development of this thesis in *The Institution of Christian Religion,*
I.xviii: "That God doth so vse the seruice of wyched men, and so boweth their mindes to
put hys iudgements into execution, that yet styll himselfe remayneth pure from all spot."
See Roy W. Battenhouse, *Marlowe's Tamburlaine* (1941) pp. 99 ff. In his *History of the
World* Raleigh takes a very moral view of the fall of princes: the misfortunes of such
monarchs as Henry IV and Richard III are interpreted to mean that wrong-doing always
entails punishment. See C. F. Tucker Brooke, "Sir Walter Ralegh as Poet and Philosopher,"
*ELH,* V (1938), 104.

[30] See Willard Farnham, *"The Mirrour for Magistrates* and Elizabethan Tragedy," *JEGP,*
XXV (1926), 66-78. Mr. Farnham has developed the subject admirably in his *Medieval
Heritage of Elizabethan Tragedy* (1936). After the endless *Mirror for Magistrates* the tra-
dition was continued by such works as Antony Munday's *Mirrour of Mutabilitie* (1579) and
Thomas Beard's *Theatre of Gods Iudgements* (1597, 1612, 1631). The theme of mutability
—treated with increasing *Weltschmerz* toward the end of the sixteenth century—was a
favorite one. See Spenser's "Prologue" to bk. V of *The Faerie Queene* and the fragmentary
"Two Cantos of Mutabilitie"; Justus Lipsius, *Tvvo Bookes of Constancie,* I.xv, xvi; Louis
Le Roy, *Of the Interchangeable Covrse, or Variety of Things in the Whole World* (trans.
R. A., 1594); John Norden, *Vicissitudo Rerum* (1600); John Donne, "First Anniuersarie,"
*Poems* (1912), I, 231 ff.

[31] *The Institution of Christian Religion,* I.xvi (fol. 57ʳ).

fashionably toyed with skepticism—atheism, the godly called it[32]—but in his old age, in prison, he relapsed into a cynically pious resignation. God, the author of all our tragedies, "hath written out for us and appointed us all the parts we are to play." Therefore,

certainly there is no other account to be made of this ridiculous world, than to resolve that the change of fortune on the great theatre is but as the change of garments on the less: for when, on the one and the other, every man wears but his own skin, the players are all alike.[33]

If Du Bartas was right in concluding that God chastises even the faithful "to draw deuout sighes from calamitie," [34] then Thomas Beard's explanation of God's curious ways is surely legitimate: even the saints with the "fagots flaming about them" are consoled by their trust in providence; and as for sinners, they can only "gnash their teeth, fret themselues, murmur against God, and blaspheme him, like wretches, to their endlesse perdition." [35]

Thus in a perfectly designed theocratic universe it is the lot of man to adjust himself to eternal providence. Since God has "set degrees and astates in all his glorious workes," Sir Thomas Elyot argues that the body politic, with its higher and its lower, its fortunate and its wretched, serves to mirror God's divine plan.[36] In concurring, La Primaudaye speaks for all the faithful:

The beautifull and great frame of the vniuersall globe; whereof the diuinities, order, and equall firmenesse of all the seuerall parts, together with one perfect

[32] There has been a good deal of work done on "The School of Night," the allegedly atheistic group of wits headed by Raleigh. See Arthur Acheson, *Shakespeare and the Rival Poet* (1903), which raised the question of the allegory in *Love's Labour's Lost;* cf. Quiller-Couch's and Wilson's development in their edition of the play (the New Shakespeare, 1923, pp. xxiii-xxxiv); G. B. Harrison's essay in his edition of *Willobie his Avisa* (1926); M. C. Bradbrook, *The School of Night* (1936); F. A. Yates, *A Study of Love's Labour's Lost* (1939); the Variorum ed. of Shakespeare's *Sonnets* (ed. Hyder Edward Rollins, 2 vols., 1944), II, 310.

[33] *The Works* (1829), II, xlii-xliii. In closing a long discussion of evil in Stoic terms, Justus Lipsius (*Tvvo Bookes of Constancy*, 1939, II.13) makes a specific analogy between the lives of wicked men and a tragedy: "This wicked man prospereth. That tyrant liueth. Let be awhiles. Remember it is but the first Act, and consider aforehande in thy mind, that sobs and sorrows will ensue vppon their sollace. This Scene will anon swimme in blood, then these purple and golden garments shalbe rowled therein. For that Poet of ours [i.e. God] is singular cunning in his art, and will not lightly transgresse the lawes of his Tragedie." See Lily B. Campbell, *Shakespeare's Tragic Heroes: Slaves of Passion* (1930), pp. 3-24.

[34] *Deuine Weekes*, p. 24; cf. Calvin, *The Institution of Christian Religion*, I.xvii (fol. 64ᵛ-65ʳ).

[35] *The Theatre of Gods Ivdgements*, p. 541.

[36] *The Boke Named the Gouernour* (ed. Henry Herbert Stephen Croft, 1883), I, 4.

harmony obeying the gracious and soueraigne gouernment of their Creator, by good right deserue to bee called pure, for without so excellent a disposition, there would be nothing els but an vncleane, and polluted disorder and confusion.[37]

The stars in their course, the king on his throne, the peasant in his hut all point to the same great truth of a divinely ordered universe. It was when Copernicus dislodged the stars from their courses, when the king lost his throne and the peasant tired of his hut, when villains like Machiavelli challenged the assumptions of political morality, when the inherited theocratic values of the Middle Ages wore thin, that traditionalists like La Primaudaye could only conclude that universal decay and corruption had set in. But that crack-up would follow the Renaissance. Conservatives like La Primaudaye die hard, and in the sixteenth century the principle of order was the inherited mainstay of many a better man than he.

As we shall see presently, it was much easier for Catholics than for Protestants to accept the *status quo*. In fact, ever since Augustine, and until our own day, it has not been uncommon for Catholics to look with considerable complacency upon the inequalities and social ills of the race. Erasmus was anything but a Jeffersonian democrat, but—with the notable exception of Vives[38]—almost alone in the sixteenth century he deplored the misery of the downtrodden in a ruthless hierarchal society.[39] His Protestant contemporaries, eager to rise in the world and increasingly contemptuous of ecclesiastical checks against "usury," were more outspoken.[40] Toward the end of the century, some of them advocated civil disobedience as a religious duty. In one of the most notorious of their tracts—Christopher Goodman's *How Superior Powers Oght to be Obeyd* (1558)—the argument is referred directly to God. His people should, by right, be ruled "by no other Lawes and ordinances, then by such as

---

[37] *The French Academie*, p. 898; cf. Louis Le Roy, *Of the Interchangeable Covrse, or Variety of Things in the Whole World*, fol. 12ᵛ.

[38] See the eloquent *De Subventione Pauperum, Sive de Humanis Necessitatibus, Opera Omnia Ordinata a Gregorio Majansio* (1782-1790), IV, 420-94. This has been translated by Margaret M. Sherwood as *Concerning the Relief of the Poor; or, Concerning Human Need* (1917).

[39] See, for example, two of the most famous (and frequently reprinted) of the *Adagia*: "Scarabaeus aquilam quaerit" and "Aut regem aut fatum nasci oportet"; cf. Preserved Smith, *Erasmus*, pp. 199 ff. Cardinal Pole, as reported by Starkey (*England in the Reign of King Henry the Eighth*, p. 9), takes a more typical and calmer view of economic inequalities.

[40] For example, John Knox in *The First Blast of the Trumpet* (1558) and John Ponet in *Treatise of Politique Power*. But not all Protestants were subversive. As a good aristocrat, Sir Philip Sidney expresses his anti-democratic bias rather openly in the *Arcadia* (II.25-26); cf. Edwin A. Greenlaw, "Sidney's *Arcadia* as an Example of Elizabethan Allegory," *Anniversary Papers by Colleagues and Pupils of George Lyman Kittredge* (1913), p. 335; William Dinsmore Briggs, "Political Ideas in Sidney's *Arcadia*," *SP*, XXVIII (1931), 137-61.

God had geuen them." [41] Consequently, He is pleased by rebellion under certain conditions. "Yf God geue you grace" to resist the tyrannies of Catholics and overweening civil authorities, "you may be certayne and sure to finde vnspeakable conforte and quietnes of conscience, in the mydle of your danger and greatest rage of Satan." [42]

Such seditious talk is, however, more characteristic of the seventeenth than of the sixteenth century. Two notables of the Tudor age were advocates of the principle of order—Elyot in politics and Hooker in theology. Elyot thought politically, and wrote to establish the proposition that disorder is chaos. Like the patterned universe, like the moral microcosm that is man, a "publicke weale is a body liuing, compacte or made of sondry astates and degrees of men, whiche is disposed by the other of equite and gouerned by the rule and moderation of reason." [43] The cosmic sweep of system running into system—the four elements, the creatures "assendynge upwarde," the stars in their courses—teach the great lesson: order is divine. The moral is written plainly in the book of nature. Everywhere we see "discrepance of degrees, whereof procedeth order." Moreover, "take away ordre from all thynges what shulde than remayne?" [44] Elyot could have known Copernicus, but he writes like John of Salisbury when he fuses the Neoplatonic and Aristotelian traditions of hierarchies to uphold a stratified society. As the son of the judge of common pleas, the friend of More and the client of Wolsey, Henry's ambassador to the court of Charles V, and a member of Parliament, Elyot was a graceful product of the ruling class whose apologist he became. But although his career as a politician throws a good deal of light on his political morality, it does not lessen his importance as a spokesman for the principle of order. To him, order means due degree and equality means chaos. If God's plan were disrupted so that the rabble were deprived of their betters' restraining influence then men would be animals, the strong preying upon the weak. "Than were all our equalitie dasshed, and finally as bestes sauage the one shall desire to see a nother." [45]

Elyot's is the genuine voice of all conservatives at all times. On the assumption of a political order corresponding to the moral and the physical order of the universe he tried valiantly to hold the dyke against change.

[41] *How Superior Powers Oght to be Obeyd* (with a bibliographical note by Charles H. McIlwain, The Facsimile Text Society, 1931), p. 163.

[42] *Ibid.*, p. 217.

[43] *The Gouernour*, I, [1].

[44] *Ibid.*, I, 3.

[45] *The Gouernour*, II, 209-12. This section bears the marginal heading, "Obedience due to gouernours."

But nearly a century later, long after Machiavelli had cynically repudiated the moral basis of political conduct, and after Calvin had taught all up and coming Protestant burghers the advantages of economic leveling, we still hear the plaintive tones of the old tradition. In his contempt for the common man, Coriolanus is one of the most vehemently articulate anti-democrats on record. For the Hydra-headed rabble—unfit for war, incapable of government, too base for gratitude—he has only blows and scorn.

> You common cry of curs, whose breath I hate
> As reek o' th' rotten fens, whose loves I prize
> As the dead carcasses of unburied men
> That do corrupt my air, I banish you! [46]

If that tantalizing mob scene in *Sir Thomas More* is Shakespeare's, then Coriolanus and More must be accounted cousins-german both dedicated to the proposition that God intends rulers to rule, subjects to obey. When More tells the mob that their insurrection is a sin against God [47] his trite but powerful rationalization of a hierarchal society echoed the arguments of a thousand years. But the failure of the Stuarts is enough to remind us that their power was waning and soon to be spent.

Richard Hooker, one of the most luminous characters of the sixteenth century, gave a definitive statement to the principle of order. His stately *Of the Laws of Ecclesiastical Polity* (1594-1597) is more than a defense of the Anglican *via media* against querulous Puritans: it becomes the most sustained and noble plea in our language for an orderly universe comprising orderly social and religious institutions at the disposition of an orderly God. "The being of God is a kind of law to his workings," [48] says Hooker, and the eternal law laid up in the bosom of God is manifest

---

[46] III.iii.120 ff.

[47] *Sir Thomas More . . . An Anonymous Play of the Sixteenth Century Ascribed in part to Shakespeare* (ed. John Shirley, n.d.), II.ii:

> For to the king God hath his office lent
> Of dread, of justice, power and command,
> Hath bid him rule and willed you to obey. . . .
> What do you then,
> Rising 'gainst him that God himself installs,
> But rise 'gainst God? What do you to your souls
> In doing this, O desperate as you are?
> Wash your foul minds with tears, and those same hands,
> That you like rebels lift against the peace,
> Lift up for peace, and your unreverent knees
> Make them your feet to kneel to be forgiven.

See *Coriolanus*, I.i.99 ff.

[48] *Of the Laws of Ecclesiastical Polity*, I.ii.2.

throughout all creation. When Hooker permits himself to speculate on the consequences of a lawless universe, he is terrified. What if nature "should intermit her course"?

if the frame of that heavenly arch erected over our heads should loosen and dissolve itself; if celestial spheres should forget their wonted motions, and by irregular volubility turn themselves any way as it might happen; . . . if the moon should wander from her beaten way, the times and seasons of the year blend themselves by disordered and confused mixture, the winds breathe out their last gasp, the clouds yield no rain, the earth be defeated of heavenly influence, the fruits of the earth pine away as children at the withered breasts of their mother no longer able to yield them relief: what would become of man himself, whom these things now do all serve? See we not plainly that obedience of creatures unto the law of nature is the stay of the whole world? [49]

Hooker's God, like Aquinas', is rational, and the object of rational knowledge. Natural law controls the operation of things in nature; celestial law of things in heaven; reason of rational creatures like man; divine law of moral conduct; human law (combining reason and divine law) of man's secular activity. But the workings of all these kinds of law leads to the same truth: "God being the author of nature, her voice is but His instrument."

Of Law there can be no less acknowledged, than that her seat is the bosom of God, her voice the harmony of the world: all things in heaven and earth do her homage, the very least as feeling her care, and the greatest as not exempted from her power: both Angels and men and creatures of what condition soever, though each in different sort and manner, yet all with uniform consent, admiring her as the mother of their peace and joy. [50]

Is it surprising, then, that even on his deathbed Hooker prayed for the reign of law? [51]

### A LITTLE LOWER THAN THE ANGELS

Great as was the solace of a theocratic, hierarchal universe, [52] even greater was the thought of man's place in that universe. As a special

[49] *Ibid.*, I.iii.2.

[50] *Ibid.*, I.xvi.8.

[51] Izaak Walton, *Lives* (The Temple Classics, 1898), II, 91. On Hooker, see Hardin Craig, *The Enchanted Glass* (1936), pp. 24 ff.; Henry Osborne Taylor, *Thought and Expression in the Sixteenth Century* (1920), II, 135 ff.; for an admiring account of Hooker's political thought see J. W. Allen, *A History of Political Thought in the Sixteenth Century* (1928), pp. 184 ff. For Hooker's sociological views see the *Laws,* I.lix-lxxxix, VIII.i-iv. A more pedestrian statement of the principle of order is William Baldwin's—he of *The Mirror for Magistrates*—in his *Treatise of Morall Philosophy* ("Enlarged" by Thomas Palfreyman, 1640?), p. 53a.

[52] Another indication of the assumption of a hierarchal universe was the very popular

creation he was only a little lower than the angels. As Starkey has it, when we consider man and his works, "we schal nothyng dowte of hys excellent dygnyte, but playnly affyrme, that he hath in him a sparkful of Dyvynyte, *and* ys surely of a celestyal *and* dyuyne nature." [53] Everything pointed to man's preëminence: his possession of an immortal soul, his distinguishing faculty of rational understanding, his status as emperor of the earth and master of all lower forms of creation. In a geocentric universe, the earth was the hub of creation, and man was the darling of God's providence. The stars in their majestic circlings, the world, and everything on it—"all laide, O glorie! at the foote of man." [54] In Sir Thomas More's *Utopia,* religion was nothing less than the realization of this fact.[55]

The miracle of man is nowhere seen more clearly than in the notion of the microcosm. Just as the hierarchal universe comprises all levels and degrees, so man, the little world mirroring the great, is himself the mark of God's benevolent providence. In a universe presumed to be orderly, and presumed to exemplify everywhere the delicate correspondences between higher and lower, the argument from analogy could never fail to charm. The wonder of the macrocosm is reproduced in the microcosm. The fact of harmonious concord, as Sir John Fortescue explained, could not be denied:

In this order hot things are in harmony with cold, dry with moist, heavy with light, great with little, high with low. In this order angel is set over angel, rank upon

belief in demonology and astrology. And as Browne and Burton show, it was not confined to the superstitious and illiterate. On this level, the principle of cosmic order was predicated on the correlation and interaction of the natural and the supernatural realms. There were few as cynical as Edmund in calling astrology the excellent foppery of the world; such works as *The Compost of Ptholomeus* and such quacks as Dr. Robert Fludd commanded wide followings. A whole galaxy of tragic heroes—Marlowe's, Chapman's, Shakespeare's—were prepared to admit the influence of the stars on their destinies, and the ghost of the elder Hamlet taxed the credulity of neither Shakespeare's audience nor the Prince of Denmark. There were scores of contemporary treatises on the subject: e.g. R[obert] H[arrison]'s translation of Lavater, *Of Ghostes and Spirites Walking by Night* (1572, 1596); Reginald Scot, *The Discoverie of Witchcraft* (1584); Thomas Nash, *The Terrors of the Night* (1594); James I, *Daemonologie* (1598). See J. Dover Wilson, *What Happens in Hamlet* (1935), ch. III *passim;* W. A. Notestein, *A History of Witchcraft in England from 1558 to 1781* (1911); M. A. Murray, *The Witch-Cult in Western Europe* (1921); Montague Summers, *The History of Witchcraft and Demonology* (1926). For contemporary astrology see Andrew Boorde, *The Pryncyples of Astronomye in Maner a Pronosticacyon* (1550?); John Maplet, *The Diall of Destiny* (1581); "Arcandam," *The Most Excellent Profitable, and Pleasaunt Booke to Finde the Fatall Destiny of Everyman* (1562 ff.). See E. F. Bosanquet, *English Printed Almanacks and Prognostications, a Bibliographical History to the Year 1600* (rev. ed., 1928).

[53] *England in the Reign of King Henry the Eighth,* p. 12.
[54] George Chapman, "Petrarchs Seven Penitential Psalms" *The Poems* (ed. Phyllis Brooks Bartlett, 1941), III.5.        [55] *Utopia* (The English Reprints, 1869), p. 146.

rank in the kingdom of heaven; man is set over man, beast over beast, bird over bird, and fish over fish, on the earth, in the air and in the sea: so that there is no worm that crawls upon the ground, no bird that flies on high, no fish that swims in the depths, which the chain of this order does not bind in most harmonious concord.[56]

Sir John wrote in the fifteenth century, but even in the seventeenth Francis Bacon found it necessary to express his contempt for the still popular notion: "as if there were to be found in man's body certain correspondences and parallels, which should have respect to all varieties of things, as stars, planets, universals, which are extant in the great world." [57] But Bacon fancied himself an iconoclast; most men were still content to see the intricate variety of nature mirrored in man.

> For in man's self is Fire, Aire, Earth, and Sea,
> Man's (in a word) the World's Epitome,
> Or little Map, which heere my Muse doth trie
> By the grand Patterne to exemplifie.[58]

He has "in his soule the image of God," explained one man of medicine, "and in his bodie the modell of the whole world." [59] In beholding the "wonderfull composition and disposition" of his body he should always be reminded of its creator's providence.[60] It was just as if God, said Mornay, "to set forth a mirror of his workes" showed His own infinity in man's immortal soul and the "hugenesse of the whole World together" in his physical being.[61]

And thus man's optimistic appraisal of himself: if he was an animal, he was also a God. His body, combining the elements and the humors of the material creation, might be perishable; but his reason, like God's, was divine; and his soul was immortal. From Pico's *Oratio* to Milton's *Areopagitica* the theme was endlessly developed: man alone has reason, and by his reason he may learn to know the God who has so signally distinguished him. This great gift, like everything else, is part of God's providence: "desiderabat artifex esse aliquem qui tante operis rationem perpenderet, pulchritudinem amaret, magnitudinem admiraretur." [62] Man may wallow in the mud, but he reaches to the stars.

---

[56] Quoted by Tillyard, *The Elizabethan World-Picture*, p. 24. See George P. Conger, *Theories of Macrocosms and Microcosms in the History of Philosophy* (1922), pp. 53 ff.

[57] *Advancement of Learning*, bk. II (*Works*, VI, 241).

[58] Du Bartas, *Deuine Weekes*, p. 205.

[59] Laurentius, *Discourse on the Preservation of the Sight*, p. 80.

[60] *The French Academie*, p. 346.

[61] *A Worke Concerning the Trunesse of Christian Religion*, p. 209.

[62] Pico della Mirandola, "Oratio," *Opera*, f. 55ᵛ.

> I know I am one of Nature's little kings,
> Yet to the least and vilest things am Thrall. . . .
> I know my self a MAN,
> Which is a *proud,* and yet a *wretched* thing.[63]

Sir Thomas Browne, in one of his great purple patches, made literature of a commonplace: "We are onely that amphibious piece between a corporeal and spiritual Essence, that middle form that links those two together, and makes good the Method of GOD and Nature." Man is the "great and true *Amphibium,* whose nature is disposed to live, not onely like other creatures in diverse elements, but in divided and distinguished worlds." [64]

To the seventeenth century it would become a major problem to determine man's role in these divided and distinguished worlds, and to adjudicate between the corporeal and spiritual elements in his nature. But before the demon of doubt arose, and the new mechanics reduced all activity to body acting upon body, the man of the Renaissance could, even while modestly confessing to his carnal nature, rejoice in his pre-eminence. He bore the "Image of th' Almightiest" and therefore was almost divine.[65] God leaves His "print" on all creation, explains Sir John Davies, but on His special creation He confers the highest distinction: "Thy whole image Thou in Man hast writ."

> There cannot be a creature more diuine,
> Except (like Thee) it should be infinit.[66]

Even Sir Walter Raleigh, whose experience with his fellows should have taught him better, clung to the consoling thought of man's divinity. Man, the microcosm, is

internally endued with a divine understanding, by which he might contemplate and serve his Creator, after whose image he was formed, and endued with the powers and faculties of reason and other abilities, that thereby also he might govern and rule the world, and all other God's creatures therein.[67]

To show the wide, uncritical acceptance of this Renaissance optimism I have quoted mainly from the hack-writers and the harmless drudges,

---

[63] Sir John Davies, *Nosce Teipsum* in *Complete Poems* (ed. Alexander B. Grosart, 1876), I, 24. See Louis I. Bredvold, "The Sources Used by Sir John Davies for 'Nosce Teipsum'," *PMLA,* XXXVIII (1923), 745-69.

[64] *Religio Medici,* pp. 38-39; cf. p. 61: "We are all monsters, that is, a composition of Man and Beast."

[65] Du Bartas, *Deuine Weekes,* p. 235.

[66] *Nosce Teipsum* in *Complete Poems,* I, 81.

[67] *History of the World,* I.ii.5. See E. A. Strathman, "Sir Walter Raleigh on Natural Philosophy," *MLQ,* I (1940), 48-62, on the more orthodox elements in Raleigh's thinking.

but in closing this chapter, I, like every one else, must fall gratefully into the lap of Shakespeare. Hamlet's encomium is a tissue of commonplaces, but it says in a dozen lines what La Primaudaye needed nearly a thousand pages to say. Even though, in his discontent, the natural world seemed a sterile promontory and a pestilent congregation of vapors, Hamlet wonders why he cannot see it for what it is—the earth a goodly frame, the air a brave o'erhanging firmament, a majestical roof fretted with golden fire. And as for man, the glory of the universe, his grandeur is apparent.

What a peece of worke is a man, how noble in reason, how infinit in faculties, in forme and moouing, how expresse and admirable in action, how like an Angell in apprehension, how like a God: the beautie of the world; the paragon of Animales.[68]

It is also to Shakespeare that we must go for the tersest statement of the assumption that made Renaissance optimism possible—the assumption of the principle of order. In Ulysses' speech to the Grecian leaders[69] are compounded all the elements that gave meaning and merit to a hierarchal universe.

> The heavens themselves, the planets, and this centre
> Observe degree, priority, and place,
> Insisture, course, proportion, season, form,
> Office, and custom, in all line of order;
> And therefore is the glorious planet Sol
> In noble eminence enthron'd and spher'd
> Amidst the other, whose med'cinable eye
> Corrects the ill aspects of planets evil
> And posts, like the commandment of a king,
> Sans check, to good and bad. But when the planets
> In evil mixture to disorder wander,
> What plagues and what portents, what mutiny,
> What raging of the sea, shaking of earth,
> Commotion in the winds! . . . O, when degree is shak'd,
> Which is the ladder to all high designs,
> Then enterprise is sick! How could communities,
> Degrees in schools and brotherhoods in cities,
> Peaceful commerce from dividable shores,
> The primogenity and due of birth,

---

[68] II.ii.305 ff. I have followed the pointing of Q2 because it, unlike that of the Folio and virtually all modern editions, shows that *apprehension*, and not *action*, is appropriate to angels. On the indefinite article before *man* see G. L. Kittredge's note in his edition of *Hamlet* (1939), p. 189.

[69] *Troilus and Cressida*, I.iii.85 ff.

Prerogative of age, crowns, sceptres, laurels,
But by degree, stand in authentic place?
Take but degree away, untune that string,
And hark what discord follows! Each thing meets
In mere oppugnancy.

And from this alternative, Ulysses, good conservative that he was, shrank in horror. It was well he did so, for those who accepted the alternative laid upon themselves the obligation of constructing a new universe on the ruins of the old. This assignment, as the seventeenth century would discover, had its perils no less than its rewards.

# XV

## THE USES OF NEOPLATONISM

### FLORENTINE NEOPLATONISM

BEFORE THE ENTHRONEMENT OF THE NEW SCIENCE in the seventeenth century, Neoplatonism had for several generations been a focus of Renaissance optimism.[1] As it developed from Ficino and Pico della Mirandola it was anything but a simple restatement of a very old tradition, for it followed two widely divergent lines: the examination of the cosmos for the purpose of tracing the hierarchies of being in sober analytical fashion, and the celebration of that high knowledge that comes by intuition and revelation—by the Augustinian illumination of the soul that approaches the Godhead directly.[2] The first of these tendencies was of great importance in supplying a motive and a point of view for men like Copernicus and Kepler, and the second—more mystical and more theosophical—is reflected in various ways in the literature of the Renaissance.

By the end of the Middle Ages—say, the thirteenth century—the *modus operandi* for ascertaining truth had been tacitly determined to nearly everyone's satisfaction. All that pertained to the supersensuous and abstract (therefore the permanent and universal) was marked off as the area of theology and dogma; all that pertained to the physical and the sensible was conceded to be the legitimate object of secular thought. For the Middle Ages the Augustinian distinction between the realm of grace and the realm of nature, with its corollary dualism of body and soul and the two-fold truth of a natural and revealed religion, had remained fairly stable. In the Renaissance, however, there were several factors tending to break down these hoary dualisms. Under the impact of a revived Neoplatonism the spiritual was thought to constitute the

---

[1] See Nesca A. Robb, *Neoplatonism of the Italian Renaissance* (1935); Paul Oskar Kristeller, *The Philosophy of Marsilio Ficino* (1943); John Smith Harrison, *Platonism in English Poetry* (1903); Taylor, *Thought and Expression in the Sixteenth Century*, II, 274 ff.; Walter Raleigh's introduction to Castiglione's *Book of the Courtier*, pp. lxx ff.; Boas, *The Major Traditions of European Philosophy*, pp. 159 ff.; Erwin Panofsky, *Studies in Iconology* (1939), pp. 129 ff. For an excellent bibliographical guide to the subject see Paul Oskar Kristeller and John Herman Randall, Jr., "The Study of the Philosophies of the Renaissance," *JHI*, II (1941), 471-72.

[2] See Robb, *Neoplatonism in the Italian Renaissance*, p. 17.

source and true reality of the physical, and nature, as Emerson was to say, to be the symbol of spirit. As men tried to understand the physical they were driven beyond surfaces to its supersensible reality. The two halves of experience were fused, and natural philosophy, the legitimate domain of secular speculation, proved to be an avenue of the meta-physical. Consequently, much Renaissance "philosophy" is theosophical. Ficino and Pico (and, across the Alps, Reuchlin) came to employ an erudite and fantastic numerology to demonstrate the correspondence be-tween nature and spirit; and Bembo, in Castiglione's fourth book, had no trouble whatever in passing from the experience of physical beauty to a rapturously mystical absorption into the Godhead. The temporal micro-cosm was seen by some to reflect the mathematical harmony and beauty of the spiritual macrocosm,[3] so that all experience merged into a con-tinuum. Mystic and naturalist alike learned to reverse the Nicene formu-lary: they approached God through nature rather than nature through God, and the upshot was a pervasive optimism by which everything was construed as good, and man as potentially divine.

We must now trace some of these developments systematically.

During the Middle Ages Plato had meant little more than Chalchidius' four-century version of the *Timaeus*. Even Petrarch, who knew no Greek but venerated Plato from afar, may have been ignorant of the *Meno* and *Phaedo* (ca. 1157) of Henricus Aristippus' redaction. From Petrarch to Ficino, Italian humanism had been mainly philological and Latin. Such of Petrarch's successors as Marsigli and Salutati were, like their master, Ciceronian in their Latinity, Augustinian in their theology. But after Chrysoloras had taught in Italy at the end of the fourteenth century, a knowledge of Greek became more common. The Greeks sent to the Councils of Ferrara (1438-1439) and Florence (1439-1442) were such zealous literary missionaries that two of them, George of Trebizond and Bessarion, stayed in Italy. About the same time, Georgius Gemisthus (Plethon) encouraged Cosimo de' Medici to establish the Florentine Academy to further Platonic studies. Plethon's *De Platonicae atque Aristotelicae Philosophiae Differentiae* both exalted Plato at the expense of Aristotle and revived interest in Neoplatonists like Plotinus and Por-phyry. Then for a generation warfare raged. George of Trebizond ac-cused Plethon of fostering a neopaganism, and in his *Comparatio Pla-*

---

[3] Note, for instance, the *De Docta Ignorantia* of Nicholas Cusanus (1401-1464), whom Ernst Cassirer has interpreted as one of the seminal forces of Renaissance mysticism. See Cassirer's *Das Erkenntnis Problem in der Philosophie und Wissenschaft der Neueren Zeit* (1922), I, 21 ff. and his "Giovanni Pico della Mirandola," *JHI*, III (1942), 140 ff., 321; cf. Windelband, *A History of Philosophy*, pp. 345-74; August Reikel, *Die Philosophie der Renaissance* (1925), pp. 55-69.

*tonis et Aristotlis* (1464) damned all forms of Platonism as cordially as he defended Aristotelian naturalism. Bessarion, more temperate and more scholarly, answered him with the famed *In Calumniatorem Platonis* (1469), which undertook to exonerate Plato of the charge of paganism and even to make of him an acceptable, if involuntary, Christian. Thus by the time Ficino appeared, the Italian intellectuals were ripe for a philosophic synthesis.

Ficino, the true saint of Italian humanism, and Pico, his dazzling disciple, were both dead by 1499, but they represent the twin peaks of Florentine Neoplatonism. To them both, Plato was the "Attic Moses," and they attempted, by reconciling the philosophy of Plato with the divinely revealed word of God, to fuse pagan and Christian thought into an optimistic idealism. True humanists, they wished to adduce to the support of their religious faith the best of secular thought. Ficino declared his intention of reëstablishing the dignity of God's gift, philosophy, and thus save religion from "execrabile inscitia." [4] In 1463 he began the twenty-year task of translating Plato, steeped himself in Augustine, and made his great synthesis of Christianity and Platonism in his *Theologica Platonica* and *De Christiana Religione.* Inspired by Pico's visit to Florence in 1484, he began his version of Plotinus and the Neoplatonists, which he concluded with his commentary on the *Enneads* eight years before his death in 1499. As for Pico, he gloried in his erudition: not only from Hermes Trismegistus, the Chaldaeans, the Pythagoreans did he draw his mystic lore; he proposed to go further and achieve a harmony of Plato and Aristotle, "a multis ante hac creditam a nemine satis probatum." [5] But he died in 1494 having completed only a part (*De Ente et Uno*) [6] of his ambitious *Symphonia Platonis et Aristotelis.*[7]

Both Ficino and Pico shared the Neoplatonic metaphysics that construed all being as receding concentric circles emanating from God, at once the source and apex of creation. Obviously, such a universe could be only good.

---

[4] See Robb, p. 63; Kristeller, *Ficino,* pp. 320 ff.

[5] "Oratio quam elegantissime de Hominis . . . ," *Opera,* fol. 58ʳ.

[6] This fragment has been translated, with a useful introduction, by Victor Michael Hamm as *Of Being and Unity* (1943).

[7] On the thesis that Pico is merely a late representative of the Scholastic tradition see Avery Dulles, *Princeps Concordiae* (1941); this view has been challenged by Ernst Cassirer, "Giovanni Pico della Mirandola," *JHI,* III (1942), 123-44, 319-46. Another attempt to synthesize all philosophies was that of Agostino Steuco, or Augustinus Steuchus Eugubinus (1496-1549); in *De Perenni Philosophia* he argues that man, inherently noble but in these later days fallen from his former excellence, might regain all through a study of philosophy. See Don Cameron Allen, "The Degeneration of Man and Renaissance Pessimism," *SP,* XXXV (1938), 208.

All things are in themselves good, because they are from it [the eternal good]. They are also good for us in so far as they are related to it. But they rightly become evil and hard for us because we abandon it most wrongly and follow those things that are necessarily in it and are preserved by it.[8]

This, of course, is the standard Neoplatonic view that we have encountered so often before, for Neoplatonists are nothing if not repetitious: the incorporeal is better than the material, and therefore man should direct his will toward spirit rather than matter. But nonetheless, the whole cosmic hierarchy—God, the angels, the soul, body, and quality in the lowest (that is, matter uninformed by spirit) [9]—are delicately adjusted one to the other in the best of all possible worlds. Pico, reducing the categories of being, was content with only three realms: the supercelestial region occupied by intelligence ("mentibus decorarat"), the heavenly spheres with eternal souls, and the lower physical world filled with a host of creatures ("omnigena animalium turba").[10]

All this is common enough, of course, but the importance accorded man by Ficino and Pico is extraordinary. Ficino places soul (the attribute of man) centrally in the five orders of being because it is the nexus between the highest and the lowest—the "third essence" that is the "mirror of divine things, the life of mortal things, and the connection between the two." Of all the wonders of nature, this is the greatest: "all other things under God are always in themselves of one certain kind of being; this essence is at once all of them. . . . the center of nature, the middle point of all that is, the chain of the world, the face of all, and the knot and bond of the universe." [11] Pico's statement of the preëminence of man's active intellect is even more striking. Whereas all other things are by their natures bounded and prescribed, man is placed by God in the center of the ranks of being so that he can, as he wills, raise himself to God or fall as low as the beasts. "O summam dei patris liberalitatem, summam & admirandam hominis foelicitatem." [12]

This view of man's status and potentialities was the basic Neoplatonic gift to the Renaissance. Man, medially situated between spirit and matter,

---

[8] Quoted by Kristeller, *Ficino*, p. 66.

[9] Ficino, *Theologica Platonica*, III.12 (trans. in part as *Platonic Theology* by Josephine L. Burroughs, *JHI*, V, 1944, 227-39).

[10] Pico, "Oratio," *Opera*, fol. 55ᵛ-56ʳ. In Pico's *Heptaplus*, a commentary on the first chapter of Genesis, there are three degrees of emanation from the pure being of God: mind or spirit, the incorruptible celestial realm of the nine spheres, and the material world with nine orders of being ascending from formless matter. See Ernst Cassirer, *Individuum und Kosmos in der Philosophie der Renaissance* (1927), pp. 82 ff.

[11] *Theologica Platonica*, III.2. (*JHI*, V, 231); cf. Kristeller, *Ficino*, pp. 407 ff.

[12] Pico, "Oratio," *Opera*, fol. 56ʳ.

is able through his active intellect to attain almost deific excellence by subordinating the baser to the higher element in his complex nature. His highest good is union with God; his highest knowledge is knowledge of God. "Oportet nostram felicitatem in eo versari: ut Deo abque medio haereamus." [13] Pico's majestic *Oration on the Dignity of Man* insists upon man's high function of raising himself; for although sensible things are passive and thus determined, man alone initiates movement: he is, as it were, supernatural and contingent on nothing save himself.[14] In Cassirer's words, Pico thus revived the Pelagian heresy, and denied original sin. Man does not even require the gift of grace, as both Spenser and Milton were Neoplatonic enough to suggest. After the Red Cross Knight has descended from the Mount of Contemplation, where he achieved the holiness of spirit,[15] he is self-sufficient; and Guyon, having learned to fortify himself through temperance, has no real need of Arthur's aid.[16] As the Guardian Spirit says in *Comus,* if a mortal is truly virtuous he needs no divine assistance.[17] In Pico's view, each man is the center of the world, the focus from which radiate all the interdependent forces of the universe, and he attains his knowledge of pure being through his own efforts. His highest intellection consists not of mathematical analysis or Aristotelian observation, but of a *scientie abdita*. His intelligence arranges and classifies the "phantasms" of sense, but it is his suprasensible knowledge which reaches to the infinite and the absolute: the highest knowledge is mystical knowledge, the ultimate dignity of man. "Intelligo de illo intelligere abdito, quod est sine phantasmate, vel adminiculo sensus aut phantasiae et non adhuc de quocumque tali, sed intelligere abdito, directo, et permanente." [18]

Ficino's *Theologica Platonica* offers a stirring argument for man's immortality on precisely these grounds: immortality is man's so that he may at length fulfill his proper function—so difficult when he is shackled to the flesh—of enjoying the pure contemplation of God, a consummation granted to the good and denied to the wicked.[19] If he uses his native gifts properly, man is Godlike in his possession of a rational soul. Just

---

[13] Quoted from Ficino by Robb, p. 68.

[14] This, as Cassirer says ("Giovanni Pico della Mirandola," *JHI,* III, 1942, 321) is the real basis of Pico's unrelenting opposition to astrology, which put man under the control of forces beyond his power and thus denied him freedom.

[15] *Faerie Queene,* I.x.53 ff.

[16] *Faerie Queene,* II.i.8 ff.

[17] *Comus,* ll. 1018 f.; cf. Harrison, *Platonism in English Poetry,* pp. 61-64.

[18] Quoted by Cassirer, "Giovanni Pico della Mirandola," *JHI,* III (1942), 144.

[19] See Kristeller, *Ficino,* pp. 324 ff.; cf. his "Ficino and Pomponazzi on the Place of Man in the Universe," *JHI,* V (1944), 220-27. See Ernst Cassirer, "Ficino's Place in Intellectual History," *JHI,* VI (1945), 483-501—a review of Kristeller's *Ficino.*

as God is above all things, so man seeks to conquer the universe. "As for our desire for victory, we can easily recognize the immeasurable splendor of our soul from the fact that even dominion over this world will not satisfy it, if after having subdued this world, it learns that there is still another which it has not yet subdued." [20] Likewise, just as God created everything, man can shape materials to his own purposes, imitating the function of God and imposing beauty and form on the lower orders of creation. "Therefore the power of man is almost similar to that of the divine nature, for man acts in this way through himself." [21] Truly, concludes Ficino, man is the vicar of God.

### BELLEZZA DEL SPIRITO

An adequate study of Neoplatonism in the English Renaissance is yet to be written, and when it is it will touch, even if obliquely, on most of the literature between More and Milton. The Neoplatonism of men like Ficino and Pico was relatively austere and philosophical: hence its appeal as a body of moral and humanistic doctrine to moralists like Colet and Erasmus.[22] For men of letters—and of course one thinks first of Spenser—the morality of Neoplatonism, so compatible with Christianity, was strengthened by its aesthetics. It was, therefore, as a body of aesthetic-moral thought, prevailingly optimistic, that Neoplatonism reaches everywhere in the sixteenth century. All we can do in a sketch like this is suggest some of the main lines that its development took.

It is difficult to say how much of what passes for Neoplatonism in the sixteenth century was Neoplatonic and how much derived directly from Plato.[23] The point of view was Platonic, but its justification—or rationalization—was Neoplatonic. If there were any basic tendencies in so sprawling body of thought they were 1) to elevate the spiritual over the physical and 2) to approach the spiritual through the physical. For both notions Plato furnishes abundant precedent.

The core of all varieties of Platonism—to hold spirit superior to matter

---

[20] *Theologica Platonica*, XIV.4 (*JHI*, V, 238).

[21] *Ibid.*, XIII.3 (*JHI*, V.233).

[22] See Seebohm, *The Oxford Reformers*, pp. 39, 151 ff.

[23] Harrison's book (*Platonism in English Poetry*) is weakened because he fails to treat this problem. Oddly enough, the translations of Plato in the sixteenth century are negligible. Phillippe de Mornay made a version of the supposititious *Axiochus* in his *Six Excellent Treatises of Life and Death* (English translation, 1607), and Edw. (Edmund?) Spenser perhaps translated the same dialogue in 1592 (ed. F. M. Padelford, 1934). But on the alleged Spenser translation see Marshall W. S. Swan, "The *Sweet Speech* and Spenser's (?) *Axiochus*," *ELH*, XI (1944), 161-81. See Palmer, *List of English Editions and Translations of Greek and Latin Classics Printed before 1641* (1911), p. 86. A fragmentary translation of Plotinus did not appear until Thomas Taylor published his version in 1794.

and to consider the physical as a determent to the attainment of spiritual excellence—had entered so thoroughly into the fabric of Christian thought that its formulation in the *Dialogues* need hardly be cited. The *Phaedo,* however, comes to mind immediately. That dialogue, based on the antithesis of body and soul, matter and idea, contains a terse statement of Platonic values: the material is inconstant and imperfect, and what man learns about it through sensation tends to degrade his soul, which may have knowledge of spiritual absolutes.

And were we not saying long ago that the soul when using the body as an instrument of perception, that is to say, when using the sense of sight or hearing or some other sense (for the meaning of perceiving through the body is perceiving through the senses)—were we not saying that the soul too is then dragged by the body into the region of the changeable, and wanders and is confused; the world spins round her, and she is like a drunkard, when she touches change?

Very true.

But when returning into herself she reflects, then she passes into the other world, the region of purity, and eternity, and immortality, and unchangeableness, which are her kindred, and with them she ever lives, when she is by herself and is not let or hindered; then she ceases from her erring ways, and being in communion with the unchanging is unchanging. And this state of the soul is called wisdom? [24]

Truly, then, the attainment of wisdom—which is also virtue—is to chastize the flesh and to ignore the world—in short, is to learn the art of dying.

The source of the second basic Platonic concept in the Renaissance—the approach to the holiness of spirit through matter—was of course Diotima's beautiful speech in the *Symposium,* probably responsible for more poetry, good and bad, than any other passage ever written. As the soul, with its vitalistic function of *eros,* takes delight in the beauty of physical forms it is gradually elevated until it perceives what every wise man must know: that physical beauty is but a reflection of the eternal and absolute beauty of spirit, the apex of being and the fusion of truth and goodness. Impelled by his desire, man first loves physical beauty, but he soon perceives that true beauty lies further. He catches a vision of

beauty absolute, separate, simple, and everlasting, which without diminution and without increase, or any change, is imparted to the ever-growing and perishing beauties of all other things. He who from these ascending under the influence of true love, begins to perceive that beauty, is not far from the end. And the true order of going, or being led by another, to the things of love, is to begin from the beauties of earth and mount upwards for the sake of that other beauty, using these as steps only, and from one going on to two, and from two to all fair forms, and

[24] *Phaedo,* 79.

from fair forms to fair practices, and from fair practices to fair notions, until from fair notions he arrives at the notion of absolute beauty, and at last knows what the essence of beauty is.[25]

Although Plato's doctrine of the purity of spirit and the impurity of matter had been both a philosophical and religious commonplace for centuries it was too ascetic for the Renaissance, when men had learned to glory in the forms, sounds, colors, and textures of the world around them. This joy in the material universe was accompanied, however, by a compulsion—the result of fifteen centuries of Christian teaching—to pass beyond the surface of nature to the spiritual content of nature. It was here that Neoplatonism came to the aid of the Renaissance artist and moralist: a system that construed the universe, even the physical world, as a series of emanations participating to a greater or lesser degree in the purity of spirit made it possible for man to have his cake and eat it too. As a Neoplatonist, one could revel in the sensuous beauty of the physical world and all the while have as his ultimate goal the beauty and virtue of spirit. One could observe with considerable erotic satisfaction the shapely breasts of one's mistress, and yet declare that he loved her most for the beauty of her soul. In the *Epithalamion* Spenser's lush account of the bride's goodly eyes, forehead ivory white, paps like lilies budded, leads to the praise of her spiritual beauty which is the true source of her outward charms.

> But if ye saw that which no eyes can see,
> The inward beauty of her lively spright,
> Garnisht with heavenly guifts of high degree,
> Much more then would ye wonder at that sight,
> And stand astonisht. . . .[26]

For the Neoplatonist, then, the appreciation of the world's surface beauty could, as the fourth book of Castiglione's *Courtier* shows, develop into a blinding mystical knowledge of the beauty and goodness of spirit. Neoplatonism served, thus, as both an aesthetic and moral discipline. By mitigating the asceticism of *echt* Platonism and of Augustinian Christianity it enabled man to take a legitimate delight in the

---

[25] *Symposium*, 211.

[26] *Epithalamion*, ll. 184 ff. Artegall's growing reverence and love for Britomart (*Faerie Queene*, IV.vi.21 ff.) is a more pretentious statement of the same theme. Their encounter begins, oddly enough, with a fight, but when, with a sword-stroke, he had "her ventayle shard away," he stayed his blows, dropped his weapon, and fell to his knees: his wonder at her beauty then became religion.

world and the flesh by rationalizing such delight as the first necessary step toward that condition of virtue which spiritual wisdom makes possible.

Before it ran its course in the seventeenth century, Neoplatonism degenerated into mere literary affectation. Most of the Elizabethan sonneteers are insipid enough, but their inane Petrarchism compares rather favorably with the Neoplatonic cult of Charles' court on the eve of the Civil War.[27] Only with genuinely religious men like Herbert and More did the Platonic tradition retain its vitality. This vitality consisted, for about a century and a half, of the optimistic idealism with which Neoplatonism enable the man of the Renaissance to view himself and the world about him.

A large element in the optimism of the Renaissance, and particularly in the cosmologies built on the principle of order, was Neoplatonism. Through the great Platonic doctrine of spirit as the creative principle working on matter, the Neoplatonists explained the beauty and order of the universe as a result of love. It was love that first caused God to share his perfection with lower forms of creation, and it is love inspired by beauty, that causes man to seek to return again to the perfection of God.

According to Ficino, love first moved God to create the material universe.

Absoluta perfectio, in summa dei est potentia. Eam divina intelligentia contemplatur, atque inde voluntas eadem cupit extra se propagare: ex quo propagandi amore creata ab eo sunt omnia.[28]

By its shaping and informing influence, love imposes order, beauty, and design on the chaos of brute matter; as a result, the physical universe is the testament of God's excellence. According to Spenser, it was love that, controlling the discordant elements and tempering

[27] See Kathleen M. Lynch, "Conventions of Platonic Drama in the Heroic Plays of Orrery and Dryden," *PMLA*, XLIV (1929), 456-71. The chatty report of James Howell (quoted by Harrison, *Platonism in English Poetry*, pp. 155-56) suggests the degradation of courtly Platonism: "The Court affords little News at present, but that there is a Love call'd Platonick Love which much sways there of late: it is a Love abstracted from all corporeal gross Impressions and sensual Appetite, but consists in Contemplations and Ideas of the Mind, not in any carnal Fruition. This Love sets the Wits of the Town on work; and they say there will be a Mask [D'Avenant's *Triumph of Love*] shortly of it, whereof Her Majesty and her Maids of Honour will be part." Note Spenser's contempt for the affectations of Platonism in the dedicatory epistle to the *Fowre Hymnes*.

[28] *Commentarium in Convivium*, III.2, quoted by Lilian Winstanley (ed.), *The Fowre Hymnes* (1907), p. lx; cf. Kristeller, *Ficino*, pp. 263 ff.

Their contrarie dislikes with loved meanes,
Did place them all in order, and compell
To keepe them selves within their sundrie raines,
Together linkt with adamantine chaines.[29]

But not only was God motivated by love in creating the universe as a mirror of the realm of spiritual perfection;[30] man too is motivated by his love of the beauty of nature to seek the ultimate wisdom of spiritual illumination. As Bruno explains, the true beauty of spirit shines through the body to create a harmony of soul and body.

Tutti gli amori (si sono heroici . . . ) hanno per oggetto la divinitá, tendeno alla divina bellezza, la quale prima se communica all' anime, et risplende in quelle, et da quelle poi ò (per dir meglo) per quelle poi si communica alli corpi: onde é che l'affetto ben formato ama gli corpi ò la corporale bellezza, per quel che é indice della bellezza del spirito.[31]

But not only this: love is the compulsion behind man's gradual ascent to wisdom. An object of beauty inspires love in man precisely because it evokes in him the mysterious intimations of his own immortality. It serves to remind him dimly (through the Platonic theory of recollection) of the ideal beauty of pure form which he had perhaps known before his birth, and which he feels the compulsion to regain. Whatever excites man's desire does so because it is shaped by that "wondrous Paterne" whereof

as every earthly thing partakes
Of more or lesse, by influence divine,
So it more faire accordingly it makes,
And the grosse matter of this earthly myne,
Which clotheth it, thereafter doth refyne,
Doing away the drosse which dims the light
Of that faire beame which therein is empight.[32]

Spenser's *Fowre Hymnes* is the most sustained essay in Neoplatonism of the English Renaissance.[33] Taken together, these poems constitute

[29] "An Hymne in Honour of Love," ll. 86 ff.; cf. "Colin Clouts Come Home Againe," ll. 841 ff.
[30] See "An Hymne of Heavenly Love," ll. 25 ff.
[31] Quoted from *De Gli Heroici Furori* (1585) by Winstanley, p. lxv.
[32] "An Hymne in Honour of Beautie," ll. 43 ff.; cf. l. 133: "For soule is forme and doth the bodie make."
[33] In addition to Lilian Winstanley's edition of the *Fowre Hymnes*, already cited, see the series of articles by Josephine W. Bennett on Spenser's Neoplatonism: "Spenser's *Fowre Hymnes:* Addenda," *SP,* XXXII (1935), 131-57; "Spenser's Garden of Adonis," *PMLA,*

an enchiridion of Neoplatonic cosmology and ethics. Even though so thorough-paced a Platonist as A. E. Taylor has questioned if Spenser even knew Plato at first hand,[34] the *Hymnes* and (more sporadically) the *Faerie Queene* are shot through and through with ideas that formed the fabric of Renaissance Platonism. The two hymns in honor of love and beauty, which Spenser perhaps revised in his last years to make them less erotic, are concerned respectively with the function of love in evolving a harmonious and orderly universe from chaos and with defining the true beauty of spirit as the ultimate object of man's desire. Of the second pair, "An Hymne of Heavenly Love" deals with the special creation of man by God and with man's capacity of attaining, by the ascent to ever higher objects of desire, a spiritual knowledge of his creator. When man, whom God "made by love out of his owne like mould," [35] learns to direct his desire towards spirit rather than matter he may rise to the ultimate knowledge of God's beauty and goodness. Thenceforth earthly glory will seem but "durt and drosse" compared to "that celestiall beauties blaze" which illuminates the spirit.[36] The final "Hymne of Heavenly Beautie" completes the quartet by treating of the mystical ecstasy to be achieved through the contemplation of God. Such a vision is possible to man—and this is his glory—when he mounts, step by step, from the "easie vew/Of this base world" up through the starry skies and the angelic hosts to the "bright Sunne of Glorie."

> Faire is the heaven where happy soules have place,
> In full enjoyment of felicitie,
> Whence they doe still behold the glorious face
> Of the Divine Eternall Majestie;
> More faire is that where those Idees on hie
> Enraunged be, which Plato so admyred,
> And pure Intelligences from God inspyred.[37]

The second element of Neoplatonic optimism—its flattering estimate of man and his capacities—is implicit in its cosmology. Spenser was a Protestant, and there is a good deal of strenuous Protestantism in the

XLVII (1922), 46-80; "Spenser's Venus and the Goddess of Nature in the *Cantos of Mutabilitie*," *SP*, XXX (1933), 160 ff. See also Harrison, *Platonism in English Poetry, passim*, and a pair of articles, old but still useful, by Jefferson B. Fletcher: "A Study in Renaissance Mysticism: Spenser's 'Fowre Hymnes,'" *PMLA*, XXVI (1911), 452-75 and "Benivieni's 'Ode of Love' and Spenser's 'Fowre Hymnes,'" *MP*, VIII (1911), 545-60 (the *Ode* itself is translated, pp. 547 ff.).

[34] "Spenser's Knowledge of Plato," *MLR*, XIX (1924), 208-10.
[35] "An Hymne of Heavenly Love," l. 116.
[36] "An Hymne of Heavenly Love," ll. 274 ff.
[37] "An Hymne of Heavenly Beautie," ll. 78 ff.

attitude of the Red Cross Knight; but his mystical ethics of purification, illumination, and perfection[38] has little in common with the theology of the great Reformers.[39] If the universe is the creation of a wise, benevolent God—Platonically, the orderly shaping of matter according to the prototypic ideas in the eternal mind of God—then man, stimulated by the beauty around him, may rise to beatitude. Ascending stepwise from more to less physical objects of desire, he may at last attain his consummation in the ecstatic knowledge of the ultimate beauty, wisdom, and truth which are one in the mind of God. Spenser calls this consummation "Sapience," the dominating concept of the great "Hymne of Heavenly Beautie."

Whatever the majestic figure of Sapience meant to Spenser—perhaps a fusion of the Holy Ghost and Plato's heavenly beauty[40]—it represents the goal of man's ethical discipline. It is the highest of God's attributes, and when man, at the end of his spiritual pilgrimage, comes to share it, he has the deific capacity of seeing the true relation between material and spiritual beauty.[41] Sapience wears a golden crown as the "signe of highest soveraignty," [42] and her preëminence is unchallenged.

> Both heaven and earth obey unto her will,
> And all the creatures which they both containe:
> For of her fulnesse, which the world doth fill,
> They all partake, and do in state remaine,
> As their great Maker did at first ordaine,
> Through observation of her high beheast,
> By which they first were made, and still increast.[43]

"Leave me, O Love, which reachest but to dust," cried Sir Philip Sidney. As a good Protestant he was torn between the desires of his flesh and of his soul, but as a good Platonist he trusted in his capacity to attain the

---

[38] See Edwin Greenlaw, "Spenser's Influence on *Paradise Lost*," *SP*, XVII (1920), 345 ff.

[39] The question of Spenser's indebtedness to the Protestant ethic is complicated by his eclecticism: one can prove him to have been everything from a Zeal-of-the-land Busy to a Florentine Platonist. For discussions of his Protestantism see E. Buyssens, "The Symbolism of the Faerie Queene, Book I," *PQ*, IX (1930), 403-406; cf. his "Spenser's Allegories," *TLS*, XXXIII (1934), 28. See also F. M. Padelford's trio of articles: "Spenser and the Puritan Propaganda," *MP*, XI (1913), 85-106; "Spenser and the Theology of Calvin," *MP*, XII (1914), 1-18; "Spenser and the Spirit of Puritanism," *MP*, XIV (1916), 31-44. For a much stronger statement see Paul N. Siegel, "Spenser and the Calvinist View of Life," *SP*, XLI (1944), 201-222. H. S. V. Jones ("The 'Faerie Queene' and the Medieval Aristotelian Tradition," *JEGP*, XXV, 1926, 298) would put Spenser in the central tradition of Renaissance art—"conservative, mediaeval, and Catholic."

[40] See C. G. Osgood, "Spenser's Sapience," *SP*, XIV (1917), 167-77.

[41] Ll. 267 ff.

[42] Ll. 190-91.

[43] Ll. 197 ff.

spiritual beatitude of beauty: his desire was fixed on the changeless and timeless love that drew him to heaven.[44] Although even Spenser confesses that sometimes spirit finds matter intractable,[45] he never questions that the beauty of matter results from the infusion of spirit. Therefore man's high destiny is clear: with his capacity for love and with his God-given faculty of reason (even if stained with sin),[46] he transcends the beauty of matter to arrive finally at the beauty of spirit. This is his function and his glory.[47]

### THE ECLECTIC OPTIMISM OF THE FAERIE QUEENE

The Platonism of the *Fowre Hymnes* is apparent to all who run and read, but the *Faerie Queene* is different. It is a monument to the English Renaissance—a sprawling, ungainly depository of many literary and intellectual traditions. Ever since Ruskin, in the *Stones of Venice,* undertook to work out its allegory[48] it has been a favorite parlor game of scholars to unravel its strands, ascertain its sources, and reveal its meaning. Although the vast scholarship expended on the *Faerie Queene* has been—some of it—of a high order and fascinating as a charade, it has established little more than that Spenser had a multitudinous and rather untidy mind, and that consistency was not the virtue he most hankered after.

Spenser's own announced intention, in the letter to Raleigh, to build his poem on Aristotelian ethics has served to confuse rather than clarify the allegory: owing to his disinclination (or incapacity) to follow his sources clearly, Spenser had provided work for many scholars who have tried to untangle his mental operations. Spenser had no great interest in Aristotle at all;[49] he actually followed the *Ethica Nicomachea*—if rather freely;[50] he was allegorizing England's role in European politics;[51] he

[44] Sonnet cx.    [45] "An Hymne in Honour of Beautie," ll. 141 ff.

[46] "An Hymne of Heavenly Love," ll. 120 ff.

[47] J. B. Fletcher has suggested ("A Study in Renaissance Mysticism: Spenser's 'Fowre Hymnes'," *PMLA*, XXVI, 1911, 456-57) that Spenser has fused Neoplatonism and Calvinism: those who attain the vision of mystic love correspond to Calvin's elect. The suggestion reveals, I think, a certain unfamiliarity with the *Institute*.

[48] See the variorum edition of *The Works of Edmund Spenser*, I (1932), 422-24. Of course, Ruskin was by no means the first; back of him lay Rymer and Blackmore, Warton, Upton, and Hurd.

[49] J. J. Jusserand, "Spenser's 'twelue priuate morall vertues as Aristotle hath deuised'," *MP*, III (1906), 373-83.

[50] W. F. De Moss, "Spenser's Twelve Moral Virtues 'according to Aristotle'," *MP*, XVI (1918), 23-38, 245-70; cf. Lilian Winstanley (ed.), *The Faerie Queene: Book II* (1919), pp. li ff.

[51] Ray Heffner, "Spenser's Allegory in Book I of the Faerie Queene," *SP*, XXVII (1930), 142-61; cf. Philo M. Buck, Jr., "On the Political Allegory in the Faerie Queene," *The University Studies of the University of Nebraska*, XI (1911), 159-92.

was allegorizing Calvin's *Institute*.[52] And so on *ad infinitum*.[53] The task of determining accurately what Spenser was trying to do in the *Faerie Queene* is fascinating but endless. Nonetheless, it is possible to trace a fundamental Platonism through most of his work. In the *Fowre Hymnes* it is obvious; in the *Faerie Queene,* though it is less obvious, it is pervasive.

For one thing, Spenser's incorrigible tendency toward allegory implies an essentially Platonic interpretation of experience. George Santayana has said somewhere that genuine idealism springs from a contempt of the world; if so, Spenser was not a genuine idealist. A man of the Renaissance, he loved the surface, the color, the texture of things; but he felt the compulsion to seek the highest reality in spirit rather than matter, and his Platonism enabled him to satisfy his yearning. Moreover, it gave him a literary form. He saw everything as the reflection of some higher and more spiritual reality; consequently, as Miss Winstanley has said, he was able to construct his great poem as Plato's Demiurge constructed the universe: "the ideas first, and afterwards, the sensuous world, which is at once their symbol and their shadow. It is Platonism which, more than anything else, gives its real unity to *The Faerie Queene*." [54] The Red Cross Knight and Una, Guyon and his Palmer, Artegall and Britomart—all the innumerable *dramatis personae*—allegorize ideas and values; as personifications they derive their validity from Spenser's Platonic metaphysics in which the physical thing reflects the spiritual truth.

Although I do not purpose to enter the wood of error that constitutes Spenserian allegory, I must point out some of the Platonic ideas that inform the *Faerie Queene*. Under the pressure of his Puritanism and Platonism Spenser works miraculous transformations in the Aristotelian virtues. For example, Holiness, the subject of the first and most carefully organized book, is scarcely Aristotelian at all. The Red Cross Knight, a champion who sets out to destroy evil wherever he finds it, attains his sanctity at long last when he recognizes Una's true beauty. Platonically her beauty, like that of Sapience in the hymn, is the beauty of wisdom; and it is visible to the Red Cross Knight only after his purification. Until he becomes something more than a "man of earth" and elevates

[52] E. Buyssens, "The Symbolism of the Faerie Queene, Book I," *PQ*, IX (1930), 403-406.
[53] Among the mountains of Spenserian scholarship one should not forget the important work of F. M. Padelford: *The Political and Ecclesiastical Allegory of the First Book of the Faerie Queene* (1911) and "The Spiritual Allegory of the 'Faerie Queene', Book One," *JEGP*, XXII (1923), 1-17; cf. C. G. Osgood, "Comments on the Moral Allegory of the Faerie Queene," *MLN*, XLVI (1931), 502-507.
[54] *The Faerie Queene: Book II*, p. xii.

his soul from the "frail infirmities" of sense,[55] he is incapable of love with a spiritual object. In the House of Holiness[56] he had learned the three Christian virtues of faith, hope, and charity (Fidelia, Speranza, and Charissa); and the soul-wisdom he acquires on the Mount of Contemplation[57] completes his education in holiness. He descends from the Mount to finish the job he has started—the rescue of Una's parents from the dragon—but he vows to return to the contemplative life.[58]

Even Guyon, the exemplar of the extremely Aristotelian virtue of continence, is an incipient Platonist. For Guyon, continence is not, as Aristotle suggests, temperance in bodily pleasures; it becomes something very like Platonic justice—the moderation and rational control of the whole organism. Just as the charioteer of the Phaedrus must guide his unruly steeds, Guyon must moderate rationally, with the assistance of his dour little Palmer, among the soul-elements of spirit and appetite. He not only controls his anger when Archimago falsely accuses the Red Cross Knight of rape, but also his more righteous anger against Furor and his haggish mother Occasion.[59] He takes warning from Furor, whose

> reason, blent through passion, nought descryde,
> But as a blindfold bull at randon fares,
> And where he hits, nought knowes, and whom he hurts, nought cares.

Finally, Guyon has to combat the intentional and malicious anger of Pyrocles, whom at first he refuses to fight, but whom, when he does fight, he subdues without losing his own rational self-control—"tempring the passion with advizement slow." [60]

But having learned to temper his anger rationally, Guyon proceeds to a sterner discipline—that of harmonizing all his desires under the sovereignty of reason. For as Mr. Lewis has reminded us, the theme of the second book is not the ascetic eradication of bodily desires but the "defence of Health or Nature against various dangers." [61] What Guyon

---

[55] I.x.52.

[56] I.x.3 ff.

[57] I.x.53 ff.

[58] I.x.64. In Annibile Romei's *Courtiers Academie* (trans. J. K[eper], 1598) Signor Francesco Patritio is a man very learned and "especially in Platonical philosophy." He delights to instruct the Countess of Scandiano in the love of beauty, and his thesis is that all "the beauty of this worldly frame, and all the parts thereof, dependeth on ideal form in mind divine comprehended" (quoted by Lewis Einstein, *The Italian Renaissance in England*, 1913, pp. 84-85).

[59] II.i.8 ff.

[60] II.iv.3 ff.

[61] C. S. Lewis, *The Allegory of Love: A Study in Medieval Traditions* (1936), p. 337.

must learn is, quite simply, *mens sana in corpore sano,* the great motif of humanistic balance. He resists the temptation of Phaedria's frothy wantonness (which soon passed the "bonds of modest merimake");[62] he is not even much tempted by the gross worldly goods laid before him in the House of Mammon;[63] and at last in Acrasia's Bower he meets successfully the last and greatest of his tests—that of sensual beauty and desire not sanctified with spiritual wisdom, unproductive of natural pleasure. His instruction in Alma's house of temperance[64] is a good preparation for his perilous voyage to Acrasia's Bower. With the trusty Palmer at his side he sails safely by such traps as the Gulf of Greedinesse,[65] the Rock of vile Reproach,[66] the Wandering Isles and the voluptuous Phoedria,[67] the Quicksand of Unthriftyhed,[68] and the piteous cries of a woman feigning distress.[69] As they near the Bower of Bliss, Guyon is more sorely tried by the maiden swimming with "her two lilly paps aloft displayd";[70] indeed, the Palmer is compelled to rebuke "those wandering eyes of his." [71] But when they at last come upon the witch Acrasia and her paramour lying in dreadful lubricity, uninterested in and presumably incapable of the benison of natural enjoyment, then Guyon's course is clear. Rushing upon the voluptuaries with a "subtile net," Guyon and the Palmer proceed to the work of righteous destruction, demolishing the bowers and palace of Acrasia and releasing her victims so that by regaining their rational self-control they may change from beasts into men again.[72]

*The Faerie Queene* is, then, neither strictly Aristotelian nor strictly Platonic; it is not strictly anything, for it is at once pagan and Christian, Catholic and Protestant. Spenser is the great eclectic. The concept of continence in the second book is ostensibly Aristotelian, but there is much more to Guyon than his mere abstinence from excess: in his moral courage, his balance, and his reasonableness, he is very like Plato's ideal man of justice. Even Britomart, the exemplar of chastity in the third book, is a Platonist in spite of herself. Her chastity is not dry and acidulous, but rather passionate and vitalistic, striving nobly for a noble object. Britomart very nearly approaches the Platonic *eros* that under the com-

---

[62] II.vi.21.
[63] II.vii.
[64] II.xi.
[65] II.xii.3.
[66] II.xii.8.
[67] II.xii.11 ff.
[68] II.xii.13.
[69] II.xii.27-29.
[70] II.xii.66.
[71] II.xii.68.
[72] II.xii.83 ff. See Lewis, p. 332, and, for an analysis of Book Two in Aristotelian terms, F. M. Padelford, "The Virtue of Temperance in the Faerie Queene," *SP*, XVIII (1921), 334-46. On the terminal episode see Merritt Y. Hyghes, "Spenser's Acrasia and the Circe of the Renaissance," *JHI*, IV (1943), 381-99.

pulsion of love seeks ever higher (that is, more spiritual) objects of desire. She represents that love that

> to the highest and the worthiest
> Lifteth it up, that els would lowly fall.[78]

Even in the fourth book, devoted to the typically Aristotelian virtue of friendship, we find the sharply pointed contrast between the false Florimell and the true Florimell: between the frail beauty of the body and the genuine beauty of the spirit.

Actually, the question of Spenser's reliance on Aristotle or on Plato for his ethics is for our purposes dwarfed by a larger certainty—that he was profoundly influenced by the humanistic appraisal of man to which both Aristotle and Plato subscribed. Spenser was a good enough Protestant to construe virtue as active rather than passive, but he knew enough about pagan humanism to believe that man had within him the seeds of his own virtues. Spenser's heroes could enjoy the world, but only under the discipline of their self-mastery; and their self-mastery consisted in developing rationally and harmoniously that generic excellence that is their birthright as men.

[78] III.v.2. See F. M. Padelford, "The Allegory of Chastity in the 'Faerie Queene'," *SP*, XXI (1924), 367-81.

# XVI

## CHRISTIAN HUMANISM

### CHRIST AND CICERO

As a MOVEMENT dedicated to the restoration of both pagan and Christian morality, Christian humanism was another focus of optimism and conservatism. Like Renaissance Neoplatonism, it comprised a set of values that drew their strength from the past. If we may say that Erasmus and Milton, *mutatis mutandis,* were advocating the same principles, we may say that Christian humanism was the last great orthodox statement of man's preëminence in a theocratic universe. For Copernicus was a contemporary of Erasmus, Galileo of Milton, and long before *Paradise Lost* was published the apostles of the new science and of the Protestant version of Augustinian theology were clamoring for a revaluation of man's place in nature.

Like Neoplatonism, Christian humanism looked behind rather than before. Working with proud erudition on the accumulated data of nearly two thousand years of pagan and Christian thought, it attempted one final affirmation of the dignity of man under the old dispensation. Like Neoplatonism, it was syncretistic. On the threshold of an era that was to demand a reorientation of values, it gathered together the strength of a rational philosophy and a revealed religion for the last completely confident pronouncement of faith in God and man. To reconcile Saint Paul and Plato, Saint Jerome and Cicero, the humanists invoked both their learning and their piety; but that the Christian commonwealth of which they dreamed was never more than a dream was inevitable in the age of Henry VIII and of Calvin, when ruthlessness and power, rather than scholarship and moderation, were the highest virtues.

The essential fact of northern humanism was its conservatism. We should not be beguiled by the apparent audacity of Erasmus' attacks on the Schoolmen and his tampering with a textually corrupt Bible; for in their anti-Scholasticism and in their scholarship the humanists tried to check recent corruptions in order to attain a more primitive purity, both of dogma and of letters. Their aim was to revive, to recover, and to reconstruct—not to build a new edifice from new foundations.[1]

[1] See Douglas Bush, "Two Roads to Truth: Science and Religion in the Early Seventeenth Century," *ELH,* VIII (1941), 83; cf. his *The Renaissance and English Humanism* (1939), *passim.*

The humanists shared the Renaissance enthusiasm for the study and revival of classical forms in art and letters—a program which ultimately led other men to the reëxamination of the physical world around them. The humanists' interest in this matter was twofold: not only to cultivate the elegance, style, and formal graces of classical art, but to employ them *suaviter modo* in the service of a traditional and majestic faith. The Schoolmen had written atrocious Latin about tedious and trivial subjects. If only, one can hear Erasmus sigh, they could combine the eloquence of Cicero and Quintilian with the simple piety of Saint Jerome. It was this piety, a genuine reverence for primitive Christianity stripped of its corruptions and recovered from Scholastic accretions, that distinguished northern humanism from Italian humanism.[2] Erudition was common to both varieties, but in the south it became pagan and worldly while in the north the medieval tradition of pious learning was continued.

In their attack on merely secular scholarship the men of the north revealed their conservatism. Petrarch had been a good Christian as well as a savant, but his successors were often mere antiquarians, until presently the whole tone of Italian humanism became philological and critical. Men like Guarino and Poggio were notable not as moralists but as indefatigable searchers after ancient manuscripts.[3] Petrarch had cherished good Latin, and rejoiced to uncover lost treatises of Cicero, but he was never so brazenly secular as Politan and Bembo (who, oddly enough, attained a cardinalate). It was Bembo, in fact, who advised a correspondent not to read Saint Paul, lest his style be ruined.[4] It was because Ficino and Pico passed beyond mere scholarship to philosophic synthesis that they commanded the respect of Colet and Erasmus. For these northern humanists held learning without piety to be a perversion of the intellect. The young Erasmus himself toiled as the sedulous ape, but in his riper years he unmercifully lampooned irreverent pedantry in his *Ciceronianus* (1528).[5]

In this dialogue, Nosophonus, the Ciceronian, tells Bulephorus and Hypologus that the great love of his life is Cicero: "all eloquence except Ciceronian is distasteful to me. This is the nymph for love of whom I am pining away."[6] He makes exhaustive studies of Ciceronian diction and syntax, and forswears all other. "A Ciceronian he will not be in whose books there is found a single little word which he cannot show in the writing of Cicero."[7] When Nosophonus writes a letter, it is agony. He

<hr>

[2] See Hulme, *The Renaissance*, pp. 261 ff.
[3] See Burckhardt, pp. 89 ff.
[4] See F. Funck-Bretano, *The Renaissance* (1936), pp. 72-73.
[5] *Ciceronianus*, trans. Izora Scott, 1908.
[6] P. 21.        [7] P. 27.

is lucky to form a single proper sentence in a whole night's toil.[8] Now to Bulephorus (that is, Erasmus), this is impious balderdash. In his judgment, such pedantry is folly.

Wherever I turn I see things changed, I stand on another stage, I see another theater, yes, another world. What shall I do? I, a Christian, must speak to Christians about the Christian religion. In order that I may speak fittingly, shall I imagine that I am living in the age of Cicero and speaking in a crowded senate in the presence of the senators on the Tarpeian Rock?[9]

Nosophonus' idolatry is, moreover, ignorant. Cicero was a great orator and lawyer, "but in some other things he was of the second rank—an indifferent poet, rather a poor translator from the Greek, of uncertain promise in other fields."[10] Even worse, such pedantry is irreligious: the De Amicitia and De Senectute are good Latin and sound morality, but as for the De Natura Deorum and the De Divinatione . . . A man's studies should strengthen his faith, not undermine it. "His est totius eruditionis et eloquentiae scopus."[11] Men like Nosophonus are corrupting true religion.

We are Christians only in name. The body is baptized in sacred water but the mind is unwashed; the forehead is signed with the cross, the mind curses the cross; we profess Jesus with our mouths, we wear Jupiter Optimus Maximus and Romulus in our hearts.[12]

The Ciceronianus, trifle though it is, tells us much about the temper of northern humanism. Though of great erudition and stylistic elegance, it attacks the affectations, the absurdities, and the blasphemies that make conduct ridiculous and impious. Behind all of Erasmus' satire lay the

---

[8] Later in the dialogue (p. 105), Nosophonus attacks Erasmus for his glibness: he "degrades and hurries everything." On the affectations of humanistic scholarship see J. Huizinga, Erasmus (1924), p. 298.

[9] P. 62.

[10] P. 69.

[11] Quoted by Taylor, Thought and Expression in the Sixteenth Century, I, 165. Etienne Dolet, who was to die at the stake, scurrilously answered the Ciceronianus. For him, he said, Christ and Cicero were enough. Erasmus' fears, however, were justified: some of the most frequently reprinted of the ancients were such subversive rationalists or Stoics as Aurelius, Epictetus, Plutarch, and Seneca. See George T. Buckley, Atheism in the English Renaissance (1932), pp. 3, 11 ff.; Henri Busson, Les Sources et le développement du rationalisme dans la littérature française de la renaissance (1922), pp. 16 ff. For bibliographies of Renaissance translations of the classics see V. de Sola Pinto, The English Renaissance (1938), pp. 187 ff.; Henrietta R. Palmer, List of English Editions and Translations of Greek and Latin Classics Printed before 1641; F. Seymour Smith, The Classics in Translation (1930).

[12] P. 73.

same impulse of piety, and the purpose of those bagatelles that have most charmed posterity—the *Praise of Folly* and the *Colloquies*—was always the correction of error towards attaining a Christian life. Thus, Erasmus would attack rascally monks as eagerly as rascally innkeepers. His own early education in a monastery had made him suspicious, but his real objection to extravagant clericalism was that it distorted Christ's simple prescription for the good life. Schoolmen who hide behind the barricade of "scholastic definitions, arguments, corollaries"[13] are no better than the monks who peddle indulgences, or than their victim who chooses "rather to venture the whole Stress of his Salvation upon a Skin of Parchment than upon the Amendment of his life."[14] Erasmus mocked ritualists "who beg those things of the Saints, which they dare not ask of a good man."[15] And he applauded Saint Jerome's maxim that it is no great matter to have made a pilgrimage to Jerusalem, but a very great thing to have lived well.[16]

The fact is that the kind of primitive Christianity preached by Erasmus was the antithesis of the pomp, corruption, ritualism, and venality of contemporary Catholicism. "*Erasmus?*" says a character in one of the *Colloquies*. "They say he's Half a Heretick."[17] But like his friend Colet, Erasmus had at the core of his thinking a winsome, almost naive, piety. "Whatsoever is pious, and conduces to good Manners, ought not to be called profane."[18] To know God and the Bible, to injure no one, to exercise charity, to practice patience—these constituted his Christianity.[19] In "The Gospel-Carrier" Cannius says, with artful simplicity, that merely to mouth scraps of the Gospel is not enough. "A man does not carry it in his Heart, that does not love it with all his Soul; and nobody loves it as he ought, that does not conform to it in his life." To which Polyphemus replies: "These Subtleties I don't understand."[20] Perhaps some of these teachings were remembered by the Bishop of Augsburg when he said that most of what he knew of Christ he had learned from Erasmus.[21]

In his own day, Erasmus' prodigious literary labors were often regarded with as much distrust as were his lampoons. And perhaps justly, for they had the same purpose—to purify and strengthen the Christian faith. By his scholarship Erasmus hoped to enable every Christian to read the

[13] *The Praise of Folly* (trans. Hoyt Hopewell Hudson, 1941), p. 78.
[14] "Of Rash Vows," *The Colloquies* (trans. N. Bailey, 1878), I, 55; cf. II, 361.
[15] "Concerning the Profitableness of Colloquies," *The Colloquies*, II, 372.
[16] *Ibid.*, II, 360; cf. II, 1 ff.
[17] "The Young Man and the Harlot," *The Colloquies*, I, 297.
[18] "The Religious Treat," *The Colloquies*, I, 182.
[19] "The Child's Piety," *The Colloquies*, I, 87; cf. II, 362.
[20] "The Gospel-Carrier," *The Colloquies*, II, 172-73.
[21] See P. S. Allen, *Erasmus: Lectures and Wayfaring Sketches* (1934), p. 72.

Bible in its philological purity, just as he hoped, in those countless hortatory and inspirational tracts (like *The Education of a Christian Prince* and the *Adagia*) to show that the good life is one of rational piety. The man was a born propagandist, and in the *Paraclesis* (the preface to his version of the New Testament) he justified his efforts:

Platonists, Pythagoreans, and the disciples of all other philosophers, are well instructed and ready to fight for their sect. Why do not Christians with yet more abundant zeal espouse the cause of *their* Master and Prince? Shall Christ be put in comparison with Zeno and Aristotle—his doctrines with their insignificant precepts? [22]

Lorenzo Valla, whom Erasmus worshipped for his erudition, had used his talent to denounce the spurious and to confirm the true. Not only had he dared to say of the Vulgate that it was faulty in style and grossly inaccurate in translation; he had, to the consternation of some, shown that the Donation of Constantine was a forgery, and he had questioned the authenticity of the Pseudo-Dionysius.[23] His audacities were without precedent, but Erasmus applauded and emulated him. To Leo X he explained his textual revision of the Vulgate, which seemed impious to many: "by this labour we do not intend to tear up the old and commonly accepted edition, but to emend it in some places where it is corrupt, and to make it clear where it is obscure." [24] How better could a man employ his learning, he asked.

To say, then, that humanists like Erasmus indulged in neopaganism because they were seduced by the literary elegancies of the classics would be patently absurd. Always uppermost in their thought was the preservation and the restoration of Christian faith; and this goal could be reached, as they thought, by cultivating a literary heritage that through carelessness or ignorance had been almost lost. For Erasmus, the man of learning, the path was clear: his learning was to be used in the service of his faith. Just as the practice of Christianity was to be freed from the absurdities of monasticism and Scholasticism, so the theology and holy texts were to be purged of textual corruption. The phrase *bonae litterae* is virtually the leitmotif of Erasmus' innumerable letters, pamphlets, manuals, and editions, but he never practiced the art of literature for its

[22] Quoted by Seebohm, *The Oxford Reformers*, p. 326. See *A Book Called in Latin Enchiridion Militis Christiani and in English The Manual of the Christian Knight* (1905), "The Epistle," *passim*, and esp. pp. 15 ff.

[23] See *The Cambridge Modern History*, II (1904), 664; cf. Smith, *Erasmus*, pp. 15-16.

[24] *The Epistles*, no. 434 (II, 316). Long before, Saint Jerome had to meet the charge that he took liberties with the Bible; he countered that though he dared not "correct" the words of Christ, he freely reconstructed the obviously corrupt texts (*Letters*, no. XXVII; cf. his very sensible remarks on translation, *Letters*, no. LVII).

own sake. He could only mock professional aesthetes: when they find a new word in Cicero, "O Jupiter! what exulting then, what triumphs, what panegyrics, as if they had conquered Africa or captured Babylon." [25] As the *Enchiridion* shows, "godly learning" should be synonymous with "learned godliness."

Erasmus himself was tireless in sacking antiquity for his own purpose, but his purpose was moral instruction: his mission was to show how learning and literary style—in a word, *eloquentia*—could be used in the service of piety. The numerous editions of the *Adagiorum Collectanea* from 1500 on represented more than erudition; they demonstrated the proposition that in the works of pagan antiquity there is much that a wise man may use in attaining virtue. Although he was ignorant of science, Erasmus denounced it because it distracted man's thoughts from moral philosophy.[26] When he wrote of so unholy a thing as politics, and for such ruthless opportunists as Charles V and Henry VIII, it was on the assumption that political activity is basically moral. The *Enchiridion* is probably the last great credo of political morality before the secularization of Machiavelli. It was "not composed for any display of genius or eloquence," Erasmus told Colet, "but only for the purpose of correcting the common error of those who make religion consist of ceremonies and an almost more than Jewish observance of corporeal matters, while they are singularly careless of things that belong to piety." [27] *Piety* and *eloquence* ring like a refrain through thousands of pages. They were the very attributes that made Saint Jerome so great, and it was scandalous that his works were so little known. "Good Heavens! shall the names of Scotus, Albertus, and writers still less polished be shouted in all the schools, and that singular champion, exponent and light of our religion, who deserves to be the one person celebrated,—shall he be the only one of whom nothing is said?" [28]

Erasmus' English friends show much the same temper of mind. Sir Thomas More, who has received more praise than he deserves, was characterized by an extreme, even fanatic, orthodoxy coupled with a genuine interest in Latin style. In many ways, he reminds one of Savonarola: they were both men of intransigent orthodoxy who probably welcomed martyrdom, and they may both be fairly charged with piety mounting (or deteriorating) almost to fanaticism. Perhaps there are a

[25] *The Praise of Folly*, p. 71.
[26] See Smith, *Erasmus*, p. 35.
[27] *The Epistles*, no. 180 (II, 376).
[28] *The Epistles*, no. 134 (I, 289); cf. Smith, *Erasmus*, pp. 190 ff.

few arguments against heresy in Plato and Aristotle, Savonarola admits, but "they and other philosophers are now in Hell. An old woman knows more about the Faith than Plato. It would be good for religion if many books that seem useful were destroyed." [29] In matters of dogma, More was equally severe. Although those celebrated passages of sweetness and light in *Utopia* urge the utmost tolerance in religion, it is hard to reconcile More's principles with his practices. To him, Tewkesbury, who had translated Luther and had died for his audacity, was only a "stinking martyr." [30] Under the urbane surface of the Lord Chancellor there lurked a medieval ascetic. As soon as he was called to the bar, More had inaugurated a course of lectures on Augustine's *De Civitate Dei*,[31] and a little later, having fallen into disfavor with Henry VII, he seriously considered becoming a Carthusian brother, in preparation for which he resorted to a hair-shirt and to sleeping on bare boards with a log for a pillow.[32]

More, like the young Erasmus who had imitated Innocent III's *De Contemptu Mundi*, followed the literary tradition of a morbid asceticism in his *Four Last Things*—but it was a product of his maturity, and he must have meant it. A characteristically macabre *memento mori*, complete with the dance of death, the book is a vehement essay in primitive Christianity. Weighing the comfort of Scripture against that of pagan philosophers, More concludes that the seventh chapter of Ecclesiastes "containeth more fruitful advice and counsel to the forming and framing of man's manners in virtue and the avoiding of sin, than many whole and great volumes of the best of old philosophers or any other that ever wrote in secular literature." [33] The acrid realism of his treatment of death is far from what some have praised as the *joie de vivre* of the Renaissance man. The true Christian, says More, will think earnestly of the dance of death on the walls of Saint Paul's—the "loathly figure of our dead bony bodies, bitten away the flesh." [34] The best death one can hope for is to be

[29] Cited by Burckhardt, pp. 250-51. In 1497 at the Carnival, Savonarola burned in the Piazza della Signoria women's cosmetics together with manuscripts of Petrarch, Boccaccio, and Pulci. The inclusion of Pulci is understandable, but why the Petrarch of the *Secretum*, or the Boccaccio of the *De Viribus*?

[30] See Smith, *Erasmus*, p. 93. R. W. Chambers (*The Place of St. Thomas More in English Literature and History*, 1937, pp. 42 ff.) has argued against Foxe, Froude, Acton, and many others that More's advocacy of religious persecution is quite consonant with the liberalism of *Utopia*. As a lawyer, he explains, More urged persecution because he feared violence and sedition. For More's opinion of heretics, see William Roper, *The Lyfe of Sir Thomas Moore, Knighte* (ed. Elsie Vaughan Hitchcock, EETS, vol. CXCVII, 1935), pp. 34-36.

[31] Roper, p. 6.        [32] Roper, p. 6.

[33] *The English Works of Sir Thomas More*, I (1931), 459.

[34] *Ibid.*, I, 468.

lying in thy bed, thy head shooting, thy back aching, thy veins beating, thine heart panting, thy throat rattling, thy flesh trembling, thy mouth gaping, thy nose sharping, thy legs cooling, thy fingers fumbling, thy breath shortening, all thy strength fainting, thy life vanishing, and thy death drawing on.[85]

Is it not odd that two flowers of Christian humanism, More and Pico, ended their lives like third-century ascetics rather than men of the Renaissance?

The religious orthodoxy of the humanists, though violent in More, was conspicuous in all his friends and spiritual brethren. Petrarch admired Ciceronian Latin, but he worshipped Augustine. Ficino translated Plato, but only that the whole world might learn his piety. Pico fell under the ban of Innocent VIII when he announced his nine hundred theses, but only thirteen of them were questioned and a majority were lifted from such eminently acceptable sources as Albert, Aquinas, and Scotus. In fact, Pico's life, in the account of his nephew which was translated by More, was almost like the plot of a morality play: the brilliant but worldly young man of prodigal gifts who at last was saved by true religion. John Colet, a truly beatific man, had been charmed by the Florentines who revived Neoplatonism to buttress their piety. In his exegesis of Genesis, he drew heavily on Pico's *Heptaplus,* and as his commentary on first Corinthians shows, he was carried away by the treatises of the Pseudo-Dionysius. The movement of his thought was antirationalistic and anti-Scholastic, and towards a warm, intoxicating blend of primitive Christianity and mysticism. He sharply snubbed young Erasmus, who had professed a great admiration for Aquinas. "Unless his spirit had been somewhat worldly," explained Colet gravely, "he would not surely have corrupted the whole teaching of Christ by mixing with it his profane philosophy." [36]

Erasmus, the most cosmopolitan of them all, could always be counted on to speak for the true believers. When he humanistically insisted on the dignity of man, he argued from the fact of man's vicarious importance through Christ's atonement and God's grace.[37] In sober fact he attributed boyish misbehavior to original sin.[38] Although he did not like Luther's Augustinian severity, he was a good enough Catholic to uphold the Church's position on the sad dogma of man's native depravity.[39]

---

[85] *Ibid.,* I, 468.

[36] Quoted by Seebohm, *The Oxford Reformers,* p. 107. For Erasmus' famous praise of Colet and the English group see *The Epistles,* no. 110 (I, 226).

[37] *Enchiridion,* ch. XXVII.

[38] See Taylor, *Thought and Expression in the Sixteenth Century,* I, 162.

[39] *Enchiridion,* ch. VIII. See also ch. XXXVII.

Erasmus' forte was irony, and his only passionately held conviction was for simple piety; yet he would always rise to be numbered among the faithful. His innate conservatism would permit no less: it was better to make one's peace with a traditional if corrupt Church than to expose oneself to danger in following the new and the radical. In the famous colloquy "An Enquiry Concerning Faith," Barbatus fears doctrinal commitments and institutionalized religion, only to be warned that through the Church alone can one receive the grace essential for salvation.[40] Erasmus could mock the extravagances of an arrogant and venal clergy, but he could never permit himself to question the creed which conferred their power upon them.

### ERASMUS AND LUTHER

In his reaction to the Reformation that convulsed his time, Erasmus, the prince of the northern humanists, most clearly showed his orthodoxy and conservatism. Like Sir Thomas Browne a century later, he was temperamentally unable to do other than follow the great wheel of his Church. Although the issue for Erasmus was mainly doctrinal, it elicited more than a doctrinal response: his innate love of moderation and tradition, and his revulsion from violence were traits of character rather than religious convictions. Frederic Seebohm, in his famous book, supports the thesis that Erasmus, Colet, and More were, in their own fashion, reformers. In their genuine desire for a reformation of clerical abuses and for a return to what they perhaps romantically construed as primitive piety, they were. But in their genteel and even timid iconoclasm they were dwarfed by titans like Luther and Calvin. In the angry tumult of the real reformers, the correction of abuses was necessary but paltry; they wished to abandon the whole tradition of a rational theology and replace it—with violence, if need be—with a religion of Augustinian subjectivism and revelation. To these dread limits the humanists could not go. Just as the crudities of the *Epistolae Obscurorum Virorum* (1515-17)—even though it defended Reuchlin against the Schoolmen—offended Erasmus' delicacy, so the violence of Luther's reforms offended his sense of decorum and moderation.

The rock on which Erasmus and Luther split was the question of free will. Luther (and Calvin) could be satisfied only with a complete reversal of Thomistic rationalism: that man should presume to know God through his puny reason was to them as abhorrent as that God Himself was circumscribed by reason. Erasmus, however, could not think of God save as essentially rational, or of man as essentially good if only he

---

[40] *The Colloquies*, I, 329.

used his God-given reason in the service of his piety. The whole of man's excellence was epitomized in his faculty of reason, and to think of him as congenitally depraved and therefore unable to use his reason in choosing the good was a libel on human dignity.

Erasmus' attitude toward Luther was sympathetic at the beginning. In general he approved the ninety-five theses, and, as all Europe knew, he tirelessly urged the reform of papal abuses. "The Roman Curia," he wrote Colet in 1518, "is incapable of a blush, for what can be more shameless, than this constant supply of Pardons?" [41] But as all Europe knew also, he detested the Augustinian doctrine of total depravity.[42] Emotionally, he was the heir of Aquinas, who had been unable to accept the notion that God imposed punishment for sins beyond man's control. Providence, Aquinas had argued, produces every grade of being: some things are strictly determined by "necessary causes," but others, like man, react to "contingent causes." [43] Thus, "guilt proceeds from the free-will of the person who is reprobated and deserted by grace. In this way the word of the prophet is true—namely, *Perdition, O Israel, is thy own.*" [44]

The promulgation of Leo's bull *Exsurge* coincided with Erasmus' rising doubts about Luther's position on free will. After 1520 the disputants had finished their skirmishing and were ready for battle. As late as 1519, in his famous letter to young Albert of Hohenzollern, Cardinal Archbishop of Mainz, Erasmus had equivocated so as to please both sides. But Luther's attack on the sacraments in his notorious *Prelude on the Babylonian Captivity of the Church* and his burning of the canon law (10 December, 1521) was a profound emotional shock to a man who revered tradition as Erasmus did. With Luther's answer to Leo, the *Refutation of the Bull,* the issue was clear, and one can imagine the vast relief of the papacy when Erasmus finally agreed to write against Luther in his *De Libero Arbitrio* (1524).[45]

Erasmus' treatise was a skillful and erudite restatement of the Thomistic position. He cajoled and satirized; he quoted the fathers; he squeezed every drop of evidence from the Scriptures.[46] But throughout one can

---

[41] *The Epistles,* no. 757 (III, 298).

[42] As, for instance, in his commentary on Romans, V:2: "Wherefore since sin entered the world through one man." See Smith, *Erasmus,* pp. 170-71.

[43] *Summa Theologica,* I.22.4.

[44] *Ibid.,* I.23.3.

[45] *Opera Omnia* (1703-1706), IX, 1215-1248. For a very able account of the controversy between Erasmus and Luther see Smith, *Erasmus,* ch. IX; cf. Robert H. Murray, *Erasmus & Luther: Their Attitude to Toleration* (1920), pp. 213-37.

[46] For instance, note his interpretation of the verse from Genesis: "Non permanebit spiritus meus in homine in aeternum, quae caro est" (*Opera Omnia,* IX, 1235).

see that he—like most disputants before and since—was seeking rational grounds for an intuitive attitude. At the core of his faith was the conviction of Cardinal Pole: ignorance is vice and knowledge is virtue; and the alleged bondage of the will is merely bondage to ignorant opinion which may be rectified by "dylygent instructyon *and* wyse conseyl." [47] Why did God—as He surely did—give to man a free will?

Ut sit quod merito imputetur impiis, qui gratiae Dei volentes defuerint, ut excludatur a Deo crudelitas & injustitiae calumnia, ut excludatur a nobis desperatio, ut excludatur securitas, ut exstimulemur ad conandum. [48]

The wisdom and goodness of God are manifest in man's ability to choose rationally between alternatives. Grace is of course indispensable, but a free will is too.

Ergo meo quidem judico, quod ad *Liberum Arbitrium* attinet, quae didicimus e sacris Litteris, si in via pietatis sumus, ut alicriter proficiamus ad meliora, relictorum obliti: si peccatis involuti, ut totis viribus enitamur, adeamus remedium poenitentiae, ac Domini misericordiam modis omnibus ambiamus, sine qua nec voluntas humana est efficax, nec conatus . . . [49]

It was Luther, however, who had the last word. *The Bondage of the Will,* his reply to Erasmus, was one of the most influential books of the century. Calvin, who of course read it, must have rejoiced in a passage like this:

God foreknows nothing subject to contingencies, but he foresees, foreordains, and accomplishes all things by an unchanging, eternal, and efficacious will. By this thunderbolt free will sinks shattered in the dust. [50]

Luther would not commit himself to a strict determinism—a man may walk abroad or stay within doors—but he would not subtract an iota from God's sovereignty or from man's complicity in the sin of Adam. In his *Table Talk* he frequently mused on Erasmus' folly.

Aber wir wissen noch nicht recht, was wir nach dem Fall unser ersten Aeltern worden sind und von Mutter Leibe mit uns bracht haben; nehmlich ein gar verruckte, verderbte und vergiste Natur an Leib und Seel und an allen ihren Kräften. Da is nichts Guts an, wie die Schrift sagt. Und ist das mein endliche Meinung, wie in allen meinen Schriften zu sehen ist, sonderlich wider Erasmum Roterodamum,

[47] *England in the Reign of King Henry the Eighth,* pp. 30-31.
[48] *Opera-Omnia,* IX, 1248.
[49] *Ibid.,* IX, 1216. For a short but eloquent statement of Erasmus' belief in the dignity of man see the *Enchiridion,* ch. XXVII.
[50] Quoted by Smith, *Erasmus,* pp. 352-53.

der furnehmsten unter allen Gelehrten einen in der Welt: Wer des Menschen freien Willen vertiheidingen will, dass er etwas in geistlichen Dingen vermöge und mit wirken könne, auch im geringsten, der hat Christum verläugnet. Dabei bleib ich und weiss, dass es die gewisse Wahrheit ist.[51]

At the Heidelberg Debate (April, 1518) Luther had insisted that "free will, after the fall, was only a name, and that when a man acted according to his own being he sinned mortally."[52] It was inevitable that one holding this opinion should consider Erasmus no better than an Arian.[53] But Erasmus loved *eloquentia* rather than doctrine, and he feared violence and rebellion more than Luther's contempt: he could only shudder at a theology that humiliated man's reason and shamelessly upset the *status quo* of religious polity. In a rare moment of candor he gave Richard Pace the truth rather than urbane chit-chat:

All men have not strength for martyrdom. I fear lest, if any tumult should rise, I should imitate Peter [in denying his Lord]. I follow the just decrees of popes and emperors because it is right; I endure their evil laws because it is safe. I think this is allowable to good men, if they have no hope of successful resistance.[54]

In everything Erasmus writes, said Luther in a letter to Spalatin in 1521, "he is thinking of peace, not of the cross."[55] But by that time he must have known he could expect nothing from the first scholar of Europe, and thereafter it became his favorite diversion to deride him. He repeated against Erasmus the old scandal that he was "filius monachi et nonnae."[56] He charged that in those glittering epistles Erasmus did nothing except "die Freunde lobet und die Feinde und Widersacher schilt und läftert."[57] When he learned that Erasmus had at long last decided to take sides against him he wrote him condescendingly that obviously God had not granted him courage enough to fight openly with His champions—in spite of which Luther and his followers had "tolerated and even respected the mediocrity of God's gift in you."[58] And when Erasmus finally died, long after the events of 1521 and even as Calvin was girding his loins, Luther pronounced his valediction more in

[51] *Tischreden (Werke, 1883 ff.)*, VI, 119.
[52] Quoted by Smith, *Erasmus*, p. 339.
[53] *Tischreden*, I, 377; cf. III, 620-21.
[54] *Opus Epistolarum Des. Erasmi Roterodami* (ed. P. S. Allen, 1906 ff.), no. 1521 (translated by Smith, *Erasmus*, p. 243). This letter, written in 1521, was not reprinted until the eighteenth century.
[55] *Luther's Correspondence and Other Contemporary Letters* (trans. Preserved Smith and Charles M. Jacobs, 1913-1918), II, 56; cf. II, 190.
[56] *Tischreden*, IV, 574.
[57] *Ibid.*, VI, 252.
[58] *Luther's Correspondence*, II, 228.

sorrow than in anger: "Er starb auch dahin sine crux et sine lux." [59] But Erasmus died in the bosom of his Church, and so he would have claimed the victory after all.

## "PRYUATE STUDYS"

If Erasmus' role in the Reformation teaches us anything, it is that the humanists were trying to salvage tradition. They were unwilling to undertake any fundamental revaluation of man or his institutions, but they were eager to preserve and purify the best features of the *status quo*. Their ethics, therefore, were personal rather than sociological. Like young Henry Adams they were optimists who believed that the universe was essentially moral and essentially rational, and that man's well-being was to develop (by education) his innate moral and rational faculties.

A truly learned man, the humanists assumed, would be a good man. Indeed, all the evils of society could be attributed to the fact that "the moost part of al [men] be vnlearned. And a greate number hathe learning in contempte." [60] If only men would learn to act rationally, sighs Erasmus again and again, there would be no war, no avarice, no bestiality, no impiety. For the humanists the Socratic equation of knowledge and virtue still made sense. Merely because he was eager for wisdom, Pico became both wise and good: though "yet a child and beardless, he was both reputed, and was indeed, both a perfect philosopher and a perfect divine." [61] About the objects of knowledge there was no question. They were the revealed truths of God in the Scriptures and the complementary truths of classical thought. When Erasmus was drawing up a reading program for a "Christian prince"—the very phrase was a contradiction in terms in the sixteenth century—he included Solomon's Proverbs and Ecclesiasticus (both, incidentally, more redolent of literature than dogma), to be followed by Plutarch, Aristotle, and Cicero.[62] And he admired Colet's taste in literature as much as he did his saintly character: "libros Ciceronis avidissime devorarat et Platonis Plotinique libros non oscitanter excusserat." [63]

Roger Ascham, himself a tutor of royalty, was like Erasmus a schoolmarm at heart. His plan for perfection was a little more commodious. One needs to "dwell in these few bookes onelie": the Bible, Cicero, Plato, Aristotle, Xenophon, Isocrates, and Demosthenes. And if he does so, he "must nedes proue an excellent man." [64] It was that simple. The hu-

---

[59] *Tischreden*, V, 310.     [60] More, *Utopia*, "The Epistle," p. 25.

[61] *The English Works of Sir Thomas More*, I, 351.

[62] *The Education of a Christian Prince* (trans. Lester K. Born, 1936), pp. 200-201.

[63] Quoted by Seebohm, *The Oxford Reformers*, p. 15, n. 1.

[64] *The Scholemaster* (ed. Edward Arber, 1927), p. 129.

manists were all fast impaled on the assumption—by no means obsolete in certain quarters—that a good book must be about good things; the function of literature was moral discipline. The corollary to this proposition still haunts literary criticism: a good writer must be a good man. In the dedication to *Volpone,* Jonson, firmly anchored in the classical tradition even if he was no Saint Anthony, pointed out that if we reflect "impartially, and not asquint," we must grant the "impossibility of any man's being the good poet without first being a good man."[65] Of course, Milton's whole career was built on this creed, and no man was more aware of its demands. Thus, Milton's defense of Spenser (a better teacher than Aquinas) and Ascham's attack on the Arthurian tales (bawdry and open manslaughter) were in the same humanist tradition.

Similarly, the humanists were valiant in defending against the obscurantists books that were proper though pagan. Sidney insisted that a good poet is "indeed the right Popular Philosopher,"[66] and his academic friend Gabriel Harvey urged instruction in "ye choisist and purist authors"—Cicero and Caesar, Terence and Virgil.[67] Long before, in More's day, there were those at Oxford who were so narrow in their piety as to think that teachers of Greek were *diabolos maximos,* their students *diabolos minutulos.* They were of course opposed by More, who went so far as to threaten them with the displeasure of Archbishop Warham, Cardinal Wolsey, and even the king himself.[68] Characteristically, Erasmus used his irony to advance the cause of pagan literature. There is so much good morality in Plutarch, he observed gently, that it is amazing "how such evangelical Notions should come into the heart of a Heathen."[69] Even if he was unable to take the field with Luther, he was genuinely humbled before the piety and wisdom of Cicero's *De Senectute,* and when he closed Plato's account of Socrates' death he could only murmur, *Sancte Socrates, ora pro nobis.*

Thus for the humanists the magic phrase *bonae litterae* became an ethical principle. Without Greek, Colet told Erasmus, we are nothing.[70]

[65] *The Complete Plays* (Everyman's Library, n.d.), I, 400.

[66] *Apologie for Poetrie* in *Elizabethan Critical Essays* (ed. Gregory Smith, 1904), I, 167.

[67] *Letter-Book* (ed. Edward John Long Scott, Camden Society Publications, N.S., no. 33, 1884), p. 181; cf. p. 53.   [68] See Seebohm, *The Oxford Reformers,* p. 459.

[69] "The Religious Treat," *The Colloquies,* I, 198. On the humanists' desire to interpret the classics as moral treatises see Busson, *Les Sources et le développement du rationalisme,* pp. 3-9. A hack-writer like William Baldwin, in his *Treatise of Morall Philosophy,* assembled a collection of purple passages alphabetically culled from Aristotle to Zeno. He explained (p. 39b) that next to the Bible, there is nothing "more true" than such "godly doctrine."

[70] See Allen, *Erasmus: Lectures and Wayfaring Sketches,* p. 83. More's Raphaell Hythlodaye (*Utopia,* p. 29) much preferred Greek to Latin. As a student of philosophy, "he knew that ther is nothyng extante in Latine, that is to anye purpose, sauynge a fewe of Senecaes, and Ciceroes dooynges."

Learning in those balmy, pre-Baconian days meant little more than familiarity with a literary canon and ease in handling a couple of languages, but it was the key to the good life. When More chose the rulers of his Utopia—"ambassadours, priestes, Tranibores, and finallye the prince him selfe"—from the "company of the learned" [71] he was providing for both sound morality and good government. Although the humanists were bookish, they were anything but philosophical. Just as most of them preferred piety to dogma, they preferred ethics to metaphysics and epistemology. They venerated "learning" (which, according to Ascham, "teacheth more in one yeare than experience in twentie"),[72] but they were impatient with knowledge that was conceptual rather than moral.

Consequently they were Alexandrian rather than Attic. Men of erudition and blameless lives, they were not original thinkers. Whoever said that Erasmus looked as if he were descended from a long line of maiden aunts knew a good deal of the temper of northern humanism. Erasmus and his friends hankered for what was safe and settled; conformity was for them a virtue, and respect for authority, religious and literary, was their creed. In the high Renaissance, the Faustus-mood of radical individualism passed them by. Even Ascham's Anglicanism does not strike one as the achievement of a hard-fought moral struggle: he was neither a Loyola nor a Luther. And the English saint of humanism, Sir Thomas More, could lose all his gentle charm in prescribing torments for the heretics who dared to upset the *status quo*.

When Ascham declared the principles of the ideal schoolmaster to be "three speciall pointes, Trothe of Religion, honestie in liuing, right order in learning," [73] he epitomized the humanist ideal. To these men, the past was a field full of fair flowers, ready for plucking.[74] One had only to fashion the bouquets, taking care not to stray into *terra incognita*. Ascham explained airily that he was neither a Stoic nor an Anabaptist, and could appreciate "a merie, plesant, and plaifull nature" as well as

---

[71] *Utopia*, pp. 86-87.

[72] *The Scholemaster*, p. 61.

[73] *Ibid.*, p. 23.

[74] Lewis Mumford (*The Condition of Man*, pp. 179 ff.) develops the thesis that humanism, especially in Italy, was a product of the cult of luxury that attended the rise of capitalism and of political absolutism. "The acquisition of culture now became a by-product of the acquisitive impulse itself: it rested on a boundless capacity to collect and pile up physical treasures. In one's home, the sign of culture was to be surrounded by fragments, reproductions, or ornamental simulcra of the antique world: in conversation one would trot out quotations from one's favorite classic authors, in the original language, to prove that one had spent one's time almost exclusively in their company."

the next man—if, he adds quickly, "no outrage be committed, against lawe, me[a]sure, and good order." [75]

Law, measure, and good order were shibboleths for nearly all the early humanists. Erasmus' well-advertised disapproval of war, for instance, was based upon these principles. Everywhere he saw order and decorum and degree; why, he asked wearily, should they be disturbed? "Animals destitute of reason, live with their own kind in a state of social amity. Elephants herd together; sheep and swine feed in flocks." [76] Only man, the rational animal. . . .

On the medieval analogy between the body politic and the human organism, the prince should rule his people as the mind should rule the body, and mind is of course the instrument of reason. Why, then, do men not read the right books, learn right reason, and live in rational tranquillity? [77] Reason was a term much bandied about, then as now, but the humanists seem never to have arrived at a very satisfactory definition of it. It was universally commended as a very good thing, and in some way related to reading, in the original, the proper authors; moreover, its function was to point men towards "Trothe of Religion" and right order in learning. But beyond these amiable commonplaces the humanists rarely ventured.

Erasmus insisted that *institutio* is what makes a man a man: uneducated, he is a "wild beast," but properly trained he is a "divinity." [78] But living amid the political chicanery of the sixteenth century, Erasmus could only piously hope that the properly educated prince "loves and honors virtue as the finest quality of all, the most felicitous, the most fitting a prince; and that he loathes and shuns moral turpitude as the foulest and most terrible of things." [79] Thomas Lupset charged Cardinal Pole, "drowynyd in the plesure of letturys *and* pryuate studys," with retreating to his books and thus neglecting a realistic treatment of his country's needs.[80] But this indictment would have seemed absurd to Erasmus. A prince, as the leader of men, should embody man's proudest virtues—the hoary quartet of wisdom, magnanimity, temperance, and

---

[75] *The Scholemaster*, pp. 63-64.

[76] Quoted from *The Complaint of Peace* by Lester K. Born in his edition of *The Education of a Christian Prince*, pp. 10-11.

[77] In his muddy allegory *Euthymiae Raptus* Chapman reflects on the blight of war and decides that until man acquires true wisdom and learning, and thus approaches God, will he cease to fight with his kind. The notion was, of course, a commonplace.

[78] Quoted from *De Pueris Instituendis* by Taylor, *Thought and Expression in the Sixteenth Century*, I, 162.

[79] *The Education of a Christian Prince*, p. 148.

[80] *England in the Reign of King Henry the Eighth*, pp. 2-3.

integrity—and how else could he learn these except by being a scholar-prince? [81]

Because the humanist gloried in the role of *laudator temporis acti* it is perhaps irrelevant to expect incisiveness or intellectual independence from him. Erasmus and his friends were, nearly all of them, men of personal charm, of urbanity in an age of violence, of erudition, of temperate lives. Moreover, they were disinterested in their quest for the life of reason. Erasmus, answering his old preceptor's charge of worldliness when he abandoned the monastic life, spoke the truth as he knew it: "Pecuniae studium numquam me attigit. Famae gloria nec tantillum tangor. Voluptatibus, esti quondam fui inclinatus, numquam servivi. Crapulam et ebrietatem semper horrui fugique." [82] But the tone is negative; the sins are not those of commission. This cautious, inhibitive strain is too basic and too persistent for an age racked with new problems demanding urgency and daring. The pallid synthesis that the humanists sought came, after all, to very little in an era sundered by the Reformation and swayed dangerously by the winds of so many conflicting doctrines. For better or worse, men of violence and of decision triumphed: Loyola and Calvin influenced the lives of unborn generations while Erasmus and More yearned wistfully for the serenity of compromise and tradition. [83]

---

[81] *The Education of a Christian Prince*, pp. 150-51.

[82] *Selections from Erasmus: Principally from the Letters* (ed. P. S. Allen, 1908), p. 57.

[83] See Douglas Bush, *The Renaissance and English Humanism*, p. 83. For a charming and erudite essay on the temper of sixteenth-century politics see P. S. Allen, "Force and Fraud," *The Age of Erasmus* (1914), pp. 167 ff.

# XVII

IN AN AGE OF SHIFTING AND DISLOCATED VALUES like the Renaissance, no man could assess himself solely in religious, philosophical, or economic terms. The ripeness that Edgar told mad old Lear was the sum of wisdom could not be reached even by a Faustus. Between Petrarch and Milton, however, there was homogeneity of a sort, and it consisted of the generally optimistic view of man arrived at through various disciplines and in various ways. If Neoplatonism led to one such optimistic evaluation—idealistic and mystical—of the nature and capacities of man, then faculty psychology led to another, based on different and generally naturalistic assumptions, but coming to similarly optimistic conclusions.

In the Renaissance there was available for the common man as for the savant a convenient body of knowledge and a convenient terminology to explain man's functioning. Derived in the main from antiquity, faculty psychology was almost universally used for a more or less "scientific" and naturalistic analysis of man regarded as the sum of his faculties of sense, will, and reason. The science of this psychology employed, as we shall see, crude personification and anthropomorphism, but as a principle of explanation it was no more inaccurate than and just as handy as many others that have served us since. Like Ptolemaic astronomy, the faculty psychology derived from Galenic physiology would today have only a dusty antiquarian interest but for the fact that it once did not seem crude. In trying to trace the history of man's opinion of himself we cannot afford to neglect the formulae by which he expressed his opinion.

The juxtaposition of Neoplatonism and faculty psychology is handy because they represent the twin polarities of mysticism and naturalism. Plato had established the notion—perpetuated for the unlettered in Christian theology—that the soul was different from and superior to the body because it was capable of a high kind of wisdom and was exempt from the disorders and imperfections of matter. Such mystical doctrines as transmigration, Platonic recollection, ecstatic vision, and Christian immortality are some of the monuments to this conviction. Broadly speaking, the other great tradition which western Europe had inherited from antiquity was the Aristotelian-Galenic naturalism predicated on a close and organic relationship of soul and body. In the Renaissance, the incompatibility of these two attitudes toward the soul was ignored: the grafting of a naturalistic psychology onto the Platonic-Christian dualism of body and soul produced a curious hybrid, but it discommoded no one. Virtually no one, sometimes not even the professed Neoplatonic mystics, consistently held to the Platonic notion of the soul as a separate *eidos,* apart from and unaffected by the body. Most of the notable psychological treatises of the Renaissance—those of Vesalius, Bright, Laurentius, Huarte, Burton, Harvey—though the work of good Christians, were written on the assumption of body-soul interaction, and not Platonic dualism.[1] It is this naturalistic psychology that we shall now examine.

Galen (A.D. 130-200?) had summarized for antiquity all that was known about the human body, and as Chaucer's Physician as well as Bartholomaeus Anglicus' *De Proprietatibus Rerum* make plain, his memory was kept green for more than a thousand years.[2] Early in the sixteenth century Thomas Linacre, a flower of English humanism and the first president of the Royal College of Physicians, used his Greek (newly learned in Italy) to turn Galen's works into Latin.[3] Within two generations there were other translations by R. Copland (1541), W. Turner (1568), G. Baker (1574), and J. Jones (1574), in addition to the more or less popular redactions and medical self-helps like those of Elyot, Boorde, Recorde, and Vicary. Better-known men like Bright, Bacon, and Burton never ventured far from the assumptions of Galenic psychology.

Indeed, when Bacon, with characteristic trumpetings, announced that his analysis of human conduct was to be thoroughly naturalistic—for man should properly be considered part of the great "continent of nature"[4]—he was merely restating what had been held axiomatic for centuries: that between man's physical and mental functions existed the

---

[1] See Timothy Bright, *A Treatise of Melancholie* (reproduced from the 1586 edition with an introduction by Hardin Craig, 1940), p. xii. Burton's careful catalogue of sources for his anatomy (I, 168) and his psychology (I, 290) is a check list of standard works.

[2] Bartholomaeus Anglicus' thirteenth-century compendium was early (1398) Englished by John de Trevisia; his version was the basis of Stephen Batman's redaction, which appeared (1582) as *Batman uppon Batholome.* See G. E. S. Boyar, "Bartholomaeus Anglicus and his Encyclopaedia," *JEGP,* XIX (1920), 168-89.

[3] Linacre translated six of Galen's works between 1517 and 1524; the first three were *De Sanitate Tuenda* (1517), *Methodus Medendi* (1519), and *Galeni Pergamensis de Temperamentis et de Inequali Intemperie* (1521). For other versions see Palmer, *List of English Editions and Translations,* pp. 48 ff.

[4] *Advancement of Learning,* bk. II (*Works,* VI, 236).

closest correlation and mutual reaction. What Bacon called the "sympathies and concordences between the mind and body" [5] formed the very matrix of the Galenic doctrine.[6] Just as the body works upon the mind with "bad humours" and "gross fumes," explained Robert Burton, the mind "most effectually works upon the body, producing by his passions and perturbations miraculous alterations, as melancholy, despair, cruel diseases, and sometimes death itself." [7] The very specific dietary regimens contrived by scholars like Elyot and by physicians like Boorde and Laurentius clearly testify to the common belief that mind and body interact most intimately. For instance, Elyot's "Counsayle of phisyche" for the relief of dolor and melancholy urges abstinence from anger, unpleasant sights and odors, laxatives, dry winds, "moche companieng with women," old beef or mutton, "harde chese," beans and "peason," coarse bread, "greatte fyshes of the see," "wyne redde and thycke," onions, and leeks.[8] Even though Platonism was very congenial to Elyot the moralist,[9] Elyot the physician did not scruple to resort to a therapy incompatible with Plato's conception of the soul.

The naturalistic view of the integration of all man's parts and faculties

---

[5] *Ibid.*, bk. II (*Works*, VI, 237).

[6] See, for instance, *On the Natural Faculties*, II.8: "Now in reference to the *genesis of the humours*, I do not know that anyone could add anything wiser than what has been said by Hippocrates, Aristotle, Praxagoras, Philotimus and many others among the Ancients. These men demonstrated that when the nutriment becomes altered in the veins by the innate heat, blood is produced when it is in moderation, and the other humours when it is not in proper proportion."

[7] *The Anatomy of Melancholy*, I, 288; cf. Iohn Huarte, *Examen de Ingenios* (1616), p. 63; Huarte insists that the physical differences between men, especially in their qualities of moistness, heat, and dryness, determine "all the difference of mans wits"; otherwise, "all men should partake equally vnderstanding" (p. 75).

[8] *The Castel of Helthe* (facsimile of the 1541 ed. with an introduction by Samuel A. Tannenbaum, 1937), ff. 65ʳ-65ᵛ; cf. Andrew Boorde, *A Compendyous Regyment or a Dyetary of Helth* (ed. F. J. Furnivall, EETS, Ex. Ser., no. 10, 1870), pp. 287 ff.; Laurentius, *A Discourse of the Preservation of the Sight*, pp. 104 ff.; Bright, *A Treatise of Melancholie*, p. 159. This close body-soul relationship was pointed out, in its bearing on Shakespeare's plays, by Richard Loening in his "Ueber die physiologischen Grundlagen der Shakespeare'schen Psychologie," *Jahrbuch der Deutschen Shakespeare Gesellschaft*, XXXI (1895), 1-37. For example (pp. 35-36): "Alle seelischen Konflikte bei Shakespeare, in der Tragödie wie in der Komödie, bestehen in dem um die Herrschaft über Entschluss und Wollen geführten Kampfe zwischen der in der Ewigkeit gegründeten Vernunft und dem auf irdischer, Körperlicher Basis beruhenden individuellen Temperament, oder wie der Dichter es mehrfach ausdrückt: zwischen Blut und Urteil." S. Singer ("Ueber die physiologischen Grundlagen der Shakespeare'schen Psychologie," *Jahrbuch der Deutschen Shakespeare Gesellschaft*, XXXVI, 1900, 65-94) argued that Shakespeare learned his psychology not from books but from the common lore of the time—"das die Anschauungen Shakespeares über diese Punkts nicht die gelehrten, sondern die volkstumlichen seiner Zeit waren" (p. 65).

[9] See Friedrich Dannenberg, *Das Erbe Platons in England bis zur Bildung Lylys* (1932), pp. 195 ff.

—a kind of physiological monism—was based on the venerable notion that all created matter is composed of the four elements of earth, air, fire, and water. To Empedocles' four irreducible components (named *stoicheia* by Plato and rendered as *elementa* by the Latins) Aristotle had added the fifth element (quintessence) to account for the stuff of souls and stars. And for the natural science of the Renaissance, these served very well to account for the physical constitution of all created things: both man and the universe he inhabited, both microcosm and macrocosm. When Cleopatra, just before her suicide, announced that she was fire and air, having surrendered her other elements to baser life, she could be sure everyone in the audience would understand her. The function of the four elements in determining man's nature and temperament was a commonplace.[10] Each element had two properties: earth is dry and cold, water is cold and moist, air is hot and moist, and fire is hot and dry. Man, the microcosm, has four corresponding humors, or subtle fluids: blood (like air) is hot and moist, choler (like fire) is hot and dry, phlegm (like water) is cold and moist, and melancholy (like earth) is cold and dry. As the elements and the humors distilled from the elements are mixed in a man, so his temperament or complexion (we should say personality or character) is determined. Jonson's Crites has a "divine" temper because all the elements and humors are peaceably met, without emulation of precedency;[11] and Antony, in his eulogy of Brutus, comments on a similarly happy (and extraordinary) state of affairs.[12] Not everyone had Bacon's candor in defining the soul as "a corporeal substance, attenuated and made invisible by heat," clothed with the body, and "refreshed and repaired by the spirituous blood of the arteries";[13] but virtually everyone accepted the naturalistic assumption of a very intimate correlation between the state of the body and the state of the soul. Without the four elements and the corresponding four humors the Renaissance physiologist and moralist would have had a hard time.[14]

[10] See, for example, Huarte, *Examen*, pp. 63 ff.; La Primaudaye, *The French Academie*, p. 341; Laurentius, p. 84.

[11] *Cynthia's Revels*, II.1. Mercury continues: "he is neither too fantastically melancholy, too slowly phlegmatic, too lightly sanguine, or too rashly choleric; but in all so composed and ordered, as it is clear Nature went about some full work, she did more than make a man when she made him."

[12] *Julius Caesar*, V.v.68 ff. See P. Ansell Robin, *The Old Physiology in English Literature* (1911), pp. 27 ff. See Ruth Lelia Anderson, *Elizabethan Psychology and Shakespeare's Plays* (1927), pp. 30 ff.

[13] *De Augmentis*, IV.3 (*Works*, IX, 50).

[14] Note, for instance, Timothy Bright's naturalistic orthodoxy (sig. iij*): "I have layd open how the bodie, and corporall things affect the soule, & how the bodie is affected of it

A corollary of this Aristotelian-Galenic tradition of naturalism was faculty psychology. As its name implies, mental operations and modes of conduct were thought of and personified as the result of certain physiological conditions. As Aristotle had long ago pointed out, man has a vegetable, a sensitive, and a rational soul, each with its own faculties.[15] And although there was considerable disagreement on the minutiae of classification, the main schematic lines of this psychology were agreed upon: 1) the vegetable soul has the faculties of nutrition, growth and reproduction; 2) the concupiscible part of the sensitive soul works through the five external senses and the three internal senses of common sense, imagination, and memory; the irascible part, which originates action in response to the stimuli of sense, has the faculties of appetite and locomotion; 3) the rational soul, man's proudest possession, has the faculties of understanding and will. To explain the interrelation of these levels of soul was the mastering concern of sixteenth-century physiologists and moral philosophers. Although the great problem lay in the correlation between the rational and sensitive souls—that is, between man as an animal and man as a special creation—the vegetable soul, functioning on the level of nutrition and reproduction, was not left to languish below the salt. Given a naturalistic physiology, the processes of the vegetable soul were extremely important in determining the physical basis of man's higher flights of reason and will.

Consequently the vegetable soul had to be analyzed closely by those physiologists attempting to account naturalistically for human behavior. Since all four humors—melancholy, phlegm, choler, and blood [16]—are

againe." See Bright's long discussion (pp. 39 ff.) on the body-soul relationship. On Bright's attitude see Richard Loening, "Ueber die physiologischen Grundlagen der Shakespeare'schen Psychologie," *Jahrbuch der Deutschen Shakespeare Gesellschaft*, XXXI (1895), 4 ff.; cf. G. B. Harrison's essay on Elizabethan melancholy affixed to his edition of Nicholas Breton's *Melancholike Humours* (1929), pp. 57 ff. On the alleged verbal similarities between Bright and Shakespeare see Mary Isabelle O'Sullivan, "Hamlet and Dr. Timothy Bright," *PMLA*, XLI (1926), 667-79; on the relation between Bright and Thomas Burton see Paul Jordan-Smith, *Bibliographia Burtoniana* (1931), pp. 63-65.

[15] The acceptance of Aristotelian psychology was so wide that citation is superfluous. But see, *inter alia*, Huarte, *Examen*, pp. 32 ff.; Mornay, *A Worke Concerning the Trunesse of Christian Religion*, pp. 211-12; Sir Walter Raleigh, "Treatise of the Soul," *Works*, VIII, 571-91. For discussions see Edward Dowden, "Elizabethan Psychology," *Essays Modern and Elizabethan* (n.d.), p. 519; Anderson, *Elizabethan Psychology and Shakespeare's Plays*, pp. 8 ff. Miss Lily B. Campbell has pointed out (*Shakespeare's Tragic Heroes*, p. 65) that some authorities, like Plutarch in "Of Moral Vertue," distinguished the "spirituall, intelligible and reasonable" soul from the "brutish, sensuall, erronius" soul; but by further dividing the latter into vegetable and concupiscible parts, they in effect restated the Aristotelian psychology.

[16] See Levinus Lemnius, *The Tovchstone of Complexions* (trans. T[homas] N[ewton], 1633), pp. 14-15.

"engendered" from food and drink and thus ultimately from the four elements,[17] and since they are conveyed by the three spirits distilled in the liver, heart, and brain, the functions of the vegetable soul are intimately related to those of the higher faculties.

### THE VEGETABLE SOUL

The nutritive or vegetable soul was the seat of the humors which could (and often did) influence the whole course of a man's life. Although the humors should work for the preservation of the body,[18] the excess of any one of them would distemper the whole organism. Such an excess could result from any one or a combination of various factors— climate, age, geography, even time of day.[19] Although any of the four humors could be dangerous (for "grose disease / Soone growes through humours superfluite")[20] the most feared was melancholy: the sober treatises of Bright, Laurentius, and Burton are monuments to its power. Its natural form was bad enough: rising from that "pudle of the splene" melancholy passed to the heart and then to the brain where it often sadly excited the imagination with "monstrous fictions"—the result being all manner of irrational conduct indicative of grief "against reason."[21] It could become "of such an exculcerating, and fretting qualitie, that it wasteth those partes, where it lighteth."[22] And it could lead, suggests Huarte darkly, "to treasons and treacheries."[23] But in spite of their potential dangers, the humors served the beneficent and essential function of nourishing the natural heat, the power by which all creatures "live, are nourished, encreased, preserved and procreated."[24] Derived so intimately from the elements, the humors were the vehicle of the vitalistic motor activity that made life possible.[25]

---

[17] Burton (I, 170), enlarges the list of humors to include serum, sweat, and tears; but Laurentius' list of four (p. 84) is much more orthodox.

[18] Burton, I, 169.

[19] See Anderson, *Elizabethan Psychology and Shakespeare's Plays*, pp. 34 ff.

[20] Spenser, "The Ruines of Rome," st. xxiii.

[21] Bright, p. 82; cf. pp. 125 ff.

[22] Bright, p. 32; cf. Burton, I, 199 ff.

[23] *Examen*, p. 95. For a discussion of the dread "melancholy adust," a particularly virulent form of melancholy, see Campbell, *Shakespeare's Tragic Heroes*, pp. 75 ff.

[24] Lemnius, *Touchstone of Complexions*, p. 12; cf. La Primaudaye, *The French Academie*, p. 341.

[25] I must bury in a footnote what could be the topic for a large book—the dramatic use of the humor psychology, especially for purposes of satire. Jonson, of course, is *facile princeps* among his contemporaries in his employment of this psychology, and the classical statement of the theory is the "Induction" to *Every Man Out of His Humour, Complete Plays* (Everyman's Library, 1910), I, 62-63. But in earlier non-dramatic prose the use of humors to explain conduct is not uncommon (see Charles Read Baskervill, *English Elements in Jonson's Early Comedies*, 1911, pp. 34 ff.); as early as Lyly's *Midas* (1589) faculty

The spirits, in addition to the humors and the natural heat, were also a property of the vegetable soul. The three principal organs of the body—the liver, heart, and brain—manufactured respectively the natural, vital, and animal spirits;[26] through them the natural heat was "conveid and sent" to all parts of the body.[27] Each kind of spirit represented a successively finer rarefication of the blood which, nourished by the chyle in the intestines, collected in the liver. (Spenser's Alma, showing her guests through her castle, very properly pointed out the pantry and kitchens—the digestive parts of the body.) [28] In the liver, then, the blood was first distilled into the natural spirits.[29] But passing through the *vena cava* to the heart, its organ of distribution, it is, in the left ventricle, turned into vital spirits—"clearer, brighter, and subtiller than any corporal or bodely thing." [30] These vital spirits have as their "office," explains Huarte, "to stir vp the powers of man, and to give them force and vigour that they may be able to worke." [31]

The vital spirits rise from the heart to the brain—always, it seems, by something conveniently called "secret channels"—and are finally distilled

psychology was used to explain distempered personalities. Chapman, whom Jonson so much admired, often resorts to the humors for comic and satirical purposes (see Paul V. Kreider, *Elizabethan Comic Character Conventions as Revealed in the Comedies of George Chapman*, 1935, pp. 144 ff.). After such romantic comedies as *A Tale of a Tub* and *The Case Is Altered*, Jonson turned enthusiastically to realistic humor comedy, by which the inner man is revealed through externalities and mannerisms. From 1595 to 1609 there was a literary fad of humor books, such as there had been of "anatomies" and of sonnet-cycles earlier. Some pertinent examples are Chapman's *Humourous Day's Mirth* (1599), Jonson's humor comedies, Samuel Rowland's *Letting of Humours Blood in the Head-Vaine* (1600), John Davies' *Humours Heau'n on Earth* (1605), and Rowland's *Humours Looking Glasse* (1608). There are, of course, many others. For Marlowe's use of the faculty psychology, see Carroll Camden, "Marlowe and Elizabethan Psychology," *PQ*, VIII (1929), 69-78, and "Tamburlaine: The Choleric Man," *MLN*, XLIV (1929), 430-35. For Shakespeare's use of this psychology see Ruth Lelia Anderson's book already cited.

[26] See Burton, I, 172-73; cf. Bright, pp. 47-48.

[27] Lemnius, *Tovchstone of Complexions*, p. 12.

[28] *The Faerie Queene*, II.lx.27 ff. See C. L. Powell, "The Castle of the Body," *SP*, XVI (1919), 197-205, for analogues to Spenser's House of Temperance; cf. P. Ansell Robin, "Spenser's House of Alma," *MLR*, VI (1911), 169-73 (on the interpretation of II.ix.22).

[29] See Thomas Vicary, *The Anatomie of the Bodie of Man* (ed. F. J. Furnivall and Percy Furnivall, EETS, Ex. Ser., no. 53, 1888), p. 69. Lemnius (*Tovchstone*, p. 15) points out that if the ingested food is bad, "then is the meat altered and changed into vaporous belching, stinking fumes, and fulsome breathing, which ascending up out of the stomake, disturbe and hurt the braine and minde." See Robin, *The Old Psychology in English Literature*, pp. 107 ff.

[30] Vicary, p. 58.

[31] *Examen*, pp. 30-31; cf. Rabelais' account (III.4) in orthodox Galenic terms. As an example of the action of the vital spirits, Huarte (p. 31) says if a man sees a "faire woman" and desires the "venerious act," then vital spirits "run forthwith to the genitall members, and raise them to the performance." Lemnius (*Tovchstone*, pp. 16-17, 22-23), uses the same example.

for the third time into animal spirits. These are "more excellent then the other and before the rest in dignity." [32] As Pierre Charron, the friend of Montaigne, put it, the vital spirits are "raised" by the arteries to the brain, where they are "concocted and reconcocted, elaborated and made subtile by the help of the multiplicity of small *Arteries*, as fillets diversly woven and interlaced, by many turnings and windings, like a labyrinth or double net." [33]

Whatever the physiological details—and there was a good deal of disagreement[34]—one thing is clear: the three grades of spirit, corresponding to Aristotle's three grades of soul, were the bridge connecting man's physical and mental parts. Timothy Bright, in fact, suggests very strongly that they may be identified with the soul.[35] Without them, at least, there could be no correlation between the acts of the soul and acts of the body. Today we should call them the nervous system—which jargon probably means little more to most of us than Burton's did to his contemporaries: spirit is a "most subtle vapour, which is expressed from the *blood,* and is the instrument of the soul, to perform all his actions; a common tie or *medium* betwixt the body and the soul." [36]

### THE SENSITIVE SOUL

Above the vegetable lay the sensitive soul, the *bête noire* of faculty psychologists. A necessary medium for transmitting the data of sense to the higher faculties of the rational soul, it continually lurked to usurp the functions of reason and thus make a man a beast. Indeed, it is through the sensitive soul that man is linked with animals, for it is common to both; and when man, prostituting the reason and will, permits the promptings of his sensitive soul to motivate his conduct he becomes no better than a beast. In a way, then, the sensitive soul is the pivotal faculty of the human organism.

The sensitive soul is the seat of appetite, by which man reacts to the stimuli of externals; and of motion, by which he expresses his reaction. Its concupiscible or coveting part works through the five outward and three inward senses (common sense, imagination or fantasy, and memory). The irascible part articulates the motions of the body, for it controls the affectations or motions by which a man seeks the objects his

---

[32] Lemnius, *Tovchstone*, p. 23.

[33] *Of Wisdom* (trans. Samson Lennard, 1670), p. 14.

[34] For instance, see Huarte's careful anatomy of the brain (*Examen*, pp. 25 ff.); cf. La Primaudaye, *The French Academie*, pp. 410 ff.

[35] P. 35.

[36] I, 170. See Bright, p. 35 and (on the physiology of the spirits) Bacon, *Sylva Sylvarum*, X.901 ff. (*Works*, V, 119 ff.).

appetite desires and shuns those it dislikes.[37] It is through the senses, the "readie servants" [38] of the reason and will, that man experiences the outer world and reacts to it. Both concupiscence and irascibility are modes of the same faculty; functioning properly, they are the "trustie spyes and faithfull reportmen" [39] that convey to their sovereign, reason—and the metaphor is repeated endlessly—the data of sense for discrimination and judgment, after which they execute the mandates of their superior. When, however, the senses become the "cutthroates of reason" [40] the entire economy of man's psychology is disrupted. Degree, order, and priority are overthrown, and the result, in psychology as in politics, is chaos.

> What warre so cruel, or what seige so sore,
> As that which strong affections doe apply
> Against the forte or reason ever more,
> To bring the sowle into captivity? [41]

Of course the faculty psychologists were ready with an explanation. When the data of sensation (either from the five senses or the memory) are presented to the imagination, that faculty should straightway submit them, "under the forme of Good or Evill," [42] to the understanding for appraisal and judgment. The understanding or reason having adjudicated the matter, animal spirits "flocke from the brayne, by certaine secret channels to the hearte, where they pitch at the dore, signifying what an object was presented." [43] From this point on, the vegetable soul articulates the muscles, ligaments, and bodily parts so as to implement in motion the decision (either of attraction or revulsion) reached by the reason. But in the crucial role of the imagination hides the danger. Because it can misconstrue or distort the data of sensation, it can throw the whole response of the organism into disequilibrium. And when the heart is called into play, to act upon the information sent from the brain by animal spirits, it can solicit the aid of the humors and thus unbalance (physiologically and psychologically) the intricate structure of man.[44]

---

[37] Burton, I, 176.

[38] Sir John Davies, *Nosce Teipsum* in the *Complete Poems*, I, 34.

[39] Laurentius, p. 6; cf. Elyot, *The Gouernour*, I, 26.

[40] Laurentius, p. 11; cf. La Primaudaye, *The French Academie*, pp. 364 ff.

[41] *The Faerie Queene*, II.xi.1. For Spenser's analysis of the five senses see II.xi.7 ff.

[42] Nicholas Coeffeteau, *A Table of Humane Passions* as quoted by Campbell, *Shakespeare's Tragic Heroes*, p. 67.

[43] Thomas Wright, *The Passions of the Minde in Generall* (1630), pp. 45-46.

[44] The heart was especially suspect. See Spenser, *Amoretti*, 50:
> Is not the hart of all the body chiefe,
> And rules the members as it selfe doth please?

The sovereignty of the rational faculty thus jeopardized by the erroneous report of the imagination (which is itself often "drowned in the corporeal organs of sense"),[45] man is put "farre under the condition of brute beasts." [46] As Burton warns,

if the imagination be very apprehensive, intent, and violent, it sends great store of spirits to or from the heart, and makes a deeper impression, and greater tumult; as the humours in the body be likewise prepared, and the temperature itself ill or well disposed, the passions are longer and stronger: so that the first step and fountain of all our grievances in this kind is a *laesa imaginatio,* which, misinforming the heart, causeth all these distemperature, alteration and confusion, of spirits and humours.

Then the body fails in "sense and motion; so we look upon a thing, and see it not; hear, and observe not; which otherwise would much affect us, had we been free." [47] And this is man's ultimate degradation: he can suffer no ignominy greater than that by which his divine reason is subverted by the passions of his animal parts.

The psychology of this disruption of man's faculties is like a drama in which the imagination is the villain. Dr. Johnson said that if it were not for the imagination, Sir, a man would be as happy in the arms of a chambermaid as of a duchess, but he also said, in the more edifying *Rasselas,* that all power of fancy over reason is a degree of insanity. The moral philosopher of the Renaissance never treated the faculty of imagination lightly. It was notoriously suspect, and the opprobrium that still clings to our word *fantasy* reflects the distrust with which it was long regarded. In literary criticism the defense of or attack on the imagination became the theme of nearly every scribbler,[48] but its power was more than merely aesthetic.

Properly, the imagination should serve, as everyone agreed, merely as

Donne (*Devotions upon Emergent Occasions,* no. 11, "Nobilibusque Trahunt," The Abbey Classics, n.d., p. 70) remarks that although the heart, liver, and brain are the three chief organs, they do not constitute a "triumvirate" because the heart is sovereign, and "in the throne, as king, the rest as subjects, though in eminent place and office."

[45] Burton, I, 297.

[46] Bright, sig. ij[r].

[47] Burton, I, 290-91. For a notable discussion of the potential dangers of sensation see Montaigne's great *Apology for Raymond Sebond* in *The Essays* (trans. E. J. Trechmann, 1927), II, 35 ff.

[48] Bacon (*Advancement of Learning,* bk. II, *Works,* VI, 258-59) was notoriously suspicious of the literary uses of imagination, and even Spenser ("Tears of the Muses," ll. 553 ff.) echoed a critical commonplace when he urged poets to discipline their imagination lest they pike up "heapes of huge words" and thus make a "monster of their fantasie." For a typical statement of the results of false imaginings see the dialogue between Guazzo and Annibel in the first book of *The Civile Conversation* (trans. George Pettie and Barth. Young, The Tudor Translation, 1925), I, 18 ff.

the messenger or *nuntius* between sense and reason: it was the agent which transmitted the data of sensation to the superior faculties for judgment. Although it was the highest faculty of animals (the *ratio brutorum*, according to Burton),[49] in man it should be under the surveillance and discipline of the understanding, and be like a mirror to give a true reflection of externals.[50] "For Sense sendeth over to Imagination before Reason have judged: and Reason sendeth over to Imagination before the Decree can be acted; for Imagination ever precedeth voluntary Motion." [51] It can retain the impressions of sense, even though the objects of sense be absent, and—here is the hazard—it can even make new configurations of its own that have no reference to reality. Thus it produces not only dreams, but also the many monstrous and prodigious things that sometime drive men to madness. The ghosts and demons that stalk through Elizabethan drama are many of them the misbegotten products of a diseased imagination. As Chapman's Clermont explains to Guise, the ghost he had seen came from his own fantasy:

> The imagining power
> (Stirr'd up by forms hid in the memory's store,
> Or by the vapours of o'erflowing humours
> In bodies full and foul, and mix'd with spirits)
> Feigns many strange, miraculous images.[52]

The imagination is the most perilous of man's faculties, for when subverted by fumes and humors and powerful sensory drives it becomes "false and corrupt," preferring falsehood to truth and "deluding the soul with false shews and suppositions." [53] Unless controlled by the reason, "it troubleth and moueth all the sence and vnderstanding, as a tempest doth the sea." [54]

Plastic and mobile as it is, the sensitive soul falls all too easily into error. Then like "naughty servants" the senses wantonly assume the role of master,[55] and

---

[49] I, 182; cf. I, 291.

[50] Fulke Greville, "A Treatise of Humane Learning," st. 10-11 (in *Poems and Dramas*, ed. Geoffrey Bullough, 2 vols., n.d.).

[51] Bacon, *Advancement of Learning*, bk. II (*Works*, VI, 258). In a famous pronouncement (*Advancement*, bk. II, *Works*, VI, 389-91, 409 ff.) Bacon declared it the function of rhetoric—so highly valued by the Elizabethans—to apply reason to imagination for the better moving of the will. See Karl Wallace, *Francis Bacon on Communication & Rhetoric* (1943), *passim* (and esp. the bibliography, pp. 229 ff.); Craig, *The Enchanted Glass*, ch. VII.

[52] *The Revenge of Bussy D'Ambois*, V.i.41 ff.

[53] Burton, I, 292.

[54] La Primaudaye, p. 415.

[55] Wright, *The Passions of the Minde in Generall*, p. 8; cf. Greville, *Caelica*, xcvi; "A Treatise of Humane Learning," st. 5 ff.

> the state of man,
> Like to a little kingdom, suffers then
> The nature of an insurrection.[56]

And this is passion—the excessive physiological response to the externals of sense.[57] Motion is the legitimate function of the sensitive soul acting under the guidance of reason, and even affection is the mild disturbance stimulated by sensual desires unchecked by reason; but passions (or perturbations) are like "so many wild horses" that tear a man to pieces.[58] "Blindnesse of vnderstanding, peruersion of will, alteration of humours," and disease are some of the effects of passion.[59] Though all are bad, the physical results are most spectacular. The passion of anger, explains Elyot, "doth superfluously heate" the members so that at best "tremblynge" and "outragious swearynge" follow. But "immoderate" passions are worse: "they do not only annoye the body, & shorten the lyfe, but also they do appaire, and somtyme lose utterly a mans estimation." The ultimate result is the "displeasure of almighty god."[60] God's wrath is proper, for through passion man degrades himself most impiously, so that his whole organism deteriorates.

> Of all Gods workes, which doe this world adorne,
> There is no one more faire and excellent,
> Then is mans body both for powre and forme,
> Whiles it is kept in sober government;
> But none then it more fowle and indecent,
> Distempred through misrule and passions bace:
> It growes a monster, and incontinent
> Doth loose his dignity and native grace.[61]

There are a few discreet men, remarks Burton, who can control their passions by religion, philosophy, and moral precept.

But most part, for want of government, out of indiscretion, ignorance, they suffer themselves wholly to be led by sense, and are so far from repressing rebellious inclinations, that they give all encouragement unto them, leaving the reins, and using all provocations to further them: bad by nature, worse by art, discipline,

---

[56] *Julius Caesar*, II.i.67-69.

[57] According to Charron (*Of Wisdom*, p. 66) passion is "a violent motion of the *Soul* in the sensitive part thereof, which is made either to follow that which the *Soul* thinketh to be good for it, or to fly that which it takes to be evil."

[58] Burton, I, 75; cf. I, 81. Bacon is very explicit on the physical effects of passion; see *Sylva Sylvarum*, VIII.713 ff. (*Works*, V, 13 ff.).

[59] Wright, *The Passions of the Minde in Generall*, p. 47.

[60] *The Castel of Helthe*, f. 62ʳ-62ᵛ.

[61] *The Faerie Queene*, II.ix.1.

custom, education, and a perverse will of their own, they follow on, wheresoever their unbridled affections will transport them, and do more out of custom, self-will, than out of reason.[62]

When the passions are regnant, says Bacon craftily, a man's true nature reveals itself, for then he is "out of his precepts," [63] and his soul is swept as by a raging wind.[64] Othello, surely a great and worthy man, admits to his own infirmity when he rebukes his quarreling men.

> My blood begins my safer guides to rule,
> And passion, having my best judgment collied,
> Assays to lead the way.[65]

As Hamlet realizes to his horror, his mother has become a monster by surrendering to her erotic passions; and Florizel, even worse, is so dominated by his passion that he is willing to renounce his succession to the throne.[66] It is praise indeed, then, when Brutus says of Caesar that he has not known him

> when his affections sway'd
> More than his reason.[67]

Even though there was little agreement on the subject, to catalogue the passions was a favorite pastime of Renaissance moralists. Generally they were classified as concupiscible (love-hatred, desire-aversion, joy-sadness) and irascible (hope-despair, courage, fear, and anger).[68] These categories of six "coveting" and five "invading" passions, which had been established by Aquinas, provided the theme for many elaborate varia-

[62] I, 297-98; cf. La Primaudaye, p. 439.

[63] Essays, "Of Nature in Men" (Works, XII, 212).

[64] Advancement of Learning, bk. II (Works, VI, 336).

[65] II.iii.203 ff.

[66] The Winter's Tale, IV.iii.483 ff.

[67] Julius Caesar, II.i.20-21. Illustrations from Shakespeare and from Elizabethan drama could be, and have been, multiplied endlessly. See Campbell, Shakespeare's Tragic Heroes, sect. II (pp. 109 ff.), where Hamlet is treated as a victim of the passion of grief, Othello of jealousy, Lear of wrath, Macbeth of fear. See also Murray W. Bundy, "Shakespeare and Elizabethan Psychology," JEGP, XXIII (1924), 516-49; Anderson, Elizabethan Psychology and Shakespeare's Plays, passim. Mr. Craig (The Enchanted Glass, pp. 128 ff.) has made an elaborate analysis of Heywood's Woman Killed with Kindness to show the effects of passion on character. See also his "Shakespeare's Depiction of the Passions," PQ, IV (1925), 289-301.

[68] See Burton, I, 297-98; Wright, pp. 19 ff.; Charron, Of Wisdom, pp. 70 ff. (a very elaborate classification of passion); cf. Campbell, Shakespeare's Tragic Heroes, pp. 69 ff. Bright (pp. 81 ff.) distinguishes between simple and compound passions (for example, hate and hope produce anger). See Du Bartas, Deuine Weekes & Workes, pp. 349 ff.

tions. In spite of a waxing neo-Stoicism towards the end of the sixteenth century, there were few dissenters from the Aristotelian notion that not all passions were harmful. Aquinas had decreed that the "passions of the soul, in so far as they are contrary to the order of reason, incline us to sin; but in so far as they are controlled by reason, they pertain to virtue." [69] And even though Shakespeare's contemporaries generally used a tighter (or narrower) definition of passion to mean the excessive re-action of the sensitive soul to externals, they were not prepared to admit that all the passions were destructive. So long as they were properly sub-ordinated to reason, the passions constituted a natural function of the soul. Although they could "force" the soul "through the evill disposed instrument of the bodie," explains Bright, normally they were a neces-sary adjunct to man's supreme function of understanding.[70] Earlier, Elyot had decided that the passion of joy could be healthful by bringing the humors "to an equall temperance" and drawing the "natural heat outward." [71] Bacon did not object to passion *per se*, but because a man in passion takes a short view and looks to immediate good through im-mediate action rather than to the ultimate good which is discerned by the understanding. Consequently they should be disciplined by exercise, habit (the Thomistic *habitus*), education, imitation, and the like,[72] so that man could attain the goal of moral philosophy: the subordination of passion to reason. "Finis itidem Ethicae affectus ita componere, ut rationi militent, non autem eam invadant." [73]

### THE RATIONAL SOUL

A Platonist, an Aristotelian, a Christian humanist would all agree that man's rational soul was his crown and his beatitude, and as such that it should enjoy what Spenser called its "dew regalitie." [74] Through his reason, the faculty of his highest level of soul, man may attain genuine knowledge, or live a life of temperance and rational well-being, or be-come like the God whose divine attribute of reason he alone among ani-mals shares. If, as every good theist maintained, the universe is rational like its creator, then the reason natural to man is the supreme evidence of theocracy.[75] In naturalistic faculty psychology no less than in Neo-platonic mysticism—in virtually all the great modes of sixteenth-century

[69] *Summa Theologica*, II.24.2.
[70] P. 39.
[71] *The Castel of Helthe*, f. 66ʳ.
[72] *Advancement of Learning*, bk. II (*Works*, VI, 338).
[73] *De Augmentis*, VI.3 (*Works*, IX, 132).
[74] *The Faerie Queene*, II.i.57.
[75] For instance, see Hooker, *Of the Laws of Ecclesiastical Polity*, I.ix.1.

thought except Calvinism—man's reason was accounted his supreme attribute. "For nothing is more excellent than reason whereof God hath made man partaker, so ther is nothing more beseeming reasō thē to know love & honor God." [76] Not all free-thinkers in the Renaissance were so pious as La Primaudaye, but they nearly all agreed in chanting the glory of man's reason, either as the instrument of Christian virtue or as the key to that rational self-control which is the sum of moral excellence. In making man, God has endued him with His own divinity—the "right reson" by which he governs himself "according to hys excellent nature and dygnyte." Otherwise, the "affectys and vycyouse desyrys" of his "erthy body" would make him live no better than a "brute best." [77]

Faculty psychology had an explanation for this supremacy. As the highest level of soul, the rational has the attributes of reason and will: reason, that it may, operating on the data of sensation, discern truth and falsity, similarities and dissimilarities, and thus arrive at the generalized and abstracted knowledge that lies beyond particulars;[78] will, that it may implement its conclusions through action. For reason is the "skilfull horserider" [79] that by controlling the lower faculties can attain both truth (theoretical reason) and goodness (practical reason).[80] Located in accordance with its supremacy, reason has its seat in the brain,[81] "as in the highest & safest fortress of the whole frame of man, to reigne amidst all the other senses, as Prince and Lord ouer them all." [82] There, proud sovereign that it is, reason rules her "handmaides" memory and imagination; and they, proud courtiers enjoying "the priviledges of renowned excellencie, doe lodge within her royall pallace, and that very neare her owne person." [83]

---

[76] La Primaudaye, *The French Academie*, p. 423.

[77] Starkey, *England in the Reign of King Henry the Eighth*, p. 165.

[78] See Raleigh, "Treatise of the Soul," *Works*, VIII, 587; cf. La Primaudaye, pp. 416-18. La Primaudaye's analysis of induction (p. 418) is, for its date, very interesting. See Laurentius (p. 16): the reason receives the data of sense divorced from particulars—"the formes of things naked and voide of substance"; therefore the understanding alone of man's faculties "comprehendeth the universall world." See *ibid.*, p. 76.

[79] Laurentius, p. 7; cf. Du Bartas, *Deuine Weekes*, pp. 50, 83; Milton, *Paradise Lost*, V, 482 ff., VII, 507 ff.; Sir John Davies, *Complete Poems*, I, 101-102. Note Octavian's remark in *The Courtier* (p. 307) that reason has such power "that she maketh the sense alwaies to obey and by wonderous meanes and wayes" exerts her discipline over all the lower faculties.

[80] La Primaudaye, p. 423. Bacon (*De Augmentis*, V. 1, *Works*, XI, 61) says the lesser faculties are concerned with ethics and conduct, reason with knowledge; cf. *Advancement*, bk. II (*Works*, VI, 260-61).

[81] See Huarte, *Examen*, pp. 25 ff.          [82] La Primaudaye, p. 416.

[83] Laurentius, pp. 74-75; cf. Charron, *Of Wisdom*, p. 67. For Calvin's detailed, but ironic, account of this orthodox conception of the sovereign reason see *The Institution of Christian Religion* (trans. Thomas Norton, 1561), II.ii (fol.11-12).

But reason, if it is to play any part in man's practical conduct, must employ the services of the will—"that facultie and vertue of the soule, whereby we desire that which is good, and eschew euill by the direction and guiding of the reason." [84] It is a revealing comment on Renaissance optimism that :he will, notoriously and traditionally the most corruptible of man's faculties, was then generally held to be the instrument of virtue, and virtually the prince consort of reason itself. If appetite expresses lust and irrational desires, says Hooker, then will is the means by which man exerts his rational control over the data of sense, for the object of will is "the good which reason doth lead us to seek." Will, in short, is the nexus between judgment and sensation. "Appetite is Will's solicitor, and the Will is Appetite's Controller." [85] Coeffeteau, less cryptically, explains the will as the "Queene of the powers of the soule" which regulates conduct according to the dictates of reason. The data of sense are relayed by common sense, memory, and imagination "under the forme of good or euill" to the higher faculties of the soul. Once under the scrutiny of reason these data are instantly "enlightened with the Light of the understanding," and then "purged from the sensible and singular conditions" which the imagination has failed to divest them of, and thus conceptualized. It is then that the will, ideally under the guidance of the understanding, sets in motion the reaction of the body according to the verdict of the understanding.[86]

In spite of the high position accorded the will, however, it was never forgotten by traditionalists that reason was supreme; only the iconoclasts would deny that in man as in God there is no higher attribute. Duns Scotus, combating Thomistic raionalism, had made will the highest attribute of God, and his spiritual heirs—men like Machiavelli and Calvin—based their thinking on the primacy of the will; hence the emotional shock of their political theory and theology. They, like Iago, would argue that 'tis in ourselves we are thus and thus, that will is the gardener of the body, and that the power and corrigible authority of all our actions lie in our will. But to urge this voluntarism was to subvert the immemorial sovereignty of reason and thus to demolish the traditional symbol of man's dignity, his divine faculty of understanding.

Men like Hooker, Shakespeare, Bacon, and the swarm of faculty psychologists clung to the old humanistic belief in the superiority of reason to will; they are, therefore, spokesmen of the Renaissance optimism

---

[84] La Primaudaye, p. 441.

[85] *Of the Laws of Ecclesiastical Polity*, I.vii.3; cf. Dowden, "Elizabethan Psychology," *Essays Modern and Elizabethan*, p. 332.

[86] Quoted from *A Table of Humane Passions* by Campbell, *Shakespeare's Tragic Heroes*, p. 67; cf. Castiglione, *The Courtier*, pp. 342-43.

I have been trying to describe. For if man is a rational creature, and if his reason is served by his will, then his possibilities for virtuous conduct are infinite. From Ficino to Milton the stream runs clear. As a good Platonist, Ficino had attributed to man's intellect a divine faculty of working "in a manner which is universal, absolute, simple, distinct, pure, stable." For him the will, which "moves soul and body to action in order that they may approach the desired objects," was clearly subordinate.[87] But as Milton's Raphael explained, it was precisely because man was endued with the "Sanctitie of Reason" that he could govern himself and all the lower creatures, and even claim a magnanimity to correspond with heaven's.[88] To know the variations on this theme is to know the greatest monuments of Renaissance literature.

In faculty psychology, then, the will, which had been theologically slandered for centuries, was generally applauded as that irascible faculty of the rational soul whose object is what the judgment declares is good. It was an appetite, Raleigh conceded, but an appetite which makes us

desire that good which the understanding comprehendeth to be such indeed or in appearance, and flieth the contrary. This is our will, which we use to stir us up to seek God and heaven, and heavenly things, by which we rest also in these things, and are delighted and satisfied in them, being gotten. This is a part of the reasonable soul: this is one point by which we are men, and do excel all other creatures living upon the earth.[89]

Raleigh's encomium is based, of course, on the assumption that the will is free, superior to contingency, and at liberty to choose between genuine alternatives. As the humanists had for two centuries maintained against certain severe theologians[90]—as Erasmus had notoriously maintained against Luther—unless the will of man is free, man's dignity is a myth, his optimism an illusion. "What is prodigious," says Gelli, is that "there is no object or force either terrestrial or celestial, that can command her [that is, the will] to will otherwise than she pleases." [91] It was inevitable that Calvin, being what he was, had fixed on this very point in order to destroy the last vestige of man's confidence in himself: by declaring man's free will eternally in bondage "soubz le joug de peché" [92] he had in effect

---

[87] *Platonic Theology*, XIV.3 (*JHI*, V, 237-38).

[88] *Paradise Lost*, VII, 507 ff.

[89] "Treatise of the Soul," *Works*, VIII, 586-87.

[90] See Robb, *Neoplatonism of the Italian Renaissance*, p. 39; cf. Du Bartas, *Deuine Weekes*, p. 93; Milton, *Paradise Lost*, III, 92 ff.

[91] Battista Gelli, *The Circe . . . Consisting of Ten Dialogues Giving a lively Representation of the Various Passions, and many Infelicities of Humane Life* (trans. Thomas Brown, 1702), p. 288.

[92] *Institute*, I, 82.

invalidated his claim to rational self-government and thus reduced him to the condition of innate depravity which has for centuries been the solace of all good Calvinists.

Not even the most optimistic humanist would argue, however, that the will was under all conditions a faculty inexorably striving for the goods ascertained by reason. As a mediate faculty lying between sense and reason, the will was particularly vulnerable; it could, and often did, let the objects of sense rather than the objects of reason determine its conduct, and when it did, the result was disastrous. For the will could, as even Bacon admitted, "colour and infect the understanding" in numberless and sometimes imperceptible ways.[93] When this occurred, the natural—that is, rational—functioning of the soul collapsed into that disorder which is the theme of Ulysses' mighty plea to the Grecian leaders: to prevent will from deteriorating into that appetite which is "an universal wolf."[94] In an orderly, hierarchal universe, which was the necessary assumption of Renaissance optimism, the dislocation and corruption of the will was as heinous as the collapse of the due degrees of astronomy, of the state, of society. It should never happen—and ideally never did—but when it did (as when Antony sank into disgrace and ruin) it was because man "would make his will / Lord of his reason."[95] Such villains as Iago and Edmund are all the more dangerous because they know their victims' weakness and work on them to bring about the insurrection of their will.[96] When they succeed, tragedy is inevitable. Othello and Gloucester are men who have let slip their reason, and consequently they are no longer men at all.

In faculty psychology, then, we find another statement of Renaissance optimism. Though antipodal to the mysticism of the Platonists, it arrived through ostensibly naturalistic assumptions and analyses at a comparable evaluation of man's dignity. In its analysis of passion and perverted will, faculty psychology was perhaps more realistic than Neoplatonism about man's potential frailties. But the frailties could be construed only as aberrations. Man's proper function was reason, and his intricately constructed soul, rising step by step from its material basis to its apex or rational knowledge, was held by no means to be the least of God's wonders in a universe of which every part was a testament to the providence and sagacity of its supremely rational creator.

[93] *Novum Organum*, I.49 (*Works*, VIII, 82).
[94] *Troilus and Cressida*, I.iii.119 ff. "Will" frequently (in *Troilus and Cressida* nearly always) means physical desire.
[95] *Antony and Cleopatra*, II.xiii.3-4.
[96] See Bundy, "Shakespeare and Elizabethan Psychology," *JEGP*, XXIII (1924), 539.

## XVIII

IN THE SIXTEENTH CENTURY the various systems of thought we have examined—humanism, Neoplatonism, naturalistic faculty psychology—inevitably tended to coalesce. A humanist might be, and often was, a good Platonist; a zealot like La Primaudaye or an empiricist like Bacon (enchanted by his look into the future) did not scruple to use the jargon of faculty psychology; an eclectic like Spenser leaped nimbly from the Neoplatonism of the *Fowre Hymnes* to the hybrid Protestantism, Platonism, and Aristotelianism of the *Faerie Queene*. Whatever their persuasion, most men of the Renaissance (except the extreme Calvinists hoping against hope for election) were agreed that good conduct for man consisted in using his gift of reason to discipline his sensuous appetites and to arrive ultimately at the high truth of spirit or of conceptual knowledge. Further, they were agreed on the assumption that made possible their optimistic evaluation of man: the assumption that reason was natural to man. In the sixteenth century the intellectual streams of European culture flowed together for the last time before the success of the new science in the seventeenth century threw all in doubt. Christianity, Platonism, Aristotelianism, Stoicism met and merged; and thus Ficino, Erasmus, Spenser, even Bacon could maintain at least a nominal Christianity while advocating this or that form of neopaganism. The Renaissance was indeed the era of synthesis.

This coalescence of diverse intellectual disciplines was obvious in ethical theory. Most men of the sixteenth century, except outright skeptics and atheists, could have given reasonably sincere lip service to the ethics of More's *Utopia*. There would inevitably have been some quibbling of the definition of terms—for nomenclature has always been the pitfall of thought—but the basic principles would have been as sweetly reasonable to Sir Thomas Elyot as to Rabelais. Man's felicity, said More, is the result of a virtuous life, and a virtuous life consists of living according to nature, that is, rationally, after the pattern of God.

For they [the Utopians] define vertue to be life ordered according to nature, and that we be here vnto ordeined of god. And that he dothe followe the course of nature, which in desiering and refusinge thinges is ruled by reason. Furthermore that reason doth chiefly and principallye Kendle in men the loue and veneration of the deuine maiestie.[1]

This passage of More's is a useful point of departure for a sketch of sixteenth-century Christian ethics because it suggests nearly all the main lines that ethical theory was to follow for the next hundred years. Whether men argued for the good life based on temperance and moderation, or on the Thomistic *habitus* of virtue, or on the rational control of passion, or on the Ciceronian-Italianate concept of decorum and gentility,[2] they could virtually all subscribe to More's definition of virtue, adjusting their devious ethical values to the fundamental assumption of a benevolent and omnipotent Christian God, the author and model of man's divinely rational virtue, the object of his highest knowledge. Morality and epistemology coalesced, and for the last time Aristotle's concept of "Intellectual Virtue" had meaning for Christendom. Man's innate right reason was the key both to piety and wisdom, which indeed were one.

In a century of such tumultuous intellectual activity there were all shades of Christian piety, from extreme asceticism to an urbane revival of Neo-Stoical deism. Beyond the fringes, moreover, lay the bifurcated monster of skepticism and fideism which was eventually to produce Pascal, but which in the sixteenth century was represented by a man like Pierre Charron: he could write both *Les Trois Verités* (a universally admired defense of the Roman Church) and *De la Sagesse* (a textbook of mechanistic sensationalist psychology bitterly denounced by the Jesuits for its impiety). The wonder is that there was any homogeneity whatever in so many diversified, overlapping, and conflicting ethical systems; but there was homogeneity of a sort, and it is our business to trace a few of its important manifestations.

First, the outright zealots. Jan van der Noot, whose grim *Theatre for Voluptuous Worldlings* (1569) provided grist for the mill of young Edmund Spenser, may be allowed to speak for those who urged something very like a *contemptus mundi* as the height of moral wisdom. Although his point of view would seem to most men of the Renaissance too otherworldly for comfort, it did not lack advocates.

No kynde of affection, enuie, hate, anger, sorowe or payne, shal trouble you, ye shal put away al wickednesse, & make no accompt of worldly matters, but youre conversation shall be in heauen.[3]

---

[1] Page 107. For some seminal classical analogues see Plato, *Timaeus,* 30, 47; Aristotle, *Eth. Nich.,* 1138, 1177.

[2] See Campbell, *Shakespeare's Tragic Heroes,* pp. 93 ff.          [3] Sig. Si$^r$.

This was at once too simple and too rigorous for those who, not wishing to lose their hope of heaven, none the less were not disposed to dismiss this world and this life like fourth-century cenobites. The man of the Renaissance was generally pious—after his own fashion—but he also had an insatiable interest in the world about him. Hence the various optimistic regimens that enabled him to interpret his luscious beauties of the physical universe into a witness of God's providence; hence the various ethical theories that enabled him to live in the world as a Christian while enjoying it as a man.

Secondly, then, there were many rich developments of what might be called Christian humanism. Sir Thomas Elyot was certainly a Christian, certainly a distinguished and well-fed personage, and a thorough-paced Platonist.[4] As a man of medicine he wrote a typical analysis of human conduct in the jargon of faculty psychology, but as an intimate of the nobility he used *The Gouernour* to articulate an ethical and political theory not unpleasing to his great patrons at the top of a stratified society. The pattern of his ethics lies in the notions of Ciceronian decorum and gentility; it is essentially a class morality of *noblesse oblige* that informs so many of the courtesy books of the Renaissance. It would have meant nothing to Shakespeare's father in his Stratford tannery, but it would have seemed the essence of good taste to Henry VIII's courtiers.

The nature and condition of man, wherin he is lasse than god almightie, and excellinge nat withstanding all other creatures in erthe, is called humanities; which is a generall name to those vertues in whome semeth to be a mutuall concorde and loue in the nature of man.

This being so, it follows then that man's chief virtues are those dictated by both his rational and social needs. Benevolence, beneficence, and liberality each contribute to the ideal ruler's master-virtue of "begnitie or gentilnes" which insures the perpetuation of an orderly, hierarchal society.[5] The variations of this aristocratic ethic are innumerable, and when we find Gabriel Harvey reporting in the *Letter-Book* that during the 'seventies the Italianate-Ciceronian courtesy books were all the rage among the gilded youths at Cambridge, we should not be surprised at the aberrations and deterioration of so common an attitude. In effect, etiquette supplanted ethics, and humanism had sunk low indeed when Guazzo could recommend "Learning" as the *summum bonum:*

[4] See Friedrich Dannenberg, *Das Erbe Platons in England bis zur Bildung Lylys* (1932), pp. 195 ff.; Kurt Schroeder, *Platonismus in der Englischen Renaissance vor und bei Thomas Eliot* (1920), pp. 85 ff.

[5] *The Gouernour*, II, 88-89; cf. Bacon, "Of Goodness and Goodness of Nature," *Essays* (*Works*, XII, 118).

Alas you wyll be but ungentle Gentlemen, yf you be no Schollers: you wyll doo your Prince but simple service, you wyll stande your Countrey but in slender steade, you wyll bryng your selves but to small preferment, yf you be no Schollers.[6]

Whatever its affectations, however, the great Renaissance ideal of gentility had nobility of a kind, even though it was at best snobbish and at worst ludicrous. In a gentleman like Sir Philip Sidney, a devout Christian and a flower of the dying tradition of chivalry, we find the purest form of the ethics of gentility. But in his writing he had little to add to the maxims of the courtesy books. Basilius, king of Arcadia, is a good ruler and a good man because his kingly virtues of wisdom, courage, and magnificence are matched by "those which stirre affection": truth, meekness, courtesy, mercy, and liberality.[7] This catalogue of virtues, grown hoary with time, was of course the support to the master-virtue of piety—and here, of course, Sidney links hands with van der Noot, with Spenser, with nearly all his contemporaries. Spenser's piety, like his more secular virtues, has an aristocratic cast. He, like Elyot a great gentleman who knew the value of decorum, elevated piety into a sort of Neo-Stoical resignation. Elyot speaks admiringly of the strength derived from the "cōtempt of fortune in sure quietnesse and most perfite felicitie,"[8] and Sidney eloquently preaches his doctrine that "it can never be said, that evil hapneth to him, who falles accompanied with vertue." Ostensible disaster is only the mercy of God, Who demands reverence and not curiosity.[9] The famous prayer of Pamela's—apocryphally of such comfort to Charles I on the scaffold—breathed the same kind of gentle Neo-Stoicism which merged imperceptibly into the grateful acceptance of God's inscrutable providence. "Let calamitie be the exercise, but not the overthrowe of my virtue."[10]

Sidney, both in life and death, was a symbol of the Renaissance, and his ethical theory may therefore be taken as representative for a great body of sixteenth-century thought. Although he lived and died gloriously, he lived mainly on inherited values and he exemplified a way of life that within a few decades of his death would be shattered as a worthless anachronism by Cromwell's soldiers. For Sidney as a man of action, for Milton as a man of letters, the massive humanistic fusion of the glory of God with the glory of man was still meaningful. For them both, as for the typical man of the sixteenth century, there was no difficulty

---

[6] *The Civile Conversation*, I, 8.
[7] *Arcadia*, I.3.
[8] *The Castel of Helthe*, fol. 65ʳ.
[9] *Arcadia*, I.4.
[10] *Ibid.*, III.6.

whatever in adjusting Christian piety to a superb confidence in human dignity. Thus Renaissance ethics had a twin polarity, suitable both for the ills amenable to the exercise of man's native reason and for the ills amenable only to the ministrations of a benevolent God.[11]

This kind of bifurcated ethics employed the sovereignty of reason for disturbances in the order of nature, and the grace of God for spiritual afflictions. It was as humanistic as the Renaissance, heir to fifteen centuries of Christianity, dared to be, and until the rise of the new science it maintained a kind of precarious preëminence. It not only preserved intact the glory of God; it also affirmed the possibility and desirability of man's controlling the complex functions of his organism through his innate capacity for reason. By ringing the various changes upon it man could make his proper obeisance to God and still satisfy his secular craving for individualism, subjectivism, and personal dignity. At the very opening of the Renaissance, Petrarch, a man of impeccable and even Augustinian piety, had argued in his *De Remediis Utriusque Fortuna* for the classical and Stoical virtue of philosophic self-control—a concept that could and did develop presently into the identification of virtue with that rather prissy decorum that Cicero's *De Officiis* had bequeathed to so many Renaissance moralists. In an age productive of men whose lust for fame and conviction of excellence demanded an ethical prop, Cicero's equation of morality with rational decorum and gentility was extremely congenial: "quod consentaneum sit hominis excellentiae in eo, in quo natura eius a reliquis animantibus differat." [12] In this notion of rational self-discipline the Renaissance found its ambiguous but generally satisfactory reconciliation of human and divine spheres of influence. Moderation, said Bishop Hall, is "the very elliptic line, under which reason and religion move without deviation." [13]

This is not the place to analyze all the shadings of this humanistic ethics that posited human reason almost as high as God's grace. But in one book, blatantly typical in its optimistic evaluation of man, we can trace the main lines of the argument. *The Circe* of Battista Gelli, the friend of Castiglione, is a series of frisky if prolix dialogues between Ulysses and the beasts on Circe's island. Posing to each unfortunate the choice of reverting to manhood or staying as he is, Ulysses has a neat opportunity of justifying the condition of man to those who have perhaps forgotten their former blessings. The oyster, once a fisherman, argues

---

[11] This is perfectly illustrated by Dr. Timothy Bright. See his *Treatise of Melancholy*, pp. 184-85, 242.

[12] *De Officiis*, I.xxvii.

[13] *Christian Moderation*, sect. I, *The Works* (ed. Philip Wynter, 1863), VI, 388.

that beasts (and presumably even bivalve mollusks) are obviously better
endowed physically than "that Sorry Two-legged Animal call'd man." [14]
Disgusted at this "Tinsel reasoning" Ulysses turns to the mole (once a
plowman) who also refuses his offer: he, for one, has no wish to return
to his former hunger and drudgery; his flaming (and for the sixteenth
century, extraordinary) discourse on social inequality is an impressive
performance. Ulysses next approaches a snake (once "reckon'd of the
most Topping Physicians of Greece")[15] only to be rebuffed once more,
this time because of man's susceptibility to bodily ailments. And so on
through a long list of prospects, each of whom, for one good reason or
another, scornfully refuses to change the happiness of a beast for the
miseries of a man.[16] The noble horse remembers his fear and intemperance as a man, and argues eloquently against man as the most passion-
driven of animals.[17] But Ulysses, though discouraged, reflects that because
man alone among animals stands erect and looks upward, he must be
destined for a "Felicity that will exalt him above the human state." [18]
And so he continues his quest.

Finally he comes upon the elephant, formerly a philosopher at Athens,
who is at least open to persuasion and willing to argue the question of
man's preëminence. It is in this last dialogue that Ulysses rises to the
height of his eloquence; his defense of man is a tissue of commonplaces,[19]
but it is a classical statement of the Renaissance conception of human
dignity.[20] The elephant, who seems to have been an Aristotelian in the
old bad days, points out that man's "boasted understanding" can work
only through the senses, and that sensation is by no means the unique
attribute of humans. It is true, Ulysses admits, that man uses sensation
for intellection, but it is also true that he transcends his bodily faculties
to arrive at the knowledge of those ideas which are the "proper essence"
of physical nature.[21] Man's unique faculty, then, is his understanding of

[14] *The Circe* (trans. Thomas Brown, 1702), p. 13.

[15] P. 42.

[16] This notion of the superiority of animals to man, at least in certain aspects, was not
uncommon. See Elyot, *The Gouernour*, II, 167; Sir Walter Raleigh, "The Sceptic," *Works*,
VIII, 551; La Primaudaye, *The French Academie*, p. 913; Montaigne, *The Essays*, I, 444 ff.

[17] A commonplace of Neo-Stoicism. See Charron, *Of Wisdom*, pp. 98 ff.

[18] Pp. 198-99. This argument for man's preëminence because of his erect posture is at
least as old as Plato (*Timaeus*, 90, 92). See F. E. Robbins, *The Hexaemeral Literature*, p.
10, n.3, also pp. 56, 71. In the Renaissance it appeared everywhere: see La Primaudaye,
*The French Academie*, II.28, *passim*; Pedro Mexio, *The Treasvrie of Avncient and Moderne
Times* (trans. Thomas Milles, 1613), I.7; Thomas Heywood, *The Hierarchie of the Blessed
Angells*, p. 338 (cf. p. 375); Milton, *Paradise Lost*, VII, 508 and XI, 9.

[19] See Giuseppe Tofannin, *Il Cinquecento* (1929), pp. 262 ff.

[20] *The Circe*, pp. 259 ff.

[21] *Ibid.*, p. 269.

ideas. This, superior to fancy, superior to imagination, is his real dignity; equipped with reason and with his free and inviolate will to act upon the dictates of his judgment, he is clearly the crown of all creation. He may sink as low as a beast, says Ulysses (perhaps gazing intently at the elephant), or he may rise almost to God.

If despising all the allurement and obstacles he finds from his body, he seriously applies his thoughts to the contemplation of divine things, he shall almost make himself a God. Who then can behold Man and not be surprized with admiration, him I say who is not only superior to all other creatures, and Lord of this Universe, but has this peculiar privilege granted him by nature to do whatever he pleases.[22]

Not even the Aristotelian elephant can withstand this kind of salesmanship: he asks to become a man again, and after he and Ulysses have exchanged congratulations on their mutual blessedness as men, Ulysses conveniently cribs from Lorenzo de' Medici a deistic hymn to the "Great Nature of the World" that encompasses such wonders as the perfection of the heavens and the "Perfection of our Intellect." Together then the two men board the waiting ship to sail to Greece.

Although Gelli's optimistic evaluation of human nature and conduct is generally Platonic it may stand as typical of an extremely common Renaissance attitude that took many forms: Florentine Neoplatonism, the Christian humanism of Erasmus, the ethics of gentility and nobility in the courtesy books, even the naturalism of faculty psychology. In all these fashionable systems the primacy of human reason as the arbiter of human conduct was a basic assumption.

This generalization may be made to cover even a man like Pierre Charron, whose works reveal a curious mixture of Catholic piety, skepticism, and Neo-Stoicism. Like his friend Montaigne, Charron was skeptical of man's capacity for either rational or virtuous conduct. He thought the "number of fools are infinite,"[23] and that the heart of man is as unchecked as the sea.

It is infinite, diverse, inconstant, confused, and irresolute, yea, many times horrible and detestable, but ordinarily vain, and ridiculous in its own desires.[24]

Charron would agree with Gelli's horse that man is of all animals most racked and torn by passion, and yet he confidently prescribes a life of reason in his "altogether pleasant, free, bucksome, and if I may so say,

---

[22] *Ibid.*, pp. 289-91.
[23] *Of Wisdom*, p. 211.
[24] *Ibid.*, p. 79.

wanton" [25] ethical system. This strongly Neo-Stoical system, predicated on a sensationalist and materialistic psychology, would be quite meaningless without the assumption that a life of rational well-being is possible for man. There are, says Charron, four paths to the attainment of wisdom: 1) to remain free of the "external errours and vices of the world" while maintaining a "plain, entire, and universal liberty of the mind"; 2) to practice always a "true and essential probity" in following a "certain end and course of life"; 3) to cultivate the virtues of self-control, equanimity, and prudence; and 4) to maintain in one's soul a "true tranquility of spirit, the crown of wisdom, and the sovereign good." [26]

It is true but unimportant that "reason" meant one thing to Charron and Lipsius—for a man to direct himself "in all things according to nature" [27] so as to achieve that supreme virtue of the "Constancie" [28] that is "valiant, noble, and glorious impassibility" [29]—and that it meant something else altogether to Ficino and Spenser. What is important is that nearly everyone believed "reason," of one kind or another, to be natural for man, and man therefore to be capable of attaining a good life through the cultivation of his native faculties. (Calvin, Machiavelli, and the extreme skeptics would dissent, but they would form a small minority.)

Spenser, thus, is a typical man of the Renaissance in his ethics. By turns a mystic and an Aristotelian—yet always loitering in the shade of Plato—he insisted on the preëminence of reason, the unique faculty which man of all animals shares with God. Like Milton, Spenser makes the humanistic assumption that all virtues—the holiness of the Red Cross Knight, the temperance of Guyon, the chastity of Britomart, the justice of Artegall—are active, not passive. They require that a man go forth and conquer the world, and not withdraw from it. Spenser's hero is always the wayfaring Christian who, like Milton, has no regard for a fugitive and cloistered virtue, unexercised and unbreathed.[30] The Bower of Bliss is one of the lushest essays in Renaissance sensualism on record, but its very sensuousness heightens the moral of Guyon's temperance. He neither flees before temptation nor succumbs to it, but with the help of his Palmer's reason overpowers it. Guyon's victory is the victory of the Renaissance man, wonderfully equipped to display the active strength of his rational soul. Guyon—and even the Red Cross Knight, who gets

---

[25] *Ibid.*, "Preface," [sig. A8ʳ].
[26] *Ibid.*, pp. 208-209; cf. Burton's prescription for wisdom, *Anatomy of Melancholy*, II, 119 ff.
[27] Charron, *Of Wisdom*, "Preface," [sig. B1ʳ].
[28] See Lipsius, *Tvvo Bookes of Constancie*, I.v.
[29] Charron, p. 215.
[30] See Edwin Greenlaw, "A Better Teacher than Aquinas," *SP*, XIV (1917), 202 ff.

into one mess after another—embodies the ethical values of an Elizabethan far removed from Spenser intellectually: when Bacon said that we
"must know, that in this theatre of man's life it is reserved only for God
and Angels to be lookers on," [31] he was voicing the characteristic confidence in man's capacity to conduct his life with dignity and success.
Bacon's *summum bonum* is hardly Spenser's, yet they tacitly agree that
man, *as man,* is capable of attaining it.

### NEO-STOICISM

The history of ideas, like the history of music, is astonishing for the
virtually infinite variations and permutations of a few basic factors.
That thousands of tunes have been written from the twelve tones of our
scale is no more astonishing than that for about twenty centuries men
have been working out combinations and developments of perhaps half
a dozen basic ideas.

Although the rise of Neo-Stoicism in the late Renaissance is but an
eddy in the stream of man's intellectual history, it is a clear example of
the principle of recurrence, of the tendency of each age to reshape its
intellectual legacy for its own purposes. In antiquity, as we have seen,
Stoicism was one of the last great efforts to abstract philosophical permanence from the tensions and contradictions of man's experience. As
a drastic superimposition of law and security on the flux of life it was,
though a patchwork, extremely useful for the Roman lawyers who had
not forgotten the simple virtues of the Republic but who had somehow to
administer an empire. In the late Renaissance, on the eve of the victory
of the new science, Stoicism was revived that certain men might believe
they could rely on the constancy of their own indomitable souls in a
world characterized by aggression, compromise, and disorder. Much of
the flinty charm of Stoicism—for Zeno, for Cicero, for Boethius, for
Lipsius, for Chapman—has been, as Léontine Zanta has said, that it has
"de quoi séduire un homme jeté dans la lutte et aux prises avec toutes les
difficultés." [32] Justus Lipsius, one of the prophets of Neo-Stoicism, is a
case in point: a quiet scholar, he lived in what seemed to him and to
many others hideously tumultuous times. Born a Catholic, he became a
Lutheran at Jena, a Calvinist at Leyden, and finally a Catholic again.
But through all the exigencies and changes of an untidy life he cherished
—somewhat ironically—the Neo-Stoic ideal of constancy as man's highest
virtue. Is it not true that Stoicism, even more than most philosophical
and religious systems, is a pathetic rationalization of one's desires?

---

[31] *Advancement of Learning,* bk. II (*Works,* VI, 314).
[32] *La Renaissance du Stoicisme au XVI° Siècle* (1914), p. 335.

Generically, Renaissance Neo-Stoicism marks another stage in the humanistic rediscovery of antiquity. Like Platonism, however, Stoicism had woven itself so tightly into the Christian fabric, with its veneration for natural law and its disregard for the frailties of the flesh, that most good Christians were like Petrarch in the fourteenth and Phillippe de Mornay in the sixteenth century: they were, among other things, Stoics in spite of themselves. The great Stoic doctrine of the control of passion by reason, with its aesthetic corollary of the control of imagination by judgment, very quickly became a commonplace of Christian humanism. It remained for men like Lipsius and Guillaume Du Vair to rationalize their Stoicism and to think of it as a moral and intellectual discipline distinct from and perhaps even superior to Christianity. When this happened, the seams began to split, for the humanistic synthesis of paganism and Christianity had gone too far.

It is not hard to account for the appeal of Neo-Stoicism to men of the late Renaissance. At least ostensibly compatible with the Christianity to which it had contributed so much, Stoicism, as a phenomenon of the late sixteenth-century, was in the main humanistic tradition of Renaissance ethics in its glorification of reason as man's proudest glory. But what was an urbane and flattering commonplace for most moral philosophers became for the Neo-Stoic a burning conviction of preëminence that elevated him above Church, above state, even above human nature. Of all the neo-pagan cults of the Renaissance, Neo-Stoicism provided the most chest-thumping rationalization of individualism; for an age productive of individuals who were perhaps more intense than virtuous, Neo-Stoicism provided a rhetorically splendid justification of a common attitude.

The popular appeal of this individualism is reflected more clearly in the mighty line of Marlowe, Shakespeare, and Chapman than in the sober prose of Lipsius or Du Vair. These men who wrote plays for a living beat the drum for that kind of self-reliance and autonomous glory that permitted one to rise above both good luck and disaster to achieve the complete realization of personality. Events may conspire against a man, and fickle Fortune—that wanton goddess of unreason that bends a whirling universe to her purposes—may humble the mighty and raise the unworthy; yet there lies within a man the staying-power, the *quiddam suum ac proprium,* that permits him to rise above circumstance. Such a man, as Hamlet tells Horatio, takes Fortune's buffets and rewards with equal thanks: his real glory is that strength that comes from the realization of his own identity.

In Lipsius' hymn to Constancy we can yet hear some of the proud tones of Neo-Stoicism:

Being firmelie setled against all casualties, bearing thy selfe vpright in all misfortunes, neither puffed vp nor pressed downe with either fortune, thou maist challenge to thy selfe that great title, the neerest that man can haue to God, To be immooueable.[33]

As Mr. Eliot has said, this kind of individualism may be nothing but a way of cheering oneself up,[34] but both as an ethical discipline and a theory of dramatic characterization it proved useful. The conception of character implicit in both Marlowe's and Shakespeare's[35] tragic heroes is partly Neo-Stoical, but it remained for George Chapman—a bookish man whose knowledge of character is characteristically literary—to capitalize on this fashionable kind of individualism.[36]

But that is perhaps too harsh: although an indifferent playwright, Chapman was an honest man who made a hard living by writing. Even though we cannot quite believe his Clermont, there is every reason to think he represents Chapman's sincere effort to draw a truly "good" man. Chapman was learned, and like most learned men an incorrigible pedagogue; also he was a Christian who never quite succeeded in subordinating the moralist to the artist. His characters are usually moral abstractions, his plays vehicles for moral instruction.

That is why his Stoicism is so flamboyant. There are other elements in his thought, of course: he draws heavily on Neoplatonism for his rigorous dualism of body and soul,[37] passion and reason, nature and grace.[38] But Stoicism colors the syncretistic pattern of his thought, and

[33] *Tvvo Bookes of Constancie,* I.vi.
[34] "Shakespeare and the Stoicism of Seneca," *Selected Essays* (1932), p. 112.
[35] Mr. Eliot's denial of consistent Neo-Stoicism in Shakespeare is of course valid. Shakespeare merely used Neo-Stoicism as he used skepticism and cynicism in his creation of character.
[36] Even though M. Schoell has raised serious objections to Chapman's reputation as a savant (*Études sur l'humanisme continental en Angleterre à la fin de la renaissance,* 1926) his borrowings from Ficino and Comes hardly justify Legouis' strictures on his "pédantisme" and "paresse intellectuelle."
[37] Thus in *The Revenge of Bussy D'Ambois* (V.v.170-73):
> The garment or the cover of the mind,
> The human soul is; of the soul, the spirit
> The proper robe is; of the spirit, the blood;
> And of the blood, the body is the shroud.
The idea was of course a commonplace, but could Chapman have been reading Erasmus' *Enchiridion,* ch. VII?
[38] See Royal W. Battenhouse, "Chapman and the Nature of Man," *ELH,* XII (1945), 89-92—a very able discussion.

informs his concept of character. Indeed, a man like Clermont is so Stoic that we almost forget his author was a Christian. For Chapman's ethical ideal demands the "complete" man who in his quest for tranquillity (should we say "salvation"?) is compelled to repudiate nature. He embodies a Promethean, and typically Renaissance compulsion toward fulfillment, but he achieves his goal by renouncing his very humanity, so that when he has learned to live by reason he has virtually ceased to be a man at all. He has become the Stoic sage.

Thus Chapman's Byron is a study of the character who in the Bussy plays became a mechanical monster. Byron is the Renaissance great man, the Marlovian hero who urges self-realization as man's highest moral obligation. Byron urges his fellows to be free and untruss their slaveries,[39] and he himself rises to a titanic contempt for all except his self-sufficiency. He despises Fortune and the intrigues of the Valois court, and as a "man of spirit beyond the reach of fear" [40] he will seek to evade nothing. His "great heart" will not down; it is like the sea that, reacting to its own internal heat and to the inexorable motion of the tides, "never will be won" until it is "crown'd with his own quiet foam." [41] Bussy is a Stoic individualist, beyond fear, beyond human frailties, including, it seems, conscience. Superbly self-confident, he disregards all obstacles until at last he is consumed in his own fire. A superman who baits the king and his courtiers, and even the Senecan demon conjured up from hell, he finally, as Mr. Parrott has said, consents rather than yields to death. A man of "noblesse"—how often that word occurs[42]—he is alone in a vulgar world, and glorious even in defeat. He refuses to beg for life, but he does regret that an early death cuts short his career of self-realization.[43]

In the sequel, *The Revenge of Bussy D'Ambois,* even Bussy's Neo-Stoical individualism is topped by Clermont's. Though Bussy still hankered after fame in spite of his self-sufficiency, his brother Clermont has learned to despise even that last infirmity of noble mind. Though he bears meekly the taunts of the inane courtiers, he loathes them as the "breathing sepulchres of noblesse." [44] As a man of infinite internal resources, and like Bussy in his self-reliance, he is content to contain his fire "as hid in embers" [45]—for all the world, as Guise comments admir-

[39] *The Conspiracy and Tragedy of Byron* in *The Tragedies* (ed. Thomas Mac Parrot, 1910), III.iii.130 ff.

[40] *Bussy D'Ambois,* I.i.46.

[41] I.ii.157 ff.

[42] Note Chapman's dedication (Parrott, p. 77) of *The Revenge* to Sir Thomas Howard for his "undoubted virtue and exceeding true noblesse."

[43] V.iv.90 ff.

[44] *The Revenge of Bussy D'Ambois,* II.i.153.

[45] II.i.94.

ingly, like another Brutus.[46] His goal, as he sententiously declares in the approved Senecan fashion, is to live at one with nature: all the "discipline of manners and of manhood" is contained in this precept.

> A man to join himself with th' Universe
> In his main sway, and make (in all things fit)
> One with that All, and go on round as it.[47]

Indeed, so complete is Clermont's identification with the Stoic sage that Chapman puts into his mouth tags from Epictetus which he conveniently glosses in the marginalia.[48] Guise, whose only function seems to be to comment on Clermont, is lavish in his encomium: a "firm inexorable spirit," as contemptuous of the mighty as of the "idolatrous vulgar," Clermont is the wise man who knows himself and speaks the truth. In short, he is the "Senecal man." [49]

But for all this, Clermont is something of a prig—as perhaps most Stoic sages are. When his friends marvel at his comprehension of women he explains nobly that he, even as they, first "takes fire out of the frail parts of my blood"; once his lust is satisfied, however, "I love them then out of judgment." [50] Such a man has to die a Stoic as he has lived—with suicide. This Clermont does. Having avenged his brother's murder (after three long acts of irrelevancies to postpone the revenge until the end of the play) he learns that Guise, his friend and patron, lies foully murdered. Happily, Clermont is not tempted to undertake a new program of extermination; instead he gravely talks himself into suicide. Unable to live longer in a world gone mad, or to subject himself "to all the horrors of the vicious time," [51] he finds at last his consummation in death and thus remains, as he thinks, master of his fate.

Chapman's "Senecal man" is a poetic redaction of Neo-Stoic ethics, but Chapman was not an original thinker. To understand Neo-Stoicism better we should turn to its more systematic spokesmen across the Channel.

One of the effects of the humanistic exploration of pagan literature had been the revival of interest in the Roman Stoicism of Cicero, Seneca, and Epictetus.[52] On the Continent this revival burgeoned into a system of

[46] II.i.103.
[47] IV.i.137 ff.
[48] On Chapman's borrowings from Epictetus see Schoell, pp. 99 ff., 248 ff.
[49] IV.iv.16 ff.
[50] V.i.154 ff.
[51] V.v.149 ff.
[52] Cicero's philosophic works had been printed at Venice in 1471 (ten years before Caxton published Tiptoft's translation of the *De Amicitia*), Seneca's *Epistles* at Strassburg

thought that, though not original, attracted both ardent advocates and ardent opponents. It was too pagan for good Christians and too Christian for good neopagans. Justus Lipsius (1547-1606) was a Belgian who taught up and down Europe, became famous for his work on Seneca and Tacitus, and changed his religion to suit his patrons; Guillaume Du Vair (1556-1621) was an eminent French lawyer whose distinguished career was in statesmanship and diplomacy; but they have lived for posterity because they achieved a more or less systematic formulation of Neo-Stoicism.[53]

One must expect to find no startlingly original ethical theory in these men. They revived the old Stoic catchwords and wrote variations on the old Stoic themes of fortitude and self-reliance. Already, Rabelais and Montaigne had shown how Stoicism could be dallied with. Rabelais' notorious inscription over the Abbey of Thélème had, after all, been little more than a restatement of the Stoic formula of *sequere naturam*.[54] And his commendation of Pantagruel's mental equilibrium is a potpourri of the well-rubbed precepts of such worthies as Cicero and Marcus Aurelius. Pantagruel, it will be recalled,

never vexed or disquieted himself with the least pretence of dislike to anything, because he knew he must have most grossly abandoned the divine mansion of reason, if he had permitted his mind to be never so little grieved, afflicted or altered on any occasion whatsoever.[55]

And so on. Montaigne's Stoicism was for the most part confined to his salad days, and it was orthodox enough until he matured into the great and characteristic skepticism of his middle period. The tone of the early essays, as M. Villey has said, is "imperieux, pressant, il vous harcèle: sa morale est tendue, inflexible." [56] Montaigne's youthful confidence in the sovereignty of reason is refreshing: he quotes Seneca like the scholar he

in 1475, and Politan's Latin version of Epictetus in 1493. Of course, Plutarch was immensely popular in England long before Philemon Holland published *The Morals* in 1603. As Mlle. Zanta has said (p. 9), Cicero and Seneca became more than models of Latin prose; they became "des amis, des conseilleurs, auprès desquels on peut trouver consolation et apprendre cet art de la vie." See Rudolf Kirk's introduction to Lipsius' *Tvvo Bookes of Constancie* (1939), pp. 15 ff. and Henrietta R. Palmer, *List of English Editions and Translations of Greek and Latin Classics*, under the relevant name-entries.

[53] Lipsius' *La Constance* (trans. in 1593 by Sir John Stradling as *Tvvo Bookes of Constancie*), *Manuductio*, and *Physiologia Stoicorum;* Du Vair's *Sainte Philosophie, Philosophie Morale du Stoique* (trans. in 1598 by T[homas] I[ames] as *The Moral Philosophie of the Stoicks* and in 1664 by C. Cotton as *The Morall Philosophy of the Stoics*), and *Constance.* On the Stradling translation of Lipsius see Morris W. Croll, "Attic Prose: Lipsius, Montaigne, Bacon," *Schelling Anniversary Papers* (1923), pp. 124-27.

[54] See Zanta, pp. 21 ff.

[55] III.ii.

[56] *Les Sources & l'evolution des éssais de Montaigne* (1908), II, 55.

was, as much charmed with his literary elegance as with his morality. Montaigne indulges in all the stock attitudes of Stoicism: pity is an error,[57] sadness is "degrading and cowardly,"[58] the passions are lethal.[59] The fact is that Montaigne's Stoic pose is somewhat literary and precious, and it is well for his reputation that he lived to write that monument of skepticism, *The Apology for Raymond Sebond.*[60]

When we recall the rather fastidious Stoicism of such giants as Rabelais and Montaigne—to say nothing of lesser fry like La Boëtie, Jean de Coras, Louis le Caron—it is clear that Lipsius and Du Vair may not be hailed as the men who single-handed revived the ethics of Zeno and Seneca. But they did take their Stoicism seriously, and summarized an attitude that had been a more or less modish accomplishment of men of letters. When Lipsius celebrates his Constancy as the "right and immoueable strength of the minde, neither lifted vp, nor pressed downe with externall or casuall accidentes," and as the true mother of Patience ("a voluntarie sufferance without grudging of all things whatsoeuer can happen to, or in a man"),[61] he was articulating a brand of Neo-Stoic individualism with a powerful appeal to men battered by an uncertain world. His "foure principall affections" of desire, joy, love, and sorrow, arising from such false goods as riches and honor, or from such false evils as poverty and infamy, could exert no sway over one who had come to believe that nothing could help or hurt "the inner man, that is, the minde."[62] The "dissentions, stirs, & a continual conflict" arising from the "iarring concord"[63] of man's bodily and mental parts could not move him who had, in effect, repudiated the body for the mind. For such a monster of prefection the sovereign good was, as Du Vair said, "l'estat et disposition d'une âme pure et innocente, et son action parfaicte, bien herueuse at toute celeste."[64] In the Renaissance as in antiquity, the Stoics were not afflicted with self-doubt.

This was all very well; indeed it represented but a difference of degree from the rational optimism of the commonplaces of Christian humanism. But when Stoic ethics collided with Christianity, as it inevitably did, there was cause for alarm among the faithful. Neo-Stoicism was ostensibly Christian, and men like Lipsius tried very hard to demonstrate how

[57] *The Essays*, I, 4.
[58] *Ibid.*, I, 7.
[59] *Ibid.*, I, 17-18.
[60] For further instances of Montaigne's Stoicism see I, 26, 34, 40-41, 44, 51, 72-74, 75-90. See Fortunat Strowski, *Montaigne* (2d ed., 1931), pp. 83-118.
[61] *Tvvo Bookes of Constancie*, I.iv.
[62] *Ibid.*, I.vii.
[63] *Ibid.*, I.v.
[64] Quoted by Zanta, p. 274.

sweetly compatible were pagan morals and Christian faith. In spite of all the disclaimers, however, the fact remained that Neo-Stoicism elevated reason so high that it could only lead to a natural religion that accommodated the supernatural with difficulty, if at all. In spite of its liberalism and its eclecticism the Renaissance was, on the whole, reluctant to subscribe to this kind of deism. The sixteenth century was much too close emotionally to the Middle Ages to forego its notions of an anthropomorphic deity benevolently keeping his eye on each sparrow. The attenuated deity of the Neo-Stoics was too remote for men who had not yet entirely forgotten their Augustinian heritage.

Lipsius, however, worked valiantly to identify Stoic reason with Christian faith, and Du Vair argued that even though Stoicism could not supplant Christianity it could purify its crudities and corruptions. Oddly enough, in fact, to be a Stoic is to be a Christian, for by submitting to reason and to nature man submits to God, and thus achieves happiness. God made us "maistre pour estre membres de ce bas monde, toutes les parties dequel observans l'office et le mouvement qu'il leur adonnés servent à sa gloire." [65] Such deistic optimism was, as we have seen, hardly confined to Neo-Stoicism; men of Lipsius' persuasion had to answer a much more serious charge, and one which they wriggled hard to evade. That was the charge of mechanistic determinism.

Lipsius takes the trouble to list four points on which he differs from the pagan Stoics: he would not subject God to destiny, he would relax his determinism to allow for God's miracles, he would not deny contingency, he would not abridge man's claim to free will.[66] This bill of particulars centers about the hotly contested question of Stoic fate, a question recognized by both Neo-Stoics and their opponents as crucial. If the universe is, as the ancient Stoics held, strictly materialistic and strictly deterministic, then how could God be saved from and elevated above the inexorable causality that governs all things? Lipsius' answer to this question shows how seriously the Neo-Stoics went about their business. There are, he insists,[67] varieties of destiny: 1) mathematical, by which the movements of the stars and planets are controlled; 2) natural, by which a man begets a son instead of a serpent; 3) violent fate, the strictly Stoic "necessitie of all thinges and actions, which no force can withstand or breake"—in other words, the necessity that God decrees for the workings of a "stedfast and stable nature"; and 4) true destiny, the eternal decree of God's providence which encompasses destiny, "being as it were

[65] Quoted by Zanta, p. 284.
[66] *Tvvo Bookes of Constancie*, I.xx.
[67] *Ibid.*, I.xviii-xix.

a disposing and bestowing abroad of that vniuersall prouidence, by particulars. Therefore Prouidence is in God, and attributed to him alone: Destinie in the things, and to them is ascribed."

As a Christian, Lipsius has the candor to admit that the pagan Stoics, however wise, were sometimes injudicious in talking of fate; none the less they of all the ancients were most aware of the majesty and glory of God. "And if in treading this trace of Destinie they went somewhat astray, it was thorough [sic] a laudable and good desire they haue to withdrawe blind men from that blind Goddesse, I meane FORTVNE." [68] Paradoxically, it is precisely God's providence that ensures true liberty and prevents chaos. It is the equivalent of the natural reason that informs the universe, and if a man would be deific he has merely to follow nature, which is to submit to providence. Man has free will, of course, and the fact that God in His wisdom has foreknowledge of the event in no way jeopardizes his freedom. God "fore-saw it (I say) not forced it: hee knewe it, but constrayned not: he fore-tolde it, but not prescribed it." [69] To deny any part of God's foreknowledge is to deny His providence, the grossest impiety and a thing unthinkable.

So in this fatall vessell wherein we all sayle, let our willes wrangle and wrest as they list, they shal not turne her out of her course, nor anie thing hinder the same. That highest will of all willes must holde and rule the raynes, and with the turne of a hande direct this chariot whither soeuer it pleaseth.[70]

Thus emerges the paradox of Neo-Stoicism. Of all forms of Renaissance neopaganism worked into the fabric of Christianity it advocated the most ruthless individualism; yet it also put man's freedom under the severest check. The Neo-Stoics could urge the utmost liberty for man's conscience and conduct precisely because they could not conceive of freedom without law. And the law which no man could break was that providence or destiny which determined the course of all things in nature. Therefore to follow nature released man from the bondage of the trivial restrictions of society and morality for the sublime bondage of natural law. There is in God, then,

a watchfull and continuall care (yet without cark) whereby he beholdeth, searcheth, and knoweth all thinges: And knowing them, disposeth and ordereth the same by an immutable course to vs vnknowne. And this is it which here I cal PROVIDENCE, whereof some man through infirmitie may grudge or complaine: but not doubt, except he be benummed of his senses, and besotted against nature.[71]

[68] Ibid., I.xviii.
[70] Ibid., I.xx.
[69] Ibid., I.xx.
[71] Ibid., I.xiii.

Although the Neo-Stoics may have thought they thus exonerated their Christian God from the charge of being subject to fate, their ethics presented yet another stumbling-block to the orthodox. Their conception of man's freedom under natural law led to that coldness and callousness necessary for a blatant individualism but antithetical to the ethical tenderness of Christianity. The popular aversion to Neo-Stoicism was centered more on this inhuman harshness of an individualistic ethics than on the relatively abstruse question of determinism. Marlowe made many of his heroes ruthless Stoic individualists, but he could rouse the rabble with a typical overstatement of the Stoic's toughness. "First be then voyd of these affections," Barabas instructs Ithamore,

> Compassion, loue, vaine hope, and hartlesse feare,
> Be mou'd at nothing, see thou pitty none,
> But to they selfe smile when the Christian moane.[72]

Is not death in a caldron too good for such a man?

No one who has read enough Renaissance history to distinguish between Henry VIII and John Calvin can argue seriously that humanitarianism was a flourishing sentiment in the sixteenth century; none the less, the virtues—passions, said the Stoic contemptuously—of pity and love were generally accounted to be integral parts of the Christian ethic. But the Stoic moralist had no choice: if complete self-realization through submitting to nature meant the eradication of all passion, then even the passions sanctioned by religion must go. For as Charron had said, one religion is much like another and they are all negligible compared to the genuine piety of comprehending one's place in nature. As for the Christian virtues, pity constituted a subversion of reason just as much as lust or anger. The wise man, says Lipsius, will permit himself to entertain rational compassion for the distress of others, but "with discretion and care, that he infect not himselfe with other mens contagion: and that (as Fencers vse to say) hee beare not others blowes vppon his owne ribbes." [73] Excessive grief over the misfortunes of one's country or of one's friends is ignoble, and based on opinion rather than reason. The wise man will acknowledge that he should, as a matter of custom or convenience, love, defend, or perhaps even die for his emotional allegiances, but even so his emotions should not lead him to "lament, waile and dispaire." [74]

It was this pose of unchristian and inhuman passivity that was the butt

---

[72] *The Jew of Malta*, ll. 934 ff.
[73] *Tvvo Bookes of Constancie*, I.xii.
[74] *Ibid.*, I.xi.

of countless orthodox moralists in the sixteenth century. For conventional ethics were generally either Platonic or Aristotelian, or a combination of the two, and prescribed not the violent eradication of passion but its moderation and discipline by reason. It is not surprising, therefore, to find a pungent anti-Stoicism one of the stock themes of Erasmus' *Praise of Folly*.[75] Passion is natural to man, being a function of his sensitive soul, and the Stoics who would outlaw it demand an unnatural and mechanical perfection. Seneca, that "double-strength Stoic," says Folly, proved the Stoic sage to be "a marble simulacrum of a man, a senseless block, completely alien to every human feeling."[76] And near the end of the century, Tranio's low pun echoes the common man's impatience at the ideal of Stoic virtue. He urges Lucentio, elated at the prospect of a life of pure reason, to practice a sensible moderation.

> Good master, while we do admire
> This virtue and this moral discipline,
> Let's be no Stoics nor no stocks, I pray,
> Or so devote to Aristotle's checks
> As Ovid be an outcast quite abjur'd.[77]

Roger Ascham, the Protestant humanist, sees as a sign of God's providence the fact that the writings of such atheistical rascals as Stoics and Epicureans ("fondest in opinion, and rudest in vtterance") were first condemned and forgotten, and are now out of both use and memory.[78] Dr. Timothy Bright, though a spokesman for the Stoical mechanistic psychology, was vastly annoyed at those monsters who, "with a Stoical prophanes of Atheisme," deny the claims of conscience, "against which they themselues labour to shut vp their hard heartes, & with obstancie of stomach to bear out that whereof they tremble with horror."[79] Thomas Wright, another psychologist, argued that passion should not be extirpated "(as the Stoicks seemed to affirme)" but instead "be moued, & stirred vp for the seruice of vertue."[80]

And so the swelling chorus rose. Bacon thought that "to seek to extinguish anger utterly is but a bravery of the Stoics."[81] La Primaudaye rejected Stoicism because it inculcated a kind of odious individualism that makes a man the means of his own salvation, lifting "him vp in a

---

[75] See, for instance, pp. 14, 15, 22, 26, 47, 51, 79.
[76] *The Praise of Folly*, p. 39.
[77] *The Taming of the Shrew*, I.i.29 ff.
[78] *The Scholemaster*, p. 118.
[79] *A Treatise of Melancholie*, p. 188.
[80] *The Passions of the Minde in Generall*, p. 17.
[81] *Essays*, "Of Anger" (*Works*, XII, 271).

vaine presumption . . . which in the end cannot but be the cause of his vtter vndoing." [82] Du Bartas, advancing the attack on another salient, shuddered at the impious Stoic doctrine of determinism and fate which bind

> With Iron Chaines of strong *Necessitie*
> Th' Eternals hands, and his free foot enstocke
> In *Destinies* hard Diamantin Rocke.[83]

Fulke Greville, though a zealous Protestant, was enough of a Renaissance *honnête homme* to resent the Stoic's contempt for honor and fame.[84] Robert Burton, after considerable study of the subject, concluded darkly that passion is so intrinsic and overpowering an element in human nature that a man who is free of it is "either a god or a block," [85] and moreover that Zeno was "mad" to think the Stoic sage other than a fantastic abstraction.[86] Sir Thomas Browne, with characteristic urbanity, simply denied that Stoic ethics made sense. "The Stoics that condemn passion, and command a man to laugh in Phalaris his Bull, could not endure without a groan a fit of the Stone or Colick." [87]

In spite of such attacks, however, there was a perceptible swing to Neo-Stoicism in the early seventeenth century. The humanistic ethics of balance, moderation, and rational harmony gave way, in Jacobean drama, to a mechanistic Stoic psychology and an ethics that threw grave doubts on man's capacity for harmonizing the elements of his nature. Moreover, the incipient deism of the age of science found an easy outlet in Stoicism—so much so that Sir Thomas Browne grumbled that Stoicism, preached from a pulpit, passed for current divinity. Could he have been thinking of that reclaimed satirist, Joseph Hall, who occupied the bishop's palace in Norwich?

But the seventeenth century lies beyond the limits of this book, and the Neo-Stoicism that erupted at the end of the sixteenth is enough to show that the urge was still strong to synthesize those elements of both pagan and Christian culture that enabled man to view himself with considerably more satisfaction than would be possible in another fifty years. Men like Lipsius and Chapman, at least, must have thought that carpentry and consolidation of the traditional systems was still possible, even if to others it was clear that the Renaissance synthesis was tottering and that a radically new analysis of the universe and man's place in it was next in order.

---

[82] *The French Academie*, p. 7.          [83] *Deuine Weekes*, p. 132.
[84] "Fame and Honour," st. 20 ff.          [85] I, 289.          [86] I, 135.
[87] *Religio Medici*, p. 60. See Henry W. Sams, "Anti-Stoicism in Seventeenth- and Early Eighteenth-Century England," *SP*, XLI (1944), 65-78.

# XIX

## THE PROTESTANT VIEW OF MAN

### THE REVIVAL OF AUGUSTINIAN INDIVIDUALISM

I HAVE SUGGESTED THAT RENAISSANCE OPTIMISM was developed, in the main, from the great medieval principle of order which was codified in the natural theology of Aquinas and buttressed by the rich tradition of pagan humanism. But what may we say of the apparenttly antithetical views of the Reformation: the conviction of man's depravity and impotence? Was this theology not new in the Renaissance? Does it not invalidate our thesis that the major elements of Renaissance thought were derived from the past? Did it not require a radical revaluation of human dignity?

The fact is, as anyone who has read *De Civitate Dei* must know, that the theology of the Reformers was a return through the Thomistic synthesis of the late Middle Ages to a still earlier set of principles formulated by Augustine. Furthermore, even the antirationalistic theologies of Luther and Calvin, uncongenial as they were to the kind of optimism we have described, explored new (or at least rediscovered) grounds for human dignity: they placed a new and heavy emphasis on individualism and made it possible for the middle-class culture emerging from the late Middle Ages to expend its best energies in economic activity. Thus the two great reformers—hagridden with a sense of sin and preaching a theological determinism which denied man any voice in rational self-discipline before the awful fact of predestination—provided a fresh impetus for optimism of a sort. Luther developed a new rationale for religious individualism in his reversal to Augustinian mystical cognition; and Calvin, by his theological sanction for intense economic activity, rationalized that department of human conduct that (at least until our own day) has resulted in thundering supremacy of a Protestant, capitalistic culture. Although both men broke with the Thomistic rationalism of the late Middle Ages, each provided a compensatory device, and on the whole the influence of Protestantism can hardly be said to have been toward causing man to retire from the world and resign himself to his well-merited damnation.

It is not uncommon to find the Reformation cited as the signal of man's spiritual liberation from the rusty tradition of Rome.[1] Like so many generalizations it is at best only a half-truth. It is obvious that the iconoclasm of Luther and Calvin achieved a notable change in the economic coördinates of religion, and that they tore most of northern Europe away from the ritual of the Catholic Church. But theologically their service to liberalism is more questionable. Humanists like Erasmus spoke tartly of piercing the web of Scholastic frippery in order to return to the font of all virtue and wisdom—the Bible itself. The Reformers, also theological primitivists, actually did so, and the result was something from which the humanists recoiled in urbane horror. It was one thing for Erasmus, in his great effort to propagate the Bible, to work unceasingly on Saint Jerome, the father of the Vulgate, but he had no stomach for an Augustinian Christianity based on Saint Paul.

Luther's religious individualism was a genuine contribution to sixteenth-century thought. His central principle of justification by faith recalled Augustine's doctrine of spiritual illumination, but he dared to do what Augustine did not: he sought to make the transaction between God and man a matter of individual responsibility by dispensing with a monopolistic redemptionist institution. Through the mystic union of the believer with Christ, all lesser allegiances were abolished; the priesthood of each believer made superfluous all intermediaries—sacramental, clerical, political. It was through this audacious doctrine that Luther mainly shocked his contemporaries. After his attack on the seven sacraments in the *Prelude to the Babylonian Captivity*, the hand of every traditionalist was raised against him.

*Principio neganda mihi sunt septem sacramenta et tantum tria pro tempore ponenda, Baptismus, Poenitentia, Panis, et haec omnia esse per Romanam curiam nobis in miserabilem captivitatem ducta Ecclesianque sua tota libertate spoliatam* quanquam, si usu scripturae loqui velim, non nisi unum sacramentum habeam et tria signa sacramentalia, de quo latius suo tempore.[2]

These sentiments were so repellent to Henry VIII, that valiant man of God, that he enlisted the help of some of the leading clergymen of his realm to refute such heresy in his *Defense of the Seven Sacraments*—a treatise which Erasmus professed to admire.[3] For his pains, as everyone knows, Henry won for himself and for his successors the title of Defender of the Faith. But more than faith was involved in Luther's individualism, even though he himself was unwilling to follow all its implications. If

---

[1] For instance, Franz Alexander, *Our Age of Unreason* (1942), pp. 123 ff.
[2] "De Captivate Babylonica Ecclesiae Praeludium," *Werke* (Weimar ed.), VI, 501.
[3] *The Epistles*, I, 423-24.

a man may dispense with authority and institutions in matters of religious conscience, why not in matters of political conscience? In the Separatists of the seventeenth century we may trace some of the democratic implications of Luther's Protestant individualism. Luther himself hedged and retracted during the Peasants' Revolt, but a spiritual descendant like Roger Williams dared to put his doctrine of freedom of conscience to the test.

Because his basic principle was that all Christians were members of the "spiritual estate," one of Luther's first objectives was to combat the mechanization of grace through the sacraments.[4] It was against this heresy that Leo promulgated the bull *Exsurge Domine* in 1520. Luther made the signal innovation of preaching salvation through personal faith rather than salvation through the "work" of participating in those sacraments which automatically invoked grace (*ex opere operato*). His great translation of the Bible, which established the language and laid a linguistic basis for German nationalism, was one of the fruits of this conviction; and the profoundly subjective tone of his theology led, through Quietism, to its sublimated (or attenuated) form in Kantian metaphysics. Like Augustine, whom he revered and quoted endlessly, Luther insisted on the necessity of divine illumination flooding the soul of the worshipper: all else was vain. The tonsure, ordination, and consecration of the clergy "may make a hypocrite or an anointed puppet," he said, "but never a Christian or a spiritual man."[5] The true Christian is passive before his God, relying wholly on his faith for his salvation.[6]

Ostensibly, Calvin too followed the star of liberal individualism. He retained only the two sacraments of baptism and communion—those indispensable exterior signs by which God manifests His good will to us "pour soustenir et confermer l'imbecillité de nostre Foy."[7] But actually, liberty was a concept foreign to the tyrant of Geneva. Luther had emphasized Augustine's doctrine of mystical illumination, but Calvin's

---

[4] For a terse statement of the doctrine of justification by faith see *Luther's Correspondence and Other Contemporary Letters*, II, 199 ff.; cf. Preserved Smith, "Luther's Development of the Doctrine of Justification by Faith Only," *Harvard Theological Review*, VI (1913), 407-25.

[5] "To the German Nobility," *Documents Illustrative of the Continental Reformation* (ed. B. J. Kidd, 1911), p. 63.

[6] Note Donne's remark (*LXXX Sermons*, 1640, no. 67, p. 677): "To come to God there is a straight line for every man every where." In Luther's individualism, as in Augustine's, there is a strong mystical element. From Master Eckhart on, Germany had proved congenial to those—like the League of the Friends of God and the Brothers of the Common Life—who wished to substitute a primitive Christianity of personal purity and the conscious imitation of Christ for the dogma, ritual, and intellectuality of an organized church. It should not be forgotten that Luther himself translated the *German Theology*, the monument of German mysticism.

[7] *Institution de la religion Chrestienne*, II, 565.

heart warmed more readily to those massive doctrines of original sin, predestination, and election. As Parrington has said, his thinking was formed by notions of oriental despotism and sixteenth-century monarchism, modified by the medieval conception of a city-state.[8] If we may see Luther in Roger Williams, we have only to contemplate the theocratic magistrates of Boston to observe the political implications of Calvinism. John Cotton and John Winthrop were sober, pious men, but they had as much interest in democracy as in the Pope's well-being.

But if the Reformation liberated the individual ritually (and, as we shall see, helped to liberate him economically), it bound him theologically to the rigors of a revived Augustinian sense of sin. The reversal to this essentially antirationalistic theology was, in fact, the main alternative to the Scholastic tradition which the Reformers held in such contempt. As Luther wrote from Wittenberg in 1517:

Our theology and St. Augustine are progressing happily and prevail at our University. Aristotle is at a discount and is hurrying to everlasting destruction. People are quite disgusted with the lectures on the Sentences [of Peter Lombard], and no one can be sure of an audience unless he expounds this theology, i.e. the Bible or St. Augustine, or some other teacher of note in the Church.[9]

Adolf Harnack has said that without a revival of Augustinianism the Reformation would have been impossible: Luther's cardinal doctrine of justification by faith alone and Calvin's restatement of the doctrines of original sin and predestination reach back through the rational theology of Aquinas to the Bishop of Hippo.

In our day, George Santayana has voiced the dilemma of a man nurtured in the Catholic Church who could no longer embrace it intellectually even though he clung to it emotionally. For Calvin there were no such emotional allegiances. He had the mind of a lawyer and logician. Repelled by a Church that had become fat and comfortable, a theology that had become rational, Calvin had to make a drastic revaluation of his faith. He had to revise the concept of both God and man, and when he had done so, the result was uncommonly like the theological absolutism of Augustine. Calvin viewed man as a creature whose only hope was to fling himself before an awful God no longer dozing behind the veil of the temple: God became real, Hebraic, and terrifying; man was reduced again to the sinful spawn of Adam, groveling in his total depravity

---

[8] Vernon Louis Parrington, *Main Currents in American Thought* (1930), I, 13.

[9] Quoted by Hartmann Grisar, *Luther* (trans. E. M. Lamond, 1913-1917), I, 305. Even though Grisar, as a Catholic, is somewhat unsympathetic to Luther, his mammoth study is indispensable.

and incapable of anything except more sin. And so for Calvin as for Augustine, the two basic facts of religion were a God of power and righteous anger rather than love and bland rationality, and a man of impotence and sin rather than virtue and rational self-sufficiency. For Aquinas' optimistic theology that had made both God and man, in varying degrees, rational and capable of a rational *rapprochement,* Calvin substituted the Augustinian (and Scotist) theology of God as unconditioned will, contingent upon nothing and least of all upon reason. In consequence, man suffered a terrible reduction to the sinful and guilty object for the working of God's inscrutable will.

In this revision—and reversal—of the common humanistic optimism concerning man and his potentialities, both Luther and Calvin denied the assumptions and implications of Renaissance optimism. Inevitably, then, they detested the comfortable, traditional theology of men like Erasmus. Things had not come to the pretty state described by Gibbon of the "enlightened" clergy of the eighteenth century: they had to mouth the doctrines of original sin, faith, and predestination "with a sigh, or a smile." [10] But even the sixteenth-century humanists, though of course Catholic, could not accept the Reformers' Augustinian derogation of man. Personally and ideologically the Reformers and the humanists were poles apart. As Allen has said, Luther "could buy a Homer, and lament that he had no time to read the classics; but his heart was set, in his chamber and in his pulpit, on cultivating a sense of sin." [11] Both his and Calvin's dogmas denied, *au fond,* the humanistic dignity of man which was based on the cardinal assumption of man's rational self-control. After Luther had tried to enlist Erasmus' aid, only to be rejected, he ridiculed him, with typical delicacy, as a hollow nut that fouls the mouth. Not only did Erasmus retaliate with gentle irony—by his marriage, he suggested, Luther "vult, opinor, affligere carnem" [12]—he wrote his famed *De Libero Arbitrio Diatribe* (1524) as a frontal attack on Luther's barbarous theology.[13] In his rejoinder a year later, *De Servo Arbitrio,* Luther enthusiastically developed those calumnies on man that must have made Erasmus writhe.

Si enim credimus verum esse, quod Deus praescit et praeordinat omnia, tum neque falli neque impediri potest sua praescientia et praedestinatione, Deinde nihil fieri,

[10] *The Decline and Fall of the Roman Empire,* V, 402.

[11] *Erasmus: Lectures and Wayfaring Sketches,* p. 83.

[12] Kidd, *Documents Illustrative of the Continental Reformation,* p. 180. On this point, as on all others concerning Luther, Grisar is copious: see II, 115 ff. for Luther's attack on the impossible ideal of chastity; cf. III, 241-73.

[13] After Erasmus' treatise was published, says Grisar (II, 261), "many cultured laymen breathed more freely, as though relieved of a heavy burden, when the authoritative voice of the great scholar was at last raised against Luther in defence of free-will, that basic truth of sane human reason and pillar of all religious belief."

nisi ipso volente, id quod ipso ratio cogitur concedere; simul ipsa ratione teste nullum potest esse liberum arbitrium in homine vel angelo aut illa creatura.[14]

In a famous simile, Luther construes man's enslaved will as the very basis of all religious belief. Either Satan or God controls the impotent will of man, and man himself is nothing more than a saddle horse. "If God mounts into the saddle, man wills and goes forward as God wills . . . but if the devil is the horseman, then man wills and acts as the devil wills. He has no power to run to one or the other of the two riders and offer himself to him, but the riders fight to obtain possession of the animal."[15] One thinks of Swift's Houyhnhnms using the domesticated Yahoos as beasts of burden.

Luther at least had the humanist Melanchthon in his camp,[16] but with Calvin there could be no possible compromise. At the opening of the second book of the *Institute,* when he is about to launch into his great attack on the dignity of man, Calvin ironically cites the Socratic "know thyself" as one of the necessities of religious belief. But his reasons are unsocratic. The pagan moralists, says Calvin, urge man to know himself "that he shoulde not be ignorant of his owne dignitie and excellencie: and nothing els do thei will him to beholde in him selfe, but that whereby he may swell with vaine confidence, & be puffed vp with pride." When man really knows himself, however, his pride lies trailing in the mud. The "heauy sight of oure filthines & shame doth thruste it selfe in presence." There are always those flattering pseudomoralists (the humanists?) who hide man's true vileness—and there are always fools to believe them. "For ther is nothynge that mans nature more coueteth, than to be stroked with flattery." But let no man think to find true self-knowledge in such vanity: it is the "worste kynde of ignoraunce."[17]

Calvin's central concept of an inscrutable and omnipotent God demanded the utter degradation of the human race. The sum of wisdom is not our vaunted reason (too puny to conduct us to God, too feeble to comprehend His power); it is certainly not classical learning (Calvin himself quickly abandoned such youthful indiscretions as his humanistic

[14] *Werke* (Weimar ed.), XVIII, 786. See Grisar's elaborate and extremely unflattering analysis (II, 264 ff.). Luther had been developing his denial of free will from the beginning of his career, and in 1520 had stated his main arguments in his *Assertio omnium articulorum.*

[15] Quoted by Grisar, II, 274; cf. Luther, *Werke,* XVIII, 635.

[16] Although Melanchthon followed the orthodox line of Lutheran determinism in his *Loci communes rerum theologicarum* (1521), he subsequently changed his ground completely. See Alexander Smellie, *The Reformation in Its Literature* (1925), pp. 108 ff.

[17] *The Institution of Christian Religion,* II.i (fol. 1-2). Both the pagination and signatures of the Norton translation of 1561 are extremely erratic. See J. Bohatec, "Calvin et l'humanisme," *Revue Historique,* CLXXXIII (1938), 207-41, and CLXXXV (1939), 71-104.

commentary on Seneca's *De Clementia*);[18] it is to know God in his majesty and man in his impotence: God as the source and being of all "verité, sapience, bonté, justice, jugement, misericorde, puissance, et saincteté"—man as a creature made in the image of God but through his fall marked now by "imbecilité, misere, vanité, et vilanie." [19] For every sensible man the primary fact of life should be the realization of Adam's fall that "enkyndeled the horryble vengaunce of God vpon all mankynde." [20]

The importance Calvin ascribed to the "chute" is tremendous. Adam once shared ("a été faict participant") God's wisdom and holiness; he was even endowed with free will. But by choosing to transgress the divine injunction he cursed himself and all his posterity with a crime beyond speech and beyond expiation.

Pourtant au lieu de sapience, vertu, saincteté, verité, justice, desquelz ornemens il estoit vestu, ayant la semblance de Dieu, sont survenues horribles pestes, à scavóir ignorance, faiblesse, ordure, vanité, injustice: desquelles non seulement il a esté enveloppé en sa personne: mais aussi a empesché toute sa posterité.[21]

Caught between Adam's sin and God's omnipotent wrath, man is powerless. He cannot evade his hereditary stain, and even his capacity to escape its consequence—eternal damnation—must attend God's will. By his shameful nature he is condemned to wrongdoing, and he can escape punishment not through his own efforts but only through the arbitrary exercise of God's mercy, which he can never merit. Of himself, he is as powerless to free himself from the coils of his innate depravity as an infant—who, incidentally, is routed straight to hell from its first moment. Infants not only "brynge with them their owne damnation from their mothers wombe" as heirs of Adam; they are also sinful

by their owne faulte. For though they haue not as yet brought forth the fruytes of theyr owne iniquitie, yet they haue the seede thereof enclosed within them: yea their whole nature is a certayne seede of Sinne: therefore it can not be but hatefull and abhominable to God.[22]

[18] See Quirinus Breen, *John Calvin: A Study in French Humanism* (1931), pp. 67 ff.

[19] *Institute*, I, 1.

[20] *The Institution of Christian Religion*, II.i (fol. 3). It has been suggested that Carlyle's lamentable style should perhaps be forgiven because of his chronic indigestion. Similarly, Calvin's theology should perhaps be judged in the light of his ailments—the "stone, the Gout, the Hemorrhodes, a Phthysike feuer, shortness of winde, beside the ordinary disease of the Miegraine." See Theodore de Beza, *A Discovrse . . . containing the life and death of M. Iohn Caluin . . . Turned out of Frenche into English, by I.S. In the yeare of our Lord*, M.D.LXIIII [London, 1578?], sig. C3ᵛ.

[21] *Institute*, I, 33-34.

[22] *The Institution of Christian Religion*, II.i (fol. 4ᵛ).

Even a faithful Christian is an impotent toad. Internally he is racked by the unceasing war between his intelligence and his will. The one should discriminate between possibilities, the other execute decisions by pursuing the good and avoiding the evil. Ideally, the intelligence is the "gouverneur et capitaine de l'ame," and should lead man to a realization of his own infamy and of God's sublimity.[23] But through man's corruption, these faculties which should work harmoniously have become "deux combatons" whose unequal struggle (for our reason is a pallid and polluted thing) hurls his "en bas."[24] Consequently, man is doubly damned. "Nous . . . ne pouvons rien de nous mesmes."[25] He is left only with his excoriating knowledge of original sin:

the inheritably descendynge peruersnesse and corruption of our nature, poured abroade into all the partes of the soule, whyche fyrste maketh vs gilty of the wrath of God, and then also bryngeth forth these workes in vs, whyche the Scripture calleth the workes of the flesh.[26]

Calvin's contempt for the human race and his adoration of God are codified in his doctrine of predestination. Through it, he dramatized man's impotence and God's sovereignty—and the political implications of this relationship are extremely interesting—with a force that has not yet spent itself, as the work of some modern theologians and dismayed intellectuals shows.[27] In his doctrine of the Elect, for which he drew on Pauline and Augustinian sources, Calvin went as far as one may go in announcing the incomprehensible sovereignty of God, the desolate frailty of man. Through Adam's fall, to which his free will led him, human nature is "vuide et destituée," capable only of "toute espece de mal."[28] God, in his omnipotence, of course has no compulsion to save any human from the damnation the race has incurred. "Nostre perdition donc precede de la couple de nostre chair: et non pas de Dieu."[29] But because He is, among other things, a God of "misericorde," He takes pity and chooses

[23] *Institute*, I, 42.
[24] *Ibid.*, I, 82.
[25] *Ibid.*, I, 105.
[26] *The Institution of Christian Religion*, II.i (fol. 4ʳ).
[27] The revival of Calvinism among contemporary intellectuals is notable. See Philip Blair Rice, "Thomas Mann and the Religious Revival," *The Kenyon Review*, VIII (1945), 361-77; Randall Jarrell, "Freud to Paul: The Stages of Auden's Ideology," *Partisan Review*, XII (1945), 437-57. Franz Kafka's "In the Penal Colony" might be construed as an allegory of Calvinism: it describes the infernal machine that finally destroys the officer who operates it; and K., the hero of *The Trial*, feels so keenly the guilt for the unspecified crime with which he is charged that at last he submits without a struggle to his execution. T. S. Eliot's views on original sin are, of course, too well-known to cite.
[28] *Institute*, I, 37.
[29] *Ibid.*, I, 38.

—arbitrarily, for He is above contingency—to permit some to be saved, however unjustly and irrationally. He elects His saints, and they can no more resist His irresistible grace than the damned majority can evade their eternal torment. Thus through predestination, which Calvin himself had the decency to call a *decretum quidem horribile,* some are chosen for salvation, others for real and fiery damnation.

Nous appelons Predestination le conseil eternel de Dieu par lequel il a determiné ce qu'il voulait faire d'un chacun homme. Car il ne les crée pas tous en pareille condition: mais ordonne les uns à vie eternelle les autres à eternelle damnation.[30]

This transaction depends upon nothing but God's will. It is impious to justify it, or to circumscribe it with human criteria of reason.

Thys counsel as touching the elect, we say to be groūded vpon his [i.e. God's] free mercie without any respect of the worthinesse of man: but whom he appointeth to damnatiō, to them by hys iugement which is in dede iust and irreprehensible but also incōprehensible, ye entrie of lyfe is forclosed.[31]

That one man is elected for salvation while another (whose life is perhaps one of incessant but futile good works) is damned may perplex us, but it pleases God. "But if you proceed further to ask why He pleased," warns Calvin, "you ask for something greater and more sublime than the will of God, and nothing such can be found." [32] God's majesty is celebrated by the piety of the elect (whose piety is forced upon them); it is exalted by the sinfulness of the damned.[33] Each man is what he is because God has willed it so. The "seul plaisir de Dieu" is the ultimate fact of the universe.[34]

The doctrine of predestination has a sort of terrifying sublimity. In an age of aggression, of murderous economic and nationalistic exploitation, it served to remind man, feeble man, that his destiny lay ultimately be-

---

[30] *Ibid.,* II, 471.

[31] *The Institution of Christian Religion,* II.xxi (fol. 242ᵛ).

[32] Quoted by Georgia Harkness, *John Calvin: The Man and His Ethics* (1931), p. 70. It should be said that Catholic theologians deny the soft impeachment that Calvin's theology is Augustinian. For Calvin, original sin is not, as for Catholics, Adam's transmitted guilt, or the deprivation of grace, or concupiscence; "it is a profound and complete subversion of human nature; it is the physical alteration of the very substance of the soul. Our faculties, understanding, and will, if not entirely destroyed, are at least mutilated, powerless, and chained to evil" (Eugène Portalié in *The Catholic Encyclopedia,* II, 101). At the Synod of Dort (1618-1619) the rigors of Calvinistic theology were codified into the five doctrines of unconditional election, limited atonement, total depravity, irresistibility of grace, and final perseverance of the saints. See Schaff, *The Creeds of Christendom,* II, 550-97.

[33] See Troeltsch, *The Social Teachings of the Christian Churches,* II, 583.

[34] *Institute,* II, 479.

yond himself. As such, it was a radical departure from the humanistic tradition of rational self-control as the key to human conduct. Like the *danse macabre,* predestination was a dramatic *memento mori* that humiliated man without in any way restricting his activites. If all man's deeds are as nothing against the will of a capricious and omnipotent God, then man is in effect free, either to wallow in his sense of sin or to find surcease in febrile temporal activity. In short, predestination implied a kind of Stoic determinism which released man from any sort of responsibility.[35] And as we shall presently see, if Calvin destroyed any anthropocentric basis for salvation, he at least legitimatized gainful economic activity. The Protestant world, which since the Renaissance has devoted its best energies to buying cheap and selling dear, has therefore found the substitution of economic for moral freedom a very good bargain.

For a certain type of mind Calvinism still exerts a cobra-like charm. It exemplifies deific democracy, for all men are equal in God's sight and neither good words nor secular glory can insure election. Grace can come only to him who has faith ("particular redemption"), and only the elect are capable of faith. In a universe created and dominated by a God like Calvin's, the elect may feel blissfully secure: they have a paid-up insurance policy good for eternity, and against the irresistible grace of God nothing can prevail. To a man like Jonathan Edwards, predestination was a "delightful doctrine, exceeding bright, pleasant and sweet." But to one like Milton, nurtured and sustained by the humanistic confidence in man's dignity based on moral and rational responsibility, no such despot as Calvin's God was worthy of a good man's respect.

### THE ECONOMIC SANCTION

The theology we have described—even though more anciently medieval than the rational, humanistic kind which supported orthodox Renaissance optimism—would seem to destroy any vestige of belief in the dignity of man. And, in terms of the humanistic tradition, it did so. But there were compensations. The individualism latent in Protestant theology was congenial to other sixteenth-century signs of independence: the emergence of the national state, the new prestige of the vernaculars, the common distrust of the Scholastic tradition. But it was in its economic implications that the Reformation most clearly reveals the new individualism. For the aristocratic moral values of a small minority of wealth and learning Calvin substituted a set of sanctions for economic (and, ultimately, political) leveling which made his theology indispensable for a burgeon-

---

[35] Note Donne's remark (*LXXX Sermons,* no. 68, p. 691): beware of predestination, for it "may bring thee to thinke, that God is bound to thee, and thou not bound to him."

ing capitalistic and democratic culture. We must now examine these sanctions.

Economic interpretations of history have been popular in our time, and the Renaissance and Reformation have been the favored haunts of those who read history as the manifestation of economic tensions. At any rate, it is important to remember that what we call the Renaissance coincided with the substitution of money and wages for the medieval economy of barter;[36] and after the famous studies of Weber, Troeltsch, and Tawney[37] it became—until the inevitable reaction set in—almost a commonplace to identify the rise of capitalism with the spread of the Protestant ethic over northern Europe and America. Thus, it was once popular to say that an economy glorifying free enterprise, initiative, individual aggressiveness, and even ruthless competition demanded a religion that justified such conduct, and that Protestantism met the demand during those centuries when men were still traditional enough to feel the need of a religious sanction for their secular activity. But since the rebuttals of Pirenne and Robertson[38] the Weber thesis has necessarily been modified. Robertson, particularly, has systematically restudied the question of correlating capitalism with Protestantism to reach the conclusion that capitalism was a necessary consequence of many factors: the nascent capitalism of the late Middle Ages, the nature of the Renaissance state, the softening Catholic attitude toward usury, the influence of geographical explorations—and therefore not wholly religious. Although in the following pages I shall of course take account of these views, I think that Weber's thesis has not been entirely discredited—Tawney is a powerful advocate—and I shall support the view that while the Reformation obviously did not cause capitalism, Protestantism has certainly profited by its advent and development. Although this is clearly not the place to treat all the factors in the rise of capitalism, the conjunction of capitalism and Protestantism—not yet explained away—is nothing if not relevant to a discussion of Protestant individualism.

In the Middle Ages Europe was a land-locked continent. With the sea

---

[36] See Preserved Smith, *The Age of the Reformation*, pp. 515 ff. This is the thesis of a very readable little book by Wallace K. Ferguson, *The Renaissance* (1940).

[37] Max Weber, *The Protestant Ethic and the Rise of Capitalism* (trans. Talcott Parsons, 1930); Ernst Troeltsch, *The Social Teaching of the Christian Churches* (trans. Olive Wyon, 1931); R. H. Tawney, *Religion and the Rise of Capitalism* (1926).

[38] Henri Pirenne, *Economic and Social History of Medieval Europe* (1936), esp. pp. 162 ff., 209 ff.; Henri Pirenne, "Les Périodes de l'Histoire Sociale du Capitalisme" in *Bulletin de la Classe des Lettres de l'Académie Royale de Belgique*, no. 5, 1914, pp. [258]-299; H. M. Robertson, *Aspects of the Rise of Economic Individualism: A Criticism of Max Weber and His School* (1935). For a popular restatement of Robertson's views see Lewis Mumford, *The Condition of Man*, pp. 159 ff.

closed by the Vikings in the north and the Moslems in the south, Europe was compelled to subsist on itself. The result was a land economy with no great need for foreign markets.[39] Rural isolation found its political counterpart in feudalism, under which land was the only form of wealth and source of power; its religious counterpart was Catholicism, which insisted on a hierarchal society and combated both social and economic leveling. As usual, the Church was not entirely disinterested. With its vast real estate holdings it was, as Tawney has said, "an immense vested interest, implicated to the hilt in the economic fabric, especially on the side of agriculture and land tenure."[40] It resisted the rise of the new middle class and the extension of property to the hitherto unpropertied classes just as it resisted the Spiritual Franciscans with their audaciously naive demand for evangelical poverty. Dante had explained that both Canon and civil law were designed to check "that cupidity which grows by the amassing of riches,"[41] but in the amassing of riches the Church itself was the worst offender.

Some of the early abortive attempts at reformation were directed principally at the venality of the Church, and the severity with which the Waldensians, the Fraticelli, and the Lollards were repressed indicated how much was at stake. The nameless horrors of the Albigensian crusade must remain the most heinous canonical mass murder by an institution which has never scrupled to employ such tactics when the need was urgent. As Voltaire took malicious glee in pointing out, the wanton luxury and avarice of the Papacy, no less than its shameless exploitation of the poor, must be accounted one of the immediate causes of the Reformation. Chaucer and the author of *Piers Plowman* wrote poetry, but they also served as recorders of fourteenth-century ecclesiastical corruption.

In short, the medieval Church was able to take a complacent attitude toward social ills, and a very denunciatory one toward any economic activity tending to disturb the *status quo*. Arguing from the Pauline text of the body and its members, the Church could accommodate any sort of social and economic disequilibrium. This world, after all, was but a wretched inn for the wayfaring Christian. As late as the sixteenth century, Sir Thomas Elyot accepted as a natural necessity the existence of a "multitude, wherein be contayned the base and vulgare inhabitantes not aduanced to any honour or dignitie,"[42] and he was merely echoing a long line of impeccable ecclesiastics.

[39] Pirenne, *Economic and Social History of Medieval Europe*, pp. 1-16.

[40] P. 55. See Robertson, p. 52, on the latent capitalism of the medieval Church.

[41] *Convivio*, IV.12.

[42] *The Gouernour*, I, 2. Note also More's typically medieval contempt for money (*Utopia*, pp. 98 ff., 160-61).

Likewise, the attitude of the Church toward usury—which we have dignified with the name "interest" and made the solace of unnumbered coupon-clippers and stockholders—was one of uncompromising opposition.[43] The man who buys cheap and sells dear, says Gratian, "is of the buyers and sellers who are cast forth from God's temple."[44] Sometimes profit was treated as wages (even Aquinas speaks of the "just price"), but pure interest on a loan involving no risk was anathema. *Homo mercator vix aut numquam potest Deo placere*.[45] As a conservative, Erasmus was properly snobbish toward the class—men who conduct sordid business by sordid methods, who lie, perjure themselves, steal, and cheat, but who none the less become important because they have gold rings on their fingers.[46]

Such opprobrium was common in Shakespeare's day, and for that matter long after, as Robertson skillfully demonstrates.[47] But gradually, through the seventeenth century, those whose elders had been properly scandalized at Volpone, Shylock, and Sir Giles Overreach[48] began to take a more complacent view of the sordid business of using money to make more money. This changing attitude coincided with, even if it was not caused alone by, the spread of the Reformation through northern Europe. It would be too much to say, of course, that Luther and Calvin reconstructed the economy of Europe by establishing urban society, city-states, nationalism, lay culture, and a money-economy. But Calvin at least did formulate a theology agreeable to the new spirit of economic aggressiveness. Although the old opposition to usury changed slowly—the modification of such mental habits is always glacially slow—and although many Protestant contemporaries of Bacon persisted in their opposition, the fact remains that Calvin and his seventeenth-century followers made a change possible. Calvin might equivocate, but his interests were clear, and the class which he attracted finally evolved the proper slogans for a rationalization of modern Protestant capitalism.

[43] See Andrew Dickson White, *A History of the Warfare of Science with Theology in Christendom* (1920), II, 264 ff.; John Strachey, *The Coming Struggle for Power* (1933), pp. 30 ff.; McIlwain, *The Growth of Political Thought in the West*, pp. 162 ff. On the moderation of the Catholic view see Robertson, pp. 133 ff.

[44] Quoted by Tawney, p. 35.

[45] See Pirenne, *Economic and Social History of Medieval Europe*, p. 14.

[46] *The Praise of Folly*, p. 69. See the *Enchiridion*, ch. XXXIV.

[47] Pp. 111 ff. The attitudes of Spenser and Chapman were not at all uncommon; see *The Faerie Queene*, II.vii.46 ff.; "Virgils Epigram of Play," *The Poems*, p. 234.

[48] See C. T. Wright, "Some Conventions Regarding the Usurer in Elizabethan Literature," *SP*, XXXI (1934), 176-97; Arthur B. Stonex, "Money-Lending and Money-Lenders in England during the 16th and 17th Centuries," *Schelling Anniversary Papers* (1923), pp. 263-85. For a bibliography of the numerous Elizabethan attacks on usury see *CBEL*, I, 845. Beard's condemnation (*The Theatre of Gods Ivdgements*, pp. 474 ff.) is typical.

With Luther, however, it was quite another matter. Luther, whose thinking was as burly as his person, was incapable of coherent economic theorizing. As Allen has said, he improvised as readily as the cold, doctrinaire Calvin systematized. His economic and political thought, in the light of his theology, should have been vehemently individualistic; but actually it tended to be medieval.[49] He construed the state as the secular manifestation of God's law (*natürlich Recht*), revealed either through the Scriptures or through the divine illumination of the believer.[50] Luther was quietistic and conservative, the son of a woodcutter who never lost his respect for his betters and the institutions protecting them. Although some of his followers in the seventeenth century were as liberal politically as they were theologically, Luther himself viewed the social hierarchy as the work of God, and urged it as a religious duty to stay in one's divinely appointed place.[51] Even in his celebrated concept of "calling" (*Beruf*) he referred, like medieval theologians, to the status allotted one *sub specie aeternitatis*.[52] To this, he insisted, the good Christian should dutifully cling. Thus civil disobedience—as brought home to Luther in the horrendous Peasants' Revolt for which he was at least partially to blame—filled him with revulsion and typically violent anger.

Drumb sol hie zuschmeissen, wurgen und stechen heimlich odder offentlich, wer da kan, und gedencken, das nicht gisstigers, schedlichers, teuffelischers sein kan, denn ein auffrurischer mensch, gleich als wenn man einen tollen hund todschlahen mus, schlegstu nicht, so schleght er dich und ein gantz land mit dir.[53]

He would always take sides with the man, he thundered, "who endures rebellion and against him who rebels, however justly." [54]

[49] See Grisar, VI, 86 ff.

[50] See J. W. Allen, *A History of Political Thought in the Sixteenth Century* (1928), pp. 15 ff.; cf. Tawney, pp. 88 ff. and Troeltsch, II, 554 ff.; Luther Hess Waring, *The Political Theories of Martin Luther* (1910), pp. 61 ff. On Luther's theories of natural law see R. H. Murray, *The Political Consequences of the Reformation* (1926), pp. 65-66.

[51] See Weber, *The Protestant Ethic*, p. 160. Luther, like many great men, had no great regard for consistency. In such works as his *Treatise on Christian Liberty* he is surprisingly liberal.

[52] See Grisar, VI, 65 ff.

[53] "Wider die räuberischen und mörderischen Rotten der Bauern," *Werke*, XVIII, 358. Luther wrote two other tracts against the Peasants' Revolt in 1525: "Ermahnung zum Freiden" (which urged on the rebels pious submission to their divinely appointed superiors), *Werke*, XVIII, 279 ff., and "Ein Sendbrief von dem harten Büchlein wider die Bauern," *Werke*, XVIII, 375 ff.

[54] See Allen, *A History of Political Thought in the Sixteenth Century*, p. 19. Robertson (pp. 11 ff.) makes much of the survival of the medieval notion of living contentedly in one's divinely ordained place. "The spirit of 'calling,' " he concludes (p. 27), "did not breed a spirit of capitalism. The spirit of capitalism was responsible for a gradual modification and attrition of the Puritan doctrine; and this attrition had barely begun in England before the Restoration."

Although, as we shall see, Calvin took a much more elastic view of "calling," he equivocated on the question of civil disobedience. It is true that he, perhaps reluctantly, condoned rebellion against unjust rulers when the people acted through their legal representatives or when the tyrant's abuse ran counter to the word of God,[55] and yet as a practicing politician he was a despot. However sympathetic he was to economic freedom, he was a political absolutist—and he, unlike Locke, was unaware of the paradox. The famous last chapter of the *Institute*, "Of civile gouernement," is nothing but a plea (of course heavily buttressed by scriptural citations) for medieval absolutism. God Himself decrees

that we be subiect not only to the gouernement of those princes which execute their office towarde vs well and with suche faithfulnesse as they ought, but also of all them, which by what meane soeuer it be, haue the dominion in possession although they performe nothyng lesse thā that which perteineth to the duetie of princes.[56]

His own tight little theocracy in Geneva must have reflected his notions of the ideal secular life—one of energetic self-seeking rigidly prescribed by a saintly oligarchy whose influence reached everywhere. In his zeal to restore the primal purity of Christianity, he would abolish the distinction between the ecclesiastical and the secular. Like the magistrates of Boston, the Consistory at Geneva formed an invulnerable theocracy. "A sin was a crime against the State: a crime was a sin against the Church."[57]

Politically, Calvin was a typical man of the sixteenth century. The cruel violence with which various contemporary sects insisted on their own "reforms"—the socialism and sexual anarchy of the Anabaptists of Münster, the denial of the Trinity by the Socinians—shows the temper of the times.[58] In its great princes like Henry VIII, François I, and Charles V as well as in its turbulent religious leaders, the age expressed its bent toward absolutism. For this tendency Machiavelli was the secular and Calvin the theological apologist. Although Nashe might mourn that men divided Christ's robe, men of Calvin's stripe shared the attitude (if not the theology) of Fielding's Parson Thwackum:

When I mention religion I mean the Christian religion; and not only the Christian religion but the Protestant religion; and not only the Protestant religion, but the Church of England.

[55] See G. P. Gooch, *Democratic Ideas in the Seventeenth Century* (2d ed., 1927), p. 7.

[56] IV.xx (fol. 168ᵛ). In a theocratic universe everything was, of course, for the best. "We nede not muche labor to proue that a wicked king is the wrath of God vpon the earth" (IV.xx [fol. 169ʳ]).

[57] Mumford, *The Condition of Man*, p. 189.

[58] See Buckley, *Atheism in the English Renaissance*, pp. 43-60.

In Geneva, Calvin achieved a fantastic theocracy: a governmental elite of approved clerics regulating to a hair's breadth the life of a bustling commercial city. Not until the saints came to Boston was there a comparable spectacle. Geneva was holy, but economically it had its eye on the main chance. Calvin borrowed money to inaugurate the manufacture of cloth and velvet; later, when the competition from Lyons proved too strong, he hit upon watchmaking.[59] But such secular acumen was welded to incorrigible piety. Few men now are vastly concerned over being supralapsarians or infralapsarians, but in those palmy days it might mean the difference between living comfortably or dying painfully. For as Coleridge said of the Puritans, the Genevans would not put on a corn-plaster without scraping a text over it. From 1542 to 1546 in Geneva, a town of perhaps 16,000 persons, there were fifty-eight executions and seventy-six banishments; to observe Christmas involved a heavy fine and imprisonment; after nine in the evening, only spies, ferreting out sin, might walk abroad; a little girl of thirteen was beaten with rods for declaring her preference for Catholicism; Gruet, a theologian who was imprudent enough to disapprove of one of Calvin's innumerable tracts, was put to the rack twice daily for a month; and of course, as posterity has never forgotten, Servetus died at the stake.[60]

But for all this political despotism, Calvin evolved a theology compatible with the economic anarchy of capitalism. As a member of the burgher class and a lawyer, he had none of Luther's peasantlike regard for keeping one's place. He developed the concept of "calling" into an attitude both congenial and indispensable to the emerging capitalism of Protestantism, which has always drawn its strength from the middle class. To Calvin, calling meant the morally compulsory satisfaction of those obligations which a man's position in the world imposed upon him. We must remember, he warned, that it is the Lord's injunction to "euery man of vs in al the doinges of his life, to haue an eye to his calling, for his calling is holy, and euery mans seuerall kinde of life is vnto him as it were his standing apointed him by God."[61] But there is nothing in the Lord's

[59] See Troeltsch, II, 642.

[60] See Smith, *The Age of the Reformation*, pp. 171 ff.; Allen, *A History of Political Thought in the Sixteenth Century*, pp. 63 ff.; Harkness, *John Calvin*, pp. 34 ff. For contemporary documents on the rigors of the Genevan theocracy see Kidd, *Documents Illustrative of the Continental Reformation*, pp. 629 ff. Beza, Calvin's coadjutor and biographer, explained that it was God's providence for Calvin not to "suffer his enemies to take breath" (*A Discovrse . . . containing the life and death of M. Iohn Caluin*, sig. A4ᵛ); and besides, Servetus was a "Spaniard of so cursed memorie . . . who was not a man, but rather a horrible monster, compounded of the ancient and newe heresies, and aboue all an execrable blasphemer against the Trinitie, and namely against the Eternitie of the sonne of God" (sig. A5ʳ).     [61] *The Institution of Christian Religion*, III.x (fol. 171ᵛ).

injunction to prevent a man's rising from one "standing" to another; and Calvin's unabashed advice for every man to lay up for himself as much treasure as possible, the corruption of moth and rust notwithstanding, marks a sharp departure from the medieval, Catholic view toward economic activity. The good things that we may obtain through righteous toil signify the bounty of God; they are "apointed for oure cōmoditie, that they may be as things deliuered vs to kepe, whereof we must one day yelde an accompt. We must therefore so dispose them, that this saying may be continually found in our eares, yeld an accōpt of thy baylywike." [62]

This emphasis on stewardship and thrift—great Protestant virtues—is important, for such economic habits enable a man to keep what he has and get more. This distinction between Calvin's and Luther's views was that a man's position is not necessarily the one he is born to, but the one he achieves by his industry and frugality. The world is to be saved for God, and the best missionary is he who gains credit by conquering the world. Labor and perseverance toward a certain (economic) goal become admirable; poverty is not holy but deplorable and even sinful. For Calvin there was a sharp difference between humble Christian submission to the will of God and the Stoic disregard of such good things as the fruits of labor. A man who does not enjoy the benefits of this world is "comme une pierre." [63] Even though Christians' life on earth is but a "iorney through a straunge countrey, by whiche they trauayle towarde the kingdome of heauen," they should travel as comfortably as possible. "If we must but passe through the earth, doubtlesse we ought so far to vse the good thynges of the earth, as they may rather further than hynder our iourney." The world is slippery, and we should therefore "labour to fasten our foote there, where we maye stande safely." [64] Therefore away with that "unnaturall Philosophie" that urges us to use only the necessities of life and thus "doth niggardly bereue vs of the lawefull vse of Gods liberalitie." [65] Although salvation is reserved for the Elect, the glorification of God is every man's duty, and aggressive action pleases Him as much as prayer. The world is sanctified by good (that is, economically advantageous) works which, though they cannot purchase salvation, can testify that the worker is worthy of his reward. [66]

It is not surprising that the Genevans, the Scotch, the New Englanders (to say nothing of the dissenting Whigs who challenged the Stuarts, or the Huguenots whom Louis XIV finally drove from France in 1685

[62] *Ibid.*, III.x (fol. 171ʳ).
[63] *Institute*, II, 807.
[64] *The Institution of Christian Religion*, III.x (fol. 157ʳ).
[65] *Ibid.*, III.x (fol. 157ᵛ).
[66] See Troeltsch, II, 583 ff., 641 ff.

to his own great disadvantage) were first and foremost men of business. A man of the world, a citizen and autocrat of a prosperous commercial city, Calvin had no scruples in urging the acquisition of wealth as a Christian's duty. As Tawney has pointed out, he performed for his century what Marx did for his: he provided pious rationalizations for the economic aspirations of the new middle class (who would not be denied), and by his doctrine of predestination he posited a sort of cosmic determinism comparable to the Marxist theory of historical materialism.[67]

When questioned about usury by Claude Sachins in 1545 Calvin delivered his most famous—and influential—opinion on the problem.[68] Perhaps realizing the enormous significance his words would have, he equivocated, and yet it is clear where his sympathies lay. Nowhere, he says, does the Bible expressly condemn usury; the position of the Papists (based on the misleading texts of Ambrose and Chrysostom) was superficial; indeed—and here the legalist speaks—the whole question is merely one of equity. Although Calvin hedged himself about with reservations —it was wrong to practice usury on the indigent, to exact more interest than a man could pay, to lend money against the interests of the state, etc., etc.—nevertheless there was nothing intrinsically evil in usury.

Whence proceeds the gain of a merchant? from his own activity, diligence and industry. Who doubts that money unemployed is altogether useless? but he who asks a loan of me does not think to have it by him unoccupied after he has received it from me. It is not therefore from the money that the profit grows, but from production. And so the arguments are indeed subtile, and have a certain speciousness, but where they are examined more closely they collapse entirely.[69]

The results of this sanction, halfhearted though it was, were momentous for the history of Protestant Europe. Thrift, sobriety, industry— all virtues making for solvency—became the adornments of the true Christian, and led ideally to the consummation of the Protestant hero: the successful businessman. The sacred right of property began to assume its capitalistic sanctity. Solvency and holiness, by some odd transmogrification of the words of Christ, were thought to be synonymous. Of course, one should always remember that God in His wisdom disposes of us as He wills, and that our main effort should be to submit to His inscrutable power. But Sunday comes but once a week, as any good banker knows,

---

[67] P. 112.

[68] See Robertson, pp. 115 ff., who tries to minimize the originality of Calvin's pronouncement. The logical extension of Calvin's views are to be found, with increasing emphasis, in works like Johann Gerhard's *Locorum Theologicorum Tomus Sextus* (1610 ff.), G. Ames' *De Conscientia* (1631), and Claude Saumaise's (Salmasius') *De Usuris* (1638).

[69] Quoted by Robertson, p. 116.

and for six days out of seven man may very happily make believe that economic competition is his main function. Calvin expressly condones this major hypocrisy of our culture: "they which vse this world, should be so minded as though thei vsed it not, they y$^t$ mary wives as though they did not mary: they y$^t$ bye as though thei did not bye, as Paul teacheth." [70]

Hence the innumerable pronouncements on the righteousness of economic gain. The Protestants rationalized and even sanctified the ruthless commercialism of what, after the sixteenth century, became the acquisitive society.[71] The new *bourgeoisie* had a new theology permitting the most drastic sort of economic individualism. Such dissimilar contemporaries as Bishop Hall and John Donne both justified the new morality. One refused to condemn usury outright ("many circumstances are considerable, ere any thing can be determined");[72] the other argued that poverty is an incentive to sin, "and therefore labour wee all earnestly in the wages of some lawfull calling, that we may have our portion of this world by good meanes." [73] As Weber has shown, in the eighteenth century occurred the full flowering of burgher morality. Indeed, it is easier to find beautifully explicit formulations of the religio-economic creed in the time of Franklin than in the time of Milton; for by that time the Protestant virtues had become incarnate in scores of worthies. The eighteenth century produced both the dazzling successes and the emphatic sanctions of Anglo-Scottish capitalism. *The New Whole Duty of Man,* the burgher's enchiridion from the time of the Georges almost to our grandfathers' day, may be taken as typical of the countless equations of economic gain and godliness.

At titular dignities intitle men to an outward respect and observance, so also doth wealth and large possessions; for, when God bestows upon one man a larger fortune and possession than on another, he doth thereby prefer and advance him into an higher sphere and condition; and when God hath set him above us, it is just and fit that we should rise and give that place to him which is of God's appointment.[74]

Is it any wonder that in our own day, so godly a man as John D. Rocke-

---

[70] *The Institution of Christian Religion,* III.x (fol. 171$^r$).

[71] In England, the Parliamentary act of 1552 which had denounced and prohibited the taking of interest was repealed in 1571.

[72] "Resolutions and Decisions" in *Anglicanism* (ed. More and Cross), p. 676.

[73] *LXXX Sermons,* no. 65, p. 659. William Butler Yeats once said (*Autobiography,* p. 90) that even as a boy he was struck by the fact that Protestant Ireland "seemed to think of nothing but getting on in the world."

[74] Quoted by Robertson, p. 24. Note the advice of Melville's Captain Bildad to his sailors about whaling on the Lord's day (*Moby Dick,* ch. XXII). For some of the cognate attitudes in contemporary American culture see Robert S. and Helen Lynd, *Middletown* (1929), pp. 458 ff.

feller has declared it the "religious duty" of every man to make as much money as possible?

Thus without ignoring either Weber or Robertson we may conclude, I think, that even if Protestantism did not cause capitalism, none the less the two regimens, one religious and the other economic, have been reciprocally advantageous. Whatever their causal relationship, the genius of Protestantism has been intimately involved in the development of our modern capitalistic culture. When Bacon, ignoring the internal moral problems that the contemporary dramatists were treating in literature, urged man to go outside himself and find fulfillment in action (for knowledge is power—over things) he was, whether he knew it or not, enunciating the new burgher morality. It was a morality that was to destroy the Socratic equation of knowledge with virtue;[75] and although Protestant theology denied man's claims to the dignity based on rational conduct, it enabled him to find a new dignity in the economic exploitation of his environment. Plato's Gorgias once said, long ago, that the greatest good for man was that which "gives to men freedom in their own persons, and to individuals the power of ruling over others in their several states."[76] Socrates, for whom knowledge was virtue, challenged this; but Bacon, for whom knowledge was power, could only concur.

In spite of an economy that made it difficult, there had of course been the pursuit of wealth in the Middle Ages; but the late seventeenth century in England presents the spectacle of a whole nation addressing itself to such pursuit—and reshaping its church and state accordingly. After the failure of Laud and the Westminster Assembly, the die was cast. Only the very unworldly could any longer suggest the slightest correlation between the Sermon on the Mount and man's economic activity. The control and profitable exploitation of nature, so eloquently and brazenly preached by Bacon, became the new *summum bonum*. The Civil War in England resolved itself into a contest between the new middle class and the old hereditary aristocracy, and the Parliamentary triumph, with the subsequent explanations of Locke, demonstrated the proposition that the end of government is the protection of property. For all except a tiny old-fashioned minority, political economy, no less than theology, became secularized. The modern capitalistic state is rarely concerned with seeking its justification from religion; it has become an institution for insuring the right of each man to pursue his economic activity without interference, and to protect the goods he has acquired. Thus, as Mr. Thur-

---

[75] See Theodore Spencer, *Shakespeare and the Nature of Man* (1942), p. 206.
[76] *Gorgias*, 452.

man Arnold has said, the greatest modern heresy is the injection of social conscience—or governmental "meddling"—into our economy.[77]

By and large, the modern church has tamely concurred, revising its traditional views where revision was indicated. Mr. John Crowe Ransom has suggested that Puritanism, which has so profoundly influenced the morality of the Protestant world, has ignored an organic synthesis of all man's activities in order to insist on isolated perfection. Certainly, economic activity has become virtually the only kind for the modern man: other activities are suffered only as appendages and adornments to his prime function of making his way in the competitive struggle for gain.[78]

Although these are only fuzzy generalizations they could, I think, be established in a careful study of man's attitude toward himself after the Renaissance. It surely is not too much to say that the coalescence of religious and economic ideas developed in the seventeenth century had implications that reached far into the future. For the believer, both spiritual and temporal well-being became an entirely personal matter. Group feeling and social obligations as well as reliance on ritualistic or priestly institutions lost their strength, and the exfoliation of Protestant sects since the sixteenth century reveals the loss of unity and cohesion that, for better or worse, made Rome so strong for so long. The individual was driven to make his way, in this world and the next, in terrible isolation. After the Reformation, the feudal and ecclesiastical collectivism of northern Europe was only a memory—at least until a new kind of collectivism arose in our own time. Moreover, since modern Protestantism has subsisted largely on Augustine's bleak estimate of man's rational and moral capacities, the appraisal of human dignity in the old-fashioned terms of humanism has steadily deteriorated. But there are always compensations: in our Protestant culture we have found a new and perhaps more genuine expression of human dignity in democratic equalitarianism, and we have (to our cost) enjoyed the hazardous joys of economic individualism. The history of thought teaches us that if we lose one prop for human dignity we can always construct another.

[77] See Harold J. Laski, *The Rise of European Liberalism* (1936), pp. 19 ff. for a pungent discussion of the pursuit of wealth and its ideological implications in postmedieval thought.

[78] Some of the social effects of the Protestant ethic in the seventeenth century are interestingly discussed by Robert K. Merton in "Science, Technology, and Society in Seventeenth-Century England," *Osiris*, IV (1938), 439 ff.

ALTHOUGH A BOOK OF THIS SORT really has no end, our glance at Protestant theology is a convenient stopping-place. For to go further would be to show how after the sixteenth century the ancient belief in human dignity was subjected to questions so new and so searching that they have not yet been answered.

However, if a conclusion to these studies be wanted, it is, I think, that from Socrates to Milton men had generally agreed that there is such divinity doth hedge a man as to set him apart from all other mortal creatures. Although in the long course of two thousand years the grounds for this conviction varied to suit various climates of opinion, it has been possible to isolate some of the basic and recurrent motifs that gave continuity to the belief in human dignity.

The great Hellenic veneration for reason informed the classical conception both of the cosmos and of man's place in it. As a rational creature uniquely capable of rational knowledge of the highest truth—variously the ideal, or forms, or *physis,* or whatever—man was clearly superior to all lower orders of life, finding his highest good and his highest virtue in that knowledge which conferred upon him his dignity.

Although it underwent a formidable reëxamination from the early Church and Augustine, this majestic notion endured, *mutatis mutandis,* through the Middle Ages and on into the Renaissance. Augustine's view of man was obviously not Aristotle's, but at least it was sufficiently Platonic to enable him, while despising man for his congenital infirmities, to dignify him with the hope of salvation. For even the sinful spawn of Adam could know the transcendent truth of God (by faith if not by conceptual thought), and this was the knowledge essential for an immortality of beatitude. Toward the end of the Middle Ages, when Aquinas crowned the long Scholastic effort to synthesize the two massive traditions of Hellenic reason and Christian faith, a thinking man could enjoy a degree of assurance concerning himself and his place in nature that, to our incredulous gaze, seems sublime.

By and large, the Renaissance through the great inherited principle of order could maintain an optimism that makes us envious. The Renaissance is not entirely a misnomer—it did plant those seeds that would germinate into our modern world of materialism, clashing nationalisms, capitalism—but by taking a wider perspective than the *philosophes* of the eighteenth century were capable of, we may now admit that in the history of thought the Renaissance quite as well rung down the curtain on the old world as it served as prologue for the new. As far as the topic of this book is concerned, the era of Erasmus, Luther, Spenser, and Milton obviously venerated tradition: it was an era when old ideas were rediscovered and restated—one in which, despite its collision of ideologies, the immemorial tradition of human dignity was a bulwark and a solace.

But since this book must merely stop, rather than come to a real conclusion, it is well to stop with the transitional figures of the great Reformers. Although they jeopardized the optimism derived from a rational, natural theology, they were, chronologically and emotionally, men of the sixteenth century. Nonetheless, the political and economic extension of their views has so dominated the modern world as to make the Renaissance seem quaint; and the philosophical implications of the new science have, since the seventeenth century, been of such urgency as to unsettle if not demolish the evaluation of human nature which gave the Renaissance its central meaning.

That, however, is obviously another story.

FINIS

# BIBLIOGRAPHY

In order to keep the tail from wagging the dog I have restricted this bibliography to those works actually quoted in the text and to only the most significant works cited in the notes. There are a few cross-references (e.g. P. S. Allen-Erasmus) to facilitate the use of the bibliography, and the original date of publication has been indicated parenthetically for certain works (e.g. *The Education of Henry Adams*) that in the text have been quoted from reprints. The following abbreviations have been used in both notes and bibliography:

| | |
|---|---|
| CBEL | The Cambridge Bibliography of English Literature |
| EETS | Early English Text Society |
| ELH | English Literary History |
| JEGP | Journal of English and Germanic Philology |
| JHI | Journal of the History of Ideas |
| LCL | Loeb Classical Library |
| MLN | Modern Language Notes |
| MLQ | Modern Language Quarterly |
| MLR | Modern Language Review |
| MP | Modern Philology |
| PG | Patrologia Graeca |
| PL | Patrologia Latina |
| PMLA | Publications of the Modern Language Association |
| PQ | Philological Quarterly |
| SP | Studies in Philology |

Abelard, Pierre, *Ethics,* trans. J. Ramsay McCallum, 1935.
——, *Historia Calamitatum,* trans. Henry Adams Bellows, 1922.
Achelis, Werner, *Die Deutung Augustins,* 1921.
Adams, Henry, *The Education of Henry Adams,* The Modern Library, 1931. (Privately printed, 1907; reprinted for the Massachusetts Historical Association, 1918.)
Adcock, F. D., "The Reform of the Athenian State," *The Cambridge Ancient History,* IV (1926), 26-58.
Aeschylus, see Oates, Whitney J. and O'Neill, Eugene, Jr. (edd.), *The Complete Greek Drama.*
Agrippa, Henry Cornelius, *The Vanity of Arts and Sciences,* trans. Ja[mes] San-[ford], 1694.
Albright, Evelyn May, "Spenser's Cosmic Philosophy," PMLA, XLIV (1929), 715-59.
Alexander, Franz, *Our Age of Unreason,* 1942.
Algarotti, Francesco, *Sir Isaac Newton's Philosophy Explain'd for the Use of the Ladies,* trans. Elizabeth Carter, 2 vols., 1739.
Allen, J. W., *A History of Political Thought in the Sixteenth Century,* 1928.

Allen, P. S., *The Age of Erasmus*, 1914.

——, *Erasmus: Lectures and Wayfaring Sketches*, 1934.

—— (ed.), *Opus epistolarum des. Erasmi Roteredami*, 10 vols., 1906 ff.

—— (ed.), *Selections from Erasmus: Principally from the Letters*, 1906.

——, see Erasmus, Desiderius.

Ambrose, Bishop of Milan, *Some of the Principal Works*, trans. H. De Romestin, A Selected Library of Nicene and Post-Nicene Fathers, 2d ser., vol. X, 1896.

Anderson, Ruth Lelia, *Elizabethan Psychology and Shakespeare's Plays*, 1927.

Andreas Capellanus, *The Art of Courtly Love*, trans. John Jay Parry, 1941.

Angus, S., *The Mystery-Religions and Christianity*, 1925.

Apuleius of Madura, *The Metamorphoses or Golden Ass*, trans. H. E. Butler, 2 vols., 1910.

Aquinas, Thomas, *Selected Writings*, Everyman's Library, 1939.

——, *The Summa Contra Gentiles*, trans. the English Dominican Friars, 4 vols., 1924-1929.

——, *Summa Theologica*, trans. the Fathers of the English Dominican Friars, 2d ed., 22 vols. [1920?]-1925.

Arendzen, J. P., "Gnosticism," *The Catholic Encyclopedia*, VI, 592-602.

Aristotle, *The Works of Aristotle Translated into English under the Editorship of W. D. Ross*, Oxford University Press:

> *De Anima*, trans. J. A. Smith, vol. III, 1931.
>
> *Ethica Nicomachea, Magna Moralia, Ethica Eudema*, trans. W. D. Ross, vol. IX, 1925.
>
> *Metaphysica*, trans. W. D. Ross, vol. VIII, 1928.
>
> *Politica*, trans. Benjamin Jowett, vol. X, 1921.
>
> *Rhetorica*, trans. W. Rhys Roberts, vol. XI, 1924.

——, *On the Soul, Parva Naturalia, On Breath*, trans. W. S. Hett, LCL, 1925.

Arnim, Ioannes (ed.), *Stoicorum Veterum Fragmenta*, 4 vols., 1905-1924.

Arnold, E. Vernon, *Roman Stoicism*, 1911.

Arouet, François Marie (Voltaire), *Oeuvres complètes*, 52 vols., 1877-1885.

Ascham, Roger, *The Scholemaster* (1570), ed. Edward Arber, 1927.

Athanasius, Bishop of Alexandria, *Select Writings and Letters*, trans. Archibald Robertson, A Selected Library of Nicene and Post-Nicene Fathers, 2d ser., vol. IV, 1907.

Augustine, Bishop of Hippo, *The Works*, ed. Marcus Dods, 15 vols., 1872-1884:

> *The City of God*, trans. Marcus Dods, 2 vols., 1872-1884.
>
> *The Confessions*, trans. J. G. Pilkington, n.d.
>
> *A Treatise of Grace and Free Will*, trans. Peter Holmes, 1876.
>
> *The Enchiridion*, trans. J. F. Shaw, 1883.
>
> *The Letters*, trans. Marcus Dods and J. G. Cunningham, 2 vols., 1872-1875.
>
> *Of Marriage and Concupiscence*, trans. Peter Holmes, 1874.
>
> *On Christian Doctrine*, trans. J. F. Shaw, 1883.
>
> *On the Predestination of the Saints*, trans. Robert Ernest Wallis, 1876.
>
> *On the Soul and Its Origin*, trans. Peter Holmes, 1874.

*Background to Modern Science: Ten Lectures at Cambridge Arranged by the History of Science Committee 1936*, 1940.

Bacon, Francis, *The Works*, ed. James Spedding, Robert Leslie Ellis, Douglas Henon Heath, 10 vols., 1857 ff.

Bailey, Cyril, *The Greek Atomists and Epicurus*, 1928.

—— (ed.), *Epicurus: The Extant Writings*, 1926.

—— (ed.), *The Legacy of Rome*, 1924.

Baker, Richard B., *The Thomistic Theory of the Passions and the Influence Upon the Will*, 1941.

Bakewell, Charles M. (ed.), *Source Book in Ancient Philosophy*, 1909.

Baldwin, James Mark (ed.), *Dictionary of Philosophy and Psychology*, 3 vols., 1901-1905.

Baldwin, William, *A Treatise of Morall Philosophy. Wherein Is Contayned the Worthy Sayings of Philosophers, Emperors, Kings, and Orators . . .* (1597), "Enlarged" by Thomas Palfreyman, [1640?].

Barker, Ernest, "The Conception of Empire," *The Legacy of Rome*, ed. Cyril Bailey, 1924, pp. 45-89.

——, *Greek Political Theory: Plato and His Predecessors*, 2d ed., 1925.

Barton, G. A., *The Religions of the World*, 1937.

Baskervill, Charles Read, *English Elements in Jonson's Early Comedies*, Texas Studies in English, no. 1, 1911.

Battenhouse, Roy W., *Marlowe's "Tamburlaine": A Study in Renaissance Moral Philosophy*, 1941.

——, Chapman and the Nature of Man," ELH, XII (1945), 87-107.

Beard, Thomas, *The Theatre of Gods Iudgements*, 1631.

Beare, John Isaac, *Greek Theories of Elementary Cognition from Alcmaeon to Aristotle*, 1906.

Becker, Carl L., *The Heavenly City of the Eighteenth-Century Philosophers*, 1932.

Benedict, Ruth, *Patterns of Culture*, 1934.

Bennett, Josephine Waters, "Spenser's *Fowre Hymnes*: Addenda," SP, XXXII (1935), 131-57.

——, "Spenser's Garden of Adonis," PMLA, XLVII (1922), 46-80.

——, "Spenser's Venus and the Goddess of Nature of the *Cantos of Mutabilitie*," SP, XXX (1933), 160-92.

Bentley, Richard, *Works*, ed. Alexander Dyce, 3 vols., 1838.

Bernard of Clairvaux, *Life and Works*, ed. Dom John Mabillon, trans. J. Eales, 4 vols., 1889-1896.

Bevan, Edwyn, *Stoics and Sceptics*, 1913.

Beza, Theodore de, *A Discovrse . . . Containing the Life and Death of M. Iohn Caluin . . . Turned Out of Frenche into English, By I.S. in the Yeare of our Lord, M.D.LXIIII* [London, 1578?].

Boas, Franz (ed.), *General Anthropology*, 1938.

Boas, George, *The Major Traditions of European Philosophy*, 1929.

Boethius, Anicius Manlius Severinus, *The Theological Tractates . . . The Consolation of Philosophy*, trans. J. F. Stewart and E. K. Rand (*The Consolation*, trans. "I.T." [1609] and revised by J. F. Stewart), LCL, 1908.

Bohatec, J., "Calvin et l'Humanisme," *Revue Historique*, CLXXXIII (1938), 207-41; CLXXV (1939), 71-104.

Boissier, Gaston, *La Religion romaine d'Auguste aux Antonins*, 3d ed., 2 vols., 1884.

Boorde, Andrew, *A Compendyous Regyment or a Dyetary of Helth* (1542?), ed. F. J. Furnivall, EETS, ex. ser., no. 10, 1870, pp. 223 ff.

Bosset, Wilhelm, "Gnosticism," *The Encyclopaedia Britannica* (11th ed., 1910), XII, 152-59.

Boulting, William, *Giordano Bruno: His Life, Thought, and Martyrdom,* 1914.

Boyar, G. E. S., "Bartholomaeus Anglicus and His Encyclopaedia," JEGP, XIX (1920), 168-89.

Bradbrook, M. C., *The School of Night,* 1936.

Bredvold, Louis I., "Deism before Lord Herbert," *Papers of the Michigan Academy of Science Arts and Letters,* IV (1925), 431-43.

———, *The Intellectual Milieu of John Dryden,* 1934.

———, "The Religious Thought of Donne in Relation to Medieval and Later Traditions," *Studies in Shakespeare, Milton, and Donne,* University of Michigan Publications: Language and Literature, I (1925), 193-232.

———, "The Sources Used by Sir John Davies for 'Nosce Teipsum,'" PMLA, XXXVIII (1923), 745-69.

Breen, Quirinus, *John Calvin: A Study in French Humanism,* 1931.

Breton, Nicholas, *Melancholike Humours* (1600), ed., with an essay on Elizabethan melancholy, by G. B. Harrison, 1929.

Brewster, Sir David, *Memoirs of the Life, Writings, and Discoveries of Sir Isaac Newton,* 2d ed., 2 vols., 1860.

Brie, Friedrich, "Deismus und Atheismus in der Englischen Renaissance," *Anglia,* XLVIII (1924), 54-98, 105-68.

Briggs, William Dinsmore, "Political Ideas in Sidney's Arcadia," SP, XXVIII (1931), 137-61.

Bright, Timothy, *A Treatise of Melancholie,* reproduced from the 1586 edition with an introduction by Hardin Craig, 1940.

Brochard, Victor, *Les Sceptiques Grecs,* 1887.

Brooke, C. F. Tucker, "Sir Walter Ralegh as Poet and Philosopher," ELH, V (1938), 93-112.

Brown, Thomas, see Gelli, Battista.

Browne, Sir Thomas, *The Religio Medici & Other Writings* (1642), Everyman's Library, 1931.

Bruno, Giordano, *Innumerable Worlds* (1584) in John Toland, *Miscellaneous Works,* 2 vols., 1747, I, 316-49.

Buck, P. M., Jr., "On the Political Allegory in 'The Faerie Queene,'" *The University Studies of the University of Nebraska,* XI (1911), 159-92.

Buckley, George T., *Atheism in the English Renaissance,* 1932.

Bundy, Murray W., "Shakespeare and Elizabethan Psychology," JEGP, XXIII (1924), 516-49.

Burckhardt, Jacob, *The Civilization of the Renaissance in Italy* (1860), trans. S. G. C. Middlemore, n.d.

Burke, Kenneth, *Attitudes Towards History,* 2 vols., 1937.

Burnet, John, *Early Greek Philosophy,* 4th ed., 1930.

———, "The Socratic Doctrine of the Soul," *Proceedings of the British Academy 1915-1916,* pp. 235-59.

Burroughs, Josephine L., see Ficino, Marsilio.

Burton, Robert, *The Anatomy of Melancholy* (1621), ed. A. R. Shilleto, Bohn's Standard Library, 3 vols., 1896.

Burtt, E. A., *The Metaphysical Foundations of Modern Physical Science,* 1925.

Bury, J. B., *The Idea of Progress,* 1932.

Bush, Douglas, *The Renaissance and English Humanism,* 1939.

———, "Two Roads to Truth: Science and Religion in the Early Seventeenth Century," ELH, VIII (1941), 81-102.

Busson, Henri, *Les Sources et le développement du rationalisme dans la littérature française de la renaissance (1553-1601)*, 1922.

Butcher, A. H., *Some Aspects of the Greek Genius*, 1893.

Buyssens, E., "Spenser's Allegories," TLS, XXXIII (1934), 28.

———, "The Symbolism of the Faerie Queene, Book I," PQ, IX (1930), 403-406.

Cadoux, Cecil John, *The Historic Mission of Jesus*, n.d.

Calvin, John, *Institution de la religion chrestienne*, the text of the first French edition of 1541, ed. Abel Lefranc, Henri Chatelain, and Jacques Pannier, 2 vols., 1911.

———, *The Institution of Christian Religion, Wrytten in Latine by Maister Iohn Calvin, and Translated into Englysh According to the Authors Last Edition*, trans. Thomas Norton, 1561.

Camden, Carroll, "Marlowe and Elizabethan Psychology," PQ, VIII (1929), 66-78.

———, "Tamburlaine: The Choleric Man," MLN, XLIV (1929), 430-35.

Campbell, Lily B. (ed.), *The Mirror for Magistrates*, 1938.

———, *Shakespeare's Tragic Heroes: Slaves of Passion*, 1930.

Carlyle, R. W. and Carlyle, A. J., *A History of Medieval Political Theory in the West*, 6 vols., 1903 ff.

Carpenter, Edward, *Pagan & Christian Creeds*, 1920.

Case, Thomas, "Aristotle," *The Encyclopaedia Britannica* (11th ed., 1910), II, 501-22.

Cassirer, Ernst, *An Essay on Man*, 1944.

———, *Das Erkenntniss Problem in der Philosophie und Wissenschaft der neueren Zeit*, 3 vols., 1922.

———, "Ficino's Place in Intellectual History" (a review of Paul Oskar Kristeller, *The Philosophy of Marsilio Ficino*), JHI, VI (1945), 483-501.

———, "Giovanni Pico della Mirandola," JHI, III (1942), 123-44, 319-46.

———, *Individuum und Kosmos in der Philosophie der Renaissance* (1927).

Castiglione, Baldassare, *The Book of the Courtier* (1528), trans. Sir Thomas Hoby, ed. Walter Raleigh, The Tudor Translations, 1900.

Caxton, William, *Mirrour of the World* (1481), ed. Oliver H. Prior, EETS, ex. ser., no. 110, 1913.

Chambers, R. W., *The Place of St. Thomas More in English Literature and History*, 1937.

Chapman, George, *The Poems*, ed. Phyllis Brooks Bartlett, 1941.

———, *The Tragedies*, ed. Thomas Mac Parrott, 1910.

Charron, Pierre, *Of Wisdom* (1601), trans. Samson Lennard, 1670.

Cheney, Sheldon, *Men Who Have Walked With God: Being the Story of Mysticism Through the Ages*, 1945.

Cicero, Marcus Tullius, *De Finibus Bonorum et Malorum*, trans. H. Rackham, LCL, 1914.

———, *De Officiis*, trans. Walter Miller, LCL, 1938.

———, *De Re Publica, De Legibus*, trans. Clinton Walker Keyes, LCL, 1928.

———, *Tusculan Disputations*, trans. J. E. King, LCL, 1927.

*Clement of Alexandria*, trans. G. W. Butterworth, LCL, 1919.

Cochrane, Charles Norris, *Christianity and Classical Culture: A Study of Thought and Action from Augustus to Augustine*, 1940.

Coffin, Charles Monroe, *John Donne and the New Philosophy*, 1937.

Coleridge, Samuel Taylor, *The Table Talk and Omniana*, ed. T. Ashe, Bohn's Standard Library, 1884.

Conger, George P., *Theories of Macrocosms and Microcosms in the History of Philosophy*, 1922.

Cook, Arthur Bernard, *Zeus: A Study in Ancient Religion*, 3 vols., 1914-1940.

Copernicus, Nikolaus, see Rosen, Edward.

Cornford, Francis MacDonald, *Before and After Socrates*, 1932.

———, *From Religion to Philosophy: A Study in the Origins of Western Speculation*, 1912.

———, *Greek Religious Thought: From Homer to the Age of Alexander*, 1923.

———, "Mystery Religions and Pre-Socratic Philosophy," *The Cambridge Ancient History*, ed. J. B. Bury, S. A. Cook, F. E. Adcock, IV (1926), 522-78.

———, "Mysticism and Science in the Pythagorean Tradition," *Classical Quarterly*, XVI (1922), 137-50.

Coulton, G. G., *Ten Medieval Studies*, 3d ed., 1930.

Craig, Hardin, *The Enchanted Glass: The Elizabethan Mind in Literature*, 1936.

———, "Shakespeare's Depiction of the Passions," PQ, IV (1925), 289-301.

———, see also Bright, Timothy.

Croll, Morris W., "Attic Prose: Lipsius, Montaigne, Bacon," *Schelling Anniversary Papers* (1923), pp. 117-50.

Crump, C. G. and Jacob, E. F. (edd.), *The Legacy of the Middle Ages*, 1938.

Cumming, W. P., "The Influence of Ovid's Metamorphoses on Spenser's 'Mutabilitie' Cantos," SP, XXVIII (1931), 241-56.

Cumont, Franz V. M., *Les Religions orientales dans le paganisme romain*, 2d ed., 1909.


Dampier-Wetham, William Cecil, *A History of Science and its Relations with Philosophy & Religion*, 1930.

Dampier-Wetham, William Cecil and Dampier-Wetham, Margaret (edd.), *Cambridge Readings in the Literature of Science*, 2d ed., 1928.

Dannenberg, Friedrich, *Das Erbe Platons in England biz zur Bildung Lylys*, 1932.

Dante, Alighieri, *Convivio*, trans. William Walrond Jackson, 1909.

———, *The Latin Works*, The Temple Classics, 1929.

———, *The Inferno*, The Temple Classics, 1932.

———, *The Paradiso*, The Temple Classics, 1936.

———, *The Purgatorio*, The Temple Classics, 1933.

D'Arcy, Martin Cyril, *Thomas Aquinas*, 1933.

Davidson, William L., *The Stoic Creed*, 1907.

Davies, Sir John, *Complete Poems*, ed. Alexander B. Grosart, 2 vols., 1876.

De Burgh, W. G., *The Legacy of the Ancient World*, 1924.

Demos, Raphael, *The Philosophy of Plato*, 1939.

De Moss, W. F., "Spenser's Twelve Moral Virtues 'according to Aristotle,'" MP, XVI (1918), 23-28, 245-70.

De Wulf, Maurice, *History of Medieval Philosophy*, trans. Ernest C. Messenger, 2 vols., 1925-1926.

———, "Nominalism, Realism, Conceptualism," *The Catholic Encyclopedia*, XI, 90-93.

Dickinson, G. Lowes, *The Greek View of Life*, 12th ed., 1919.

Dickinson, John (trans.), *The Statesman's Book of John of Salisbury: Being the Fourth, Fifth, and Sixth Books, and Selections from the Seventh and Eighth Books, of the Policraticus,* 1927.

Diels, Hermann (ed.), *Die Fragmente der Vorsokratiker,* 5th ed., 3 vols., 1934 ff.

Dilthey, Wilhelm, *Weltanschauung und Analyse des Menschen seit Renaissance und Reformation* (vol. II of *Gesammelte Schriften*), 3d ed., 1923.

Diogenes Laertius, *The Lives and Opinions of Eminent Philosophers,* trans. C. D. Yonge, Bohn's Classical Library, 1901.

Donne, John, *Devotions upon Emergent Occasions, Together with Death's Duell,* The Abbey Classics, n.d.

———, *LXXX Sermons,* 1640.

———, *Fifty Sermons,* 1649.

———, *Poems,* ed. H. J. C. Grierson, 2 vols., 1912.

Douglas, Andrew Halliday, *The Philosophy and Psychology of Pietro Pomponazzi,* ed. Charles Douglas and R. P. Hardie, 1910.

Dowden, Edward, *Essays Modern and Elizabethan,* n.d.

Du Bartas, Guillaume de Salluste, *Deuine Weekes & Workes,* trans. Joshua Sylvester, 1605.

Duchesne, Louis, *Early History of the Christian Church,* trans. from the fourth French edition, 3 vols., 1909-1924.

Dudden, F. Holmes, *Gregory the Great,* 2 vols., 1905.

Dudley, Donald R., *A History of Cynicism,* 1937.

Dulles, Avery, *Princeps Concordia: Pico della Mirandola and the Scholastic Tradition,* 1941.

Dunbar, H. Flanders, *Symbolism in Medieval Thought and its Consummation in the Divine Comedy,* 1929.

Dunning, William Archibald, *A History of Political Theories: Ancient and Medieval,* 1902.

Durand, Dana B.; Baron, Hans; Cassirer, Ernst; *et al.,* "Originality and Continuity of the Renaissance," JHI, IV (1943), 1-74.

Durant, Will, *Caesar and Christ,* 1944.


Einstein, Lewis, *The Italian Renaissance in England,* 1913.

Eliot, T. S., *Selected Essays, 1917-1932,* 1932.

Elsee, Charles, *Neoplatonism in Relation to Christianity,* 1908.

Elyot, Sir Thomas, *The Boke Named the Gouernour* (1531), ed. Henry Herbert Stephen Croft, 2 vols., 1883.

———, *The Castel of Helthe.* Facsimile of the 1541 edition, with an introduction by Samuel A. Tannenbaum, 1937.

Epictetus, *The Discourses of Epictetus: With the Encheiridion and Fragments,* trans. George Long, n.d.

Epicurus, *The Extant Writings,* ed. and trans. Cyril Bailey, 1926.

Erasmus, Desiderius, *Ciceronianus,* trans. Izora Scott, 1908, Columbia University Contributions to Education: Teachers College series, no. 21.

———, *The Colloquies,* trans. N. Bailey, ed. E. Johnson, 2 vols., 1878.

———, *The Education of a Christian Prince,* trans. Lester K. Born, 1936.

———, *The Epistles,* ed. and trans. Francis Morgan Nichols, 3 vols., 1901-1918.

———, *Opera Omnia,* ed. Jean Le Clerc, 10 vols., 1703-1706.

———, *Opus Epistolarum,* ed. P. S. Allen, 10 vols., 1906 ff.

————, *The Praise of Folly,* trans. Hoyt Hopewell Hudson, 1941.

————, *Selections from Erasmus: Principally from the Letters,* ed. P. S. Allen, 1908.

————, see also Allen, P. S.

Erdmann, Johann Eduard, *A History of Philosophy,* trans. Williston S. Hough, 2d ed., 3 vols., 1891.

Euripides, see Oates, Whitney J. and O'Neill, Eugene, Jr., *The Complete Greek Drama.*

Eusebius, Bishop of Caesarea, *The Ecclesiastical History,* trans. Kirsopp Lake and H. J. Lawler, 2 vols., LCL, 1926-1932.

*Eusebius,* trans. A. C. McGiffert and E. C. Richardson, A Select Library of Nicene and Post-Nicene Fathers of the Christian Church, vol. I, 1904.


Fahie, J. J., "The Scientific Works of Galileo," *Studies in the History and Method of Science,* ed. Charles Singer, 2 vols., 1921.

Farnham, Willard, *The Medieval Heritage of Elizabethan Tragedy,* 1936.

————, "*The Mirrour for Magistrates* and Elizabethan Tragedy," JEGP, XXV (1926), 66-78.

Ferguson, Wallace K., *The Renaissance,* 1940.

Ficino, Marsilio, *Platonic Theology* (ca. 1482), trans. in excerpts by Josephine L. Burroughs, JHI, V (1944), 227-39.

Fife, Robert Herndon, "The Renaissance in a Changing World," *Germanic Review,* IX (1934), 73-95.

Figgis, John Neville, *The Political Aspects of S. Augustine's "City of God,"* 1921.

Fisher, George Park, *History of Christian Doctrine,* 1909.

Fletcher, Jefferson B., "Benivieni's 'Ode of Love' and Spenser's 'Fowre Hymnes,'" MP, VIII (1911), 545-60.

————, "A Study in Renaissance Mysticism: Spenser's 'Fowre Hymnes,'" PMLA, XXVI (1911), 452-75.

Forbes, Elizabeth Livermore, see Pico della Mirandola.

Frazer, Sir James George, *The Fear of the Dead in Primitive Religions,* 1933.

————, *The Golden Bough: A Study in Magic and Religion,* 1931.

————, *The Worship of Nature,* 2 vols., 1926.

Friess, Horace L. and Schneider, Herbert W., *Religion in Various Cultures,* 1932.

Frith, I., *Life of Giordano Bruno the Nolan,* revised by Moriz Carriere, 1887.

Fuller, B. A. G., *A History of Ancient and Medieval Philosophy,* 1938.

Funck-Brentano, F., *The Renaissance,* 1936.


Galen, Claudius, *On the Natural Faculties,* trans. Arthur John Brock, LCL, 1916.

Gasellee, Stephen (ed.), *An Anthology of Medieval Latin,* 1925.

Gelli, Battista, *The Circe . . . Consisting of Ten Dialogues Giving a Lively Representation of the Various Passions, and Many Infelicities of Humane Life* (1549), trans. Thomas Brown, 1702.

Gibbon, Edward, *The History of the Decline and Fall of the Roman Empire,* ed. H. H. Milman, 6 vols., 1862.

Gibson, Edgar C. S., *The Three Creeds,* 1912.

Gierke, Friedrich von, *Political Theories of the Middle Ages,* trans. F. W. Maitland, 1900.

Gilson, Étienne, *La Philosophie au moyen age,* 1930.

——, *The Philosophy of St. Thomas Aquinas,* trans. Edward Bullough, rev. G. A. Elrington, 1929.

Glover, T. R., *The Conflict of Religions in the Early Roman Empire,* 3d ed., 1909.

Gomperz, Theodore, *Greek Thinkers,* trans. L. Magnus and G. G. Berry, 4 vols., 1901-1912.

Gooch, G. P., *Democratic Ideas in the Seventeenth Century,* 2d ed., 1927.

Goodman, Christopher, *How Superior Powers Oght to be Obeyd* (1558), with a bibliographical note by Charles H. McIlwain, The Facsimile Text Society, 1931.

Grabman, Martin, *Die Geschichte der scholastischen Methode,* 2 vols., 1909-1911.

Graves, Frank P., *Peter Ramus and the Educational Reformation of the Sixteenth Century,* 1912.

Greenlaw, Edwin A., "A Better Teacher than Aquinas," SP, XIV (1917), 196-217.

——, "Sidney's *Arcadia* as an Example of Elizabethan Allegory," *Anniversary Papers by Colleagues and Pupils of George Lyman Kittredge,* 1913, pp. 327-337.

——, "Spenser and Lucretius," SP, XVII (1920), 439-64.

——, "Spenser's Influence on *Paradise Lost,*" SP, XVII (1920), 320-59.

——, "Spenser's Mutabilitie," PMLA, XLV (1930), 684-703.

Gregory the Great, *Selected Epistles,* trans. James Barmby, A Select Library of Nicene and Post-Nicene Fathers, 2d ser., vol. XIII, 1905.

Greville, Fulke, First Lord Brooke, *Poems and Dramas,* ed. Geoffrey Bullough, 2 vols., n.d.

Grisar, Hartmann, *Luther,* trans. E. M. Lamond, ed. Luigi Cappadelta, 6 vols., 1913-1917.

Grote, George, *A History of Greece* (1846 ff.), Everyman's Library, 12 vols., 1906.

Guazzo, M. Steevan, *The Civile Conversation* (1574), trans. George Pettie and Barth. Young, with an introduction by Sir Edward Sullivan, The Tudor Translations, 2 vols., 1925.

Guthrie, William Keith Chambers, *Orpheus and Greek Religion,* 1935.

Gwatkin, Henry Melvill, *Early Church History to A.D. 313.* 2 vols., 1912.

—— (ed.), *Selections From the Early Writers Illustrative of Church History to the Time of Constantine,* 1911.


Halliday, W. R., *The Pagan Background of Early Christianity,* 1925.

Hammond, William Alexander, *Aristotle's Psychology: A Treatise on the Principle of Life,* 1902.

Harkness, Georgia, *John Calvin: The Man and His Ethics,* 1931.

Harnack, Adolf, *Lehrbuch der Dogmengeschichte,* 2d ed., 3 vols., 1888-1890.

——, *The Mission and Expansion of Christianity in the First Three Centuries,* trans. James Moffatt, 2d ed., 2 vols., 1908.

——, *Monasticism: Its Ideals and History and the Confessions of St. Augustine,* trans. E. E. Kellett and F. H. Marseille, 1913.

——, "Neo-Platonism," *The Encyclopaedia Britannica* (11th ed., 1910), XIX, 372-78.

Harris, C. R. S., *Duns Scotus,* 2 vols., 1927.

Harrison, G. B., see Breton, Nicholas; also *Willobie his Avisa.*

Harrison, Jane Ellen, *Prolegomena to the Study of the Greek Religion,* 1903.

Harrison, John Smith, *Platonism in English Poetry of the Sixteenth and Seventeenth Centuries,* 1903.

Harrold, Charles Frederick, see Newman, John Henry.

Harvey, Gabriel, *Letter-Book*, ed. Edward John Long Scott, Camden Society Publications, 1884.

Haskins, Charles Homer, *The Renaissance of the Twelfth Century*, 1933.

Hasting, James (ed.), *Encyclopaedia of Religion and Ethics*, 13 vols., 1908 ff.

Hatch, E., *Influence of Greek Ideas and Usages upon the Christian Church*, 7th ed., 1898.

Hefele, Charles Joseph, *A History of the Christian Councils, from the Original Documents*, trans. William B. Clark, 2d ed., 5 vols., 1894-1896.

Heffner, Ray, "Spenser's Allegory in Book I of the Faerie Queene," SP, XXVII (1930), 142-61.

*Herodotus*, trans. Henry Cary, 1871.

Heywood, Thomas, *The Hierarchie of the Blessed Angells, Their Names, Orders and Offices*, 1635.

Hippolytus, *The Writings*, trans. S. D. F. Salmond, Alexander Roberts, and W. H. Rambant, 2 vols., Ante-Nicene Christian Library, vols. VI and IX, 1870-1879.

Hobbes, Thomas, *The English Works*, ed. Sir William Molesworth, 11 vols., 1839-1845.

Homer, *The Iliad*, trans. A. T. Murray, 2 vols., LCL, 1934-1937.

——, *The Odyssey*, trans. Sir William Marris, 1925.

Honorius Augustadunesis, *De Imagine Mundi Libri Tres*, Migne, PL, CLXXII, 121 ff.

Hooker, Richard, *Works*, ed. John Keble, 6th ed., 3 vols., 1874.

Huarte, Iohn, *Examen De Ingenios, The Examination of Men's Wits*, trans., from the Italian of M. Camillo Camilli by R[ichard] C[arew], 1616.

Huizinga, J., *Erasmus*, 1924.

——, *The Waning of the Middle Ages*, 1927.

Hulme, Edward Maslin, *The Renaissance the Protestant Revolution and the Catholic Reformation in Continental Europe*, 1914.

Hunt, R. N. Carew, *Calvin*, 1933.


*Imperatoris Iustiniani Institutionum*, ed. J. B. Moyle, 2d ed., 1890.

Inge, William Ralph, *Christian Mysticism*, 3d ed., 1913.

——, *The Philosophy of Plotinus*, 2 vols., 1918.

Irenaeus, *The Writings*, trans. Alexander Roberts and W. H. Rambant, 2 vols., Ante-Nicene Christian Library, vols. V and IX, 1869.


Jaeger, Werner, *Aristotle: Fundamentals of the History of his Development*, trans. Richard Robinson, 1934.

——, *Humanism and Theology*, 1943.

——, *Paideia: The Ideals of Greek Culture*, trans. Gilbert Highet, vols. I and II, 1939-1943.

Jarrell, Randall, "Freud to Paul: Stages of Auden's Ideology," *Partisan Review*, XII (1945), 437-57.

Jerome, Saint, *The Principal Works*, trans. W. H. Fremantle, A Select Library of Nicene and Post-Nicene Fathers, vol. VI, 1912.

Jevons, Frank Byron, *An Introduction to the History of Religions*, 5th ed., 1911.

Joad, C. E. M., *Guide to Philosophy*, n.d.

John of Salisbury, *Frivolities of Courtiers and Footprints of Philosophers: Being a Translation of the First, Second, and Third Books, and Selections from the Seventh and Eighth Books, of the Policraticus,* trans. Joseph B. Pike, 1938.

——, *The Statesman's Book . . . Being the Fourth, Fifth, and Sixth Books, and Selections from the Seventh and Eighth Books, of the Policraticus,* trans. John Dickinson, 1927.

Jones, H. S. V., "The 'Faerie Queene' and the Medieval Aristotelian Tradition," JEGP, XXV (1926), 283-98.

Jones, J. Walter, *Historical Introduction to the Theory of Law,* 1940.

Jones, Richard Foster, *Ancients and Moderns: A Study of the Background of the "Battle of the Books,"* 1936.

Jonson, Ben, *The Complete Plays,* Everyman's Library, 2 vols., 1910.

Jordan-Smith, Paul, *Bibliographia Burtoniana,* 1931.

Jowett, Benjamin, see Plato; Thucydides.

Jusserand, J. J., "Spenser's 'twelue priuate morall vertues as Aristotle hath devised,'" MP, III (1905-1906), 373-83.

Justin Martyr, *Dialogus Cum Tryphone Judea,* Migne, PG, VI, 471 ff.

——, *The First Apology,* trans. William Reeves (1717), with an introduction by John Kaye, n.d.

——, *The Writings,* trans. Marcus Dods, George Reith, B. P. Pratten, Ante-Nicene Christian Library, vol. II, 1867.

Kidd, B. J. (ed.), *Documents Illustrative of the Continental Reformation,* 1911.

—— (ed.), *Documents Illustrative of the History of the Church,* 2 vols., 1920-1923.

Krappe, Alexander Haggerty, *The Science of Folklore,* 1930.

Kreider, Paul V., *Elizabethan Comic Character Conventions as Revealed in the Comedies of George Chapman,* University of Michigan Publications: Language and Literature, vol. XVII, 1935.

Kristeller, Paul Oskar, "Ficino and Pomponazzi on the Place of Man in the Universe," JHI, V (1944), 220-27.

——, *The Philosophy of Marsilio Ficino,* trans. Virginia Conant, 1943.

Kristeller, Paul Oskar and Randall, John Herman, Jr., "The Study of the Philosophies of the Renaissance," JHI, II (1941), 449-96.

Labriolle, Pierre de, *History and Literature of Christianity,* trans. Herbert Wilson, 1925.

Lactantius Firmianus, Lucius Caelius, *The Works,* trans. William Fletcher, 2 vols., Ante-Nicene Christian Library, vols. XXI and XXII, 1871.

Landry, Bernard, *Duns Scot,* 1922.

Lang, Andrew, *Myth, Ritual, and Religion,* 2 vols., 1887.

La Primaudaye, Pierre, *The French Academie. Fvlly Discovrsed and Finished in Foure Bookes,* 1618.

Laski, Harold, *The Rise of European Liberalism: An Essay in Interpretation,* 1936.

Laurentius, Andreas, *A Discourse of the Preservation of the Sight: of Melancholike Diseases: of Rheumes, and of Old Age,* trans. Richard Surphlet, with an introduction by Sanford V. Larkey, Shakespeare Association Facsimiles, 1938.

Lecky, William Edward Hartpole, *History of European Morals,* 3d ed., 2 vols., 1926.

Lee, Sidney, *The French Renaissance in England*, 1910.

*The Legacy of Rome*, ed. Cyril Bailey, 1924.

*The Legacy of the Middle Ages*, ed. C. G. Crump and E. F. Jacobs, 1928.

Legge, F., *Forerunners and Rivals of Christianity*, 2 vols., 1915.

Lemnius, Levinus, *The Tovchstone of Complexions: Expedient and Profitable for all Such as bee Desirous and Carefull of their Bodily Health*, trans. T[homas] N[ewton], 1633.

Leonardo da Vinci, *The Literary Works*, ed. Jean Paul Richter, 2d ed., 2 vols., 1939.

Le Roy, Louis, *Of the Interchangeable Covrse, or Variety of Things in the Whole World*, trans. R. A., 1594.

Lewis, C. S., *The Allegory of Love: A Study in Medieval Traditions*, 1936.

Linforth, Ivan M., *The Arts of Orpheus*, 1941.

———, *Solon the Athenian*, vol. II (1919) of *Classical Philology*.

Lipsius, Justus, *Tvvo Bookes of Constancie*, trans. Sir John Stradling, ed. with an introduction by Rufold Kirk, notes by Clayton Morris Hall, 1939.

Loening, Richard, "Ueber die physiologischen Grundlagen der Shakespeare'schen Psychologie," *Jahrbuch der der deutschen Shakespeare Gesellschaft*, XXXI (1895), 1-37.

Lovejoy, Arthur O., *The Great Chain of Being: A Study in the History of an Idea*, 1936.

Lowie, Robert Harry, *Primitive Religion*, 1924.

Lucretius (Titus Lucretius Carus), *On the Nature of Things*, trans. H. A. J. Munro, Bohn's Popular Library, 1929.

Luther, Martin, *Luther's Correspondence and Other Contemporary Letters*, trans. and ed. Preserved Smith and Charles M. Jacobs, 2 vols., 1913-1918.

———, *Tischreden* (in the *Werke*, Weimar ed.), 6 vols., 1912 ff.

———, *Werke*, Weimar ed., 57 vols., 1883 ff.

Lynch, Kathleen, M., "Conventions of Platonic Drama in the Heroic Plays of Orrery and Dryden," PMLA, XLIV (1929), 456-71.

*Lyra Graeca*, trans. J. M. Edmonds, 3 vols., LCL, 1931-1940.

Macchioro, Vittorio D., *From Orpheus to Paul*, 1930.

McGiffert, Arthur Cushman, *A History of Christianity in the Apostolic Age*, rev. ed., 1899.

———, *A History of Christian Thought*, Vol. II: *The West from Tertullian to Erasmus*, 1933.

McIlwain, Charles Howard, *The Growth of Political Thought in the West: From the Greeks to the End of the Middle Ages*, 1932.

———, see Goodman, Christopher.

McIntyre, J. Lewis, *Giordano Bruno*, 1903.

McKeon, Richard (trans. and ed.), *Selections from Medieval Philosophers*, 2 vols., 1929-1930.

Maier, Heinrich, *Sokrates, sein Werk und seine geschichtliche Stellung*, 1913.

Mâle, Émile, *L'art religieux du XIIIᵉ siècle en France*, 5th ed., 1923.

Marcus Aurelius Antoninus, *The Communings with Himself . . . Together with his Speeches and Sayings* [i.e. *The Meditations*], trans. C. R. Haines, LCL, 1930.

Marlowe, Christopher, *Works*, ed. C. F. Tucker Brooke, 1929.

Marrou, Henri-Irénée, *Saint Augustine et la fin de la culture antique*, 1938.

Mead, George R. S., *Fragments of a Faith Forgotten*, 2d ed., 1906.

Mellone, S. H., "Scholasticism," Hasting's *Encyclopaedia of Religion and Ethics,* XI, 239 ff.

Merton, Robert K., "Science, Technology, and Society in Seventeenth Century England," *Osiris,* IV (1938), 360-632.

Mexio, Pedro, *The Treasvrie of Avncient and Moderne Times. Containing the Learned Collections, Iudicious Readings, and Memorable Obseruations,* [trans. Thomas Milles], 1613.

Michelet, Jules, *Oeuvres Complètes,* Édition Définitive, revue et corrigée, 40 vols., [1893 ff.].

Migne, Jacques Paul (ed.), *Patrologiae Cursos Completus, Series Graeca,* 161 vols., 1857 ff.

———, *Patrologia Cursos Completus, Series Latina Prior,* 291 vols., 1879 ff.

Milman, Henry Hart, *History of Latin Christianity,* 4th ed., 9 vols., 1863.

Milton, John, *Paradise Lost,* ed. Merritt Y. Hughes, 1935.

*Minucius Felix* (i.e. the *Octavius*), trans. Gerald H. Randall, LCL, 1931.

*The Mirror for Magistrates,* ed. Lily B. Campbell, 1938.

Moeller, Wilhelm, *History of the Christian Church: A.D. 1-600,* trans. Andrew Rutherfurd, 1912.

Mommsen, Theodor, *The History of Rome,* trans. William P. Dickson, 4 vols., 1874.

Montaigne, Michel Eyquem de, *The Essays,* trans. and ed. E. J. Trechmann, 2 vols., 1927.

*A Monument to Augustine: Essays on Some Aspects of his Thought Written in Commemoration of his 15th Centenary,* 1930.

Moore, Clifford Herschel, *The Religious Thought of the Greeks,* 1916.

Moore, George Foot, *History of Religions,* 2 vols., 1914-1920.

More, Louis Trenchard, *Isaac Newton,* 1934.

More, Paul Elmer, *Hellenistic Philosophies,* 1923.

———, *Platonism,* 1917.

More, Paul Elmer and Cross, Frank Leslie (edd.), *Anglicanism: The Thought and Practice of the Church of England, Illustrated from the Religious Literature of the Seventeenth Century,* 1935.

More, Sir Thomas, *The English Works,* ed. W. E. Campbell and A. W. Reed, vol. I, 1931.

———, *Utopia,* trans. Ralph Robinson, ed. Edward Arber, 1869.

Mornay, Philip of, *A Worke Concerning the Trunesse of Christian Religion* (1581), trans. Arthur Golding and Sir Philip Sidney, 1617.

Müller, Max, *Lectures on the Origin and Growth of Religion,* 1879.

Mumford, Lewis, *The Condition of Man,* 1944.

Mure, G. R. G., *Aristotle,* 1932.

Murray, Gilbert, *Five Stages of Greek Religion,* 1925.

———, *The Stoic Philosophy,* 1915.

Murray, Robert H., *Erasmus & Luther: Their Attitude to Toleration,* 1920.

———, *The Political Consequences of the Reformation,* 1926.


Nahm, Milton Charles (ed.), *Selections from Early Greek Philosophy,* 1934.

Nash, Thomas, *The Works,* ed. R. B. McKerrow, 5 vols., 1904-1910.

Nelson, Norman, "Individualism as a Criterion of the Renaissance," JEGP, XXXII (1933), 316-34.

Newton, Isaac, *Mathematical Principles of Natural Philosophy and his System of the World* (1687), trans. Andrew Motte, rev. and ed. Florian Cajori, 1934.

Newton, Thomas (trans.), *The Touchstone of Complexions* by Levinus Lemnius, 1633.

Newman, Albert Henry, *A Manual of Church History,* 2 vols., 1901-1903.

Newman, John Henry, *An Essay in Aid of a Grammar of Assent,* 1870.

———, *A Newman Treasury: Selections from the Prose Works of John Henry Cardinal Newman,* ed. Charles Frederick Harrold, 1943.

Nichols, Francis Morgan (trans. and ed.), *The Epistles of Erasmus,* 3 vols., 1901-1918.

Niebuhr, Reinhold, *The Nature and Destiny of Man: A Christian Interpretation,* Vol. I: *Human Nature,* 1941.

Nietzsche, Friedrich, *Beyond Good and Evil: Prelude to a Philosophy of the Future,* trans. Helen Zimmern, 1924.

———, *Ecce Homo and the Birth of Tragedy,* trans. Clifton Fadiman, The Modern Library, n.d.

Nilsson, Martin P., *A History of Greek Religion,* trans. F. J. Fielden, with a preface by Sir James G. Frazer, 1925.

Nock, Arthur Darby, *Conversion: The Old and the New in Religion from Alexander the Great to Augustine of Hippo,* 1933.

———, "Religious Developments from the Close of the Republic to the Death of Nero," *The Cambridge Ancient History,* X (1934), 465-511.

Norton, Thomas, see Calvin, John.


Oates, Whitney J. and O'Neill, Eugene, Jr. (edd.), *The Complete Greek Drama,* 2 vols., 1938.

Origen, *The Writings,* trans. Frederick Crombie, 2 vols., Ante-Nicene Christian Library, vols. X and XXIII, 1869.

Osgood, C. G., "Comments on the Moral Allegory of The Faerie Queene," MLN, XLVI (1931), 502-507.

———, "Spenser's Sapience," SP, XIV (1917), 167-77.

O'Sullivan, Mary Isabelle, "Hamlet and Dr. Timothy Bright," PMLA, XLI (1926), 667-79.

Owen, John, *The Skeptics of the Italian Renaissance,* 3d ed., 1908.

*The Oxford Book of Greek Verse in Translation,* ed. T. F. Higham and C. M. Bowra, 1938.


Padelford, F. M., "The Allegory of Chastity in *The Faerie Queene,*" SP, XXI (1924), 367-81.

———, *The Political and Ecclesiastical Allegory of the First Book of the Faerie Queene,* 1911.

———, "The Spiritual Allegory of the 'Faerie Queene,' Book One," JEGP, XXII (1923), 1-17.

———, "The Virtue of Temperance in the Faerie Queene," SP, XVIII (1921), 334-46.

Palmer, Henrietta R., *List of English Editions and Translations of Greek and Latin Classics Printed Before 1641,* 1911.

Panofsky, Erwin, *Studies in Iconology: Humanistic Themes in the Art of the Renaissance,* 1939.

Parrington, Vernon Louis, *Main Currents in American Thought: an Interpretation of American Literature from the Beginnings to 1920*, 3 vols., 1927-1930.

Petrarch, F., *Secret*, trans. William H. Draper, 1911.

Philo Judaeus, *The Works*, trans. C. D. Yonge, 4 vols., The Bohn Library, 1890.

Picavet, François, *Esquisse d'une histoire générale et comparée des philosophes médiévales*, 2d ed., 1907.

Pickman, Edward Motley, *The Mind of Latin Christendom*, 2 vols., 1937.

Pico della Mirandola, Giovanni, *Of Being and Unity (de ente et uno)*, trans. with an introduction by Victor Michael Hamm, 1943.

———, *Of the Dignity of Man*, trans. Elizabeth Livermore Forbes (in excerpts), JHI, III (1942), 347-354.

———, *Omnia Qvae Extant Opera*, 1557.

Pike, Joseph B. (trans.), *Frivolities of Courtiers and Footprints of Philosophers: Being a Translation of the First, Second, and Third Books and Selections from the Seventh and Eighth Books of the Policraticus of John of Salisbury*, 1938.

Pinto, V. de Sola, *The English Renaissance, 1510-1688*, 1938.

Pirenne, Henri, *Economic and Social History of Medieval Europe*, London, 1936; New York, 1937.

Plato, *The Dialogues*, trans. B. Jowett, 2 vols., 1937.

Pledge, H. T., *Science Since 1500*, 1939.

*Plotinus*, trans. Stephan MacKenna, 5 vols., 1917-1930.

Poole, Reginald Lane, *Illustrations of the History of Medieval Thought*, 1884.

Powell, C. L., "The Castle of the Body," SP, XVI (1919), 197-205.

Pseudo-Dionysius, see Migne, *Patrologia Graeca*.


Rabelais, François, *The Works*, trans. Urquhart-Le Motteux, ed. Albert Jay Nock and Catherine Rose Wilson, 2 vols., 1931.

Raleigh, Sir Walter, *The Works*, 8 vols., 1829.

Ramsay, M., *Les Doctrines médiévales chez Donne*, rev. ed., 1924.

Randall, John Herman, Jr., "The Development of Scientific Method in the School of Padua," JHI, I (1940), 177-206.

———, *The Making of the Modern Mind*, 1926.

Rashdall, Hastings, *The Idea of Atonement in Christian Theology*, 1919.

Reikel, August, *Die Philosophie der Renaissance*, 1925.

Reinach, Salomon, *Cultes, mythes et religions*, 2 vols., 1905-1906.

———, *Orpheus: A History of Religions*, trans. Florence Simmonds, 1930.

Renan, Ernest, *Marc-Aurèle et la fin du monde antique* (vol. VIII of the *Histoire des origines du Christianisme*), 1881.

Rice, Philip Blair, "Thomas Mann and the Religious Revival," *The Kenyon Review*, VII (1945), 361-77.

Ritter, Constantin, *The Essence of Plato's Philosophy*, trans. Adam Alles, 1933.

Ritter, Heinrich, *The History of Ancient Philosophy*, trans. Alexander J. W. Morrison, 4 vols., 1838-1846.

Robb, Nesca A., *Neoplatonism of the Italian Renaissance*, 1935.

Robertson, H. M., *Aspects of the Rise of Economic Individualism: A Criticism of Max Weber and his School*, 1935.

Robertson, J. M., *A Short History of Morals*, 1920.

Robbins, Frank Egleston, *The Hexaemeral Literature: A Study of the Greek and Latin Commentaries on Genesis*, [1912].

Robin, Léon, *Greek Thought and the Origin of the Scientific Spirit*, trans. M. B. Dobie, 1928.

Robin, P. Ansell, *The Old Physiology in English Literature*, 1911.

———, "Spenser's House of Alma," MLR, VI (1911), 169-73.

Rogers, Arthur Kenyon, *The Socratic Problem*, 1933.

Rohde, Erwin, *Psyche: The Cult of Souls and Belief in Immortality among the Greeks*, trans. from the 8th German edition by W. B. Hillis, 1925.

Rollins, Hyder Edward (ed.), Shakespeare's *Sonnets* (Variorum Edition), 2 vols., 1944.

Roper, William, *The Lyfe of Sir Thomas Moore, Knighte*, ed. Elsie Vaughan Hitchcock, EETS, vol. 197, 1935.

Rosen, Edward (trans. and ed.), *Three Copernican Treatises* (Copernicus' *Commentariolus* and *Letter Against Werner*, and Rheticus' *Narratio Prima*), 1939.

Ross, W. D., *Aristotle*, 2d ed., 1930.

Rostovtzeff, M., *A History of the Ancient World*, Vol. II: *Rome*, trans. J. D. Duff, 1927.


*St. Thomas Aquinas: Being Papers Read at the Celebrations of the Sixth Centenary of the Canonization of St. Thomas Aquinas*, 1925.

Sams, Henry W., "Anti-Stoicism in Seventeenth- and early Eighteenth-Century England," SP, XLI (1944), 65-78.

Schaff, Philip, *The Creeds of Christendom*, 3d ed., 3 vols., 1882.

Schoell, Frank L., *Études sur l'humanisme continental en angleterre à la fin de la renaissance*, Bibliothèque de la revue de littérature comparée, vol. XXIX, 1926.

Schweitzer, Albert, *Paul and his Interpreters: A Critical History*, 1912.

Sedgwick, Henry Dwight, *Marcus Aurelius*, 1922.

Seebohm, Frederic, *The Oxford Reformers*, 3d ed., 1896.

Semprini, Giovanni, *La Filosofia di Pico della Mirandola*, 1936.

Seneca, Lucius Annaeus, *Ad Lucilium Epistolae Morales*, trans. Richard M. Gummere, 3 vols., LCL, 1917-1925.

———, *Moral Essays*, trans. John W. Basore, 3 vols., LCL, 1933-1936.

*Sextus Empiricus*, trans. R. E. Bury, 3 vols., LCL, 1933-1936.

Shakespeare, William, *The Complete Works*, ed. George Lyman Kittredge, 1936.

Shorey, Paul, *What Plato Said*, 1933.

Sidgwick, Henry, *Outlines of the History of Ethics for English Readers*, with an additional chapter by Alban G. Widgery, 6th ed., 1939.

Sidney, Sir Philip, *The Complete Works*, ed. Albert Feuillerat, 4 vols., 1912-1926.

Sihler, Ernest G., *From Augustus to Augustine*, 1923.

Simpson, Evelyn M., *A Study of the Prose Works of John Donne*, 1924.

Singer, Charles (ed.), *Studies in the History and Method of Science*, 2 vols., 1921.

Singer, S., "Ueber die physiologischen Grundlagen der Shakespearischen Psychologie," *Jahrbuch der deutschen Shakespeare Gesellschaft*, XXXVI (1900), 65-94.

*Sir Thomas More . . . An Anonymous Play of the Sixteenth Century Ascribed in Part to Shakespeare*, ed. John Shirley, n.d.

Smith, F. Seymour, *The Classics in Translation*, 1930.

Smith, Gergory (ed.), *Elizabethan Critical Essays*, 2 vols., 1904.

Smith, Preserved, *The Age of the Reformation*, 1920.

———, *Erasmus: A Study of his Life, Ideals and Place in History*, 1923.

———, *The Life and Letters of Martin Luther*, 1911.

———, "Luther's Development of the Doctrine of Justification by Faith Only," *Harvard Theological Review*, VI (1913), 407-25.

———, see also Luther, Martin.

Smith, T. V. (ed.), *Philosophers Speak for Themselves: Guides and Readings for Greek, Roman, and Early Christian Philosophy*, 1934.

Sophocles, see Oates, Whitney J. and O'Neill, Eugene, Jr., *The Complete Greek Drama*.

Spencer, Theodore, *Death and Elizabethan Tragedy*, 1936.

——— (ed.), *A Garland for John Donne: 1631-1931*, 1931.

———, *Shakespeare and the Nature of Man*, 1942.

Spenser, Edmund, *The Complete Poetical Works*, ed. R. E. Neil Dodge, Student's Cambridge Edition, 1908.

———, *The Faerie Queene: Book II*, ed. Lilian Winstanley, 2d ed., 1919.

———, *The Fowre Hymnes*, ed. Lilian Winstanley, 1907.

———, *The Works*, the Variorum Edition, ed. Edwin Greenlaw, Charles Grosvenor Osgood, Frederick Morgan Padelford, vol. I, 1932.

Spicer, E. E., *Aristotle's Conception of the Soul*, 1934.

Sprat, Thomas, *The History of the Royal Society of London*, 4th ed., 1734.

Stace, W. T., *A Critical History of Greek Philosophy*, 1920.

———, *The Destiny of Western Man*, 1942.

Starkey, Thomas, *England in the Reign of King Henry the Eighth, a Dialogue between Cardinal Pole and Thomas Lupset, Lecturer in Rhetoric at Oxford*, ed. J. M. Cowper, EETS ex. ser., vol. 12, pt. 2, 1871.

Stewart, J. A., *The Myths of Plato*, 1905.

Stiglmayr, Jos., "Dionysius the Pseudo-Areopagite," *The Catholic Encyclopedia*, V, 13 ff.

Stonex, Arthur B., "Money-Lending and Money-Lenders in England during the 16th and 17th Centuries," *Schelling Anniversary Papers*, 1923, pp. 263-85.

Strachey, John, *The Coming Struggle for Power*, The Modern Library, 1933.

Strathmann, E. A., "Sir Walter Raleigh on Natural Philosophy," MLQ, I (1940), 49-62.

Strowski, Fortunant, *Montaigne*, 2d ed., 1931.

Sylvester, Joshua, see Du Bartas, Guillaume de Salluste.

Tarn, W. W., "Alexander the Great and the Unity of Mankind," *Proceedings of the British Academy*, XI (1933), 123-66.

Tawney, R. H., *Religion and the Rise of Capitalism: A Historical Study*, 1926.

Taylor, A. E., *Philosophical Studies*, 1934.

———, "Spenser's Knowledge of Plato," MLR, XIX (1924), 208-210.

Taylor, Henry Osborn, *Ancient Ideals*, 2d ed., 2 vols., 1913.

———, *The Classical Heritage of the Middle Ages*, 2d ed., 1903.

———, *The Medieval Mind*, 2 vols., 1911.

———, *Thought and Expression in the Sixteenth Century*, 2 vols., 1920.

Telesio, Bernardino, *De Rerum Natura*, ed. Vincenzo Spampanato, 3 vols., 1910-1923.

Tertullian, *The Writings*, trans. S. Thelwall and Peter Holmes, 3 vols., Ante-Nicene Christian Library, vols. XI, XV, XVIII, 1869-1870.

*Thucydides Translated into English*, trans. B. Jowett, 2 vols., 1881.

Tillyard, E. M. W., *The Elizabethan World Picture*, 1944.

Tod, Marcus, "The Economic Background of the Fifth Century," *The Cambridge Ancient History*, V (1927), 1-32.

Toffanin, Giuseppe, *Il Cinquecento*, 3d ed., 1929.

Toland, John, *Miscellaneous Works*, 2 vols., 1747.

Toynbee, Arnold Joseph, *A Study of History*, 6 vols. thus far, 1934 ff.

Troeltsch, Ernst, *The Social Teaching of the Christian Churches*, trans. Olive Wyon, 2 vols., 1931.

Tuve, Rosemond, "A Mediaeval Commonplace in Spenser's Cosmology," SP, XXX (1933), 133-47.

Tylor, Edward B., *Primitive Culture*, 2 vols., 1874.


Ueberweg, Friedrich, *Grundriss der Geschichte der Philosophie der Neuzeit*, 11th ed., 5 vols., 1914-1920.

Underhill, Evelyn, *Mysticism*, 12th ed., 1930.

——, *The Mystic Way: A Psychological Study of Christian Origins*, 1913.


Van der Noot, Jan, *A Theatre for Voluptuous Worldlings* (1569), Scholars' Facsimiles & Reprints, n.d.

Van Deusen, Neil, "The Place of Telesio in the History of Philosophy," *Philosophical Review*, XLIV (1935), 417-34.

——, *Telesio: The First of the Moderns*, 1932.

Vicary, Thomas, *The Anatomie of the Bodie of Man*, ed. Frederick J. Furnivall and Percy Furnivall, EETS, ex. ser., no. 53, 1888.

Villey, Pierre, *Les Sources & l'évolution des essais de Montaigne*, 2 vols., 1908.

Vossler, Karl, *Medieval Culture: An Introduction to Dante and his Times*, trans. William Cranston Lawton, 2 vols., 1929.


Waite, Arthur Edward, *Lamps of Western Mysticism*, 1923.

Wallace, Karl R., *Francis Bacon on Communication & Rhetoric*, 1943.

Walsh, Gerald Groveland, S.J., *Medieval Humanism*, 1942.

Walton, Izaak, *Lives*, 2 vols., The Temple Classics, 1898.

Warbecke, John Martyn, *The Searching Mind of Greece*, 1934.

Watkins, Edward Ingram, *Philosophy of Mysticism*, 1920.

Webb, Clement C. J., *Studies in the History of Natural Theology*, 1915.

Weber, Max, *The Protestant Ethic and the Rise of Capitalism*, trans. Talcott Parsons, 1930.

Weiner, P. P., "The Tradition behind Galileo's Methodology," *Osiris*, I (1930), 732-46.

Whibley, Leonard (ed.), *A Companion to Greek Studies*, 3d ed., 1916.

White, Andrew Dickson, *A History of the Warfare of Science with Theology in Christendom*, 2 vols., 1920.

Whitehead, Alfred North, *Adventures of Ideas*, 1935.

——, *Science and the Modern World*, 1931.

Whiting, George Wesley, *Milton's Literary Milieu*, 1939.

Whittaker, Thomas, *The Neo-Platonists: A Study in the History of Hellenism*, 2d ed., 1918.

Willey, Basil, *The Seventeenth Century Background*, 1934.

*Willobie his Avisa*, ed. G. B. Harrison, 1926.

Windelband, W., *A History of Philosophy*, trans. James H. Tufts, 2d ed., 1931.

Winstanley, Lilian, see Spenser, Edmund.

Wolf, A., *A History of Science Technology, and Philosophy in the 16th & 17th Centuries*, 1935.

Workman, Herbert B., *The Evolution of the Monastic Creed*, 1913.

Wright, Celeste Turner, "Some Conventions Regarding the Usurer in Elizabethan Literature," SP, XXXI (1934), 176-97.

Wright, Louis B., "Introduction to a Survey of Renaissance Studies," MLQ, II (1941), 355-63.

————, *Middle-Class Culture in Elizabethan England*, 1935.

Wright, Thomas, *The Passions of the Minde in Generall*, 1630.


Xenophon, *Minor Works*, trans. J. S. Watson, Bohn's Classical Library, 1878.


Yates, F. A., *A Study of Love's Labour's Lost*, 1936.

Yeats, William Butler, *The Autobiography*, 1938.


Zanta, Léontine, *La Renaissance du stoïcisme au xvi siècle*, Bibliothèque Littéraire de la Renaissance, N.S., vol. V, 1914.

Zeller, E., *The Stoics, Epicureans and Sceptics*, trans. Oswald J. Reichel, 1880.

Zilsel, Edgar, "Copernicus and Mechanics," JHI, I (1940), 113-18.

# INDEX

*The following index is selective; no effort has been made to list every occurrence of persons, places, and things, but the principal discussions and thematic developments have been suggested. The footnotes are cited only when the discussion is substantial enough to make it worth looking up. For such broad entries as the* Catholic Church *or* Humanism *or* Man *only the extended discussions could be indicated.*

Abelard, Peter, metaphysics, 191-92; ethical individualism, 192-94; and Saint Bernard, 194

Achelis, Werner, on Augustine, 168n

Adams, Henry, on the Middle Ages, 185; on *vis inertiae,* 204

Aenesidemus, 92

Aeschylus, on justice, 22-23; on religion, 24

Alexandria, as a center of Christian culture, 149

Allen, P. S., on Luther, 317

Ambrose, Bishop of Milan, *De Officiis Ministrorum,* 136; on pagan science, 137; on faith, 140; on the Church, 82, 179

Anaxagoras, cosmology, 12-13, 101

Anaximander, cosmology, 5

Anaximenes, cosmology, 5, 7,

Animism, 111-13

Anselm, Archbishop of Canterbury, on Roscellinus, 191

Anthony, and monasticism, 170

Apostles, the, their missions, 127-28

Apostles' Creed, the, 143

Apuleius, Lucius, on mystery initiations, 116n

Aquinas, Thomas, on law, 73-74; realism, 192; and Augustine, 194; and Aristotle, 194; on man's nature, 195-96; natural theology, 196-97; on the mysteries, 197; on natural law, 198; *Summa Theologica,* 198-99; achievement, 200; and Erasmus, 267-68; psychology, 287-88; economics, 325

Arcesilaus, 71, 91

Arian Heresy, the, 153-58

Aristophanes, on Euripides, 21; conservatism, 27-28; on Socrates, 33

Aristotle, on the Ionians, 5, 63; on the Pythagoreans, 8; on slavery, 20-21; on man's external goods, 21; on justice, 22; relation to Plato, 53-54; metaphysics, 53-58; teleology, 55-57; psychology, 58-61, 279; ethics, 61-68, 103; politics, 65-67; and Aquinas, 194

Arnold, Matthew, on the Renaissance, 221

Arnold, Thurman, 333

Ascham, Roger, as a humanist, 270-71, 272-73; and Neo-Stoicism, 311

Astrology, popularity in the Renaissance, 235n

Athanasian Creed, the, 160-61

Athanasius, and the Council of Nicaea, 154-58

Athenagoras, on the early Church, 133-34

Athens, its stratified society, 19; humanism, 21

Atomism, in Greek thought, 13-15

Augustine, Bishop of Hippo, and Plato, 47, 171; on slavery, 83; on Neoplatonism, 97, 136, 144, 161, 164-65; affinity with mystery-cults, 123; on paganism, 138, 139; on faith, 140; life, 159-62; *Confessions,* 161-62; epistemology, 162; *The City of God,* 163, 183; theology, 162-76; on man's nature, 165-76; on sex, 167-69; influence in the Middle Ages, 176-86; on the sacraments, 179; revival of his theology in the Renaissance, 313-22

Averroes, 194-95

Bacon, Francis, and Scholasticism, 214-16; methodology, 215-17; on religion, 226; on astrology, 237; on psychology, 276-77, 278, 287; and Neo-Stoicism, 311; morality, 332

Bacon, Roger, 221

Bartholomaeus, Anglicus, 276

Basilides, 147

Beard, Thomas, on providence, 231
Benedict, and monasticism, 170
Bernard de Clairvaux, and Abelard, 194
Bessarion, 243
Beza, Theodore, on Calvin's health, 319n; on Servetus, 328n
Boethius (Anicus Manlius Severinus), on order, 17-18; on providence, 73; in the Middle Ages, 188
Boniface VIII, on papal supremacy, 181
Bossuet, Jacques Bénigne, on original sin, 171
Boyle, Robert, on Scholasticism, 208
Bright, Timothy, on psychology, 282, 288; on Neo-Stoicism, 311
Brochard, Victor, on the Greek Skeptics, 92
Browne, Sir Thomas, on Scholasticism, 208; on nature, 225; on man's nature, 238; and Neo-Stoicism, 312
Bruno, Giordano, and Copernicus, 213; and the Church, 214; and Neoplatonism, 250
Burckhardt, Jacob, on the Renaissance, 217-18
Burke, Kenneth, on Stoicism, 83
Burton, Robert, on original sin, 171; on psychology, 277, 282, 284, 285, 286-87; and Neo-Stoicism, 312
Bush, Douglas, on Bacon, 216

Calvin, John, on nature, 224n, 226; on providence, 230; on the will, 291-92; and individualism, 315-16; theology, 316-22; and humanism, 318-19; and capitalism, 327-33; politics, 327-29
Carneades, 71, 91-92
Castiglione, Baldassare, his optimism, 223-24
Catholic Church, the, early history, 127n; as a medieval institution, 177-80; on inequality, 232; and usury, 324-25
Catullus, Gaius Valerius, on Cybele, 121
Caxton, William, on nature, 225
Celsus, on the Christians, 141
Chapman, George, on the imagination, 285; as a Neo-Stoic, 74, 303-05
Charron, Pierre, on psychology, 282; as a moralist, 294, 299-300
Christian Humanism, 258-74; as moral doctrine, 258-66, 295-99; and learning, 270-74
Christianity, and the mystery-cults, 120-24; early development, 124-41; geographical spread, 126-30; the Apostles, 127; its democratization, 130-33; its success, 133-34; and paganism, 134-41
Chrysippus, 70-71, 77, 90
Cicero, Marchus Tullius, on Socrates, 33; on

Plato, 70; on law, 73; on Epicurus, 85; on Carneades, 91; in the Renaissance, 297, 305n
Cleanthes, 70, 76, 78
Clement of Alexandria, on polytheism, 10n; on the mystery-cults, 122; on Christian democracy, 131; on paganism, 138, 139
Colet, John, his theology, 210; as a humanist, 265
Constantine the Great, and Christianity, 82; and the Council of Nicaea, 152-54
Copernicus, Nikolaus, his intentions, 207, 227; and the Church, 213-14; and Neoplatonism, 241
Council of Orange, the, 176
Courtly Love, 219-20
Cowley, Abraham, on the new science, 208-09; on Bacon, 216
Cowper, William, 121
Cusanus, Nicholas, 242n
Cybele, 120-21
Cynics, the, 71

Dante Alighieri, on Aristotle, 53; De Monarchia, 180; on the Church, 182; on astronomy, 183-84; on providence, 184; letter to Can Grande, 185; on man's reason, 195; on riches, 324
Davies, Sir John, on man's nature, 238
Democracy, in Plato, 43-44; in Aristotle, 65-67; and the early Church, 128-30; and capitalism in the Reformation, 322-33
Democritus, atomism, 14-15, 101; ethics, 14n
Demosthenes, on Solon, 18-19
Descartes, René, methodology, 208
De Wulf, Maurice, on nominalism, 191
Dilthey, Wilhelm, 220, 225
Diogenes Laertius, on Zeno, 70, on Epicurus, 85; on the Skeptics, 89
Dionysus, and the Orphic mysteries, 114-15
Dionysius the Areopagite, see the Pseudo-Dionysius
Donatist Heresy, 179
Donne, John, on Scholasticism, 208; intellectual progress, 217n; and capitalism, 331; theological individualism, 315; on predestination, 322n
Double Truth, the, in Pomponazzi, 212
Dualism, in Pre-Socratic thought, 6-9; in Plato, 47; in later Greek thought, 102; and the Council of Nicaea, 156-58; in Augustine, 164; in the Renaissance, 241-42, 276
Du Bartas, Guillaume, on order, 229; on providence, 231; and Neo-Stoicism, 312

Duns Scotus, as a realist, 192; voluntarism, 199-211, 290
Durkheim, Emile, on religion, 111
Du Vair, Guillaume, as a Neo-Stoic, 302, 306-12

Economic Individualism, and the Reformation, 322-33
Edwards, Jonathan, and Calvinism, 322
Eleatics, the, 9-13
Election, in Paul and Augustine, 174-75; in Calvin, 321-22
Eleusinian Mysteries, 116
Eliot, T. S., on Neo-Stoicism, 303
Elyot, Sir Thomas, on political order, 231, 233-34, 324; on psychology, 277, 286, 288; as a humanist, 295-96
Empedocles, 11-12, 101
Epicurus, 84-88
Epictetus, as a Stoic, 75, 77, 79; on the Skeptics, 93
Epistle to the Hebrews, the, 143-44
Epistolae Obscurorum Virorum, 266
Erasmus, Desiderius, on educational reform, 207-08; on Scholasticism, 209, 210, 261; on inequality, 232; Ciceronianus, 259-60; as a scholar, 261-62; as a moralist, 262-63; orthodoxy, 265-66; controversy with Luther, 266-70, 314, 317-18; on order, 273; and Neo-Stoicism, 311; on money, 325
Euripides, skepticism, 10, 27, 28; on slavery, 21; on the mysteries, 115
Eusebius, 134
Evil, problem of, in Augustine, 163-65; in Erigena, 190n. See Providence

Faculty Psychology, 275-92
Ficino, Marsilio, philosophy, 243-46, 249; on reason, 291
Fideism, 212
Florentine Academy, the, 242-46
Fortescue, Sir John, on order, 236-37
Fortune, equated with providence, 230-31; and Neo-Stoicism, 309. See Providence
Four Elements, the, in Greek philosophy, 12; in Renaissance science, 277-78
Four Humors, the, 277-78; 280n
Frazer, Sir James, on religion, 110-11, 112, 113n
Freud, Sigmund, on religion, 111

Galen, Claudius, psychology, 276
Gelli, Battista, on the will, 291; The Circe, 297-99

George of Trebizond, 242-43
Georgius Gemisthus. See Plethon
Gibbon, Edward, on celibacy, 169-70; on Augustinian theology, 160, 317
Gilson, Etienne, on realism and nominalism, 191
Gnosticism, its break with the Church, 129n; and humanism, 135; as a heresy of the early Church, 145-49
Gomperz, Theodore, on the Sophists, 29
Goodman, Christopher, and political disobedience, 232-33
Gorgias, 25, 29, 31
Grace, in Augustine, 172. See Calvin, John
Gratian, on usury, 325
Great Chain of Being, the, and Renaissance order, 227-35
Greeks, the, regard for order, 16-25; decline of this regard, 26-29; decline of the city-state, 69-70; civic religion, 23-25, 113-14; tragedy, 22-23
Gregory the Great, on monasticism, 169; as an administrator, 179-82
Greville, Fulke, and Neo-Stoicism, 312
Grote, George, on the Pythagoreans, 8
Guazzo, Steffano, on learning, 295-96

Hall, Joseph, on logic, 208; and Neo-Stoicism, 312; and money, 331
Harrison, Jane, on religion, 111, 113
Harvey, Gabriel, on the decay of Scholasticism, 208; as a moralist, 271; as a humanist, 295
Heraclitus, his system, 9-10, 101; on order, 18; on religion, 113
Herodotus, on the Greek character, 17; on Greek religion, 113
Heywood, Thomas, 226n
Higher Criticism, the, 124n
Homer, on order, 18; the Iliad, 23; on religion, 23, 24, 25; pessimism, 110; on immortality, 117
Honorius Augustadunesis, 184
Hooker, Richard, on order, 234-35; on reason, 290
Howell, James, on Platonic love, 249n
Huarte, John, 280
Hugo of St. Victor, 186
Huizinga, J., on the Renaissance, 221
Humanism, pervasive in Greek thought, 21-22, 100-105; in Plato, 512; in Aristotle, 58-68; decay in Greece, 84-99; and the early Church, 134-41; in Italian Renaissance, 242-46, 259. See Christian Humanism, Man's Nature, Reason

Hume, David, 111
Huxley, Thomas, 187

Imagination, in Renaissance psychology, 284-85
Individualism, in Christ's teaching, 132-33; in the Renaissance, 221, 322-23
Ionians, the, 3-6
Irenaeus, on Gnosticism, 146

Jaeger, Werner, on Greek tragedy, 22; on the Sophists, 29; on Socrates, 32; on Plato and Aristotle, 53n
Jerome, Sophronius Eusebius, on the decay of Rome, 134; on pagan literature, 137, 138-39; on sex, 169; on the Pelagian heresy, 175-76; on the Bible, 262n
Jesus Christ, development of His mission, 125-41; deification, 126-27; development in Trinitarian dogma, 143-58
John of Salisbury, on law, 180; on providence, 183; his learning, 187-88; on realism and nominalism, 192; on faith, 197; on Scholasticism, 206
John Scotus Erigena, translator of the Pseudo-Dionysius, 97; *De Divisione Naturae,* 185-86; his system, 189-90
Johnson, Samuel, on the imagination, 284
Jonson, Ben, on humours, 278n; as a moralist, 271
Justice, in Plato, 41. See Providence
Justin Martyr, on the mystery-cults, 122; on the Church, 134; on God, 144; *Dialogue with Trypho,* 159

Krappe, Alexander, on religion, 110

Lactantius Firmianus, Lucius Caelius, on the Stoics, 136; on the Christian ethos, 132, 137; on humanism, 137; on paganism, 138; on the Church, 179; on providence, 183
Lang, Andrew, 113
La Primaudaye, Pierre, on nature, 226; on providence, 229; on order, 231-32; and Neo-Stoicism, 311-12
Law, in Greek thought, 16-25; in Stoic doctrine, 72-74, 78-83; and Paul (the "Old Law"), 128-30; and the medieval Church, 180-81; in Aquinas, 73-74, 198; in Sir Isaac Newton, 209; in Richard Hooker, 234-35; and Neo-Stoicism, 309-12; and Luther, 326. See Order, Providence

Leucippus, 13-14
Lewis, C. S., on Spenser, 255
Linacre, Thomas, 276
Lipsius, Justus, as a Neo-Stoic, 80, 301, 303, 305-12; on God's punishments, 231n
Logos, in Christian doctrine, 142-58; in Plato, 150
Lovejoy, A. O., on Aristotle, 58; on order, 228
Lucian, on the Stoics, 78
Lucretius, as an Epicurean, 85, 86; on the mysteries, 121
Luther, Martin, and Erasmus, 266-70, 317-18; theology, 314-15; and *Beruf,* 326-27

Mâle, Emile, on medieval thought, 185
Manicheism, and Gnosticism, 146; and Augustine, 159, 161
Man's Nature, in Paul's view, 130; in the early Church, 140; in Augustine's view, 165-76; in the Middle Ages, 177-78; as a Renaissance commonplace, 235-40; in Florentine Neoplatonism, 241-46
Marcion, 148n
Marcus Aurelius, his Stoicism, 75, 77-78, 81
Mariolatry, and courtly love, 220
Marlowe, Christopher, and Ramus, 213n; his theory of character, 302-03; and Neo-Stoicism, 310
Marrou, Henri-Irénée, on the early Church, 159n
Meier, Heinrich, on the Sophists, 30
Melanchthon, Philip, on Scholasticism, 211; theological determinism, 318n
Menander, on man's life, 70
Michelet, Jules, on the Renaissance, 221
Microcosm-Macrocosm, in Greek thought, 19-20; in the Renaissance, 236-40, 278
Middle Ages, the, and Augustine, 176-86; its enlightenment, 187-88
Milton, John, as a moralist, 271
Minucius Felix, on the mysteries, 121; on the Christian ethos, 131; on the early Church, 134; the *Octavius,* 135
Mithraism, 121
Monarchianism, 145
Monasticism, 169-70
Montaigne, Michel Eyquem, and the Skeptics, 92; his Neo-Stoicism, 306-07
More, Paul Elmer, on Socrates, 32
More, Sir Thomas, his traditionalism, 222; on man, 236; as a humanist, 263-65, 271, 272; as a moralist, 293-94
Mornay, Phillipe de, on natural religion, 226
Müller, Max, on religion, 110

Mumford, Lewis, on the Nicene Creed, 156; on monasticism, 169; on Italian humanism, 272n

Murray, Gilbert, on the Greek mysteries, 118

Mutability, a literary theme in the Renaissance, 230n

Mystery-Cults, 6, 120-21

Mysticism, and Neoplatonism, 93-99; in Plato, 118n; in Paul, 127-28; in Augustine, 161-62; in Aquinas, 197

Naturalism, and the Ionians, 4-6; and Aristotle, 55; and the Stoics, 71; and the Epicureans, 86; and Renaissance psychology, 276-92

Natural Religion, in Aquinas, 194-200; in the Renaissance, 223-27

Neoplatonism, as a philosophic system, 93-99; in the Renaissance, 227-28, 241-57

Neo-Stoicism, popularity in the Renaissance, 293, 301-12; and Sir Philip Sidney, 296; and Christianity, 307-09

*New Whole Duty of Man, the,* 331

Newman, John Henry, on religion, 110, 139-40; on sin, 166

Newton, Sir Isaac, on natural law, 209

Nicaea, the Council of, 152-58

Nicene Creed, the, 155-58, 162

Nietzsche, Friedrich Wilhelm, his vitalism, 24n; on Stoicism, 75n

Optimism, in Greek thought, 100-05; in Christ's teaching, 131-32; in the Renaissance, 223-40

Order, in Greek thought, 5, 16-25; in Aristotle, 58-61; in the Middle Ages, 182-86; in the Renaissance, 227-35

Origen, on the mysteries, 122; on Christian democracy, 131, 134; and the early Church, 136; as a theologian, 149-52; on evil, 165

Original Sin, in Paul, 171; in Augustine, 171-75; in the Reformation, 316-22

Orphism, 4, 7, 8, 110, 112-19; and Christianity, 123-24

Pachomius, 170

Parmenides, 10-11, 101

Paschasius Radbert, 176

Passion, in Aristotle, 61-62; in Stoic doctrine, 76-77; in Augustine, 172n; in Aquinas, 195n; in Renaissance psychology, 282-88

Paul, on order, 82-83; on the mystery-cults, 122; missionary activities, 127-28; and the Old Law, 128-29; and sex, 167; on original sin, 171

Peasants' Revolt, the, and Luther, 326

Pelagian Heresy, the, 175-76

Pericles, on the citizen and the state, 17; on Athens, 21-22; on immortality, 117

Permanence and Change, as a theme in Greek philosophy, 3-4, 5, 16-25, 163; in the early Church, 144; in the Middle Ages, 188

Pessimism, in Greek thought, 110-11; in Paul, 129-30

Petrarch, Francesco, his conservatism, 221-22; as a humanist, 297

Petronius, on religion, 111

Philemon, on order, 23

Philo of Alexandria, on the Logos, 150-51

Physiology, in the Renaissance, 275-92

Pico Della Mirandola, and courtly love, 219n; last years, 222, 265; on natural religion, 227; on man, 237; his philosophy, 243-46

Pirenne, Henri, 323

Plethon, 242-43

Plato, on order, 17, 20, 25; on the Sophists, 30; and Socrates, 37; epistemology, 38-39, 50-51; metaphysics, 39-40; and his predecessors, 39-40; the mathematician, 39-40; ethics, 40-41, 44-52, 102; politics, 41-44; life, 42; psychology, 45-51; in the Middle Ages and the Renaissance, 188n, 242-43, 246-48

Plotinus, 94-96; and Erigena, 190

Pluralism, in Pre-Socratic philosophy, 11-13

Plutarch, on Stoicism, 78, 81; on the mysteries, 116

Pomponazzi, Pietro, 210-12

Porphyry, on Plotinus, 94n, 97; in the Middle Ages, 188

Posidionius, 77

Predestination, in Augustine, 174-75; in Calvin, 320-22

Propitiation, 111-12

Protagoras, 25, 29, 30

Providence, in Augustine, 163-65; in the Renaissance, 229-33; and Neo-Stoicism, 308-12; and Calvin, 230n. See teleology

Pseudo-Dionysius, the, 97-99, 184

Psyche, the, in the mystery-cults, 6; in Socrates, 33, 36; in Pato, 48-49; in Aristotle, 58-61

Psychology, in Plato, 45-50; in Aristotle, 58-61; in Stoicism, 74-78; in Augustine, 172-75; in Aquinas, 195-96; in the Renaissance, 275-92

Ptolemaic Astronomy, 183-84, 275
Pyrrho of Elis, 90, 92
Pythagoras, 6-9, 101

Rabelais, François, and Neo-Stoicism, 306
Raleigh, Sir Walter, on providence, 230n, 231; on man's nature, 238, 291
Ramus, Peter, 213
Ransom, John Crowe, 333
Rational soul, the, in Aristotle, 59-61; in Renaissance psychology, 288-92
Reason, in Anaxagoras, 12-13; in Socrates, 35; in Plato, 38-40; in Aristotle, 62-63; in the Stoics, 75; importance in Greek thought, 103-04; in the early Church, 140; in Augustine, 162, 171-72; in Scholasticism, 193, 194-200, 205-07; as a moral principle ("Right Reason"), 273-74, 297-301; in Renaissance psychology, 288-92
Realism and nominalism, 188-94; in the Renaissance, 220-21
Relativism, and the Sophists, 31
Religion, contrasted with philosophy, 110; attempts at definition, 110-12
Renaissance, the, continuity with the Middle Ages, 203-22; attempts at definition, 217-22
Renan, Ernst, on Mithraism, 121; on Gnosticism, 146n; on the early Church, 182
Right reason, see Reason
Robertson, H. M., on capitalism, 323, 325
Romei, Annibile, 255n
Roscellinus, 190-91

Savonarola, Girolamo, 264n
Scholasticism, and Abelard, 193; derogation in the Renaissance, 205-17
School of Night, the, 231n
Sebond, Raymond de, on order, 228
Seebohm, Frederic, on the humanists, 266
Seneca, Lucius Annaeus, as a Stoic, 74-78; on man's original state, 177
Sensitive soul, the, 282-88
Sextus Empiricus, on Gorgias, 31; on Skepticism, 90, 92
Shakespeare, William, on man's nature, 239; on order, 239-40; on psychology, 277n, 287-88, 292; and Neo-Stoicism, 302-03, 311
Sidney, Sir Philip, on politics, 232n; as a Platonist, 252-53; as a moralist, 271, 296-97
Simonides, 21

Sir Thomas More, 234n
Slavery, in Greek culture, 19-20; Augustine's opinion, 83
Skepticism, 88-93; and Stoicism, 71
Smith, T. V., 105
Socrates, 32-36; his achievement, 37, 101-02; on immortality, 117
Solon, 17, 18-19
Sophists, the, 25-31
Sophocles, on man, 23; his pessimism, 110
Spenser, Edmund, on nature, 225; on order, 229; as a Platonist, 248, 249-51; The Fowre Hymnes, 250-53; as a Protestant, 251-52, 254; as a moralist, 253-57, 293, 300-01; The Faerie Queene, 253-57; on psychology, 281, 286
Spirits, the, in Renaissance psychology, 281
Sprat, Thomas, 208-09
Starkey, Thomas, on Erasmus, 209; on man, 236, 289; on Cardinal Pole, 273
Stoicism, in Greece, 69-78; in Rome, 78-83; in the Renaissance, 80, 301-12; and Christianity, 81-82
Stradling, Sir John, on Scholasticism, 208
Symbolism, in medieval thought, 185-86
Syncretism, and Orphism, 114; and Christianity, 120-24
Synod of Dort, the, 321n

Tawney, R. H., 323, 330
Teleology, in Anaxagoras, 13; in Aristotle, 55-56; in Stoicism, 72-74; in Augustine, 164-65. See Order, Providence
Telesio, Bernardino, 212-13
Ten Modes of Skepticism, the, 92
Tertullian, on the early Church, 134; on paganism, 137; on faith, 140
Thales, 3, 5
Theocracy, in Geneva, 327-28
Thucydides, 28-29
Troeltsch, Ernst, 323
Tylor, Edward, on religion, 110, 111, 112

Universalism, in Greek thought, 17; and Stoicism, 78-83; in the early Church, 129-35
Usury, and the Church, 324-25

Valentinus, 147-48
Valla, Lorenzo, 262
Van der Noot, Jan, 294-95
Vegetable soul, the, in Aristotle, 59; in Renaissance psychology, 280-82
Villey, Pierre, 306

Vincent of Beauvais, 185

Vives, Juan Luis, 232

Voltaire (François Marie Arouet), on the Middle Ages, 187; on the Papacy, 324

Weber, Max, 323, 331

Whitehead, Alfred North, on the Ionians, 3; on Greek religion, 24; on Hellenistic thought, 69; on Plato's world-soul, 150; on "fundamental assumptions," 176; on the Church, 180

Will, the, in Augustine, 172-75; in Duns Scotus and his successors, 199-200; in the Renaissance, 199-200, 290-92; in the Luther-Erasmus controversy, 266-70, 318; in Calvin, 318-22

William of Champeaux, as a realist, 191, 192

William of Ockham, as a nominalist, 192

Winstanley, Lilian, on Spenser's Platonism, 254

Wright, Thomas, and Neo-Stoicism, 311

Xenophanes, 10, 90

Xenophon, 19

Zeller, Eduard, 70

Zeno the Stoic, 70-75, 76n